THE YALE EDITIONS OF
The Private Papers of James Boswell

RESEARCH EDITION

Catalogue

CATALOGUE OF THE PAPERS OF JAMES BOSWELL AT YALE UNIVERSITY, by Marion S. Pottle, Claude Colleer Abbott and Frederick A. Pottle, 3 Vols., 1993

Correspondence

Volume 1   THE CORRESPONDENCE OF JAMES BOSWELL AND JOHN JOHNSTON OF GRANGE, edited by Ralph S. Walker, 1966

Volume 2   THE CORRESPONDENCE AND OTHER PAPERS OF JAMES BOSWELL RELATING TO THE MAKING OF THE *Life of Johnson*, edited by Marshall Waingrow, 1969

Volume 3   THE CORRESPONDENCE OF JAMES BOSWELL WITH CERTAIN MEMBERS OF THE CLUB, edited by Charles N. Fifer, 1976

Volume 4   THE CORRESPONDENCE OF JAMES BOSWELL WITH DAVID GARRICK, EDMUND BURKE, AND EDMOND MALONE, edited by Peter S. Baker, Thomas W. Copeland, George M. Kahrl, Rachel McClellan, and James Osborn, with the assistance of Robert Mankin and Mark Wollaeger, 1986

Life of Johnson

JAMES BOSWELL'S
LIFE OF JOHNSON

AN EDITION OF THE ORIGINAL MANUSCRIPT

In Four Volumes

Volume 2: 1766–1776

edited by
BRUCE REDFORD
with
E<small>LIZABETH</small> G<small>OLDRING</small>

EDINBURGH UNIVERSITY PRESS
Edinburgh

YALE UNIVERSITY PRESS
New Haven and London

© Yale University, 1998
Edinburgh University Press, 1998
22 George Square, Edinburgh

Set in Goudy by the
Yale Boswell Editions, New Haven,
and printed in Great Britain by
The University Press, Cambridge

A CIP record for this book is available
from the British Library

Edinburgh University Press
ISBN 0-7486-0606-8

Yale University Press
ISBN 0-300-07969-9

Listed by the Library of Congress

The paper in this book meets the guidelines for permanence and durability of
the Committee on the Production Guidelines for Book Longevity of the
Council on Library Resources.

Published by Yale University Press with the assistance of the Annie Burr
Lewis Fund.

Boswell's Life of Johnson, *Volume 2*

General Editor: Gordon Turnbull
Associate Editor: Nancy E. Johnson

BOSWELL'S *LIFE OF JOHNSON:*
AN EDITION OF THE ORIGINAL MANUSCRIPT

IN FOUR VOLUMES

VOLUME 2: 1766–1776

The preparation of *Boswell's* Life of Johnson:
An Edition of the Original Manuscript, Volume 2

was generously supported by

the National Endowment for the Humanities,

the James J. Colt Foundation, and

the L. J. Skaggs and Mary C. Skaggs Foundation

ADVISORY COMMITTEE

General Editorial Note

The research edition of the Private Papers of James Boswell consists of three co-ordinated series: the journals in all their varieties, the correspondence, and the *Life of Johnson*. The undertaking is a co-operative one involving many scholars, and publication is proceeding in the order in which the volumes are completed for the press.

The correspondence is appearing in three kinds of volumes: *single-correspondent* volumes; *subject* volumes of letters related to a topic or theme; and *miscellaneous-correspondence* volumes of the remaining letters in chronological sequence. *Boswell's* Life of Johnson: *An Edition of the Original Manuscript* is presented in an arrangement which shows the method and progress of the composition of the *Life*. The journals and their related notes and memoranda will be presented in one chronological sequence.

The parallel 'reading' or 'trade' edition, the fourteen volumes of which were completed in 1989, consists of selected portions of the papers (primarily the journals) that were considered likely to interest the general reading public. The annotation in that series was turned in towards the text to render it more accessible to the reader.

Apart from their interest to literary scholars, many of the papers Boswell preserved are of value to a broad spectrum of eighteenth-century scholarship. The annotation of the research edition, therefore, turns out from the text and relates the documents to the various areas of scholarship which they are capable of illuminating: history (literary, linguistic, legal, medical, political, social, local), biography, bibliography, and genealogy.

Acknowledgements

Marion Wells was an indispensable resource during the early phases of work on this volume. Its timely completion is due to the energy and ingenuity of the staff at the Yale Boswell Editions; Mark Spicer, acting as copy-editor and designer, made an especially important contribution. Marshall Waingrow, who continues to serve as model and consultant, supplied the list of errata for Volume 1. The portions of the manuscript that are not at Yale are published with the kind permission of Mary Hyde Eccles, the Houghton Library, and the Rosenbach Museum and Library.

Contents

Preface

This second volume leaves the reader *nel mezzo del cammin*—on MS 550, to be precise, out of a total of 1046. But thanks to the methods perfected by Marshall Waingrow, the *selva oscura* has yielded many of its secrets.

An edition of this kind is not the appropriate vehicle for commentary on Boswell's biographical artistry; rather, it seeks to furnish the materials for such a commentary. Nonetheless, it does seem important to signal the kinds of evidence that the project continues to uncover. Like its predecessor, this volume illustrates Boswell's unremitting care for stylistic nuance: on almost every page we observe him (to adapt his own observation in the journal) giving 'life to objects' with 'many little touches'. To choose but one example from scores of possibilities: by the sensitive adjustment of adjective and verb, Boswell depicts, with the exactness of a natural history manual, the behaviour of a trapped scorpion. 'I told him that I had several times when in Italy [witnessed⟩] seen the experiment of placing a scorpion within a circle of [hot/live⟩] burning coals; that it ran round and round in extreme pain, and finding no [way to escape/outlet⟩] way to escape, retired to the center and like a true Stoick Philosopher [put/clapped its sting into its head/gave its head the fatal sting⟩] darted its sting into its head, and thus at once freed itself from its woes.' A further effect of these changes is to turn summary into free indirect speech, which preserves the resonance of Boswell's vivid speaking voice.

In contrast to Volume 1, Boswell's notes and journal have become his most important source. Therefore the biographer's virtuoso handling of conversation comes sharply into focus for the first time: we watch a dedicated craftsman shaping everything from short, stichomythic exchanges to sustained, polyphonic set-pieces. An example of the former occurs on MS 329 (in which Boswell deletes a final quip in order to keep the spotlight trained on Johnson) and of the latter on MSS 335–43 (in which Boswell expertly paces the flow of a complex exchange). In addition, this volume testifies more fully than its predecessor to Boswell's mastery of biographical structure, as he links anecdotes together (e.g. MS 421 and Paper Apart C), ponders the insertion of correspondence (MSS 359–60), and repositions blocks of narrative (MS 422).

When it is complete, this edition will enrich our knowledge of the Johnsonian circle by confirming and amplifying the 'Table of Anonymous Persons' that appears in Hill-Powell's edition (vi. 431–75). In addition, it will introduce a number of corrections into the received text of the *Life* by identifying errors that escaped notice during the process of production. Given the labyrinthine nature of the printer's copy (never were 'foul papers' fouler than these), and the fact that neither Boswell nor Malone regularly read proof against copy, the wonder is that these errata are not more widespread. A comprehensive list will appear in Volume 4, as well as a supplement to the Hill-Powell 'Table'. The front matter to the final volume will also include a section devoted to Boswell's handling of his two most important kinds of source material—his own journals and letters to and from Johnson.

A full account of the project, including Professor Waingrow's illustrated description of his method, appears in Volume 1. The reader will discover one deviation from 'the Waingrow System': the transcription of Paper Apart E (pp. 177–82) treats this section as if it were part of the main text, in order to take advantage of the full range of editorial sigla. The most important of these sigla, together with illustrative examples, are gathered together in a table that should help to signpost *la diritta via*.

BRUCE REDFORD

Summary of Editorial Sigla

Symbol		Denotes	Example
[	⟩]	Change from an original draft to a later revision.	'You may as well [talk of⟩] praise a school-master whipping a boy [for construing⟩] who has construed ill …'
	∫	Alternative word(s) or phrase(s) interlined in MS, usually at stage of first draft.	'Read over your [compositions/sermons⟩] compositions, and wherever you [find/see/meet with⟩] meet with a passage …'
ʎ	λ	A later, isolated addition, ranging in scale from a single word to several paragraphs.	'Come now ʎSirλ this is an interesting matter …'
	del	A later, isolated deletion, ranging in scale from a single word to several paragraphs.	'May it not be doubted Sir whether it be proper to publish [such *del*] letters …'
/	/	An optional—grammatically independent—word or phrase, set off as such by JB in the MS by the use of virgules.	Johnson shewed himself highly pleased/with his Majestys conversation and gracious behaviour/.
⟨	⟩	Denotes a tear in the MS; letters or words within angle brackets have been reconstructed with recourse to the printed edition.	His Lordship spoke only from a few notes, but he recollected it ⟨as far⟩ as to dictate it to me while I wrote it down.

Abbreviations and short titles

This list supplements the list in Volume 1, pp. xxxvi–xxxix, to which readers of this volume should also refer.

Corres. Walpole: The Yale Edition of Horace Walpole's Correspondence, ed. W. S. Lewis and others, 48 vols., 1937–83.

Corr. 6: The Correspondence of James Boswell and William Johnson Temple, 1756–1795, Vol. 1: 1756–1777, ed. Thomas Crawford, 1997 (Yale Research Edition, Correspondence: Volume 6).

Earlier Years: Frederick A. Pottle, *James Boswell: The Earlier Years 1740–1769,* 1966.

Fasti Angl.: John Le Neve and T. D. Hardy, *Fasti Ecclesiae Anglicanae,* 3 vols., 1854.

Journ.: JB's fully written journal. Transcribed conservatively from the MS.

Later Years: Frank Brady, *James Boswell: The Later Years 1769–1795,* 1984.

Life MS i: Boswell's Life of Johnson: An Edition of the Original Manuscript, in Four Volumes, Vol. 1: 1709–1765, ed. Marshall Waingrow, 1994.

Lond. Stage: The London Stage, 1660–1800, ed. William van Lennep and others, 5 parts in 11 vols., 1960–68.

Namier and Brooke: Sir Lewis Namier and John Brooke, *The History of Parliament, The House of Commons 1754–1790,* 3 vols., 1964.

Notes: JB's condensed journal. Transcribed conservatively from the manuscript.

Ominous Years: Boswell: The Ominous Years, 1774–1776, ed. Charles Ryskamp and F. A. Pottle, 1963.

The Life of Samuel Johnson, LL.D.

[1766]

[MS 304] Both in 1764 and 1765 it [would>] should seem [that his habitual
'loathing to write'/constitutional unwillingness to write prevailed in a most
remarkable degree. Though I wrote to him frequently in the course of these years,
while I was upon my travels I did not receive a single letter in return yet he was
5 pleased with a letter which I wrote to him from the Tomb of Melancthon>] [that
his habitual 'loathing to write'/constitutional unwillingness to write prevailed in
a most remarkable degree. I have discovered no letter except one to Reynolds[1]
and though I wrote to him frequently in the course of these two years while I was
upon my travels but did not receive a single letter in return he was afterwards
10 pleased with a letter which I wrote to him from the Tomb of Melancthon[2] >] that
he was so busily employed with his edition of Shakspeare as to have had [no leisure
for any other literary exertion or even indeed/and indeed little even for>] little
leisure for any other literary exertion or indeed even for private correspondence. I
wrote to him frequently in the course of these two years while I was upon my
15 travels but did not receive a single letter in return for which ⟨it will appear that⟩
he afterwards apologised.

He obliged his friend Dr. Percy [/now Bishop of Dromore/>] now Bishop of
Dromore with a Dedication to the Countess of Northumberland [of his Collec-
tion>] which was prefixed to his Collection of 'Reliques [MS 305] of Ancient
20 English Poetry' in which he [adapts/appropriates>] pays compliments to that
[Great House>] illustrious family in the most courtly stile. It [should not be matter
of surprise>] need not be wondered at that one who can himself write so well as Dr.
Percy should [accept of a Dedication;>] [ever accept of Johnson's help to pen a
Dedication;>] accept of a Dedication from Johnson's pen; for as Sir Joshua
25 Reynolds who we shall afterwards see accepted of the same kind of assistance, well
observed to me, 'Writing a Dedication is a knack. It is like writing an Advertisement.' In this art no man excelled Dr. Johnson.[3/4] Though the loftiness of his

---

[1] This letter (August 1764) had been inserted on MS leaf 294 (*Life MS* i. 341; *Letters of
Johnson* ed. Redford, i. 243–44).

[2] Deleted direction to the compositor, 'Take it in'. JB later inserted the text of this letter
(To SJ, 30 Sept. 1764) in a note to SJ's letter of 28 June 1777.

[3] At the instigation of Sir Joshua Reynolds, JB cancelled in the revises a leaf (Volume I,
signature Mm4, p. 272) that contained this mention of Reynolds' indebtedness to SJ, who
had supplied the dedication to the King for the *Seven Discourses* of 1778 (Hazen, *Prefaces
& Dedications*, pp. 195–97). As JB reported to EM on 29 January 1791, 'I am to cancel a leaf
of the first volume, having found that though Sir Joshua certainly assured me he had no
objection to my mentioning that Johnson wrote a Dedication for him, he now thinks
otherwise' (*Corr. 2*, p. 383). This decision was taken in time for JB to refrain from
mentioning the dedication when he came to his account of 1778.

Having decided on the cancel in order to accommodate Reynolds, JB then took the
opportunity to remove all mention of SJ's comparable role in Percy's *Reliques* (Hazen, pp.

mind prevented him from ever dedicating in his own [name>] person, he wrote a great number of Dedications for others. After all the diligence which I have bestowed, some of them have escaped my inquiries. He [said he believed>] told me he believed he had dedicated to all the Royal Family round, and it [was all one/made no difference>] was indifferent to him what was the subject of the work   5 dedicated providing only that it were inocent. He once dedicated some Musick for the German Flute to Edward Duke of York.[5] In [dedicating for>] writing dedications for others he considered himself as by no means speaking his own sentiments.

Notwithstanding his long silence, I never ceased from writing to him, when I had any thing worthy of [communication>] communicating. I generally kept   10 copies of my letters [/to him,/>] to him, that I might have a full view of our correspondence [MS 306] and never be at a loss to understand any reference in his letters. He kept my letters very carefully, and a short time before his death was attentive enough to [put them up in bundles which he sealed/in sealed bundles to be delivered>] seal them up in bundles and order them to be delivered to me which   15 was accordingly done.[6] Amongst them I found [the following one of which I had not kept a copy>] one written from Corsica in which I gave him an Account of my visit to that Island.[7]

158–68). There is no evidence to suggest that Percy requested this favour. The most plausible conjecture is that JB, who was well aware of Percy's hypersensitivity to public opinion, decided to spare him as well as Reynolds (*Corr. 3*, pp. lxxxiv–lxxxvii). By contrast, a second cancel (Volume II, signature E3, pp. 29–30) was the direct result of pressure from Percy—in this instance, to do justice to the character of James Grainger. See *post* pp. 199 and n. 3.

The effect of the cancel was undermined by an index entry that revealed the nature of the original passage: 'Percy, Dr., his "Reliques of Ancient Poetry," I.272.' Although Percy suspected JB of duplicity, EM convincingly exonerated him: 'The fact is, that the page in his book to which the Index refers is, a cancelled page; to which a reference was made by one Tomlins (who made the Index) when it was in its *original state*, before it was cancelled.... After the cancel was made, the Index was unluckily forgot to be changed or cancelled, as it should have been' (EM to Percy, 5 June 1792, *The Correspondence of Thomas Percy and Edmond Malone*, 1944, pp. 56–57).

[4] After the leaf had been cancelled, JB inserted a sentence to smooth over the transition: 'He was, however, at all times ready to give assistance to his friends, and others, in revising their works, and in writing for them, or greatly improving their Dedications. In that courtly species of composition no man excelled ...'

[5] Deleted memorandum, 'Specify some more'. It is possible that JB refers to Thomas Arne's *Monthly Melody* (1760). Although Allen Hazen doubts the attribution, he has no alternative to offer (Hazen, *Prefaces & Dedications*, pp. 243–46).

[6] Within two weeks of SJ's death, Richard Brocklesby wrote to JB, 'As soon as he was convinced of the Necessity that pressed him he sealed up all your letters in a bag and wrote on the outside to be delivered to you' (*Corr. 2*, p. 34).

[7] In order to fill the space created by the cancel, JB expanded the précis of his letter to SJ: 'Amongst them I found one, of which I had not made a copy, and which I own I read with pleasure at the distance of almost twenty years. It is dated November, 1765, at the palace of Pascal Paoli, in Corte, the capital of Corsica, and is full of generous enthusiasm. After giving a sketch of what I had seen and heard in that island, it proceeded thus: "I dare to call this a spirited tour. I dare to challenge your approbation."'

This Letter [had at last the effect of obtaining me an Answer which almost made up to me for the long series of impatience/disappointment which his silence had made me suffer. It was lying for me when I arrived at Paris in January>] produced the following answer which I found on my arrival at Paris.[8]

A MR. MR. BOSWELL chez Mr. Waters Banquier a Paris.[9]
[Paper Apart P] Dear Sir[1]
Apologies are seldom of any use. We will delay till your arrival the reasons good or bad which have made me such a sparing and ungrateful correspondent. Be assured for the present that nothing has lessened either the esteem or love with which I dismissed you at Harwich. Both have been encreased by all that I have been told of you by yourself or others, and when you return, you will return to an unaltered and I hope unalterable friend.

All that you have to fear from me, is the vexation of disappointing me. No man loves to frustrate expectations which have been formed in his favour; and the pleasure which I promise myself from your journals and remarks is so great that perhaps no degree of attention or discernment will be sufficient to afford it.

Come home however and take your chance. I long to see you and to hear you, and hope that we shall not be so long separated again. Come home and expect such a welcome as is due to him whom a wise and noble curiosity has led where perhaps no native of this Country ever was before.

I have no news to tell you that can deserve your notice, nor would I willingly lessen the pleasure that any novelty may give you at your return. I am afraid we shall find it difficult to keep among us a mind which has been so long feasted with variety. But let us try what esteem and kindness can effect.

As your Father's liberality has indulged you with so long a ramble, I doubt not but you will think his sickness, or even his desire to see you, a sufficient reason for hastening your return. The longer we live and the more we think, the higher value we learn to put on the friendship and tenderness of Parents and of friends. Parents we can have but once, and he promises himself too much, who enters life with the expectation of finding many friends. Upon some motive I hope that you will be here soon, and am willing to think that it will be an inducement to your return that it is sincerely desired by

Dear Sir / Your affectionate humble Servant
Sam: Johnson

Johnsons Court, Fleet Street
Jan: 14 1766
[MS 306 resumed] [Having received Accounts of the death of my Mother and that my Father was in deep affliction, I gave up my intention of passing the Winter at Paris and returned to London in February in my way to Scotland>] [Having received Accounts of the death of my Mother and that my Father was in great affliction, I gave up my design of passing the Winter at Paris and returned to

---

[8] Direction to the compositor, '(Take it in) ∧Letter P∧'.
[9] Deleted cue, 'Dear Sir / Apologies are seldom'.
[1] The copy is in the hand of Alexander Boswell and is corrected by JB.

London in February in my way to Scotland resolved to enter myself/become an Advocate in the Court of Session in compliance with the anxious/earnest wish of my Father who was an eminent Judge/one of the eminent Judges in/of that Court>]

I returned to London in February and found Dr. Johnson in a very good house in Johnson's Court Fleet Street *[MS 307]* in which he had accomodated Miss Williams with an Apartment on the ground floor while Mr. Levet occupied his post in the garret; [and his faithful servant Francis>] his faithful Francis was still attending upon him. He received me with [strong marks of kindness and said he hoped we should pass many years of regard>] much kindness. The fragments of our first conversation which I have preserved are ₍these₎ — I told him that Voltaire in a conversation with me had distinguished Pope and Dryden thus — Pope drives a handsom [Chariot/Post chaise>] Chariot with a couple of neat trim [bay *del*] nags Dryden a Coach, and six stately horses. ['Why Sir' said Johnson>] *Johnson.* 'Why Sir The truth is they both drive Coaches and six; but [Dryden is either galloping or stumbling, Pope goes at a constant even trot>] Dryden's horses are either galloping or stumbling, Pope's go at a steady even trot.[a] He said of Goldsmith's Traveller [/which had been published in my absence/>] which had been published in my absence "There has not been so fine a Poem since Pope's time."

₍And here it is proper to settle with authentick precision what has long floated in publick report as to Johnson's being himself the Authour of a considerable part of that Poem. Much no doubt both of the sentiments and expression were derived from [his conversation>] conversing with him and it was certainly submitted to his friendly revision; but in the year 1783 he at my request marked with a pencil the lines which he had furnished which [were only line 420, and the concluding ten lines except the last couplet but one.>] are only line 420

'To stop too fearful and too faint to go'
and the concluding ten lines except the last couplet but one which I distinguish by the italick character

'How small of all that human hearts endure
That part which Kings or laws can cause or cure
Still to ourselves in every place consign'd
Our own felicity we make or find.

[a] It is remarkable that Mr. Gray has [ch>] employed somewhat of the same image to characterise Dryden. He indeed [allows>] furnishes his car with but two horses; but they are of etherial race.

'Behold where Dryden's less presumptuous car
Wide o'er the fields of glory bear
Two coursers of ethereal race
With necks in thunder cloath'd and long resounding pace.'
ODE on The Progress of Poesy.[a1]

[a1] The four lines from Gray's ode are in the hand of EM. The rest of the note is in the hand of JB.

> With secret course which no loud storms annoy
> Glides the smooth current of domestick joy.
> *The lifted ax, the agonising wheel,*
> Luke's iron crown and Damien's bed of steel
5 > To men remote from power but rarely known
> Leave reason faith and conscience all our own.'
He added 'These are all of which I can be sure' and they bear a small proportion
to the whole which consists of 438 verses. [The couplet which Goldsmith himself
inserted into the concluding sentence is
10 > The lifted ax the agonising wheel
> Luke's iron crown and Damien's bed of steel
He here mentions>] Goldsmith in the couplet which he inserted mentions *Luke* as
a person quite well=known and superficial readers have passed it over quite
smoothly; while those of more [attention/research>] attention have been as much
15 at a loss with *Luke* here as with *Lydiat* in [*The Vanity of Human Wishes*>] 'The
Vanity of Human Wishes'. The truth is that Goldsmith was himself in a mistake.
In the *Respublica Hungarica* there is an account of a desperate rebellion headed by
two brothers of the [names of *Luke* and *John*>] name of Zeck George and Luke.
When it was quelled, the punishment inflicted not upon *Luke* but upon [*John*>]
20 George, was having a red hot iron crown (*corona ferrea candescente*) put upon his
head.[2] The same severity of torture was exercised on the Earl of Menteith[3] one of
the Murderers of King James I of Scotland.
  Dr. Johnson [also favoured me by marking>] at the same time favoured me by
marking the lines which he furnished to Goldsmith's 'Deserted Village', [and
25 these>] which are only the four last
> That trade's proud empire hastes to swift decay,
> As ocean sweeps the laboured mole away:
> While self=dependent power can time defy,
> As rocks resist the billows and the sky. λ
30   Talking of education, [he said 'People have now adays>] 'People have now
adays (said he) got [into *del*] a strange opinion that every thing should be taught by
lectures. Now, I [can never>] cannot see that lectures can do [so/as>] so much
good as reading [MS 308] the Books [from which/whence>] from which the
lectures are taken. I know nothing that can be best taught by lectures except
35 where experiments are ₍to be₎λ shewn. You may teach Chymistry by lectures. ——
You might teach making of shoes by lectures.'
  At night I met him at the Mitre Tavern that we might renew our social
intimacy at the Original Place [which seemed as it were sacred to it *del*]. But there

---

[2] Deleted footnote, 'For this explanation I am obliged to Mr Maconochie Advocate and
Professor of the Law of Nature and Nations at Edinburgh'. Allan Maconochie (1748–
1816), raised to the Bench as Lord Meadowbank (1796), became Professor of Public Law
and Law of Nature and Nations at the University of Edinburgh in 1779.
[3] In reviewing the revises, JB corrected 'Menteith' to 'Athol'. He had confused an ally
with an enemy: Malise Graham, 12th Earl of Menteith, spent 26 years in prison as hostage
for James I, whereas Walter Stewart, 19th Earl of Atholl, was implicated in the murder of
the King. Before his execution in 1437, Atholl was forced to wear a crown of iron.

was now a considerable [change on>] difference in his way of living. Having had an illness in which he was advised to leave off wine, he had ⌃from that period⌄ continued to abstain from it, and drank only water or lemonade.

I told him [how>] that a foreign friend of his [/whom I had met abroad/>] whom I had met with abroad was so wretchedly perverted to Infidelity that he treated the   5
hopes of immortality with brutal [levity/contempt>] levity and said, 'As man dies like a dog let him lye like a dog.[4] *Johnson*. ['*If* he dies like a dog, *let* him lye like a dog.'/'Sir, why to be sure he may lye like a dog'>] '*If* he dies like a dog, *let* him lye like a dog.' I added that this man said to me 'I hate mankind, for I think myself one of the best of them and I know how bad I am.' *Johnson*. 'Sir, he must be very   10
singular in his opinion, if he thinks himself one of the best of men; for none of his friends think him [one of the best of men>] so.' — He [MS 309] said no honest man could be a Deist; for no man could be so after a fair examination of the proofs of Christianity. I [mentioned>] named Hume. *Johnson*. 'No, Sir. Hume owned to a Clergyman in the Bishoprick of Durham, that he had never read the New   15
Testament with [/any/ *del*] attention.' I mentioned Hume's [notion/saying>] notion that all who are happy are equally happy; A little Miss with a new gown at a dancing school ball [as/and *del*] a General at the head of a victorious army, [or/and>] and an Orator after having made an eloquent speech in a [great/public>] great Assembly. *Johnson* 'Sir, that all who are happy are equally happy is not true.   20
A Peasant and a Philosopher may be equally *satisfied*, but not equally *happy*. Happiness consists in the [multiplicity/*undeciphered word*>] multiplicity of [consciousness>] [intellectual enjoyments>] agreable consciousness. A Peasant has not capacity for having equal happiness with a Philosopher.' I remember this very question very happily illustrated in opposition to Hume, by the Reverend Mr.   25
Robert Brown at Utrecht. 'A small drinking glass and a large ⌃one⌄ /said he/[5] may be equally full; but the large one [holds/contains>] holds more than the small.[6]

Dr. Johnson was very kind this evening, and said to me, '[Well *del*] You have now [passed>] lived five and twenty years and you have employed them well.' [I answered>] [O no Sir said I.>] 'Alas Sir,' said I, 'I fear not. [MS 310] Do I know   30
History? do I know Mathematicks? Do I know law?' *Johnson*. 'Why Sir, though you may know no science so well as to be able to teach it, and no profession so well as to be able to follow it, your general mass of knowledge of books and men renders you very capable to [study>] make yourself master of any science or fit yourself for any profession.' I [said>] mentioned that a Gay friend had advised me against   35
being a Lawyer, because I should be excelled by plodding Blockheads.[7] *Johnson*.

---

[4] JB refers to Giuseppe Baretti, whom he met in Venice during his Grand Tour (Mem. 9 July 1765, Journ. 13 Feb. 1766).

[5] The optional phrase markings around 'said he' were misread as parentheses, an error that went unchecked in the printing.

[6] JB here reworks a passage from his original memorandum (15 March 1764): "'The miss and the philosopher have their desires equally satisfied. This bottle and that glass are equally full. But the bottle holds more.'"

[7] This 'Gay friend' was John Wilkes (Journ. 13 Feb. 1766), whom JB would describe as his 'gay friend' a few paragraphs later ('Our next meeting at the Mitre ...').

'ʌWhyʌ Sir in the [formal>] formulary and statutory [practice>] part of law a
plodding blockhead may [succeed>] excell; but in the [equitable>] ingenious and
rational part of it a plodding Blockhead can never [succeed>] excell.' [I said 'I fear
I shall not be a good Advocate.' *Johnson.* 'Why Sir, to be sure you will not be a
good Advocate at first; and Sir no man is a good Advocate at first; and perhaps in
seven years, you will not be so good a Lawyer as your Father, and perhaps never.
But it is better to be a tolerable Lawyer than no Lawyer; and Sir you will always see
many beneath you.' *del*] I talked [of courting great men and said Sir would you
have done it?>] of the mode adopted by some to rise in the world by courting great
men and asked him whether he had ever submitted to it? *Johnson.* 'Sir, I [never
was/was never>] never was near enough to great men to court them. [I should
have done it. *del*] [MS 311] You may [court/be prudently attached to>] be
prudently attached to great men, and [yet/still>] yet independent. You are
[not/never>] not to do what you think wrong; and Sir you are to calculate and not
pay too dear for what you get. You must not give a shilling's worth of court for
sixpence worth of good. But if you can get a shilling's worth of good for sixpence
worth of court, you are a fool if you do not pay court.'
     He said 'If Convents should be allowed at all, they should [only be/be only>]
only be retreats for persons unable to serve the publick, or who have served it. It
is our [duty>] [duty first>] first duty to serve society, and after we have done that, we
may attend wholly to the salvation of our own souls. A youthful passion for
abstracted devotion should not be encouraged.
     I talked of second sight and other [predictions of things /the fulfilment of/
which may happen by chance>] mysterious manifestations the fulfilment of which
I suggested might happen by chance. *Johnson.* 'Yes, Sir, but they have happened
so often that mankind have agreed to think them [real>] not fortuitous.'
     I talked to him a great deal of what I had seen in Corsica, and of my
[intention/design>] intention to publish an Account of it. He encouraged me by
saying, 'You cannot go to the bottom of the subject; but all [MS 312] that you tell
us [is what we do not/dont know>] will be new to us. Give us as many anecdotes
as you can.' [Rousseau with whom I had passed some time in his wild retreat
having been mentioned and I having quoted some remarks made by Mr. Wilkes
whom I had met in Italy, *Johnson.* It seems ʌSirʌ you have kept very good company
abroad, Wilkes and Rousseau. *Boswell.* ʌsmilingʌ My Dear Sir>]
     ʌ[Our next meeting at the Mitre/At our next meeting at the Mitre>] Our next
meeting at the Mitre was on Saturday 15 Febry when I presented to him my old and
intimate friend the Reverend Mr. Temple, then of Cambridge. [*undeciphered word
del*] I having mentioned that I had passed some time with Rousseau in his wild
retreat and having quoted some remark made by Mr. Wilkes, with whom I had
passed many pleasant hours in Italy, [Johnson>] Johnson said, 'It seems, Sir, you
have kept very good company abroad, Rousseau and Wilkes.' Thinking it enough
to defend one at a time, I said nothing as to my gay friend, but [answered with a
smile. Boswell. My>] answered with a smile, 'My Dear Sir! You don't call
Rousseau bad company. [*Johnson del*] Do you really think him a bad man?'
Johnson. 'Sir, if you are to talk jestingly of this, I don't talk with you. If you [would
be/are to be>] mean to be serious, I think him one of the worst of men; a Rascal

7

who [ought/deserves>] ought to be hunted out of society as he has been. Three or four nations have expelled him; and it is a shame that he is protected in this country.' BOSWELL. 'I don't deny, Sir, [but that novel>] [but that his novel>] but his novel may ₍perhaps₎ do harm; but I cannot think his intention was bad.' JOHNSON. 'Sir, that will not do. We cannot prove any man's intention to be bad. You may shoot a man through the head, and say you intended to miss him; but the Judge will order you to be hanged. [The>] An alledged want of intention when evil is committed will not be [allowed/sustained>] allowed in a court of justice. Rousseau Sir is a very bad man. I would sooner sign a [MS 313] sentence for his transportation than that of any felon who has gone from the Old Bailey these many years. Yes I should like to have him work in the Plantations.' ₍Boswell. 'Sir Do you think him as bad a man as Voltaire?' Johnson. 'Why it is difficult to settle the proportion of iniquity between them.'₎

This violence seemed very strange to me who had read many of Rousseau's [writings with pleasure>] animated writings with great pleasure and even edification, ₍had been much pleased with his society and₎ was just come from the Continent where he was very generally admired. ₍Nor can I yet allow that he deserves the very severe censure which Johnson pronounced upon him. His absurd preference of savage to civilised life and other singularities are proofs rather of a defect in his understanding than of any depravity in his heart. And notwithstanding the unfavourable opinion .which many worthy men have expressed of his *Confession du Foi du Curé Savoyarde*, I cannot help admiring it as [a performance full of pious submission>] [the performance of a mind full of pious submission/full of sincere reve[re]ntial submission>] the performance of a mind full of sincere reve[re]ntial submission to Divine Mystery though beset with perplexing doubts, a state of mind which after all must sometimes be admitted by every candid man.₎ On his favourite subject of Subordination, Johnson 'So far is it from being true that men are naturally equal —/that/[8] no two people can be half an hour together but [/the/ del] one shall acquire an evident superiority over the other.'

[I mentioned the advice given us by Philosophers, to take consolation by thinking of those who are in a worse situation than we are, which cannot apply to all>] [I observed of the advice given us by Philosophers, to take consolation by thinking of those who are in a worse situation than we are, that it cannot apply to all>] I mentioned the advice given us by Philosophers, to console ourselves ₍when distressed or embarrassed₎ by thinking of those who are in a worse situation than ourselves. This I observed, could not apply to all, for there must be some who have nobody worse than they are. *Johnson.* 'Why, to be Sure, Sir there are; but they dont know it. There is no being so poor and so contemptible who does not think [he has somebody beneath him>] there is somebody still poorer and still more contemptible.'

As my stay in London at this time was very short, I had not many opportunities [MS 314] of being with Dr. Johnson, but I felt my veneration for him in no degree lessened by my having seen [Multorum hominum mores et urbes/a great deal>]

---

[8] The optional word, which JB left unresolved, is printed in the revises.

Multorum hominum mores et urbes. On the contrary by having it in my power to compare him with many of the most celebrated [persons/literati>] persons of other countries, my admiration of his extraordinary mind was increased and confirmed.

5   The roughness indeed which sometimes appeared in his [manners/address>] manners was more striking to me ₍now₎, from my having been accustomed to the studied smooth complying habits of the Continent; and I clearly recognised in him not without respect for his honest conscientious zeal the same indignant and sarcastical mode of treating every attempt [₍at all₎ *del*] to unhinge or weaken good principles.

10   One [day>] evening when a young gentleman teised him with an account of the infidelity of his servant, who he said [would/could>] would not believe [₍in₎ *del*] the Scriptures because he could not read them in the original tongues [or/and>] and be sure that they were not invented.[9] 'Why, foolish fellow,' said Johnson, 'has he any better authority for almost every thing that he believes?' — [But>] 'Then 15 the vulgar Sir never can [MS 315] know they are right, but must submit themselves to the learned' — *Johnson*. 'To be sure, Sir. The vulgar are the children of the State and [must be taught/must learn>] must be taught like children.' — 'Then Sir a poor Turk must be a Mohametan just as a poor englishman must be a christian.' *Johnson*. 'Why ₍yes₎ Sir and what then. This now is such stuff as I used to talk to 20 my Mother when I first began to think myself a clever fellow; and she ought to have whipt me for it.'

   Another evening Dr. Goldsmith and I called on him, with [intention to carry/take him with us to sup>] the hope of prevailing on him to sup with us at the Mitre. We found him indisposed, and resolved not to go abroad. 'Come then' said 25 Goldsmith 'we [will not/shan't>] will not go to the Mitre tonight since we cannot have the big man with us.' [Dr. *del*] Johnson [set us down>] [ordered us>] then called for a bottle of Port [. We took a glass cordially and talked away. *del*] of which Goldsmith and I partook while now a water drinker sat by us. *Goldsmith*. 'I think Mr. Johnson you don't go near the Theatres now. You give yourself no more 30 concern about a new Play than if you had never had any thing to do with the stage.' *Johnson*. 'Why Sir, our tastes ₍greatly₎ alter. The lad does not care for the child's rattle, and the old man does not care for the young man's whore.' *Goldsmith*. 'Nay Sir. But [MS 316] your Muse was not a Whore.' *Johnson*. 'Sir I dont think she was. But as we advance in the journey of life we drop some of the things which have 35 pleased us; Whether it be that we are fatigued and don't chuse to carry so many things any farther, or that we find other things which we like better.' Boswell. 'But Sir Why dont you give us some thing in some other way?' *Goldsmith*. 'Ay Sir, We have a claim upon you.' *Johnson*. 'No, Sir. I am not obliged to do any more. No man is obliged to do as much as he can do. A man is to have part of his life to 40 himself. If a Soldier has fought a good many campaigns, he is not to be blamed if he retires to ease and tranquillity. [Sir *del*] a Physician who has [long practised>] practised long in a great city, may be excused if he retires to a small town and takes less practice. ₍Now₎ Sir the good I can do by my conversation bears the same proportion to the good I can do by my Writings that the practice of a physician

<hr/>

[9] JB reports on the scepticism of his own Swiss valet, Jacob Hänni (Journ. 16 Feb. 1766).

retired to a small town does to his practice in a great City.' *Boswell.* 'But I wonder Sir, you have not more pleasure in writing, [than not⟩] than in not writing.' *Johnson.* 'Sir, you *may* wonder.'

He talked of making verses, and [said⟩] observed, 'The great [matter/difficulty⟩] difficulty is to know when you have made good ones. ∧When composing∧ I [generally have⟩] have generally had them in my [MS 317] mind, perhaps fifty at a time, walking up and down in my room and then I [write em,⟩] wrote them down, and often from laziness have written only half=lines. I have written a hundred lines in a day. I remember I wrote a hundred lines of the Vanity of Human Wishes in a day. Doctor ∧(turning to Goldsmith) 'I am not quite idle.∧ I wrote one line t'other day; but I made [no/out⟩] no more.' *Goldsmith.* 'Let us hear it. We'll put a bad one to it.' *Johnson.* 'No Sir. I have [forgot/forgotten⟩] forgot it.'

Such specimens of the easy and playful conversation of the great Dr. Samuel Johnson are I think to be prized as exhibiting the ∧little∧ varieties of a mind so enlarged and so powerful when objects of consequence required its exertions, and as giving us a minute knowledge of his character and modes of thinking.[1]

After I had been some time [in/returned to⟩] in Scotland I wrote to him 'On my first return to my native country after some years of absence, I was told of a vast number of my acquaintance who were all gone to the land of forgetfulness and I found myself like a man stalking over a field of battel who every moment perceives some one lying dead.' I complained to him of irresolution and mentioned my having [made/taken⟩] made a vow as a security for good conduct. I wrote to him again without being able to move his indolence, nor did I hear from him till he had received a Copy of my [MS 318] inaugural Exercise or Thesis ∧in Civil Law∧ which I published at my admission as an Advocate as is the custom in Scotland. He then wrote to me as follows

To James Boswell Esq:[2]
[Paper Apart] Dear Sir

The reception of your Theses put me in mind of my debt to you. Why did you [dedicate it to a man whom I know you did not much love *del*] * * * * * * * * * * * * * * *.[a] I will punish you for it by telling you that your Latin wants correction.[b] In the beginning *spei alteræ* ∧not to urge∧ that it should be *primæ* is not grammati-

[a] The passage omitted alluded to a private transaction.
[b] This censure relates to the Dedication which was as follows.

---

[1] SJ's letters to Bennet Langton (8 Mar. 1766 and 10 May 1766), together with the extensive footnotes accompanying them, first appeared in the second edition, where they are clustered at the end of the second volume: JB received them, as well as seven others from the period 1767–1775, too late for piecemeal insertion. For the third edition, EM distributed the letters so that they appeared in their chronologically appropriate positions.
[2] Direction to the compositor, '"The Reception of your Thesis"/(Take it in and put in a note The Dedication).' The Paper Apart is in the hand of Margaret Boswell. The footnotes are in JB's own hand, as are certain corrections of his wife's transcription; these corrections are noted below.

cal *alteræ* should be *alteri*. In the next line you seem to use *genus* absolutely for what we call *family* that is for *illustrious extraction* I doubt without Authority. *Homines nullius originis* for *nullis orti majoribus* or *nullo loco nati* is I am affraid barbarous.[3] — Ruddiman is dead.

5   I have now vexed you anough and will try to please you. Your resolution to obey your father I sincerely approve; but do not accustom yourself to enchain your volatility by vows: they will sometime leave a thorn in your mind which you will perhaps never be able to extract or eject. Take this warning, it is of great importance.

10   The study of the Law is what you very justly term it, copious and generous;[a] and in adding your name to its Proffessors you have done exactly what I have always wished when I wished you best. I hope that you will continue to pursue it vigerously and constantly. You gain at least what is no small advantage security from those troublesome and wearysome discontents which are always obtruding
15 themselves upon a mind vacant unemployed and undetermined.

    You ought to think it no small inducement to dilligence and perseverance that they will please your father. We all live upon the hope of pleasing some-body and the pleasure of pleasing ought to be greatest and at last always will be greatest when our endeavours are excelled in consequence of our duty.

20   Life is not long and too much of it must not pass in idle deliberations how it shall be spent deliberation which those who begin it by prudence and continue it with subtility must after long expence of thought conclude by chance. To prefer one future mode of life to another upon just reasons requires faculties which it has not pleased our Creator to give us.

25   If therefore the Proffession you have chosen has some unexpected inconveniences console yourself by refflecting that no Proffession is without them and that all the importunities and perplexities of Business are softness and Luxury compared with the incessant Cravings of Vacancy and the unsatisfactory expedients of idleness

       Hæc sunt quæ nostra potui te voce monere;
30   *Vade, age.*

    As to your History of Corsica you have no materials which others have not or may not have. You have some how or other warmed your imagination. I wish there were some Cure like the Lovers leap for all heads of which some single Idea has obtained an unreasonable and irregular possession. Mind your own affairs and
35 leave the Corsicans to theirs.

        I am Dear Sir/your most humble Servant/Sam. Johnson
London August 21. 1766.

   [a] This alludes to the first sentence of the Procemium of my Thesis. '*Jurisprudentiæ* studio nullum uberius, nullum generosius: in legibus enum
40 agitandis, populorum mores, variasque fortunæ vices ex quibus leges oriuntur, contemplari simul solemus.'

   [3] A program containing the Latin in question was included for the printer along with a note in JB's hand: 'This follows Note on the Letter to me taken in on page 318. It must be printed exactly as here only in smaller capitals.'

To Dr. Samuel Johnson[4]
[Paper Apart] Much Esteemed and Dear Sir
                                        Auchinleck/6 Novr. 1766.
    I plead not guilty to * * * * *[a]
    Having thus I hope cleared myself of the charge brought against me, I presume   5
you will not be displeased if I escape the punishment which you have decreed for
me unheard. If you have discharged the arrows of Criticism against an innocent
man, you must rejoice to find they have missed him or have not been pointed so as
to wound him.
    To talk no longer in allegory, I am with all deference going to offer a few   10
observations in defence of my Latin which you have found fault with.
    You think I should have used *Spei Primæ* instead of *Spei alteræ*. Spes is indeed
often used to express something on which we have a future dependence, as in Virg:
Eclog. 1. [L.>] l. 14. Modo namq gemellos *Spem* Gregis ah silice in nuda connixa
reliquit. and in Georg. 3. l. 473 *Spemque* Gregemque simul for the Lambs and the   15
Sheep. Yet it is also used to express any thing on which we have a present
dependence, and is well applyed to a man of distinguished influence, our support,
our refuge, our *Præsidium* a[s] Horace calls Mæcenas. So Æneid 12 l. 57. Queen
Amata addresses her son in law Turnus *Spes*[5]

. . . .

[MS 318] It appears from his Diary that he was at ‸this year‸ Mr Thrales from   20
before Midsummer till after Michaelmas, and that he afterwards passed a month at
Oxford. He had now contracted a great intimacy with Mr. Chambers of that
University ‸now[6] Sir Robert Chambers one of the Judges in India‸. [His
publications>] He published nothing this year in his own name but the ‸noble‸[7]
Dedication to the King of Adams's Treatise on the Globes[8] was [of his writing>]   25

    [a] The passage omitted explained the transaction to which the preceding letter had
alluded.

---

    [4] Direction to the compositor, '(Take it in)'. The copy is in the hand of one of JB's
children, except for heading, date, salutation, notes, and the opening and closing sentences, which are in JB's hand.
    [5] Here the copy of the letter ends abruptly. JB has drawn a line from 'Spes' to the bottom
of the page, where he has written 'tio'. It is likely that from this point onward the original
letter was used as printer's copy.
    [6] In the third edition, EM changed 'now' to 'afterwards': Chambers had returned to
England in 1799 after twenty-five years in India.
    [7] It appears that 'noble' was deleted at the stage of the revises and then later reinstated,
with the result that an adjective intended for Adams's work was applied to Gwyn's (see
below).
    [8] At the stage of the revises, JB changed 'Adams's Treatise on the Globes' to 'Gwyn's
"London and Westminster improved"'. JB's substitution of Gwyn for Adams reflects his
confusion over the date of the *Treatise on the Globes*, which did indeed appear in 1766
(Hazen, *Prefaces & Dedications*, pp. 1–2). JB mistakenly assigns it to 1767 (see below, MS
321).

written by him;[9] and he furnished the Preface and several of the Pieces [which compose/contained in›] which compose a Volume of [Miscellanies/Miscellany›] Miscellanies by Mrs. ₍Anna₎ Williams ₍the blind Lady who had an Asylum in his house.[1] Of these pieces there are his 'Epitaph on Philips' and 'Friendship an Ode'

5　and I have in his own handwriting 'The Ant' a paraphrase from the Proverbs and from internal evidence I ascribe to him 'To Miss ＿＿ on her giving the Authour a gold and silk network purse of her own weaving' and 'The Happy Life.' — Most of them have evidently received considerable additions from his superiour pen, particularly 'Verses to Mr. Richardson on his Sir Charles Grandison' — 'The

10　Excursion' — 'Reflections on a grave digging in Westminster Abbey.' There is in this Collection a Poem 'On the death of Stephen Grey [F.R.S.›] the Electrician' which on reading it appeared to me to be undoubtedly Johnson's. I asked Mrs. Williams if it was not? 'Sir' said she, with some warmth, 'I wrote that Poem before I had the honour of Dr. Johnson's acquaintance.' I however was so much

15　impressed with my first notion that I mentioned it to Johnson repeating at the same time what Mrs. Williams had said. His answer was 'It is true Sir that she did it before she was acquainted with me; but she has not told you that I wrote it all over again except two lines.' 'The Fountains'[2] a beautiful little fairy tale in prose written with exquisite simplicity is one of Johnson's productions; and I cannot

20　withhold from Mrs. Thrale the praise of being the Authour of that admirable [performance›] poem 'The Three Warnings'.₎

[MS 319] But he wrote this year a Letter not intended for publication which has perhaps as strong marks of his sentiment and style as any of his compositions. The Original is in my possession. It is addressed to the late Mr. William Drummond

25　Bookseller in Edinburgh a Gentleman of good family ₍but small estate₎ who took arms for the House of Stuart in 1745[–6 del], and during his concealment ₍in London till the act of general pardon came out₎ obtained the acquaintance of Dr. Johnson who justly esteemed him as a very worthy man. It seems some of the Members of the Society in Scotland for propagating Christian Knowledge had

30　opposed ₍the scheme of₎ translating the Holy Scriptures into the Erse or Gaelick language from political considerations of the disadvantage of keeping up the distinction between the Highlanders and the other inhabitants of North Britain. Dr. Johnson being informed of this ₍I suppose by Mr. Drummond₎ wrote with a generous indignation as follows

35　　　　　　　　　To Mr. William Drummond[3]
[Paper Apart] Sir

I did not expect to hear that it could be in an assembly convened for the propagation of Christian knowledge a question whether any nation uninstructed

---

[9] This word is followed by an asterisk that does not seem to correspond to any marginalia.

[1] In a marginal note, JB has written, '"Translation of the Epitaph on Hanmer"'. Next to this appears a compositorial query, 'where this goes in?'

[2] This word is followed by an asterisk that does not seem to correspond to any marginalia.

[3] Direction to the compositor, '(Take it in*)'. The Paper Apart is written in the hand of Margaret Boswell, with corrections by JB.

in religion should receive instruction or whether that instruction should be imparted to them by a translation of the Holy Books into their own language. If obedience to the will of GOD is necessary to happiness, and knowledge of his will be necessary to obedience, I know not how he that withholds this knowledge, or delays it can be said to love his neighbour as himself. He that voluntarily 5 continues ignorance is guilty of all the crimes which ignorance produces; as to him that should extinguish the tapers of a light-House might justly be imputed the calamities of shipwrecks. Christianity is the highest perfection of humanity; and as no man is good but as he wishes the good of others, no man can be good in the highest degree who wishes not to others the largest measure of the greatest good. 10 To omit for a year, or for a day, the most efficacious method of advancing Christianity, in compliance with any purposes that terminate on this side of the grave, is a crime of which I know not the world has yet had an example except in the practice of the Planters of America a Race of Mortals whom I suppose no other man wishes to resemble. 15

The Papists have indeed denied to the laity the use of the bible but this prohibition in few places now very rigorously enforced is defended by arguments which have for their foundation the care of souls. To obscure upon motives merely political the light of Revelation is a practice reserved for the reformed and surely the blackest midnight of Popery is Meridian sunshine to such a reformation. I am 20 not very willing that any Language should be totally extinguished, the similitude and derivation of languages afford the most indubitable prooff of the traduction of nations and the geneology of mankind. They add often physical certainty to historical evidence and often supply the only Evidence of ancient Migrations and the Revolution of ages which left no written monuments behind them. 25

Every mans opinions, at least his desires, are a little influenced by his favourite studies. My zeal for Languages may seem perhaps rather overheated even to those by whom I desired to be well esteemed. To those who have nothing in [/their/>] their thoughts but trade or Policy present power or present Money I should not think it necessary to defend my opinions but with Men of letters I would not 30 unwillingly compound by wishing the continuance of every language however narrow in its extent or however incommodious for common purposes till it is reposited in some version of a known book that it may be always hereafter examined and compared with other languages and then permitting its disuse. For this purpose the translation of the Bible is most to be desired. It is not certain that 35 the same method will not preserve the Highland language for the purposes of learning and abolish it from daily use. When the Highlanders read the Bible they will naturally wish to have its obscurities cleared and to know the history collatoral or appendant. Knowledge always desires increase it is like fire which must first be kindled by some external agent but which will afterwards propagate 40 itself. When they once desire to learn they will naturally have recourse to the nearest language by which that desire can be gratified and one will tell another that if he would attain knowledge, he must learn English.

This speculation may perhaps be thought more subtle than the [*erasure*][4] of real

---

[4] The original word was erased and a blank space left. In the revises, as in the first three editions, the word printed was 'grossness'.

life will easily admit. Let it however be remembered that the efficacy of ignorance has been long tried and has not produced the consequence expected. Let knowledge therefore take its turn and let the patrons of privation stand awhile aside and admit the operation of positive principles.

5   You will be pleased Sir to assure the worthy man who is employed in the new translation that he has my wishes for his success, and if here or at Oxford I can be of any use that I shall think it more than honour to promote his undertaking.[5] I am sorry that I delayed so long to write.

                         I am, Sir etc.
10   SAM: JOHNSON
Johnsons Court Fleet Street
Augt. 13. 1766

[MS 319 resumed] ⟨The opposers being made ashamed of their strange conduct, the benevolent and pious undertaking was allowed to go on.⟩
15   The following Letters though not written till the year after being ⟨chiefly⟩ upon the same subject are now ⟨here⟩ inserted.

[MS 320] To Mr William Drummond[6]

. . . .

To Mr William Drummond[7]

. . . .

Mr. Cuthbert Shaw[8] [of whom I can∫could learn no more from his Bookseller
20   Mr. Flexney[9] but that he was an ingenious Writer about town who died very young from living too fast⟩] alike distinguished for his genius his misfortunes and his misconduct, published this year a Poem called 'The Race By Mercurius Spur Esq' in which he whimsically made the living Poets of England contend for ⟨preeminence of⟩ fame by running. .
25   'Prove by their heels the prowess of the Head'. In this Poem there was the following Portrait∫character[1] of Johnson.[2]

. . . .

---

[5] On 19 April 1793 the Rev. John Campbell, Minister of Kippen, Stirling, sent JB a long list of suggestions and corrections for a second edition. These included an account of the Rev. James Stuart, 'the worthy man employed in the Gaelic Translation of the New Testament' (*Corr.* 2, p. 525). Though JB assured Campbell that he had 'introduced your character of the worthy translator' (*Corr.* 2, p. 545), the identification did not appear until the third edition.

[6] Direction to the compositor, 'Dear Sir/That my letter should have had/(Take it in) Letter D2'. This Paper Apart no longer forms part of the *Life* MS.

[7] Direction to the compositor, 'I returned/(Take it in) Letter D3'. This Paper Apart no longer forms part of the *Life* MS.

[8] In the revises, a footnote is keyed to Shaw's name: 'See an account of him in the European Magazine, Jan. 1786'.

[9] William Flexney (1731–1808), best known as the publisher of Charles Churchill, had brought out JB's *Critical Strictures on Elvira* (1763) and *Letters between the Honourable Andrew Erskine and James Boswell, Esq.* (1763) (*Lit. Car.* pp. 18–19).

[1] The alternative is resolved by the printing of 'portrait' in the revises.

[2] Direction to the compositor, '(Take it in from the little Parcel of European Magazine)'.

The Honourable Thomas Hervey and his Lady having unhappily differed and being about to separate, Johnson interfered as their friend and wrote him a letter of expostulation which [cannot be found>] I have not been able to find; but the substance of it is proved by a Letter to Johnson which Mr. Hervey printed in answer to it. ⟨The occasion of this correspondence between Dr. Johnson and Mr.   5 Hervey was thus related to me by Mr. Beauclerk.³ 'Tom Hervey had a great liking for Johnson and [had put him into his will for a>] in his will had left him a legacy of fifty pounds. One day he said to me, "Johnson may want this money now more than afterwards. I have a mind to give it him directly. Will you be so good as to carry a fifty pound note from me to him." This I positively refused to do as he   10 might perhaps have knocked me down for insulting him and have afterwards put the note in his pocket. But I said if Hervey would write him a letter and enclose a fifty pound note, I should take care to deliver it. He accordingly did write him a letter mentioning that he was only paying a legacy a little sooner. To his letter he added "[*Postscript*>] *P.S. I am going to part with my wife*". Johnson then wrote to him   15 [taking no notice at all>] saying nothing of the note, but expostulating with him against parting with his wife'.

When I mentioned to Johnson this story in as delicate terms as I could, he told me that the fifty pound note was given to him by Mr. Hervey in consideration of his having written for him a pamphlet against Sir Charles Hanbury Williams, who   20 Mr. Harvey imagined was guilty of an attack upon him. [It>] But that it was afterwards discovered to be [written by>] the work by a gareteer who wrote 'The Fool'; so the pamphlet against Sir Charles was not printed.⟩

[Paper Apart] ⁴ In february [this year happened>] 1767 there happened one of the ⟨most⟩ memorable incidents of [his>] Johnson's life which [pleased>] gratified   25 his monarchical enthusiasm and which he loved to relate with all its circum-stances when requested by his freinds. This was [his being/being his>] his being honoured by a private conversation with his Majesty in the Library at the Queen's House. He had frequently visited that splendid room and noble collection of Books⁵ which he used to say was more numerous and curious than he   30 [supposed/*undeciphered word*>] supposed any person could have [got together/brought together>] made in the time which the King had [taken>] employed. Mr. Barnard, [the Sublibrarian whom he knew and esteemed>] [one of the Librarians whom he knew and esteemed and who is indeed remarkably

---

³ The information contained in the rest of this paragraph derives from JB's Notebook. In adapting his entry for the *Life*, JB chooses not to mention a difference of opinion with Topham Beauclerk: 'Beauclerc censured Mr Johnson's want of gratitude for the favour. I maintaind that there was a dignity in receiving the present as a tribute to superiour excellence' (*Note Book*, pp. 15–16).

⁴ This extensive Paper Apart, which numbers sixteen leaves, includes multiple revisions in the hand of Edmond Malone. These are designated 'EM' in the end notes.

⁵ In the first edition, a footnote is keyed to 'Books': 'Dr. Johnson had the honour of contributing his assistance towards the formation of this library; for I have read a long letter from him to Mr. Barnard, giving the most masterly instructions on the subject. I wished much to have gratified my readers with the perusal of this letter, and have reason to think that his Majesty would have been graciously pleased to permit its publication; but Mr. Barnard, to whom I applied, declined it "on his own account"'.

obliging to every body⟩] one of the Librarians whom Dr. Johnson knew and esteemed, took care that he should have every accomodation that could contribute to his ease [PA p. 2] and convenience [while/for⟩] while indulging his literary taste ⟨in that place⟩; so that he had here a very [pleasing occupation⟩] agreable
5   resource at leisure hours.

His Majesty having been informed of [these⟩] [his frequent⟩] his occasional visits was pleased to signify a desire that he should be told when Dr. Johnson [came there again⟩] [next visited⟩] next came to the library. Accordingly the next time that Johnson [came⟩] did come, as soon as he was fairly engaged with a Book on
10   which while he sat by the fire he seemed quite intent [in examining *del*], Mr. Barnard stole round to the apartment where the King was and in obedience to his Majesty's commands mentioned that Dr. Johnson was [now⟩] then in the library. His Majesty said he was [now /quite/*del*] [then *del*] at leisure, and would go to him; upon which Mr. Barnard took one of the candles that stood on the King's table and
15   lighted his Majesty through a suite [PA p. 3] of rooms till they came to a private door into the Library of which his Majesty [had the/kept a⟩] had the key. Being entered, Mr. Barnard [ran up to⟩] [advanced to⟩] stepped forward hastily to Dr. Johnson who was still in [a *del*] profound study and [said⟩] whispered him, 'Sir, here is the King.' Johnson started up and stood still. His Majesty approached him, and
20   at once was courteously easy.[a]

[a] The particulars of this conversation I have been at great pains to collect with [the utmost/all possible⟩] the utmost authenticity from Dr. Johnson's own detail to myself, from Mr. Langton who was present when he gave an account of it to Dr. Joseph Warton and several [more⟩] *other*[a1] freinds at Sir Joshua Reynolds's, from
25   Mr. Barnard, from the draft of a letter [to Bishop Warburton from⟩] *written by* the late Mr. Strahan the Printer ⟨*to Bishop Warburton*⟩ and from a Minute [⟨*of*⟩ *del*] the original of which is among the Papers of the late Sir [PA p. 4] James Caldwell[a2] and [which at the spontaneous request of Mr. Berkeley[a3] grandson of the Bishop of Cloyne⟩] a copy of which was most obligingly obtained for me from his son Sir
30   John Caldwell by Sir Francis Lumm. To all of these gentlemen I beg leave to make my grateful acknowledgements and particularly to Sir Francis Lumm who was [pleased/so good as⟩] pleased to take a great deal of trouble, and even had the Minute laid before [his Majesty⟩] the King by Lord Caermarthen ⟨now Duke of Leeds⟩ one of his Majestys Principal Secretaries of State, who communicated to
35   Sir Francis the Royal pleasure concerning it ⟨by a letter in these words 'I have the King's commands to assure you, Sir, how sensible his Majesty is of your attention in communicating the minute of the conversation previous to its publication.⟩ As there appears no objection to your complying with Mr. Boswell's wishes on the subject you are at full liberty to deliver it to that Gentleman to make such use of
40   in his Life of Dr. Johnson as he may think proper.'

[a1] This note was originally part of the main text. JB later designated it a note by placing brackets around the first and last words of the paragraph and writing in the margin 'Note' and 'All within Crotchets is a Note'. Additions in the hand of EM are singled out by the use of italic type.

[a2] Of the sources that JB mentions in his note, only one has been recovered: the

His Majesty began [PA p. 5] by observing to Dr. Johnson that he understood [he/Dr. J>] he came sometimes to [⟨undeciphered word⟩ del] the Library — [and then mentioning his having been/that his having heard that the Doctor had been>] and then mentioning his having heard that the Doctor had been lately at Oxford asked him if he was not fond of going [to Oxford>] thither? to which 5 Johnson answered that he [was indeed/liked>] was indeed fond of going to Oxford sometimes but [was likewise glad/that he also liked>] was likewise glad to come back again. The King then asked him what they were doing at Oxford? Johnson answered he could not much commend their diligence but that in some respects they were mended, for they had put their press under better regulations, and were 10 [at that time/then>] at that time printing Polybius. He was then asked whether [they had>] there were better libraries at Oxford or at Cambridge? He answered he believed the Bodleian [PA p. 6] was larger than any they had at Cambridge [but at the same time added that he hoped whether>] at the same time adding, 'I hope whether we have more books or not [/than they have at Cambridge/>] than they 15 have at Cambridge we [should>] shall make as good use of them as they do.' Being asked whether All Souls or Christs Church Library was the largest, he answered [that del] 'All Souls Library is the largest we have except the Bodleian.' 'Aye' said the King, 'that is the Publick Library.'

The King then [asked him>] inquired if he was ⟨then⟩ writing any thing [at 20 present? del] He answered He was not, for he had pretty well [told the world what he knew/exhausted what little knowledge he had gathered>] told the world what he knew, and must now [and read for more>] [read to acquire more>] read to acquire more knowledge. The King ⟨[and by thus>] [then>] as it should seem with a view to urge him to rely on his own stores as an original writer and to continue 25 his labours,⟩ [said>] [having said>] then said, [I do not think you borrow>] [that he did not think Dr. Johnson borrowed>] 'I do not think you borrow much from any

---

'Caldwell Minute', a copy of an account of the meeting written by SJ himself and sent to Sir James Caldwell. By comparing the text of the Minute with that of JB's Paper Apart, Frank Taylor has demonstrated that the Minute was JB's primary source for the conversation with the King: 'given the Minute we may by a process of elimination discover the rest, for, that removed, it can be seen that what remains contains for the most part its own indications of source in the form of words such as "Johnson observed to me", "at Sir Joshua Reynolds's", "said Johnson to his friends", "he said to Mr. Barnard", and "he afterwards observed to Mr. Langton"' (p. 246). According to Taylor, phrases such as these, together with the Minute itself, 'account for all [JB's] sources save one, Strahan's letter, and cover the whole of his account of the royal interview save ten lines' (p. 246). See 'Johnsoniana from the Bagshawe Muniments in the John Rylands Library: Sir James Caldwell, Dr. Hawkesworth, Dr. Johnson, and Boswell's Use of the "Caldwell Minute"', *Bulletin of the John Rylands Library* 35 (1952–53): 211–47.

a3 George Monck Berkeley (1763–93), son of the Reverend George Berkeley, prebendary of Canterbury, and grandson of Bishop Berkeley, was a minor writer of miscellaneous works such as *Maria, or, the generous Rustic* (1784) and *Heloise: or, the siege of Rhodes* (1788). He was also a corresponding member of the Edinburgh Society of Antiquaries. This deleted reference to Berkeley is the only record of his role in procuring a copy of the 'Caldwell Minute'. On 1 March 1786, JB 'waited on Sir Francis Lumm, who had obligingly procured me from Sir John Caldwell a minute of the conversation between the King and Dr. Johnson which was in the late Sir James Caldwell's repositories' (Journ. 1 Mar. 1786).

body.[6] Johnson said [he thought/I think>] he thought *[PA p. 7]* he had [done his share as a Writer>] [pretty well done his part as a Writer/an Authour>] already done his part as a Writer.[7] 'I should have thought so too,' said the King, 'if you had not written so well.' — Johnson observed to me upon this ∧that∧ 'No man could
5 have [paid/made>] paid a handsomer compliment; and it was fit for a King to [pay/make>] pay. It was decisive.' When asked by another freind [/at Sir Joshua Reynolds's/>] at Sir Joshua Reynolds's whether he made any reply to [this high compliment/his Majesty>] this high compliment, he answered, 'No Sir. When the King ∧had∧ said it, it was to be so. It was not for me to bandy civilities with my
10 Sovereign.' [Johnson here shewed a dignified sense of true politeness. Sir Charles Hotham[8] ∧who is∧ certainly one of the best/first judges of manners/good breeding/high breeding said>] Perhaps no man who had spent his whole life in courts could have shewn a more nice and a dignified sense of true politeness than Johnson did in this instance.
15 His Majesty [said>] having observed to him that he [thought he must have read/supposed he had read>] supposed he must have read a great deal Johnson answered that [/he thought more *[PA p. 8]* than he read/>] he thought more than he·read that he had not indeed neglected reading ∧he had read a great deal in the earlier part of his life∧ but having fallen into ill health he had not been able to
20 read much compared with others;[9] for instance he said he had not read much compared with Doctor Warburton upon which the King said that he heard Doctor Warburton was a man of [very>] such general knowledge, that you could scarce talk with him on any subject on which he was not qualified to speak, and

---

[6] After drawing a line through 'I do not think you borrow', JB changed his mind about the deletion and wrote 'stet' three times above the deleted words.

[7] JB has written 'allready contributed' and 'written my share' in the margins. Presumably these are discarded alternatives to 'already done his part'.

[8] Sir Charles Hotham (1729–94), 8th Bt., of Dalton Hall, Yorkshire, M.P. for St. Ives (1761–68) and Groom of the Bedchamber (1763–94), came from a family with a long tradition of royal service: father and grandfather had also served as Grooms of the Bedchamber (Namier and Brooke ii. 641). It is not clear whether the compliment to SJ's 'true politeness', which appears in the published *Life* to be JB's own, in fact originated with Hotham.

[9] The first draft of this passage is complex and defies representation by symbols alone. JB appears simultaneously to have entertained multiple possibilities, with the result that he embedded one set of alternative phrases within another. The inner set of alternative phrases described SJ's lack of early reading: 'he had not been able to read much compared with eg those who had/he had read little in comparison with Dr. Warburton'. Both of these fragments were considered by JB as possible endings for a phrase beginning, 'he had not indeed neglected reading but having very early in life fallen into ill health'. This entire passage — including its fluid and unresolved ending — was in turn considered by JB an alternative to the following interlined possibility: 'read a great deal early in life but was soon attacked by sickness which stopped his career.' All four of these phrases appear to have been written in the same draft and to have been deleted all at once in a later draft — the draft in which JB composed the final version transcribed above. There is no evidence that JB resolved any of his alternative phrases in an intermediate draft.

that his learning resembled Garrick's acting, in its universality.[1] His Majesty then talked of the Controversy between Warburton and Lowth which he seemed to have read and asked Johnson [what he thought/his opinion>] what he thought of it. Johnson answered, [Warburton has/that Warburton had most general Lowth most scholastick learning>] 'Warburton has most general most scholastick learning Lowth [was/is>] was the more correct scholar. [I do not/He did not>] I do not know which of them [calls/called>] calls names best.' [The King was pleased to say he judged [PA p. 9] of them very rightly/said that Dr. Johnson was of the same opinion and added you do not think then /Doctor Johnson/ that there was much argument in the case>] [The King was pleased to say he was of the same opinion adding You do not think then /Doctor Johnson/ that there was much argument in the case/So you think argument was out of the question. Indeed when you come to calling names argument must be very nearly exhausted>] The King was pleased to say he was of the same opinion adding, 'You do not think then, Doctor Johnson, that there was much argument in the case.' Johnson said he did not think there was. 'Why, [true>] truly,' said the King, 'when once it comes to calling names argument is pretty well at an end.'

His Majesty observed that Historians are in general very partial in giving the characters of Kings for they make them either very good or very bad. (This was introduced by speaking of Mr. Walpoles Historick Doubts.)[2] Johnson answered 'Kings Sir are generally spoken of in extremes. I have indeed no excuse to make for those who speak worse of Kings than they deserve; but as Kings have it much in their power to confer happiness it is easy to account how they happen/for their being often to be praised [PA p. 9] to excess from the gratitude of those upon whom their favours have been conferred, and /though it was an errour to depart from truth upon any occasion yet/ as far as errour was allowable it was so in this instance.>][3]

His Majesty then asked him what he thought of Lord Littletons [Book>] History ʌwhich was thenʌ just published. Johnson said he thought his style pretty good but that he had blamed Henry the Second rather too much. 'Why,' says the King, 'they seldom do these things by halves.' 'No Sir' answered Johnson 'not to Kings' but fearing to be misunderstood he proceeded to explain himself and immediately subjoined that for those who spoke worse of Kings than they deserved he could

---

[1] In the second edition, a footnote is keyed to 'universality': 'The Reverend Mr. Strahan clearly recollects having been told by Johnson, that the King observed that Pope made Warburton a Bishop. "True, Sir, (said Johnson,) but Warburton did more for Pope; he made him a Christian:' alluding, no doubt, to his ingenious Comments on the "Essay on Man."'

[2] In his *Historic Doubts on the Life and Reign of King Richard the Third* (1768), Horace Walpole mounted a fervent defense of the King's character and actions. Taking to task the 'prejudice and invention' of previous historians as well as the 'litterary superstition' of Shakespeare, Walpole claimed to do 'historic justice' to Richard (*Historic Doubts*, ed. P.W. Hammond, 1987, pp. 8, 11–12.)

[3] After drafting this paragraph, JB returned to the 'Caldwell Minute' and found that SJ and the King had discussed Lord Lyttelton's *History of Henry II* and not Walpole's *Historic Doubts* (which was published the year after their conversation). He therefore revised his account, substituting references to the correct title.

find no excuse, but that he could easier conceive how some might speak better of them than they deserved without any ill intention; for, as Kings had much in their power to give, those who were [much obliged to›] favoured by them would frequently from gratitude exaggerate their praises, and as this proceeded from a
5   good motive it was certainly excuseable as far as errour could be excuseable.ᴧ

His Majesty then asked him what he thought of Doctor Hill? Johnson answered that he was an ingenious man but had no veracity, and immediately [produced›] mentioned as an instance of it an assertion of Dr. Hill that he had seen objects magnified to a much greater degree by using three or four microscopes at a time
10   ᴧthan by using one.ᴧ 'Now' [said he›] (added Johnson) 'every one acquainted with microscopes knows that the more of them he looks through the less [he will see›] the object will appear.' — 'Why,' replied the King, 'this is not only telling [a falsehood/an imposition of a very gross kind›] an untruth [PA p. 11] but telling it clumsily, for if that be the case every one who can look through a microscope will
15   be able to detect him.'

['Then,' (said Johnson to his freinds when relating what had passed,) 'I began›] 'I now,' (said Johnson to his freinds when relating what had passed), 'began to consider that I was [running/depreciating/depressing›] depreciating this man down in the estimation of his Sovereign and thought it was time for me to say
20   something that might be more favourable.' [So he proceeded to tell the King/added›] He added therefore that Doctor Hill was notwithstanding a very curious Observer, and if he [would have been/would be›] would have been contented to tell the World no more than he knew he might have [made/been›] been a very considerable man and needed not to have recourse to such mean
25   expedients to raise his reputation.

The King then talked [PA p. 12] of Literary Journals, [and del] mentioned particularly the *Journal des Savans* and asked Johnson if it was well [done/executed›] done. Johnson said it was formerly [/very/›] very well done and gave some account of the persons who began it and carried it on for some [time›]
30   years, [explaining/discoursing/enlarging›] enlarging at the same time on the nature and use of such Works. The King asked him if it was well [done/executed›] done now. Johnson answered he [had no reason to think/could not say›] had no reason to think that it was. The King then asked him if there were any other literary Journals published in [this Kingdom/Britain›] this Kingdom except the
35   Monthly and Critical Reviews, and on being answered [there were no other/in the negative›] there were no other his Majesty asked which of them was the best. Johnson answered that The Monthly Review was [done/written›] done with most Care, the Critical upon the best principles, adding [PA p. 13] that [the Authours of the Monthly Review/the Monthly Reviewers›] the Authours of the Monthly
40   Review were enemies to the Church. [This the King said he was sorry to hear/The King said he was sorry to hear it›] This the King said he was sorry to hear.

The Conversation next turned on the Philosophical Transactions when Johnson observed that they had now a better method of [sorting›] arranging their materials ᴧthan formerly.ᴧ 'Aye' said the King 'they are obliged to Dr. Johnson for
45   that'; for his Majesty had heard and remembered the circumstance, which Johnson himself had forgot.

His Majesty expressed a desire to have the Literary Biography of this Country ably executed and proposed to [/Dr./>] Dr. Johnson to [do it>] undertake it. Johnson [seemed resolved to comply with the Royal requisition/signified his readiness to obey his Majesty's suggestion>] signified his readiness to comply with his Majesty's wishes.   5

During the whole of this Interview Johnson talked to his Majesty with profound respect but still in his firm manly manner, [with/in>] with a sonorous voice and never [below his breath>] in that subdued tone ⸜which is commonly used at the Levee and in the Drawing Room.⸝ [When/After his Majesty was gone>] After [then *del*] the King withdrew, [PA p. 14] Johnson shewed himself highly pleased /with his Majestys   10 conversation and gracious behaviour/.[4] He said to Mr. Barnard, 'Sir, they may talk of the King as they will; but he is the finest Gentleman I have ever seen'; ⸜and he afterwards observed to Mr. Langton 'Sir, His manners were those of as fine a gentleman as we may suppose Lewis the Fourteenth or Charles the Second.'⸝

At Sir Joshua Reynolds's where a circle of [his>] Johnson's freinds   15 [gathered/formed>] [was formed>] was collected round him to hear his Account of this ⸜memorable⸝ [interview/conversation>] interview, Dr. Joseph Warton in his frank ⸜and⸝ lively [cheerful *del*] manner was [particularly>] very active in pressing him to give the particulars. 'Come now ⸜Sir⸝, this is an interesting matter, do favour us with it.' Johnson with great good humour complied.   20

He [told them/said>] told them, 'I found his Majesty wished I should talk, and I made it my business to talk. I find it does a man good to be talked to by his Sovereign. In the first place, a man cannot be in a passion.' X X X Here some question [PA p. 15] interrupted him, which is to be regretted as he certainly would have pointed out and illustrated many particulars of advantage from being in a   25 situation where the powers of the mind are at once excited to vigorous exertion [from the hope of pleasing and tempered by reverential awe and fear of offending>] [from the hope of pleasing and restrained from intemperance from the fear of offending>] and tempered by reverential awe.

During all the time in which Dr. Johnson was [employed in   30 relating/repeating>] employed in relating to the circle at Sir Joshua Reynolds's the particulars of what passed between the King and him, Dr. Goldsmith [kept himself fast/sate >] remained ⸜unmoved⸝ upon a [sopha/settee>] sopha at some distance [not appearing/affecting not>] affecting not to join in the least in the eager curiosity of the company. He [gave>] assigned as a reason for his [uneasiness>]   35 gloom and seeming inattention that he apprehended Johnson [had withdrawn his purpose of giving him>] [did not mean to furnish him with>] had relinquished his purpose of furnishing him with a Prologue to his Play with the hopes of which he had been flattered; but [PA p. 16] it was strongly [suspected/believed>] suspected that he was fretting with ⸜chagrin and⸝ envy ⸜at the singular honour wch Dr. J.   40 had [so *del*] lately enjoyed⸝. At length [the naiveté of>] the frankness and simplicity of his natural character prevailed. He sprung from the [settee>] sopha [/and/ walked/came up>] advanced to Johnson and in a kind of flutter from imagining himself in the situation which he had just been hearing described, [he exclaimed/called out>] exclaimed, 'Well you acquitted yourself in this conversa-   45

---

[4] Printed in the revises.

tion better than I should [/have done/>] have done for I should have bowed and stammered through the whole of it.'

[MS 320] In 1767 I received no letter from him,[5] [though I wrote anxiously *del*]; nor have I discovered any ‚of theλ correspondence[a] he had except the two letters to Mr. Drummond which have been inserted [in>] for the sake of connection with that to the same Gentleman in 1766.[6] His Diary [gives no satisfaction; but>] affords no insight into his employment at this time. [He passed near/about three months at Lichfield and I cannot omit an affecting and solemn scene there as related by himself *del*]. He passed near/about three months at Lichfield and I cannot omit an affecting and solemn scene there as related by himself.[7]

. . . .

[Paper Apart CC][8] By those who have been taught to look upon Johnson as a harsh and savage character let this tender and affectionate scene be candidly read, and let them then judge whether more warmth of heart and grateful kindness is often found [am *del*] in human nature.

[MS 320] We have the following notice in his Devotional Record

August 2. 1767

'I have been disturbed and unsettled for a [MS 321] long time, and have been without resolution to apply to study or to business, being hindred by sudden snatches.'[9]

[He at all times undervalued/underrated his own labours and attainments. For this year in which he views himself as doing nothing appeared *The* ‚Englishλ *Works of Roger Ascham* to which he contributed a Dedication to the Earl of Shaftesbury and a Life of the Authour. *del*][10]

[a] It is proper here to mention that when I speak of his correspondence, I consider it independent of the voluminous collection of Letters which in the course of many years he wrote to Mrs. Thrale, which forms a separate part of his Works and as a proof of the high estimation [on which *del*] put on any thing which he wrote was sold by that Lady for the sum of Five hundred pounds.[a1]

---

[5] No Register of Letters has been recovered for the period from October 1766 to June 1769 (M 252, M 253).

[6] Initially, JB had marked an 'X' here which corresponded to a marginal note, later deleted, reading 'Take in Paper Apart.'

[7] JB deleted and then reinserted this sentence by writing 'Stet all here' in the margin. There is also a marginal direction to the compositor, 'Take in Paper Apart CC'.

[8] Direction to the compositor, '(Take in p 77 and p 78 of "Prayers and Meditations" and add what follows'.

[9] JB has marked an 'X' after 'nature', which corresponds to an 'X' at the bottom of the page; there JB has noted, 'Prayers and Meditations, p. 73'. In the revises, this note became two separate notes: one, keyed to 'snatches', reading 'Prayers and Meditations, p. 77 and 78' and a second, keyed to 'Dedication', reading 'Ibid. p. 73'.

[10] Presumably JB deleted this paragraph when he realized that a version of it had already appeared in the narrative for 1763 (*Life* MS i. 327–28).

[a1] This note is written on a Paper Apart which bears the heading 'Note (on word correspondence 320)'. JB has reiterated this point by writing 'Note For p. 320' at the foot of the page as well.

He however furnished Mr. Adams with a Dedication* to the King of that ingenious gentleman's 'Treatise on the Globes' conceived and expressed in such a manner [and? *del*] as could not fail to be very grateful to a Monarch distinguished for [his love of›] his love of ‚the‚ science.[1]

[*Paper Apart*][2] This year was published a Ridicule of his Style, under the title   5
of 'Lexiphanes.' Sir John Hawkins ascribes it to Dr. Kenrick but its Authour was one Campbell a scotch purser in the navy. The ridicule consisted in applying Johnson's 'words of large meaning' to insignificant matters, as if one should put the armour of Goliath upon a dwarf. The contrast might be laughable; but the dignity of the armour must remain the same in all considerate minds. This ‚malicious‚   10
drollery therefore it may easily be supposed could do no harm to its illustrious object.[3]

[*Note opp 322*] ‚It appears from his [notes of the state of his mind/Meditations›] notes of the state of his mind,[4] that he [suffered/was afflicted with›] suffered great perturbation and distraction in 1768. Nothing of his Writing   15
[appeared publickly›] was given to the publick this year except the Prologue to his friend Goldsmith's Comedy of '*The Goodnatured Man*' [, in which, as it was the year of a general election he ‚very ingeniously‚ runs a paralel *del*].[5] The [introduction›] first lines of this Prologue are strongly characteristical of the dismal gloom of his mind which in his case as in the case of all who are distressed with the same   20
malady of imagination transfers to others its own feelings. Who could suppose that it was to introduce a Comedy when [Mr. Bensly/an actor›] Mr. Bensly solemnly began

>   Pressed with the load of life the weary mind
>   Surveys the general toil of humankind.   25

But this dark ground might make Goldsmith's humour shine the more.‚

[*MS 322*] In [spring 1768›] [the spring of the›] the spring of this year [/having published my 'Account of Corsica with the Journal of a Tour to that Island'/›] having published my 'Account of Corsica with the Journal of a Tour to that Island' I [returned to/again visited/repaired to›] returned to London very desireous to   30
[see/meet›] see Dr. Johnson [/and hear him upon the subject/›] and hear him upon the subject. I [found/but›] found he was at Oxford with his friend Mr. Chambers

---

[1] JB originally deleted 'his love of', but later reinserted it by writing 'Stet' above it.

[2] Direction to the compositor, 'Take this in at the end of the year 1767.' This direction is written on the Paper Apart. There is no specific direction in the MS itself to indicate that the 'Lexiphanes' passage should be inserted here.

[3] SJ's letter to Bennet Langton of 10 October 1767 belongs to that group of letters first inserted at the end of the second volume of the second edition, and then moved to their chronologically appropriate places for the third edition. See *ante* p. 10 n. 1.

[4] JB has placed a cross after 'mind' which corresponds to a marginal note reading 'Note Prayers and Medit, p. ____.' By the stage of the revises, the blank had been filled with '81'.

[5] SJ's prologue to *The Good Natur'd Man*, first produced at Covent Garden on 29 January 1768, exploits a topical comparison between politician and playwright: 'Distrest alike, the statesman and the wit, / When one a borough courts, and one the pit' (*Poems* 1964, p. 265, *ll.* 9–10). References to the forthcoming General Election (March 1768) sustain the political 'paralel'.

who was now Vinerian Professor, and [occupied>] lived in New Inn Hall. Having
had no letter from him since that in which he [criticised/attacked>] criticised [the
latinity of the Dedication of my Thesis>] my latinity[6] and having been told by
somebody that he was offended at my having put into my Book an Extract of his
5   letter to me at Paris I was impatient to be with him and therefore followed him to
Oxford, where I was entertained by Mr. Chambers with a [civility/kindness>]
civility which I shall ever gratefully remember. I found that Dr. Johnson had sent
[off *del*] a letter to me to Scotland and that I had nothing to [lament/complain of>]
complain of but his being more indifferent to my anxiety than I wished him to be.
10   Instead of [copying with the circumstances of time and place what fragments of his
conversation I was happy enough to mark down/preserve/record during this
interview, I shall give it/them in continuation>] giving with the circumstances of
time and place such fragments of his conversation as I preserved during this visit to
Oxford, I shall throw them together in continuation.
15   I asked him ˏwhetherˏ as a Moralist [if *del*] he did not think that the [MS 323]
practice of the law [did not *del*] in some degree hurt [ones/our principles of
honesty>] the nice feeling of honesty. *Johnson*. 'Why no Sir, if you act properly.
You are not to deceive your clients with false representations of your opinion. You
are not to tell lies to a Judge.' *Boswell*. 'But what do you think of [pleading/arguing
20   for>] supporting a cause which you know to be bad.' *Johnson*. 'Sir you [dont>] do
not know it to be good or bad till the Judge determines it. I have said that you are
to state [/your/ *del*] facts fairly; so that your thinking or what you call knowing a
cause to be bad, must be from reasoning, must be from your thinking[3] your
arguments weak and inconclusive. But Sir that is not enough. An argument
25   which does not convince [/you/>] yourself, may convince the Judge to whom you
[plead/state>] urge it, and if it does convince him, why then Sir you are wrong and
he is right. It is his business to judge, and you are not to be confident in your
ˏownˏ opinion ˏthat a cause is badˏ but to say all you can for your client, and then
hear the Judge's opinion.'   *Boswell*. 'But Sir does not [the putting
30   on/assuming/affecting>] affecting a warmth when you have no warmth, and
appearing to be [firmly>] clearly of one opinion when you are in reality of another
opinion, does not such dissimulation [hurt>] impair one's honesty? Is there not
some [MS 324] danger that [one/a man>] a Lawyer may put on the same mask in
common life, in the intercourse with [one's>] his friends?' *Johnson*. 'Why no, Sir.
35   Every body knows you are paid for [putting on a/assuming/affecting>] affecting
warmth for your client, and it is therefore properly no dissimulation. The moment
you come from the bar you resume your usual behaviour. Sir, a man will no more
carry the artifice of the bar into the common intercourse of Society, than a man
who is paid for tumbling upon his hands will [tumble/continue tumbling>]
40   continue to tumble upon his hands, when he [ought to be/should be walking>]
should walk on his feet.'
      Talking of some of [the latest>] the modern Plays he [would allow no *character*
to *False Delicacy*>] said *False Delicacy* was totally void of *character*. He praised

---

[6] JB neglected to complete the deletion, leaving the compositor to resolve 'my latinity
... Thesis'; he did so by setting 'the latinity of my Thesis'.

Goldsmith's [*Good-Natured Man*⟩] 'Good-Natured Man' said it was the best
Comedy that had appeared since [*The Provoked Husband*⟩] The Provoked Husband, and that there had not been of late any such character exhibited on the
Stage as that of *Croaker*. I [said⟩] observed it was [just *del*] the *Suspirius* [of/in⟩] of
his Rambler. He said Goldsmith [/had/⟩] had owned he had borrowed it from   5
thence. — 'Sir' (continued he) 'there is all the difference in the World between
characters of Nature and characters of Manners; [*MS 325*] and *there* is the
difference between [those/the characters⟩] the characters of Fielding and
[those/the characters⟩] those of Richardson. Characters of manners are very
entertaining; but they are to be understood by a more superficial observer than   10
characters of Nature where a man must dive into the recesses of the human heart.'

It always appeared to me that he estimated the prolix compositions of
Richardson too highly, and that he had an unreasonable prejudice against Fielding. In comparing those two Writers he used this expression that there was as great
a difference between them as between a man who knew how a Watch was made   15
and a man who could tell the hour by looking [on/at⟩] on the dial=plate. This was
a short and figurative state of his distinction between drawing characters of Nature
and characters only of Manners. But I cannot help being of opinion that the
ₗneatₗ watches of Fielding are as well constructed as the large clocks of
Richardson and that his dial plates are brighter. Fielding's characters though they   20
do not expand themselves so widely in dissertation are as just pictures of human
nature and I will venture to say, have more striking features [*MS 326*] and nicer
touches of the pencil[. I will add and though Johnson used to quote with
approbation a saying that the virtues of Fielding's Heroes were but the vices of
Richardson's⟩] and though Johnson used to quote with approbation a saying of   25
Richardson's that the virtues of Fielding's heroes were the vices of a truly good
man, I will venture to add that the moral tendency of Fielding's writings though it
does not encourage a strained and rarely possible virtue, is ever favourable to
honour and honesty and cherishes the [benevolence⟩] benevolent and generous
affections. He who is as good as Fielding would make him is an amiable member   30
of Society, and may be [led on/conducted⟩] led on by more regulated instructors to
a higher state of ethical perfection.

Johnson [went on⟩] proceeded: 'Even Sir Francis Wronghead is a character of
manners though drawn with great humour.' He then repeated exceedingly well
all Sir Francis's credulous account to Manly of his being with the great man and   35
securing a place. I asked him if the Suspicious Husband did not furnish a well-
drawn character that of Ranger. *Johnson.* 'No Sir Ranger is just a Rake, a mere
Rake, and a lively young fellow, but no *character.*'

The great Douglas Cause was at this time a very general subject of discussion. I
found he had not studied it with much attention but had only heard parts of it   40
occasionally. He however talked of it and said, 'I am of opinion that positive [or
what is called proof that admits of no doubt⟩] proof of fraud should not be required
of the Plaintiff, but that the Judges should decide according as probability shall
appear to preponderate but allowing to the Defendant the presumption of filiation
to be strong in his favour. And I think too that a good deal of [weight/force⟩]   45
weight [should be allowed/is due⟩] should be allowed to the dying declarations,

[MS 327] because they were [voluntary and *del*] spontaneous. There is a [very *del*] great difference between what is said without our being urged to it, and what is said from a sort of compulsion. If I praise a man's book, without being asked my opinion of it, that is honest praise, [/and may be depended on/>] to which one may

5   trust. But if an Authour asks me if I like his Book, and I give him something like praise, it must not be taken as my real opinion.'

'I have not been troubled for a long time with Authours desiring my opinion of their Works. I used once to be sadly plagued with/by[7] a man who wrote verses, but who [literally/absolutely>] literally had no other notion of a verse but that it

10   consisted of ten syllables. *Lay your knife and your fork accross your plate* was to him a verse. Lay yōur knife ānd your fōrk accrōss your plāte. As he wrote a great number of verses he sometimes by chance made good ones [though/but>] though he did not know it.'

He renewed his promise of coming to Scotland and going with me to the

15   Hebrides but said he would now content himself with seeing one or two of the most curious of them. He said, 'McAulay who writes the Account of St. Kilda set out with a prejudice against prejudices, and wanted to be a smart modern thinker, and yet he affirms for a truth, that when [MS 328] a ship arrives there, all the inhabitants are seised with a cold.'[8]

20   He expatiated on the advantages of Oxford for learning. 'There is here, Sir,' ⋏(said he)⋏ 'such a progressive emulation. The [Students/Young men>] Students are anxious to appear well to their tutors. The tutors are anxious to have their pupils appear well in the College. The Colleges are anxious to have their students appear well in the University; and there are excellent rules of discipline in every

25   college. That the rules are sometimes ill observed may be true; but is nothing against the system. The members of an University may for a season be unmindful of their duty. I am arguing for the excellency of the Institution.'

Of Guthrie he said, 'Sir he [has>] is a man of parts. He has no great regular fund of knowledge; but by reading so long and writing so long he no doubt has picked up

30   a good deal.'

He said he had lately been a [long while/time>] long while at Lichfield, but [had wearied sadly>] [had been very weary of it>] had grown very very weary before he

---

[7] The alternative is resolved by the printing of 'with' in the revises.

[8] At this point, the second edition inserts a paragraph: 'Dr. John Campbell the celebrated writer, took a great deal of pains to ascertain this fact, and attempted to account for it on physical principles, from the effect of effluvia from human bodies. Johnson at another time praised Macaulay for his "*magnanimity*," in asserting this wonderful story, because it was well attested. A Lady of Norfolk, by a letter to my friend Dr. Burney, has favoured me with the following solution: "Now for the explication of this seeming mystery, which is so very obvious as, for that reason, to have escaped the penetration of Dr. Johnson and his friend, as well as that of the authour. Reading the book with my ingenious friend, the late Reverend Mr. Christian of Darking — after ruminating a little, "The cause (says he) is a natural one. The situation of St. Kilda renders a North-East Wind indispensibly necessary before a stranger can land. The wind, not the stranger, occasions an epidemic cold!" If I am not mistaken, Mr. Macaulay is dead; if living this solution might please him, as I hope it will Mr. Boswell, in return for the many agreeable hours his Works have afforded us."' A footnote is keyed to 'well attested': 'See Vol. II of this Work, p. 6'. In the third edition, the final cross-reference is omitted.

left it. ₍*Boswell*₎ 'I wonder at that [said I›] Sir, it is your native place.' *Johnson*. 'Why so is Scotland your native place.'

His prejudice against Scotland appeared remarkably strong at this time. When I talked of our [advances/progress›] advancement in Literature 'Sir' (said he) 'you have learnt a little from us, and you think yourselves very great   5 men. Hume would never have written History had not Voltaire written it before him. He is an echo of Voltaire.' ₍*Boswell*₎ 'But Sir we have Lord Kames.' ₍*Johnson*₎ 'You *have* Lord Kames. Keep him ha ha ha. We dont envy you him. Do [MS 329] you ever see Dr. Robertson?' ₍*Boswell*₎ 'Yes₍Sir.' *Johnson*₎ 'Does the dog talk of me?' —₍*Boswell*₎ 'Indeed he does and loves you.'   10 [I pushed him on the merit of Dr. Robertson's History. He answered 'Sir I love Robertson and I wont talk of his Book.'›] Thinking that I now had him in a corner, and solicitous for the literary fame of my country, I pressed him for his opinion on the merit of Dr. Robertson's History of Scotland. But to my surprise he escaped — 'Sir, I love Robertson and I won't talk of his Book.'   15

It is but justice both to him and Dr. Robertson to add that though he indulged himself in this sally of wit, he had too good taste not to be fully sensible of the merits of that admirable Work.

A Book maintaining the future life of Brutes [on the authority›] by an explication of certain parts of the Scriptures written by Mr. Deane a Divine of   20 the Church of England was mentioned, and ₍the doctrine₎ insisted on by a Gentleman [₍one of Johnson's friends₎ *del*] who seemed fond of curious speculation.[9] Johnson, who did not like to hear of any thing concerning a future state which was not authorised by the regular [standards›] canons of Orthodoxy, scouted[1] this talk and being offended at its continuation, he   25 watched an opportunity to give the gentleman a blow of reprehension. So when the poor Speculatist with a serious metaphysical pensive face addressed him 'But really Sir when we see a very sensible dog we dont know what to think of him', Johnson rowling with joy at the thought, which beamed in his eye turned quickly round and replied, 'No Sir. And when we see a very foolish   30 *fellow* we dont know what to think of him.' [Then up he rose bounced away›] He then up rose strided to the fire, and stood ₍for some time₎ laughing and exulting. [The Gentleman did not shrink; but when the merriment was/had abated gravely persevered saying '₍Well₎ But you Sir do not know what to think of a very sensible dog.' *del*]   35

I told him that I had several times when in Italy [witnessed›] seen the experiment of placing [MS 330] a scorpion within a circle of [hot/live›] burning coals; that it ran round and round in extreme pain, and finding no [way to escape/outlet›] way to escape, retired to the center and like a true Stoick Philosopher [put/clapped its sting into its head/gave its head the fatal sting›]   40

---

[9] JB refers to himself (Journ. 27 Mar. 1768).
[1] In his *Dictionary*, SJ provided two definitions for 'to scout': '1. To go out in order to observe the motions of an enemy privately. 2. To ridicule; to sneer.' The second he marked as colloquial: 'This is a sense unauthorised, and vulgar.' A concern for correctness may account for the substition of 'discouraged' for 'scouted' by the stage of revised proof.

darted its sting into its head, and thus at once freed itself from its woes. *This*
[will/must>] must end 'em. I said this was a curious fact as it shewed deliberate
suicide in [an insect>] a reptile. Johnson would not admit the fact. He said
Maupertuis[2] was of opinion that it does not kill itself, but dies of the heat; that it
5   gets to the center of the circle as the coolest place that its [turning/clapping>]
turning its tail in upon its head is merely a convulsion and that it does not sting
itself. He said he would be satisfied if the great anatomist Morgagni after
dissecting one upon ‸whom‸ the experiment had been tried should certify that its
sting had penetrated into its head.
10   He seemed pleased to talk of natural philosophy [, said that the>] 'That
Woodcocks' (said he) 'fly over to the Northern countries is proved because they
have been observed at sea — [that swallows>] Swallows certainly sleep all the
winter. A number of them conglobulate together by flying round and round, and
then all in a heap throw themselves under water and lye in the bed of a river.' He
15   told us one of his first Essays was a latin Poem upon the glowworm.
    Talking of the Russians and the Chinese he advised me to read Bell's travels. I
asked him if I should read Du Halde's China. 'Why yes' *[MS 331]* said he, 'as one
reads such a Book. That is to say, consult it.'
    He talked of the heinousness of the crime of Adultery by which the peace of
20   families was [broken>] destroyed. He said 'Confusion of progeny constitutes the
Essence of the crime; and therefore a woman who breaks her marriage vows is so
much more criminal than a man [/who does it/>] who does it. A man to be sure is
criminal in the sight of GOD. But he does not do his wife a very material injury if
he does not insult her; if, for instance, from mere wantoness of appetite he steals
25   privately to her chambermaid. Sir, a wife ought not greatly to resent this. I would
not receive home a daughter who had run away from her husband on that account.
A Wife should study to reclaim her husband by more attention to please him. Sir
a man will not once in a hundred instances leave his wife and go to a harlot if his
wife has not been negligent of pleasing.'[3]

---

    [2] In the second edition, a footnote praising the breadth of SJ's reading is keyed to
'Maupertuis': 'I should think it impossible not to wonder at the variety of Johnson's
reading, however desultory it may have been. Who could have imagined that the High
Church of England-man would be so prompt in quoting *Maupertuis*, who, I am sorry to
think, stands in the list of those unfortunate mistaken men, who call themselves *esprits*
forts. I have, however, a high respect for that Philosopher whom the Great Frederick of
Prussia loved and honoured, and addressed pathetically in one of his Poems,

       "*Maupertuis cher Maupertuis*

       "*Que notre vie est peu de chose.*"

There was in Maupertuis a vigour and yet a tenderness of sentiment, united with strong
intellectual powers, and uncommon ardour of soul. Would he had been a Christian! I
cannot help earnestly venturing to hope that he is one now.' For the third edition, a new,
bracketed sentence was added: '[Maupertuis died in 1759 at the age of 62, in the arms of the
Bernoullis, *tres Chretiennement.* B.]'.

    [3] In the second edition, an entirely new paragraph is inserted at this point: 'Here he
discovered that acute discrimination, that solid judgement, and that knowledge of human
nature, for which he was upon all occasions remarkable. Taking care to keep in view the

I asked him if it was not hard that one deviation from Chastity should so absolutely ruin a young woman. *Johnson.* 'Why no Sir. It is the great principle which she is taught. When she has given up that principle, she has given up every notion of female honour and virtue, which are all included in chastity.'

ₗA Gentleman/I[4] talked to him of a Lady whom he greatly admired and wished   5
to marry but [was afraid of/dreaded her superiority of talents›] dreaded her superiour talents. 'Sir,' said he, 'You need not be affraid. Marry her. Before a year goes about you'll find that reason much weaker and that wit not so bright.' Yet the Gentleman may be justified in his apprehension by one of Dr. Johnson's admirable sentences in his Life of Waller 'He doubtless praised many whom he would have   10
been afraid to marry; and perhaps married one whom he would have been ashamed to praise. Many qualities contribute to domestick happiness upon which poetry has no colours to bestow; and many airs and sallies may delight imagination, which he who flatters them never can approve.' [There are charms made for distant admiration. No spectacle is nobler than a blaze *del*].ₗ   15

He praised Signor Baretti. 'His Account of Italy is a very entertaining Book; and, Sir, I [MS 332] know no man who carries his head higher in conversation than Baretti. There are strong powers in his mind. He has not indeed [so many hooks as he might have had but so far as his hooks reach, he lays hold of objects very forcibly›] many hooks but with what hooks he has, he grapples·very forcibly.'[5]   20

ₗAt this time I observed upon the Dialplate of his watch a short greek inscription taken from the New Testament Νυξ γαρ ερχεται being the first words of our Saviours solemn Admonition to the improvement of that time which is allowed us to prepare for eternity 'the night cometh when no man can work.' He some time afterwards laid aside this dial=plate and when I asked him the reason he   25
[said//observed/›] said, [It/The inscription›] 'It might do very well upon a Clock which a man keeps in his closet, but to have it upon his watch which he carries about with him and which is often looked at by others might be censured as ostentatious.' Mr. Steevens is now possessed of the [/inscribed/›] dial plate inscribed as above [/with the inscription/ *del*].ₗ[6]   30

He remained at Oxford a considerable time; I was obliged to go back to London, where I received his letter which had been returned from Scotland.

To James Boswell Esq:[7]

. . . .

moral and religious duty, as understood in our nation, he shewed clearly from reason and good sense, the greater degree of culpability in the one sex deviating from it than the other; and, at the same time, inculcated a very useful lesson as to *the way to keep him*.' JB alludes to a comedy by Arthur Murphy, *The Way to Keep Him* (1760).

[4] Printed 'A Gentleman'.

[5] Here JB has written in 'go to back of p. 332'. By this he directs the compositor to proceed to the verso of an additional leaf (labelled '*322') that has been inserted between 332 and 333. At the top of this page JB further cues the compositor with the direction, 'belongs top 332'.

[6] This paragraph on SJ's watch does not originate in JB's journal, notes, or memoranda.

[7] Direction to the compositor, 'I have omitted / (Take it in).' JB also indicated that his response to this letter was to be included as well: 'I answered thus / My Dear Sir / I have received / (Take it in ₗBₗ).' The texts of these letters no longer form part of the *Life* MS.

Upon his arrival in London in May he surprised me ₍[one forenoon/one morning>] one morning₎ with a visit at my lodgings [and was quite satisfied with my explanation and was in the kindest and most agreable frame>] in halfmoon street was quite satisfied with my explanation and was in the kindest and most
5   agreable frame of mind. [I was elated and embracing him cried out 'Thou great Man.' He smiled and said 'Don't call names.' del] As he had objected to a part of one of his letters being published, I [put it fairly to him>] thought it right to take this opportunity of asking him explicitly if it would be [wrong>] improper to publish his letters after his death? [and I received an Answer which makes my
10   mind perfectly easy in doing what Cicero has exclaimed against in eloquent passion/passionate eloquence,[8] but which especially if being permitted[9] [Paper Apart to follow p. *332] must certainly be a valuable addition to the publick stock of entertainment while it does great honour to my illustrious friend. del] His [words were>] answer was, 'Nay ₍Sir₎ when I am dead, you may do as you will.'
15   He talked in his usual style with a rough contempt of popular liberty. 'They make a rout [said he del] about universal liberty without considering that all that is to be valued or indeed can be enjoyed by individuals is private liberty. Political Liberty is a good only [in del] so far as it produces private liberty. Now Sir there is the liberty of the press which you know is a constant topick — Suppose you and I
20   and two hundred more were restrained from [printing/publishing>] printing our thoughts what then? What proportion would that restraint upon us bear to the private happiness of the Nation?' [But Sir said I think of a hundred thousand Readers. Wretches said he. del]
This ₍mode of [arguing/ridiculing the supposed inconveniences of>] represent-
25   ing the inconveniences of restraint as light and insignificant₎ was a kind of sophistry in which he delighted to indulge himself in opposition to the extreme laxity for which it has been fashionable for too many to argue, when it is evident upon reflection that the very essence of government is restraint and certain it is that as Government produces rational happiness too much restraint is better than
30   too little. But when restraint is unnecessary and so close as to gall those who are subject to it, the people may and [MS 333] ought to remonstrate, and if relief is not granted, to resist. Of this manly and spirited principle no man was more convinced than Johnson himself.[1]
[Paper Apart K] About this time Dr. Kenrick [made an attack at him>] attacked
35   him through my sides in a pamphlet entitled 'An Epistle to James Boswell Esq occasioned by his having transmitted the moral writings of Dr. Samuel Johnson to Pascal Paoli General of the Corsicans.' I was at first inclined to answer this. But Johnson who knew that my doing so would only gratify Kenrick by keeping alive what would soon die away, ₍if left to itself,₎ would not suffer me to take any notice
40   of it.

---

[8] An untraced reference.
[9] At this point there is a direction to go on to a Paper Apart. This Paper bears the page number *332, a heading reading 'Paper Apart to follow p. 332', and it is incorporated in the MS proper.
[1] Direction to the compositor, 'Paper K'.

[MS 333 resumed] His sincere regard for Francis Barber his faithful Negro servant made him so desireous of his farther improvement that he had him now placed at a School at Bishop Stortford in Hertfordshire. [His amiable›] This humane attention does Johnson's heart much honour. Out of many letters which Mr. Barber received from his Master he has preserved three which he kindly gave   5 me and which I shall insert according to their dates.

To Mr. Francis Barber[2]

. . . .

[Paper Apart C and A] Soon after this, he supped at the Crown and Anchor Tavern in the Strand with a Company whom I collected to meet him. There were Dr. Percy now Bishop of Dromore, [the Reverend *del*] Dr. Douglas now Bishop of   10 Carlisle,[3] Mr. Langton Dr. Robertson the Historian Dr. Hugh Blair and Mr. Thomas Davies who wished much to be introduced to these eminent Scotch Literati; but on the present occasion he had very little opportunity of hearing them talk for with [much/an extreme of›] an excess of prudence for which Johnson afterwards found fault with them they hardly opened their lips, and that only to say   15 something which they were certain would not expose them to [animadversion/contradiction›] the sword of Goliath such was their anxiety for their fame when in the presence of Johnson [, who *del*]. He was this evening in remarkable vigour of mind and eager to exert himself in conversation which [P.A. p. 2] he did with great readiness and fluency, but I am sorry to find that I have   20 preserved but [little.›] a small part of what passed.

He allowed high praise to Thomson as a Poet but when [a gentleman›] one of the company said he was ₍also₎ a very good man our Moralist contested this with great warmth, accusing him of gross sensuality and licentiousness of manners. I was very much affraid that in writing Thomson's Life Dr. Johnson would have   25 treated his private character with a stern severity, but I was agreably disappointed and I may claim a little merit in it from my having been at pains to send him authentick accounts of the affectionate and generous conduct of that poet to his sisters one of whom the wife of Mr. Thomson Schoolmaster at Lanark I knew and was [favoured›] presented by her with three of his letters, one of which Dr.   30 Johnson has inserted in his life.

[P.A. p. 3] He was vehement against old Dr. Mounsey of Chelsea College as 'a fellow who swore and talked bawdy.' 'I have been often in his company,' said Dr. Percy 'and never heard him swear or talk bawdy.' Mr. Davies who sat next to Dr. Percy having after this had some conversation aside with him made a discovery   35 which in his zeal to [please/flatter›] pay court to Dr. Johnson, he eagerly proclaimed aloud from the foot of the table 'O Sir I have found out a very good reason why Dr. Percy never heard Mounsey swear or talk bawdy for he tells me he never saw him but at the Duke of Northumberland's table.' — 'And so Sir' (said Johnson loudly to Dr. Percy) 'you would shield this man from the charge of ₍swearing and₎   40

---

[2] Direction to the compositor, 'I have been very much / (Take [it *del*] in ₍B1₎) / Take in Paper marked C and A.' Paper Apart B1 no longer forms part of the *Life* MS. Paper Apart C and A is written entirely in the hand of JB and numbers six pages.

[3] In 1791 Dr. John Douglas had moved from the bishopric of Carlisle to that of Salisbury, a change reflected in the second and third editions (*Fasti Angl.* iii.245).

talking bawdy because he did not do [so/it>] so at the Duke of Northumberland's table. ₍Sir₎ You might as well tell us that [P.A. p. 4] you [had/have>] had seen him hold up his hand at the Old Bailey and he neither swore nor talked bawdy; or that you [had/have>] had seen him in the cart at Tyburn and he neither swore nor

5   talked bawdy. And is it thus, Sir, that you presume to [contradict/attempt a contradiction>] contravert what I have related?' Dr. Johnson's [reprimand>] animadversion was uttered in such a manner that Dr. Percy [was much hurt>] seemed to be displeased and soon ₍afterwards₎ left the company of which Johnson [did not take any notice/took no notice at the time>] did not at that time take any

10   notice.

       Swift having been mentioned Johnson as usual treated him with little respect as an Authour. Some of us endeavoured to support the Dean of St. Patrick's by various arguments. One in particular praised his *Conduct of the Allies*. *Johnson*. 'Sir his *Conduct of the Allies* is a performance of very little ability.' ['I don't know

15   Sir' said the gentleman. 'It has strong facts.'>] 'Surely Sir,' said Dr. Douglas, 'you must allow it has strong facts.'[4] *Johnson*. 'Why yes Sir: but what [P.A. p. 5] is that to the merit of the composition? In the Sessions Paper of the Old Bailey there are strong facts. Housebreaking is a strong fact, Robbery is a strong fact, and Murder is a *mighty* strong fact, but is great praise due to the historian of those strong facts?

20   ₍No Sir₎ Swift has told what he had to tell distinctly enough but that is all. He had to count ten, and he has counted it right.' — Then recollecting that Mr. Davies, by acting as an *informer*, had been the occasion of his talking somewhat too harshly to his friend Dr. Percy, ₍for which probably when the first ebulition was over he felt some compunction₎, he took an opportunity to give him a hit

25   [adding>] so added with a preparatory laugh. '₍Why Sir₎ Tom Davies might have written the Conduct of the Allies.' Poor Tom being thus suddenly dragged into [ludicrous/ridiculous>] ludicrous notice, in presence of the Scottish Doctors to whom he was ambitious of appearing to advantage was [sadly>] grievously mortified. Nor did his punishment rest here; for upon [after>] subsequent occasions

30   when ₍ever₎ he 'Statesman all over'[5] assumed [an over>] a strutting importance, I used to hail him '*the Authour of the Conduct of the Allies*.'

       When I called upon Dr. Johnson next morning I found him highly satisfied with his colloquial prowess the preceeding evening. 'Well,' said he 'we had good talk.' *Boswell*. 'Yes Sir, you tossed and gored several persons.'

35   [P.A. p. 6] The late Alexander Earl of Eglintoune who loved wit more than wine and men of genius more than sycophants had a great admiration of Johnson but from the remarkable elegance of his own manners was perhaps too delicately

---

[4] In the second edition, a footnote is keyed to 'facts': 'My respectable friend, upon reading this passage, observed, that he probably must have said not simply "strong facts," but "strong facts well arranged." His Lordship, however, knows too well the value of written documents to insist on setting his recollection against my notes taken at the time. He does not attempt to *traverse the record*. The fact, perhaps, may have been, either that the additional words escaped me in the noise of a numerous company, or that Dr. Johnson, from his impetuosity, and eagerness to seize an opportunity to make a lively retort, did not allow Dr. Douglas to finish his sentence.'

[5] In the third edition, an asterisk is keyed to 'over' and a note attached: 'See the hard drawing of him in Churchill's ROSCIAD'.

sensible of the roughness which often appeared in Johnson's behaviour. One evening about this time, when his Lordship did me the honour to sup at my lodgings with Dr. Robertson and several other men of literary distinction, he regretted that Johnson had not been educated with more refinement and lived more in polished society. 'No no My Lord' said Signor Baretti; 'do with him what   5
you would he would allways have been a bear.' 'True,' answered the Earl with a pleasing smile, 'but he would have been a *dancing* bear.'

To obviate all the reflections which have gone round the world to Johnson's prejudice by applying to him the epithet of a *bear*, let me impress upon my readers a just and happy saying of my friend Goldsmith, who knew him well 'Johnson to   10
be sure has a roughness in his manner; but no man alive has a more tender heart. *He has nothing of the bear but his skin.*'

[MS 333 resumed] In 1769 so far as I can discover the Publick was favoured with nothing of his composition either for himself or any of his friends. His [*Meditations*)] 'Meditations' too strongly prove that he suffered much both in body and   15
mind; yet was he perpetually striving against *evil* and nobly endeavouring to advance his intellectual and devotional improvement. Every generous and grateful heart must feel for the distresses [MS 334] of so eminent a benefactor to Mankind, and now that his unhappiness is certainly known must respect that dignity of character which prevented him from complaining.   20

His Majesty having this year [instituted/founded)] instituted the Royal Academy Johnson [was honoured with the appointment/nomination of)] had the honour of being appointed Professor of Ancient Literature[6] [of which he no doubt accepted with the greater pleasure/alacrity that his friend Sir Joshua Reynolds was put at the head of it *del*] ʎIn the course of this year he wrote some letters to Mrs.   25
Thrale.ʎ

He passed some part of the summer at Oxford, and [wrote as follows)] at Lichfield and when at Oxford wrote the following Letter,

To the Reverend Mr. Thomas Warton[7]

Dear Sir[8]   30

Many years ago when I used to read in the library of your College, I promised to recompense the College for that permission, by adding to their books a Baskerville's Virgil. I have now sent it, and desire you to reposite it on the shelves in my name.[9]

---

[6] In the second edition, a footnote is keyed to 'Ancient Literature': 'In which place he has been succeeded by Bennet Langton Esq. When that truly religious gentleman was elected to this honorary Professorship, at the same time that Edward Gibbon, Esq. noted for introducing a kind of sneering infidelity into his Historical Writings, was elected Professor in Ancient Literature, in the room of Dr. Goldsmith, I observed that it brought to my mind, "Wicked Will Whiston and good Mr. Ditton." — I am now also of that admirable institution as Secretary for Foreign Correspondence, by the favour of the Academicians, and the approbation of the Sovereign.'

[7] Direction to the compositor, 'Take it in from the Parcel ʎW,ʎ p. 22)'.

[8] For a description of JB's source for this letter, see *Life MS* i. 195 n. 6.

[9] Warton has here added to his copy of the letter a note of his own: 'It has this inscription in a blank leaf. "Hunc librum D.D. Samuel / Johnson, eò quòd hic loci / Studiis

If you will be pleased to let me know when you have an hour of leisure, I will drink tea with you. I am engaged, for the afternoon, to morrow and on friday: all my mornings are my own.[1]

I am, etc.

SAM. JOHNSON.

May 31, 1769.[2]

[MS 334 resumed] I came to London in the Autumn and having informed him that I was going to be married /in a few months/[3] I wished to have as much of his [conversation/company⟩] conversation as I could before [engaging myself in/entering upon a⟩] engaging in a state of life which [would/might⟩] would probably keep me more in Scotland and prevent my seeing him so often as when I was a single man⟩ but I found he was at Brightelmstone with Mr. and Mrs. Thrale. I was very sorry that I had not his company/him[4] with me at the Jubilee in honour of Shakspeare at Stratford upon Avon the great Poet's native town. Johnson's [double *del*] connection both with Shakspeare and Garrick founded a double claim to his presence; and it would have been highly gratifying to Mr. Garrick. Upon this occasion I particularly [regretted⟩] lamented that he had not that [warmth of/warm⟩] warmth of friendship for [MS 335] his brilliant Pupil which we may suppose would have had a benignant effect on both. When almost every man of eminence in the Literary World was happy to partake in this festival of genius, [it was hard that Johnson was not to be seen⟩] the absence of Johnson could not but be wondered at and regretted. [His only appearance there⟩] The only trace of him there was in the whimsical Advertisement of a Haberdasher who sold *Shakspearian ribbands* of various dies and by way of illustrating their appropriation to the Bard, introduced a line from the celebrated Prologue at the opening of Drury Lane Theatre.

'Each change of *many-colour'd* life he drew.'

[The ingenious Mr. Lovibond soon after the Jubilee published the following verses *del*][5/6]

---

interdum vacaret." [In⟩] Of this library, which is an old Gothic [room⟩] [structure⟩] room, he [took great deli⟩] was very fond. On my observing to him, that some of the *modern* libraries of the university were more commodious and pleasant for study, [because they were more⟩] as being more spacious and airy, he replied, "Sir, if a man has a mind to *prance*, he must study at Christ-Church and All-Souls." (T. Warton)'. In the published *Life*, JB attributed this note to himself.

[1] Warton added a note here: 'During this visit, he seldom or never dined out. He appeared to be deeply engaged in some literary work. Miss Williams was now with him at Oxford.' In the published *Life*, JB attributed this note to himself.

[2] The date of this letter has been questioned by David Fairer, who argues that 31 May 1775 is more likely. See *The Correspondence of Thomas Warton*, ed. Fairer, pp. 364–65 and Appendix D (pp. 669–71).

[3] The optional phrase, which JB left unresolved, is printed in the revises.

[4] The alternative is resolved by the printing of 'his company' in the revises.

[5] This deleted passage is followed by a direction to the compositor, also deleted, which reads '(Take them in)'.

[6] JB intended originally to quote Edward Lovibond's 'The Mulberry-Tree. A Tale,' which describes an excursion by Johnson and Garrick to see Shakespeare's mulberry tree in Stratford. The two men draw a considerable crowd, with Garrick performing from the upper

From Brightelmstone Dr. Johnson wrote me the following Letter, which they who may think that I [ought to/could>] ought to have suppressed [ʌthisʌ *del*] must have a less ardent desire for literary fame than [ʌthat whichʌ *del*] I have [ever/always>] always avowed.[7/8]

5

To James Boswell Esq.

[Paper Apart] Dear Sir

Why do you charge me with unkindness? I have omitted nothing that could do you good or give you pleasure unless it be that I have forborn to tell you my opinion of your Account of Corsica. I believe my opinion if you think well of my judgement might have given you pleasure but when it is considered how much vanity is excited by praise I am not sure that it would have done you good. Your History is like other histories but your journal is in a very high degree curious and deligh[t]ful. There is between the history and the journal that difference which there will always be found between notions borrowed from without, and notions generated within. Your history was copied from books. Your journal rose out of your own experience and observation. You express images which operated strongly upon yourself and you have impressed them with great force upon your readers. I know not whether I could name any narrative by which curiosity is better excited or better gratified.

10

15

20

I am glad that you are going to be married and as I wish[9] you well in things of less importance wish you well with proportionate ardour in this crisis of your life. What I can contribute to your happiness I should be very unwilling to withold for I have always loved and valued you and shall love you and value you still more as you become more regular and useful effects which a happy Marriage will hardly fail to produce.

25

I do not find that I am likely to come back very soon from this place. I shall perhaps stay a fortnight longer and a fortnight is a long time to a lover Absent from his Mistress. Would a fortnight ever have an end!

I am / Dear Sir your most affectionate / humble Servant / Sam Johnson / Brighthelmston Septr 9 1769

30

[Paper Apart for page 335][1] [After his return to town he was so good as to see me/indulge me frequently with his company and as he had allways approved of my keeping/making notes of his conversation I continued the practice now>] After his return to town we met frequently, and I continued the practice of making notes of his conversation, though not with so much assiduity as I wish I had done[; for

35

---

branches while 'Johnson below mutter'd strophes of Greek' (Lovibond, *Poems on Several Occasions*, London, 1785, l. 23). JB then remembered that he had mentioned the poem in his account of 1737 (*Life* MS i. 69).

[7] Direction to the compositor, '(Take it in)'. The copy is in the hand of one of Boswell's children.

[8] In the second edition, a footnote is keyed to 'avowed'; it quotes at length from the preface to JB's *Account of Corsica*.

[9] The word 'wish' is a correction, perhaps by JB, written over what appears to be 'still'.

[1] This Paper Apart is written entirely in the hand of JB and numbers ten pages in all. The cue words to the compositor indicate that JB's first thought for the opening was 'On his return'.

where is such conversation to be had from any one else *del*]. At this time indeed I had a sufficient excuse for not being able to appropriate so much time to my Journal; for General Paoli after Corsica had been overpowered by the Monarchy of France was now no longer at the head of his brave countrymen, but having with

5 difficulty escaped from his native Island [was come to Britain as the generous Asylum of unfortunate freedom>] had sought an Asylum in Great Britain and it was my duty as well as my pleasure to attend much upon him. [What particulars/parts I have committed to writing shall be faithfully communicated as I find them in my papers, without any apprehension that I shall be unreasonably

10 condemned for want of order and regular connection>] Such particulars of Johnson's conversation at this period as I have committed to writing I shall here introduce without any strict attention to methodical arrangement. ₍Sometimes₎ short notes of different days shall be blended together and sometimes a day may seem important enough to be separately distinguished.

15 [*P.A. p. 2*] He said he would not have Sunday kept with [a stiffness>] [rigidity>] rigid severity and gloom but with a gravity and simplicity of behaviour.

I told him that David Hume had [made/printed>] made a ₍short₎ collection of Scotticisms. 'I wonder' said Johnson 'that he should find them.'

He would not admit the importance of the question concerning the Legality of

20 General Warrants. [He said Such a power>] [Such a power (said he)>] 'Such a power' (he observed) 'must be vested in every government to answer particular cases of necessity, and there can be no just complaint but when it is abused for which those who administrate government must be answerable. It is a matter of such indifference a matter about which the people care so very little that were a

25 man to be sent over Britain to offer them an exemption from it at a halfpenny a piece very few would purchase it.' This was a [laxity of talking/specimen/instance of that>] specimen of that laxity of talking which I have heard him fairly acknowledge; for, surely, [while the supposed power of granting general warrants hung over our heads, we could not be considered as/of having that comfortable security>]

30 [while the supposed legal power of granting general warrants hung over our heads, we could not be considered as of having that comfortable security>] while the power of granting general warrants was supposed to be legal and the apprehension of them hung over our heads, we did not possess that security of freedom congenial to our happy constitution, and which by the intrepid [activity>] exertions of [*P.A.*

35 *p. 3*] Mr. Wilkes has been happily established. He said 'I would not give half a crown [to have half the parliament last for seven years or for life>] [to have half the members of parliament chosen for seven years or for life>] He said, 'The duration of Parliament whether for seven years or for the life of the King appears to me so immaterial that I would not give half a crown to turn the scale the one way or the

40 other. The Habeas Corpus is the single advantage which our government has over that of other countries.'

On the 30 September we dined together at the Mitre. I attempted to argue for the superiour happiness of the Savage life, upon the usual fanciful topicks. [He said>] *Johnson*. 'Sir, there can be nothing more false. The Savages have no bodily

45 advantages beyond those of civilized men. They have not better health and as to care or mental uneasiness, they are not above it but below it like bears. No Sir you

are not to talk such paradox. Let me have no more on't. It cannot entertain, far less can it instruct. Lord Monboddo one of your scotch Judges talked a great deal of such nonsense. I suffered *him*; but I will not suffer *you*.' — ₍*Boswell.*₎ 'But Sir does not Rousseau talk such nonsense?' — ₍*Boswell.*₎² 'True Sir. But Rousseau *knows* he is talking nonsence and laughs at the World for staring at him.' — ₍*Boswell.*₎ 'How so Sir.' ₍*Johnson.*₎ 'Why Sir a man who talks nonsence so well [must know/knows›] must know that he is talking nonsense. But I am *affraid* (chuckling and laughing) [P.A. p. 4] Monboddo [does/did›] does *not* know that he [is/was›] is talking nonsense.'ᵃ ₍*Boswell.*₎ 'Is it wrong then Sir to affect singularity in order to make people stare?' ₍*Johnson.*₎ 'Yes if you do it by propagating errour. And indeed it is wrong in anyway. There is in human nature a general inclination to make people stare. And every wise man has himself to cure of it, and does cure himself. If you wish to make people stare by doing better than others, why make 'em/them³ stare till they stare their eyes out. But consider how easy it is to make people stare [by being absurd/at absurdity›] by being absurd. I may do it by going into a drawing room without my shoes. You remember the Gentleman in the Spectator who had a commission of lunacy taken out against him for his extreme singularity such as never wearing a wig but a night cap. Now Sir abstractly the night cap was best; but relatively, the advantage was overballanced by his making the boys run after him.'

Talking of a London Life, he said, 'The happiness of London is not to be conceived but by those who have been in it.' ₍I will venture to say there is more learning and science within [the/a›] the circumference of ten miles from where we now sit than in all the rest of the Kingdom [besides *del*].'₎ — ₍*Boswell.*₎ 'The only disadvantage is the great distance at which people live from one another.' — ₍*Johnson.*₎ 'Yes, Sir, but that is [occasioned by/owing to›] occasioned by the largeness of it which is the cause of all the other advantages.' — ₍*Boswell.*₎ 'Sometimes I have been in the humour of wishing to retire [P.A. p. 5] to a desart.' ₍*Boswell.*₎⁴ 'Sir you have desart enough in Scotland.'

₍Although I had promised myself a great deal of instructive conversation [from›] with him on the conduct of the married state of which I had then a near prospect, he did not say much upon that topick. Mr. Seward [/has/ *del*] heard him [observe›] once say that 'a man [has/had›] has a very bad chance for happiness in

ᵃ His Lordship having frequently spoken in an abusive manner of Dr. Johnson in my company, I on one occasion during the lifetime of my illustrious friend could not refrain from [retaliating›] retaliation [by repeating›] and repeated to him this [sarcastic observation›] saying.ᵃˡ

² Although the MS reads 'Boswell,' 'Johnson' must have been intended.
³ The alternative is resolved by the printing of 'them' in the revises.
⁴ JB clearly intended to write 'Johnson'.

ᵃˡ The second edition adds a sentence to JB's footnote on Lord Monboddo: 'He has since published I dont know how many pages in one of his curious books, attempting, in much anger, but with pitiful effect, to persuade mankind that my illustrious friend was not the great and good man which they esteemed and ever will esteem him to be.' The attack appeared in volume 5 (1789) of Monboddo's *Of the Origin and Progress of Language* (1773–92).

that state, unless he marries/married[5] a woman of very strong and fixed principles of Religion.'[6] [and *del*] He maintained to me [/contrary to the vulgar notion/prejudice/>] contrary to the common notion, that a Woman would not be the worse Wife for being learned in which from all that I have observed of
5   *Artemisias* I humbly differed from him [because there is something/appears to be something in it inconsistent with feminine delicacy/gentleness without which no woman can be pleasing. *del*] That a woman should be sensible and well informed I allow to be a great advantage, and [agree with/believe the>] think that Sir Thomas Overbury[a] in his [*Wife*/Poem>] rude versification has very judiciously pointed out
10   that degree of intelligence which is to be desired in a female companion.

> 'Give *me* next *good* an *understanding wife*
> By nature *wise* not *learned* by much art
> Some *knowledge* on her side will all my life
> More scope of conversation impart,
15   Besides her inborne virtue fortifie
> They are most firmly good who best know why.'

  When I censured a gentleman of my acquaintance for marrying a second time as it shewed a disregard of his first wife, [he said/?Johnson *del*] 'Not at all Sir. On the contrary, were he not to marry again it might be concluded that his first wife
20   had [made him heartily sick of>] given him a disgust to marriage.[7] But by taking a second wife he pays the highest compliment to the first, by [proving/shewing>] shewing that she made him so happy as a married man that he [has a mind/chuses>] wishes to be so a second time.'[8] So [playfully could he evade a question which depends entirely upon feeling>] ingenious a turn did he give to this
25   delicate question. And [well did he know the nature/tender nicety of it; for>] yet on another occasion he owned that he once had almost asked a promise of Mrs. Johnson that she would not marry again, but had checked [himself/his anxious wish>] himself. Indeed I cannot help thinking that in his case the request would have been unreasonable; for if Mrs. Johnson forgot or thought it no injury
30

    [a] 'A Wife' a Poem 1614

---

[5] The alternative is resolved by the printing of 'marries' in the revises.

[6] JB draws here upon 'Communications concerning Dr. Johnson By William Seward Esq' (C2480).

[7] JB refers obliquely to his father, whose second marriage (to Elizabeth Boswell) took place on 25 November 1769. JB violently opposed the match: 'I looked on my father's marrying again as … an insult on the memory of my valuable mother' (Journ. 16 July 1769). See *Earlier Years*, pp. 441–42. In a letter to his fiancée, Margaret Montgomerie, JB reports that SJ agreed with him: 'As to my father's marrying again, he thinks it had much better not happen' (To MM, 2 Oct. 1769).

[8] As JB well knew, SJ himself had considered remarrying after Elizabeth Johnson's death. The portion of SJ's diary that he had transcribed in 1776 contains a reference to searching for 'a new wife', but JB chose to omit this information from the *Life* and emphasize instead SJ's lifelong devotion to the memory of 'Tetty' (Donald and Mary Hyde, 'Dr. Johnson's Second Wife', in *New Light on Dr. Johnson*, ed. Frederick W. Hilles, 1959, pp. 133–51).

to the memory of her first love — the husband of her youth — and the father of her children — to [make a second marriage/marry/espouse Sam⟩] make a second marriage, why should she be precluded from a third should she be so inclined. In Johnson's persevering fond appropriation of his *Tetty* even after her decease he seems totally to have overlooked the prior claim of the honest Birmingham trader. I presume that her having been married before had at times given him some uneasiness; for I remember his observing upon the marriage of one of our common friends, 'He has done a very foolish thing Sir. He has married a Widow when he might have had a Maid.'ₓ

We drank tea with Mrs. Williams. I had last year had the pleasure of seeing Mrs. Thrale at Dr. Johnson's [for a short while in a morning⟩] one morning, and had conversation enough with her to admire her talents and to shew her that I was as Johnsonian as herself. Dr. Johnson had probably [praised me. He this evening delivered me the following card in the fair handwriting of that Lady/Thralia dulcis.⁹ I preserve it as my first ticket to a great deal of most agreable society. 'Mr. and Mrs. Thrale present their best compliments to Mr. Boswell, and should think themselves highly favoured in his Company to Dinner at Stretham any day he shall think fit to appoint.' 30 Sep.⟩] been kind enough to speak well of me, for this evening he delivered me a very polite card from Mr. Thrale and her inviting me to Stretham.

On the 6 of October I [complied with/availed myself of] complied with this obliging invitation and found at [a charming⟩] an elegant Villa six miles from town, every circumstance that can make society pleasing. Johnson though quite at home, was yet looked up to with an awe tempered by affection, and seemed to be equally the care of his host and hostess [in their different ways/manners *del*]. I rejoiced at seeing him so happy.

He played off his wit against Scotland with a good humoured pleasantry [P.A. p. 6] [as giving me an/it gave me⟩] which gave me ₓthough no bigot to national prejudicesₓ an opportunity for a little contest with him. I, having said that England was obliged to us for gardeners almost all [the good ones there⟩] their good gardeners being Scotchmen. ₓJohnsonₓ 'Why Sir that is because gardening is much more necessary amongst you than with us, which makes so many of your people learn it. ₓIt is *all* gardening with you.ₓ Things which grow wild here must be cultivated with great care in Scotland. Pray now ₓ(throwing himself back in his chair and laughing)ₓ are you ever able to bring the *sloe* to perfection?'¹

I boasted that we had the honour of being the first to abolish the unhospitable and ₓtroublesome andₓ ungracious custom of giving vails to servants. ₓJohnson.ₓ 'Sir you abolished vails because you were too poor to be able to give them.'²

---

⁹ JB quotes from SJ's Latin ode to Hester Thrale, written on Skye in September 1773: it is likely that Mrs Thrale herself had given JB a copy of the ode, which he then included in his *Tour* (MS Hyde Collection; *Poems*, Yale ed., pp. 280–81).

¹ JB apparently intended at one point to make an insertion here. There is an 'X' in the margin with a circle drawn around it, which would seem to correspond to a similar marking on the verso of the previous page.

² In the margin, JB has jotted a note to himself, 'Qu if not too flat?' This is deleted and SJ's dictum (which derives from the original journal entry) remains as originally recorded.

Mrs. Thrale disputed with him on the merit of Prior. He attacked him powerfully, said he wrote of love like a man who had never felt it. His love verses were College verses. And he repeated the Song Alexis shunned his fellow swains [so ludicrously>] [with so *undeciphered word* an air>] in so ludicrous a manner [that

5   he made us laugh very heartily, and wonder>] as to make us all wonder how any body could have been [seriously *del*] pleased with such fantastical stuff. Mrs. Thrale stood to her gun with great courage in defence of amorous ditties which Johnson despised till he at last silenced her by saying, 'My Dear Lady talk no more of this. Nonsense can [P.A. p. 7] be defended but by nonsense.'[3] [This was in a

10   great measure/degree a sportive attack; for in his Life of Prior he has given him deserved praise. *del*]

     Mrs. Thrale then praised Garrick's talent for light [gay/easy/lively>] gay poetry and as a Specimen repeated his Song in [the alteration of/the altered *del*] *Florizel and Perdita* ⟨and dwelt with peculiar pleasure on this line.⟩[4]

15   I'd smile with the simple and feed with the poor.

     Johnson. 'Nay, My Dear Lady. This will never do. Poor David. Smile with the simple. What folly is that — And who would feed with the poor that can help it. No, no. Let me smile with the wise and feed with the rich.' I repeated this sally to Garrick, and wondered [to find his sensibility much irritated by it>] [to find his

20   sensibility as a poet to have been much irritated by it>] to find his sensibility as a [poetical *del*] writer not a little irritated by it. To sooth him I observed that Johnson [at times *del*] spared none of his friends, and ⟨I⟩ quoted [Horace's *foenum habet in cornu* where he represents one>] the passage in Horace in which he compares one who [attacks/satirises>] attacks his friends for the sake of a laugh [to

25   be avoided as/like a>] to a pushing ox that is marked by a bunch of hay put [upon/in to>] upon his horns ⟨*foenum habet in cornu*⟩. 'Aye,' said Garrick [of Johnson *del*] ⟨vehemently⟩, 'he has a whole mow of it.'

     Talking of History Johnson said 'We may know historical facts to be true as we may know facts [P.A. p. 8] in common life to be true. Motives are generally

30   [uncertain/unknown>] unknown. We cannot [trust to/depend upon>] trust to the characters which we find in History, unless when they are drawn by those who knew the persons as those for instance by Sallust or by Lord Clarendon.'

     He would not allow much merit to Whitefields Oratory 'His popularity Sir,' ⟨said he⟩ 'is chiefly owing to the [strangeness/peculiarity>] peculiarity of his

35   manner. He would be followed by crowds were he to wear a night=cap in the pulpit, or were he to preach from a tree.'

     ⟨I know not from what spirit of contradiction he burst out into a violent declamation against the Corsicans of whose heroism I talked in high terms. 'Sir' said he 'what is all this rout about the Corsicans. They have been at war with the

40   Genoese for upwards of twenty years and have never yet taken their fortified

---

[3] The illustrative quotation in Hill-Powell (ii. 78 n. 3) somewhat misrepresents the character of SJ's critical judgments in his 'Life' of Prior. As JB's deleted qualification suggests, SJ mingles his strictures with a good deal of 'deserved praise'.

[4] In place of *Florizel and Perdita*, JB initially seems to have intended either 'the alteration of *The Winter's Tale*' or 'the altered *Winter's Tale*'. As noted in Hill-Powell, Garrick's *Florizel and Perdita* was a condensed version of Shakespeare's play (ii. 78 n. 4).

towns. They might have battered down the walls and reduced them to powder in twenty years. They might have pulled the walls in pieces and cracked the stones with their teeth in twenty years.' It was in vain to argue with him upon the want of artillery. He was not to be resisted for the moment.ₓ

[On the evening of the 10 October>] On the evening of October 10 I presented Dr. Johnson to General Paoli.[5] I had greatly wished that two men for whom I had the highest [value>] esteem should meet. They met with a manly ease, mutually conscious of their own abilities and of the abilities one of each other. The General spoke Italian and Dr. Johnson English and understood one another very well,[6] with a little aid of interpretation from/by[7] me, in which I compared myself to an Isthmus which joins two great Continents. Upon Johnson's [entering the room/first entering the room/approach>] approach, the General said 'From what I have read of your Works Sir and from what Mr. Boswell has told me of you, I have long [had/held>] held you in great [esteem and *del*] veneration.' The General talked of language being formed on the particular notions and manners [P.A. p. 9] of a people, without knowing which we cannot know the/a[8] language. We may know the direct signification of single words; but by these no beauty of expression, no sally of genius no wit is conveyed to the mind. All this must be by allusion to other ideas. 'Sir' said Johnson, 'you talk of language as if you had never done any thing else but study it, instead of governing a nation.' The General said, ₍'Questo e un troppo gran complimento.'ₓ 'This is too great a compliment.' Johnson answered 'I should have thought so, Sir if I had not heard you talk.' The General asked him what he thought of the Spirit of infidelity which was so prevalent. *Johnson*. 'Sir this gloom of infidelity I hope is only a transient cloud passing through the hemisphere which will soon be dissipated, and the sun break forth with his usual splendour.' 'You think then' said the General 'that they will change their principles like their clothes.' *Johnson*. 'Why Sir, if they bestow no more thought on principles than on dress, it must be so.' The General said that a great part of the fashionable Infidelity was owing to a desire of shewing courage. Men who have no opportunities of shewing it as to things in this life take death and futurity as objects on which to display it.' *Johnson*. 'That is mighty [P.A. p. 10] foolish affectation. Fear is one of the passions of human nature ₍of which it is impossible to divest itₓ. You remember that the Emperour Charles V when he read upon the tombstone of a spanish Nobleman "Here lies one who never knew/felt[9] fear" wittily said "Then he has never snuffed a candle with his fingers."'

5

10

15

20

25

30

35

---

[5] *The London Chronicle* (31 October–2 November 1769) reported that SJ was introduced to Paoli on 31 October, not 10 October. According to F. A. Pottle, 'Such surviving documentation as there is rather supports the dating of *Lond. Chron.* No manuscript source for the conversation given in the *Life* under the date of 10 Oct. has been found, and the memorandum for 11 Oct., summarizing the events of the 10th, makes no mention of Johnson' (*Earlier Years*, pp. 563–64).

[6] In the margin next to this passage JB has written, 'so much to Johnson's satisfaction that he said'; because there is no mark to indicate where to insert these additional words, the compositor has queried, 'where does this come in'. The insertion was never made.

[7] The alternative is resolved by the printing of 'from' in the revises.

[8] The alternative is resolved by the printing of 'the' in the revises.

[9] The alternative is resolved by the printing of 'knew' in the revises.

ₓHe talked a few words in/of¹ french to the General; but finding he did not do it with facility, he asked for pen ink and paper and wrote the following Note.

'J'ai lu dans la geographie de Lucas de Linda un Pater noster êcrit dans une langue toutàfait differente de l'Italienne et de toutes autres lesquelles se derivent
5 du Latin. L'auteur l'appelle linguam Corsicæ rusticam; elle a peutetre passé peu a peu mais elle a certainement prevalu autrefois dans les montagnes et dans la compagne. Le même auteur dit la même chose en parlant de Sardaigne, qu'il y a deux langues dans l'Isle, une des villes, l'autre de la [compaigne>] campagne.'

The General immediately [informed/satisfied>] informed him that [the/this>]
10 the *lingua rustica* was only in Sardinia.ₓ

Dr. Johnson went home with me and drank tea till late in the night. He said General Paoli had the loftiest port of any man he had ever seen. He denied that military men were allways the [most genteel>] [highest bred>] best bred men [, for *del*]. 'Perfect good breeding,' ₓhe observedₓ [consisted>] 'consists in having no
15 particular mark of any profession but a general [elegant smoothness/elegance>] elegance of manners. Whereas in a military man you can commonly distinguish the [marks>] *brand* of a soldier, *l'homme d'epee.*'

He shunned tonight any discussion of the perplexed question of fate and freewill ₓwhich I attempted to agitateₓ. 'Sir' said he, 'we *know* our will is free, and
20 *there's* an end on't.'ₓ

[MS 335 resumed] He honoured me with his company at dinner on the 16 of October at my lodgings in ₓOldₓ Bond Street with Sir Joshua Reynolds Mr. Garrick Dr. Goldsmith Mr. Murphy Mr. Bickerstaff and Mr. Thomas Davies. Garrick played round [MS 336] him with a fond vivacity [holding by/and taking
25 hold of>] taking hold of the breasts² of his coat and [looking in>] [looked in>] looking up in his face with a lively archness, [talking how well he now was, *del*] ₓcomplimented him on the good health which he seemed then to enjoy:ₓ while the Sage shaking his head beheld him with a gentle complacency. One of the company [was late in/of coming.>] not being come at the hour that was fixed I
30 [started the/asked the usual question upon such occasions if/whether I should not order dinner>] proposed as usual upon such occasions to order dinner to be served, [and said>] adding 'Ought six people to be kept waiting for one?' 'Why yes' answered Johnson, 'if the one will suffer more by your sitting down, than the six will do by waiting.' There was a delicate humanity in this observation. Goldsmith
35 [/to divert the tedious minutes/bragged>] to divert the tedious minutes ₓstrutted aboutₓ bragging of his dress, and I believe was seriously vain of it, for, his mind was wonderfully prone to that passion. 'Come come' said Garrick, 'talk no more of that. You are perhaps the worst eheh?' Goldsmith was eagerly [breaking in>] [breaking in upon him>] attempting to interrupt him, when Garrick [went
40 on/kept laughing>] went on laughing ₓironicallyₓ, 'Nay you will allways *look* like a *Gentleman*; but I am talking of being well or ill *drest.*' 'Well ₓLet me tell youₓ' said Goldsmith. 'When my Taylor brought home my bloomcoloured coat, he said

---

¹ The alternative is resolved by the printing of 'of' in the revises.
² A deleted marginal note in JB's hand may be deciphered (and interpreted) as an experimental pair of alternatives to 'breasts': 'lapels' and 'the forepart'. These readings, however, must remain conjectural.

"Sir I have a favour to beg of you. When any body asks you who made your clothes [say›] [be pleased to say›] be pleased to mention John Phielby at the Harrow in Water-Lane.'" *Johnson*. 'Why Sir that was because he knew the strange colour would attract crowds to gaze at it, and thus they might hear of him, and see *[MS 337]* how well he could make a coat even of so absurd a colour.' 5

[When we were set down/seated our›] [When we had sat down to dinner›] After dinner our conversation first turned upon Pope. Johnson said his characters of men were [admirably/finely›] admirably drawn those of women not so well. [His pastorals he said were poor things *del*] He repeated to us in his forcible melodious manner [the character of ₍James Moore₎³ and›] the [conclusion›] 10 concluding lines of the Dunciad. [When the company were loud in praise of the lines I ventured to say›] While he was talking loudly in praise of those lines one of the company ventured to say, 'Too fine for such a Poem — a Poem on what?' *Johnson*. ₍(with a disdainful look)₎ 'Why on *Dunces*. It was worth while being a dunce then. ₍Ah Sir hadst thou lived in those days.₎ It is not worth while being 15 a dunce now when there are no wits.' *Bickerstaff* observed as a peculiar circumstance that Pope's fame was higher when [He was alive than now›] he was alive than it was then. Johnson said his Pastorals were poor things though the versification was fine. He told us with high satisfaction the anecdote of Pope's inquiring who was the Authour of his London [a Satire *del*] and saying he will be 20 soon *deterré*. He [said›] observed that in Dryden's poetry there were passages drawn from a profundity which Pope could never reach. He repeated his lines on Love (Gentle tempestous etc. *look for them*)⁴ and gave great applause to the character of Zimri. Goldsmith said that Pope's character of Addison [was drawn deep from feeling and knowledge›] shewed a deep knowledge of the human heart. 25 *[MS 338]* Johnson said that the description of the Temple in the Mourning Bride was the finest ₍poetical₎ passage he had ever read; [there was›] he recollected none in Shakspeare equal to it. — 'But' said Garrick (all alarmed for 'the God of his idolatry') 'We know ₍not₎ the extent and variety of his powers. We are to suppose there are such passages in his Works. Shakspeare must not suffer from the 30 badness of our memories.' *Johnson* diverted by this enthusiastick jealousy went on with greater [keeness›] ardour. 'No Sir. *Congreve* has *Nature*' (smiling on the tragick eagerness of Garrick). But composing himself he added 'Sir this is not comparing Congreve on the whole with Shakspeare on the whole; but only [saying›] maintaining that Congreve has one finer passage than [can be 35 found/any›] any that can be found in Shakespeare. Sir a man may have [but ten pounds/no more than ten pounds›] no more than ten guineas in the world; but he may have [those/his›] those ten [pounds›] guineas in one piece and so may have

---

³ This 'character' of James Moore appears in Book 2 of *The Dunciad* (*ll*. 35–50).

⁴ SJ repeated (and JB vaguely remembered) the lines from Dryden's *Tyrannical Love* (III. 3) that are quoted in the 'Life' of Dryden: 'Love various minds does variously inspire; / It stirs in gentle bosoms gentle fire, / Like that of incense on the altar laid; / But raging flames tempestuous souls invade, / A fire which every windy passion blows; / With pride it mounts, or with revenge it glows' (*Lives of the Poets*, ed. G.B. Hill, i. 458). The compressed quotation was deleted in the revises, when EM, unable to identify the work in question, decided to insert, '(by the former which I have now forgotten)' (*Corr. 2*, p. 331).

a finer piece than a man who has ten thousand pounds. But then he has only one
ten [pound>] guinea piece. — What I mean is that you can shew me no passage
[equal to this where moral ideas/notions are not mingled and there>] where there
is simply a [material object which produces such an effect>] description of material
5   objects without any intermixture of moral notions which produces such an effect.'
ʌMr.ʌ *Murphy* mentioned Shakespeare's description of the night before the
Battle of Agincourt, but it was observed it had *men* in it. Mʀ. *[MS 339] Davies*
suggested the speech of Juliet [imagining what she should feel if she awaked in the
tomb>] in which she figures herself awaking in the tomb of her ancestors.
10   Someone mentioned the description of Dover Cliff. *Johnson.* 'No Sir. It should be
all precipice, — all vaccuum — the crows impede your fall — the diminished
appearance of the boats and the other circumstances [may be>] [are/is>] are all very
good description; but do not [at once affect/[*undeciphered word*]>] impress the mind
ʌat once with the horrible idea of immense heigth. The impression is divided;ʌ
15   you pass on by computation ʌfrom one stage of the tremendous space to another.ʌ
Had the girl in the Mourning Bride said she could not cast her shoe to the top of
one of the pillars ʌin the Templeʌ it would not have aided the [idea/impression>]
idea but [/on/ the contrary.>] weakened it.'
    Talking of a Barrister who had a bad utterance [somebody wickedly said /that/
20   it was a loss to him that he had not been>], someone (to rouse Johnson) wickedly
said that he was unfortunate in not having been taught oratory by Sheridan.[5]
Johnson. 'Nay, Sir, if he had been taught by Sheridan he would have cleared the
room.' *Garrick.* 'Sheridan has too much vanity to be a good man.' — ([Now
mark>] [Let>] We shall now see Johnson's mode of *defending* a man[. 'No Sir *del*],
25   taking him into his own hands and [expatiating in discrimination>] discriminat-
ing.) ʌ*Johnson.*ʌ 'No Sir. — There is ʌto be sureʌ in Sheridan something to
reprehend, and every thing to laugh at; but Sir he is not a bad man. No, Sir, were
mankind to be divided into good and bad *[MS 340]* he would stand [considerably/a
considerable way>] considerably within the ranks of [ʌtheʌ *del*] good. And Sir ʌit
30   must be allowed thatʌ Sheridan excells in plain declamation though he can
exhibit no character.'
    I should [not have reported this animadversion upon Mr. Sheridan for whom I
have ever preserved a sincere regard and of whom I think>] perhaps have suppressed this disquisition concerning a person of whose merit and worth I think
35   with respect had he not attacked Johnson so [unreasonably>] outrageously in his
life of Swift, and at the same time treated us his admirers as a set of pigmies. He
[provoked the lash of wit, and I therefore have not warded it off>] who has
provoked the lash of wit cannot complain that he smarts from it.
    Mrs. Montagu [ʌasʌ the Authour of an>] a Lady distinguished for having
40   written an Essay on Shakspeare being mentioned — *Reynolds.* 'I think that Essay
does her honour.' *Johnson.* 'Yes Sir. It does *her* honour; but it would do nobody
else honour. I have indeed not read it all. But when I take up the end of a web and
find it pack=thread, I do not expect by [looking/going>] looking farther to find

---

[5] The notes upon which this conversation are based simply refer to the anonymous
barrister as 'Counsel', but they do reveal that the 'someone' who roused SJ was JB himself.

embroidery. Sir I will venture to say there is not one sentence of true criticism in [it>] her book.' *Garrick.* 'But Sir∧, surely,∧ it shews how much Voltaire has mistaken [the english>] Shakspeare, which nobody else has [done/shewn>] done.' *Johnson.* 'Sir nobody else has thought it worth while. And what merit is there in that? You may as well [talk of>] praise a schoolmaster whipping a boy [for   5 construing>] who has construed ill. No Sir, [MS 341] there is no real criticism in it, none shewing the beauty of thought as [coming from>] formed in the workings of the human heart, [from certain positions/dispositions of the mind *del*].'

The admirers of this [∧ingenious∧ *del*] Essay[a] [of *del*] may be offended at the slighting manner in which Johnson spoke of it; but let it be considered that he gave   10 his honest opinion unbiased by any prejudice, or any proud jealousy of a woman intruding herself into the chair of Criticism [∧as he might have expressed himself∧ *del*], for Sir Joshua Reynolds has told me that when the Essay first came out [and it was not known who had written it only that one of our most eminent literati said that its Authour did not know the greek tragedians in the Original>] and it was not   15 known who had written it, Johnson wondered how Sir Joshua could like it[; and one>]. At this time, Sir Joshua himself had received no information concerning the Authour except being assured by one of our most eminent literati that it was clear its Authour did not know the Greek [Tragedians>] Tragedies in the original.[6] One day at Sir Joshua's table when it was related that Mrs. Montagu in an   20 excess of compliment to the Authour of a modern Tragedy [cried>] had exclaimed 'I tremble for Shakspeare' Johnson said 'When Shakspeare has got [_____/that gentleman>] _____ for his rival and Mrs. Montagu for his defender he is in a poor state indeed.'[7] [That this Lady may have deigned to use such extravagant flattery I can believe; for I myself once heard her in a company at   25 Edinburgh say 'Edinburgh is a little London, which I like better than the great one.'[8] And this several [MS 342] eminent literary men of Scotland/scotch literary men fairly swallowed. *del*]

[a] Of which I acknowledge myself to be one, considering it as a piece of the secondary or comparative species of Criticism, and not of that profound species   30 which alone Dr. Johnson would allow to be 'real criticism.' It is besides, clearly and elegantly expressed and it has done effectually what it professed to do, namely vindicating Shakspeare from the misrepresentations of Voltaire; and considering how many young people were misled by [the *del*] his witty though false observations, Mrs. Montagu's Essay was of service to the merit of Shakspeare with a   35 certain class of readers, and is therefore entitled to praise. Johnson I am assured allowed her the merit which I have stated, saying 'it is conclusive *ad hominem*.'

---

[6] L. F. Powell suggests that JB is referring to EM (Hill-Powell vi. 429).

[7] L. F. Powell argues convincingly (*Life* ii. 486–487) that the reference is to Robert Jephson, author of *Braganza* (1775), *The Law of Lombardy* (1779), and *The Count of Narbonne* (1781). JB's 'one day' elides a conversation from 1769 with one that could not have taken place before 1775.

[8] This anecdote is not recorded in JB's journal.

Johnson [went on with his notion of true criticism 'It is what the Scotchman has attempted in›] [said›] proceeded, 'The Scotchman has taken the right method in his *Elements of Criticism*. I [don't›] do not mean that he has taught us any thing; but he has [told/given›] told us old things in a new way.' *Murphy*. 'He seems to
5   have read a great deal of french criticism, and wants to make it his own, as if he had been for years anatomising the heart of man and peeping into every crany of it.' *Goldsmith*. 'It is easier to write that Book than to read it.' *Johnson*. '[As an example of true criticism there is›] We have an example of true criticism in Burke's *Essay on the Sublime and Beautiful*, and if I recollect ⌄there is also⌄ *Du Bos*, — and
10 Bouhours who shews [all beauty to depend on truth/how all beauty depends on truth›] all beauty to depend on truth. ⌄There is no great merit in telling how many Plays have Ghosts in them, and how this ghost is better than that. You must shew how terrour is impressed on the human heart — In the description of Night in Macbeth the beetle and the bat detract from the general idea of darkness —
15 inspissated gloom.'⌄
[He said›] Politicks being mentioned he said 'This Petitioning is a new mode of distressing Government; and a mighty easy one. I will undertake to get Petitions either against quarter guineas or half=guineas with the help of a little hot wine. — There must be no yielding /to encourage this/.[9] The object is not important
20 enough. We are not to blow up half a dozen Palaces because one cottage is burning.'
The Conversation then took another turn. *Johnson*. 'It is amazing what ignorance ⌄of certain points⌄ one sometimes finds ⌄in men of eminence⌄. A wit about town who wrote latin bawdy verses asked me how England [MS 343] and
25 Scotland which were once two kingdoms were now one. And [a great Barrister›] Sir Fletcher Norton did not seem to know that there were such publications as the Reviews.
'The Ballad of Hardyknute [is nothing extraordinary›] has no great [merit/value›] merit if it be really ancient. People talk much of nature. But mere
30 obvious nature may be [shewn/copied›] exhibited with very little [merit/power of mind.'›] power of mind.'
On thursday [19 October›] October 19 I [had a long evening›] passed the evening with him at his house [by ourselves *del*]. He advised me to complete a Dictionary of words peculiar to Scotland of which I shewed him a specimen. 'Sir'
35 said he '*Ray* has made a collection of north country words. By collecting those of your country, you will do a useful thing towards the history of the language.' He bid me also go on with Collections which I was making upon the Antiquities of Scotland. 'Make a large Book, a Folio.' ⌄*Boswell*.⌄ 'But of what use will it be Sir?' — ⌄*Johnson*.⌄ 'Never mind the use; do it.'
40 I complained that he had not mentioned Garrick in his Preface to Shakespeare and asked if he did not admire him? *Johnson*. 'Yes as a Poor Player that/who[1] frets and struts his hour upon the stage — as a shadow.' ⌄*Boswell*.⌄ 'But has he not brought Shakspeare into notice?' — ⌄*Johnson*.⌄ 'Sir to allow that would be to

---

[9] The optional phrase, which JB left unresolved, is printed in the revises.
[1] The alternative is resolved by the printing of 'who' in the revises.

lampoon the age. Many [MS 344] of Shakspeare's Plays are the worse for being acted. Macbeth for instance.' — ⟨*Boswell.*⟩ 'What, Sir, [with the advantage of decoration and action?⟩] is nothing gained by decoration and action? No I do wish that you had mentioned Garrick.' — ⟨*Johnson.*⟩ 'My Dear Sir, had I mentioned him, I must have mentioned many more, Mrs. Pritchard, Mrs. Cibber —' nay and   5
⟨*Mr.*⟩ Cibber too. He too altered Shakspeare.' — ⟨*Boswell.*⟩ 'You have read his apology Sir?' — ⟨*Johnson.*⟩ 'Yes, it is very entertaining. But as for Cibber himself, [if you took⟩] taking from [his conversation/him⟩] his conversation all that he ought not to have said he was a poor creature. [He was in earnest with his Odes. I remember he brought me one to have my opinion of it, in which was this Stanza   10
      Perched on the eagles soaring wing
      The lowly Linnet loves to sing⟩]²
I remember when he brought me one of his Odes to have my opinion of it, I could not bear such nonsense and would not let him read it to [an/the⟩] the end; so little respect had I for that great man (laughing). Yet I remember Richardson wonder-   15
ing that I could treat him with familiarity.'

I [mentioned to/told⟩] mentioned to him that I had seen the execution of several convicts at Tyburn two days before, and that none of them seemed to be under any concern. *Johnson.* 'Most of them Sir, have never thought at all.' ⟨*Boswell.*⟩ 'But is not the fear of death natural to Man?' — ⟨*Johnson.*⟩ 'So much   20
so ⟨Sir⟩ that the whole of life is but keeping away the thoughts of it.' ⟨He then in a low and earnest tone talked of his meditating upon the aweful hour of his own dissolution and in what manner he should conduct himself upon that occasion. 'I know not' (said he) 'whether I [should/would⟩] should wish [to have a friend by me/that a friend should be by me⟩] to have a friend by me or have it all between   25
GOD and myself.'⟩

[MS 345] Talking of our feeling for the distresses of others — *Johnson.* 'Why Sir there [much noise is made/is much noise made⟩] is much noise made about it. But it is [not true⟩] greatly exaggerated. No, Sir, [you⟩] we have a [decent⟩] certain degree of feeling to prompt [you⟩] us to do good. More than that Providence does   30
not intend. It would be misery to no purpose.' — ⟨*Boswell.*⟩ 'But [now if I/a friend were in danger of being hanged⟩] suppose now Sir that one of your intimate friends were apprehended for an offence for which he might be hanged.'³ 'I should do what I could to [bail you; but when you were once fairly hanged I should not suffer for you/save him and give him any other assistance; but if he were once fairly   35
hanged I should not suffer for him⟩] bail him and give him any other assistance; but if he were once fairly hanged I should not suffer.' ⟨*Boswell.*⟩ 'Would you eat your dinner, that day ⟨Sir⟩?' — ⟨*Johnson.*⟩ 'Yes, Sir, and eat it as if he were eating it with me. Why there's Baretti who is to be tried for his life tomorrow, friends have risen up for him on every side yet if he should be hanged none of them will eat   40
a slice of plumb pudding the less. Sir, that sympathetick feeling goes a very little way ⟨in depressing the mind.'⟩

---

² JB had made prior use of this quotation: see *Life MS* i. 278 and n. 7.
³ By the time of the revises, '*Johnson*' had been inserted after 'hanged' and before 'I' in order to clarify the change in speaker.

I told him that I had dined lately at Foote's who shewed me a letter to him from Tom Davies ⟨telling him that he had not been able to sleep from the concern which he felt on account of *this sad affair of Baretti* [*and del*]⟩ begging of him to [think⟩] try if he could suggest any thing that would be of service to him, and at the
5   same time recommending to him an industrious young man who kept a pickleshop. *Johnson.* 'Aye Sir here you have a true specimen of human sympathy, a friend hanged or a cucumber pickled. We know not whether Baretti or the Pickle=man [has/have⟩] has kept Davies from sleep, [*MS 346*] nor does he know himself. [But Sir⟩] [And But Sir⟩] And as to his not sleeping, Sir. Tom Davies is
10   a very great man. Tom has been upon the stage, and knows how to do these things. I have not been upon the stage and cannot do those things.' ⟨*Boswell.*⟩ ['I have blamed myself/found fault with myself⟩] 'I have often blamed myself, Sir, for not feeling for others [in the keen manner that others⟩] as sensibly as many say they do.' ⟨*Johnson.*⟩ '[Why *del*] Sir, don't be duped by them any more. And Sir you will
15   find these very feeling people are not very [ready/anxious⟩] ready to do you good. They pay you by feeling.' [⟨*Boswell.*⟩ 'But I am uneasy that I do not feel enough. — ⟨*Johnson.*⟩ 'Why then keep better company and read melancholy stories/Why learn then Sir if you must be a *del*].

⟨*Boswell.*⟩ 'Foote has a great deal of humour.' ⟨*Johnson.*⟩ 'Yes, Sir.'
20   ⟨*Boswell.*⟩ 'He has a singular talent of exhibiting character.' ⟨*Johnson.*⟩ 'Sir it is not a talent; it is a vice; it is what others abstain from. It is not comedy which exhibits the character of a species as that of a Miser gathered from many misers; it is Farce which [gives/shews/exhibits⟩] exhibits individuals.' ⟨*Boswell.*⟩ 'Did not he think of exhibiting you Sir?' ⟨*Johnson.*⟩ 'Sir, fear restrained him. He knew [I'd
25   break⟩] I would have broke his bones. I would have saved him the trouble of cutting off a leg. I would not have left him a leg to cut off.' ⟨*Boswell.*⟩ 'Pray Sir is not Foote an Infidel?' ⟨*Johnson.*⟩ 'I do not know Sir that [he⟩] the fellow is an Infidel. But if he be an infidel he is an infidel as a dog is an infidel [*MS 347*] that is to say he has never thought upon the subject.'[a] — ⟨*Boswell.*⟩ 'I suppose, Sir, he
30   has thought superficially, and seised the first notions which [occurred/happened to occur⟩] occurred ⟨to his mind⟩.' — ⟨*Johnson.*⟩ 'Why then, Sir, still he is like a dog that snatches the piece next him. Did you never observe that dogs have not the power of comparing? A dog will take a small bit of meat as readily as a [big.⟩] large when both are before him.

35   [a] When Mr. Foote was at Edinburgh he thought fit to entertain a numerous scotch company with a great deal of ⟨pretty⟩ coarse jocularity at the expense of Dr. Johnson ⟨imagining it would be acceptable.⟩ I felt this as not civil to me, but sat very patiently till he had exhausted his merriment on that subject and then observed that surely Johnson must be allowed to have sterling wit and that I had
40   heard him say a very good thing of Mr. Foote himself. 'Ah my old friend Sam', cried Foote. 'No man says better things. Do let us have it.' Upon which I told the above story [Foote *del*] which produced a very loud laugh from the company. But I never saw Foote so disconcerted. He looked grave and angry and entered into a serious refutation of the justice of the remark. 'What Sir' said he 'talk thus of a man
45   of liberal education a man who was for years at the University of Oxford a man who has added sixteen new characters to the English Drama of this country.'

'Buchanan has fewer *centos* than any modern latin poet. He not only had great knowledge of the latin language but was a great [poet⟩] poetical genius. Both the Scaligers praise him.'

He again talked of the passage in Congreve with high commendation, and said, 'Shakspeare never has six lines together without a fault. Perhaps you [may/shall⟩] may find seven. But this does not refute my general assertion. If I come to an orchyard, and say there's no fruit here and then comes a poring man and finds two apples and three pears, and tells me, "Sir you are mistaken I have found both apples and Pears," I should laugh at him; what would that be to the purpose?'

ʌ*Boswell.*ʌ 'What do you think of Dr. Young's Night Thoughts Sir?' ʌ*Johnson.*ʌ 'Why there are very fine things in them.' ʌ*Boswell.*ʌ 'Is there not less Religion [among us/in the Nation⟩] in the nation now Sir than there was formerly.' — ʌ*Johnson.*ʌ ['Why I dont know not⟩] 'I do not know Sir that there is.' ʌ*Boswell.*ʌ 'For instance, there used [MS 348] to be a Chaplain in every great family, which [is not the case⟩] we/you[4] do not find now.' ʌ*Johnson.*ʌ 'Neither do you find many of the state servants which great families used formerly to have. There is a change [in/of the mode⟩] of modes in the whole deportment[5] of life.'

Next day October 20 he appeared for the only time I suppose in his life, as a witness in a Court of Justice, being called to give evidence to the character of Mr. Baretti who having stabbed a man in the street was arraigned at the Old Bailey for murder. Never did such a constellation of genius [enlighten/illuminate⟩] enlighten the aweful Sessions House Mr. Burke Mr. Garrick Mr. Beauclerk and Dr. Johnson and undoubtedly their favourable testimony had due weight with the Court and Jury. Johnson gave his evidence in a slow deliberate and distinct manner [and with a minuteness of circumstance/circumstantial minuteness *del*] which was uncommonly [impressive/clear⟩] impressive. ʌIt is well known that Mr. Baretti was acquitted.ʌ

On the 26 of October we [passed the evening together⟩] dined together at the Mitre tavern. I found fault with Foote [for making a fool of his company⟩] [for making fools of his company⟩] for indulging his talent of ridicule at the expence of his visitors, which I colloquially termed making fools of his company. — *Johnson.* 'Why, Sir, when you go to see Foote you do not go to see a Saint. You go to see a man who will be entertained at your house and then bring you on a publick stage, who will entertain you at his [MS 349] house for the very purpose of bringing you on a publick stage. Sir he does not make fools of his company. They whom he exposes are fools allready. He only brings them into action.'

ʌTalkingʌ of trade he observed 'It is a mistaken notion that a [great⟩] vast deal of money is brought into [the⟩] a nation by trade. It is not so. Commodities come for commodities; but trade produces no capital accession of wealth. [But though/yet⟩] However, though there should be [no/little⟩] little profit in money there is a considerable profit in pleasure as it gives to one nation the productions of another, as we have wines and fruits and many other foreign articles brought to us.' — ʌ*Boswell.*ʌ 'Yes Sir and there is a profit in pleasure by its

---

[4] The alternative is resolved by the printing of 'we' in the revises.

[5] The compositor set this word as 'department', and because JB did not read proof against the MS, the mistake was never caught.

[procuring/causing/giving/furnishing>] furnishing occupation to [mankind/such numbers of mankind/so many>] such numbers of mankind.' — ⟨*Johnson.*⟩ 'Why, Sir, you cannot call that pleasure to which all are averse, and which none begin but with the hope [to be idle/leave off>] of leaving off; a thing which men dislike

5   before they have tried it, and [when/after>] when they have tried it.' — ⟨*Boswell.*⟩ 'But Sir [the/our>] the mind must be employed and we grow weary [if/when>] when idle.' — ⟨*Johnson.*⟩ 'That is Sir, because [⟨from⟩ *del*] others [are/being>] are busy, we want company [/but/>] but if we were all idle there would be no growing weary; we should all entertain one another. There is indeed this in trade. It gives

10   [an opportunity for change of situation amongst men/in human life>] men an opportunity of improving their situation. If there were no trade, [those/they>] many who are poor would [MS 350] allways remain poor. But no man loves labour for itself.' ⟨*Boswell.*⟩ 'Yes, Sir. [My Father does/I know a judge who does>] I know a person who does.[6] He is a very laborious Judge and he loves the labour.'

15   ⟨*Johnson.*⟩ 'Sir, that is because he loves respect and distinction. Could he have them without labour, he would like it better.' — 'He tells me he likes it for itself.' — 'Why Sir, he fancies so because he is not accustomed to abstract.'

We went home to his house to tea. Mrs. Williams made it with sufficient dexterity ⟨notwithstanding her blindness⟩ though her manner of satisfying her-

20   self that the cups were full enough was a little awkward. She put her finger down a certain way till she felt the tea touch it.[7] In my first elation at being allowed the privilege of attending Dr. Johnson at his [late/nightly>] late visits to this Lady which was like being *e secretioribus consiliis*, I willingly drank cup after cup as if it had been the Heliconian spring. But as the charm of novelty went off, I grew more

25   fastidious ⟨; and besides I discovered that she was of a peevish temper.⟩

There was a pretty large circle [tonight>] this evening. Dr. Johnson was in ⟨[great>] very⟩ good humour, lively, and ready to talk upon all subjects. Mr. Fergusson the [Astronomer>] self=taught Philosopher told him, of a new-invented machine which went without horses[, but a *del*]. A man who sat in it, turned

30   [⟨?round⟩ *del*] a handle which worked a spring that drove it forward. 'Then Sir,' said [MS 351] Johnson, '⟨what is gained is⟩ the man has his choice whether he will move himself alone, or himself and the machine too.' Dominicetti being men- tioned, he [was violent against him, and said>] would not allow him any merit. 'There is nothing in all this boasted system. No Sir medicated baths can be no

35   better than warm water. Their only effect can be that of tepid moisture.' One of the company took the other side [very keenly *del*] maintaining that medicines of

---

[6] The deletion here confirms the speculation in Hill-Powell (ii. 99 n. 1) that JB is referring to Lord Auchinleck.

[7] In the second edition, JB softens his description of Anna Williams' tea-making: 'her manner of satisfying herself that the cups were full enough was a little awkward. She put her finger down a certain way till she felt the tea touch it' was changed to 'her manner of satisfying herself that the cups were full enough, appeared to me, a little awkward for I fancied she put her finger down a certain way, till she felt the tea touch it.' Moreover, he adds a footnote, keyed to 'it': 'I have since had reason to think that I was mistaken; for I have been informed by a Lady, who was long intimate with her, and likely to be a more accurate observer of such matters, that she had acquired such a niceness of touch, as to know, by the feeling on the outside of the cup, how near it was to being full.'

various sorts and some too of most powerful effect are introduced into the human frame by the medium of the pores, and therefore when warm water is impregnated with salutiferous substances it may produce great effects as a Bath.' This appeared to me very satisfactory. Johnson did not answer it; but talking for victory and determined to be master of the field, he had recourse to the device which 5 Goldsmith imputed to him in the witty words of one of Cibber's Comedies [/'There is no arguing with Johnson for/>] 'There is no arguing with Johnson for when his pistol misses fire he knocks you down with the but end of it.' He turned to the Gentleman, 'Well, Sir, Go to Dominicetti and get thyself fumigated; [and let>] [be sure>] but be sure that the steam be directed to thy head, for [there's>] *that* is the 10 *peccant part.*'[8]   ₍This produced a triumphant roar of laughter from the motley assembly of Philosophers Printers and dependants male and female.₎

I know not how [I came to introduce/start so wild/whimsical a supposition/fancy>] so whimsical a thought came into my mind; but I [ventured to say>] asked, 'If, Sir, you were shut up in a Castle and a newborn child with you, 15 [what/how>] what [should>] would you do?' — ₍*Johnson.*₎ 'Why Sir I should not much like my company.' — ₍*Boswell.*₎ 'But would [MS 352] you [bring it up/take the trouble of rearing it' I inquired. *Johnson.* 'Yes, I'd feed>] take the trouble of rearing it?' He seemed, as may well be supposed, unwilling to pursue the subject, but upon my persevering in my question replied, 'Why yes Sir, I would. But I must 20 have all conveniences. If I had no garden I would make a shed on the roof and take it there for fresh air. I should feed it and wash it much, and with warm water to please it, not with cold water to give it pain.' ₍*Boswell.*₎ 'But Sir, does not heat relax?' ₍*Johnson.*₎ 'Sir, [you are not to suppose/I hope you dont imagine>] you are not to imagine that water is to be very hot. I would not coddle the child. No Sir, 25 the hardy method of [breeding up>] treating children does no good. I'll take you five children from London who shall cuff five highland children. Sir, a man bred in London will carry a burthen, or run or wrestle as well as [one>] a man brought up in the hardiest manner in the country.'[9]

[Paper Apart RC] ₍*Boswell.*₎ 'Good living, I suppose, makes [them>] the 30 Londoners strong.' ₍*Johnson.*₎ 'Why Sir, I don't know that it does. Our chairmen from Ireland who are as strong men as any, have been brought up upon potatoes. Quantity makes up for quality.' ₍*Boswell.*₎ ['Would you teach your child any thing Sir?'>] 'Would you teach this child that I have furnished you with any thing?' ₍*Johnson.*₎ 'No, I should not be apt to teach it.' ₍*Boswell.*₎ 'Would not you have 35 a pleasure in teaching it?' ₍*Johnson.*₎ 'No Sir I should *not* have a pleasure in teaching it.' ₍*Boswell.*₎ 'Have you not a pleasure in teaching men? — *there* I have you. You have the same pleasure in teaching men that I should have in teaching children.' ₍*Johnson.*₎ 'Why something about that.'

₍*Boswell.*₎ 'Do you think Sir that what is called natural affection is born with 40

---

[8] SJ alludes to a couplet from Pope's *Essay on Man*: 'Imagination plies her dang'rous art, / And pours it all upon the peccant part' (Twickenham edition, ed. Maynard Mack, 1951, ii. 143–44). Cf. *Letters of Johnson* ed. Redford, iv. 192.

[9] Direction to the compositor, '(Here take in a parcel of small leaves) marked RC'. Written entirely in the hand of JB, the parcel numbers 22 pages.

us? It appears to me to be the effect of habit, [RC 2] or of gratitude for kindness. No child has it for a parent whom it has not seen.' ₍Johnson.₎ 'Why Sir I think there is an instinctive natural affection in parents towards their children.'

Russia being mentioned as likely to become a great Empire by
5   [population/populousness›] the rapid increase of population. ₍Johnson.₎ 'Why Sir I see no prospect of their propagating more. They can have no more children than they can [get/beget›] get. I know of no way to make them breed more than they do. It is not from reason and prudence that people marry, but from inclination. A man is poor. He thinks "I cannot be worse, and so I'll e'en take Peggie."' ₍Boswell.₎ 'But
10   have not nations [RC 3] been more populous at one period than [₍at₎ *del*] another?' ₍Johnson.₎ 'Yes Sir. But that has been owing to the people being less thinned at one period than [₍at₎ *del*] another whether by [migrations/emigrations›] emigrations war or pestilence, not by their being more or less prolifick. Births at all times bear the same proportion to the same number of people.' ₍Boswell.₎ 'But to consider the
15   state of our own country. Does not throwing a number of farms into one hand hurt population?' ₍Johnson.₎ 'Why no Sir. The same quantity of food being produced will be consumed by the same number of mouths though the people may be disposed of in different ways. We see [RC 4] now if corn be dear and butchers meat cheap, the farmers all apply themselves to the raising of corn till it becomes plentiful and cheap;
20   and then Butchers meat becomes dear, so that [an equality/a ballance›] an equality is allways preserved. No Sir let fanciful men do as they will depend upon it, it is difficult to disturb the system of [life/human affairs›] life.' ₍Boswell.₎ 'But Sir is it not a very bad thing [for/in›] for Landlords to oppress their tenants by [raising/racking›] raising their rents?' ₍Johnson.₎ 'Very bad. Why, Sir, it never can
25   have any general influence. It may distress some individuals. But consider this. Landlords cannot do without [RC 5] tenants. Now tenants will not give more for land than land is worth. If they can make more of their money by keeping a shop, or any other way they'll do it, and so oblige landlords to let land come back to a reasonable rent, in order that they may get tenants. [Land in England is/Land is in
30   England›] Land in England is ₍an article of₎ commerce. A tenant who pays his landlord his rent thinks himself no more obliged to him than you think yourself obliged to a man in whose shop you buy a piece of goods. He knows the landlord [lets him have his land for no less›] does not let him have his land for less than he can get from others in the same manner as the shopkeeper sells his goods. [RC 6] No
35   shopkeeper sells a yard of ribband for sixpence when seven pence is [offered for it›] the current price.' ₍Boswell.₎ 'But Sir, is it not better [that/to have›] that tenants should be dependant on landlords?' ₍Johnson.₎ 'Why Sir, as there are many more tenants than landlords [₍and a state of dependance is not a desireable state,₎ *del*] ₍perhaps strictly speaking₎ we should wish [not/no›] not. But if you please you may
40   let your lands cheap and [/have the/get their value/›] so get the value part [/in/›] in money part [/in/›] in homage. I should agree with you in that.' ₍Boswell.₎ '[I think/believe *del*] So Sir you laugh at schemes of political improvement.' ₍Boswell.₎[1] 'Why Sir most schemes of political improvement are very laughable things.'

---

[1] 'Boswell' is a mistake for 'Johnson'. It had been corrected by the stage of the revises, apparently in first proof.

He observed, [The more numerous men/mankind are/Providence has⟩] 'Providence has wisely ordered that the more numerous men are, the more difficult [is
it/it is⟩] it is [RC 7] for them to agree in any thing, and so they are governed. There
is no doubt that if the poor should reason "We'll be the poor no longer, we'll make
the rich take their turn," they could easily do it, only were it not that they cannot   5
agree. So the common soldiers though so much more numerous than their officers
are governed by them for the same reason.'

He said 'Mankind have [a strong attachment to/a regard for⟩] a strong attachment to the habitations to which they have been accustomed. You see the
inhabitants of Norway do not with one consent quit it and go to some [country in⟩]   10
part of America where there is a mild climate, and where they may have the same
produce from land with the tenth part of the labour. No Sir, [the attachment to
their accustomed dwellings⟩] their affection for their old dwellings [RC 8] and the
terrour of a general change keep them at home. [So⟩] Thus we see many of the
finest [spots in/parts of⟩] spots in the world thinly inhabited and many rugged   15
[spots/parts⟩] spots well inhabited.'

The London Chronicle which was the ₍only₎ newspaper he constantly took in
[since I was acquainted with him *del*] being brought, the office of reading it aloud
was assigned to me. I was diverted by/at² his impatience. He made me pass over
so many parts of it that my task was very easy. He would ₍not₎ suffer one of the   20
Petitions to the King ₍about the Middlesex election₎³ to be read.

I had hired a Bohemian as my servant while I remained in London, and being
much pleased with him, I asked Dr. Johnson if his being a Roman Catholick
should prevent my taking him [home to my family⟩] with me to Scotland.
₍Johnson.₎ 'Why no, Sir. If *he* has no objection, you [RC 9] can have [no   25
objection⟩] none.' ₍Boswell.₎ 'So Sir, you are no great ennemy to the
[Popish/Roman Catholick/Romish⟩] Roman Catholick Religion.' ₍Johnson.₎
'No more Sir than to the Presbyterian Religion.' ₍Boswell.₎ 'You are joking.'
₍Johnson.₎ 'No Sir, upon honour I think so. Nay Sir, of the two I prefer the
Popish.' ₍Boswell.₎ 'How so Sir?' ₍Johnson.₎ 'Why Sir, the Presbyterians have   30
no church, no Apostolical ordination.' ₍Boswell.₎ 'And do you think that
absolutely essential Sir?' ₍Johnson.₎ 'Why Sir as it was an apostolical institution,
I think it is dangerous to be without it. And, Sir the Presbyterians have no publick
worship. They have no form of prayer in which they know they are to join. They
go to hear a man pray and are to judge whether they will join ₍with him₎.'   35
₍Boswell.₎ 'But Sir, their doctrine is the same with that of the Church of England.
Their Confession of Faith and the [RC 10] Thirty Nine Articles contain the same
points; Even the doctrine of Predestination.' ₍Johnson.₎ 'Why yes Sir. Predestination was a part of the clamour of the times. So it is mentioned in our Articles but
with as little positiveness as could be.' ₍Boswell.₎ 'Is it necessary Sir to believe   40
all the Thirty Nine Articles?' ₍Johnson.₎ 'Why Sir that is a question which has
been much agitated. Some have thought it necessary that they should all be
believed. Others have considered them to be only articles of peace that is to say
you are not to preach against them.' ₍Boswell.₎ 'It appears to me Sir that

---

² The alternative is resolved by the printing of 'by' in the revises.
³ JB inadvertently wrote 'Middlex' instead of 'Middlesex'.

Predestination or what [is equivalent to it/comes to the same thing>] is equivalent
to it cannot be avoided if we hold an universal prescience[4] in the Deity.' [RC 11]
⟨Johnson.⟩ 'Why Sir does not GOD every day see things going on [and does not
prevent them/without preventing them>] without preventing them.' ⟨Boswell.⟩

5   'True Sir. But if a thing be *certainly* foreseen it must be fixed and cannot happen
otherwise, and if we apply this consideration to the human mind, there is no free
will nor do I see how prayer can be of any avail.' — He mentioned Dr. Clarke and
Bishop Bramhall on Liberty and Necessity and bid me read South's Sermons on
Prayer, but avoided the question which has excruciated Philosophers and Divines

10   beyond any other. I did not press it farther, when I perceived that he ⟨was
displeased, and⟩ shrunk from any abridgement of an attribute usually ascribed to
the Divinity, however irreconcileable [RC 12] in its full extent with the grand
system of moral government. His ⟨supposed⟩ Orthodoxy [chained down>] here
cramped the vigorous powers of his understanding. He was confined by a chain

15   which early imagination [confirmed by *del*] and long habit made him think massy
and strong, but which had he ventured to try, he could at once have snapt asunder.
      I proceeded. — 'What do you think, Sir, of [the doctrine of *del*] Purgatory as
believed by the Roman Catholicks?' ⟨Johnson.⟩ 'Why Sir, it is a very harmless
doctrine. They are of opinion that the generality of mankind are neither so

20   obstinately wicked as to deserve everlasting punishment nor so good as to merit
being admitted into the society of blessed spirits; and [that therefore/therefore
that>] therefore that GOD is graciously pleased [RC 13] to allow of a middle state
where they may be purified by certain degrees of suffering. You see Sir there is
nothing unreasonable in this.' ⟨Boswell.⟩ 'But then Sir, their masses for the dead?'

25   ⟨Johnson.⟩ 'Why Sir if it be once established, that there are souls in purgatory, it
is as proper to pray for *them* as for our bretheren of Mankind who are yet [alive>] in
this life.' ⟨Boswell.⟩ 'The idolatry of the Mass.' ⟨Johnson.⟩ 'Sir there is no Idolatry
in the Mass. They believe [GOD/the real presence of God] GOD to be there and they
adore him.' ⟨Boswell.⟩ 'The Worship of Saints.' ⟨Johnson.⟩ 'Sir they do not

30   worship Saints; they invoke them, they only ask their prayers. I am talking all this
time of the *doctrines* of the Church of Rome. I [RC 14] grant you that in *practice*
Purgatory is made a lucrative imposition and that the people do become idolatrous
as they recommend themselves to the tutelary protection of particular Saints. I
think their giving the sacrament only in one kind is criminal because it is contrary

35   to the express institution of Christ and I wonder how the Council of Trent
admitted it.' ⟨Boswell.⟩ 'Confession?' ⟨Johnson.⟩ 'Why I dont know but that is
a good thing. The Scripture says "Confess your faults one to another", and the
Priests confess as well as the [laity/people>] laity. Then it must be considered that
their absolution is only upon repentance, and often upon pennance also. You think

40   your [RC 15] sins may be forgiven without pennance upon repentance alone.'
      I thus ventured to mention all the common objections against the Roman
Catholick Church that I might hear so great a Man upon them. What he said is
here accurately recorded. But it is not improbable that if one had taken the other
side he might have reasoned differently.

---

[4] The compositor misread 'prescience' as 'presence' and this error went uncorrected
until the second edition.

ₐI must however [record/admit⟩] record that he had a respect for '*the old religion*' as the mild Melancthon called that of the Roman Catholick Church even while he was exerting himself for its reformation in some particulars. Sir William Scott informs me that he heard Johnson say 'A convert who is converted from protestantism to popery may be sincere. He parts with nothing. He is only   5
superadding to what he already had. But a convert from popery to protestantism gives up so much of what he has held as sacred as any thing that he retains, — there is [so much/such a⟩] so much *laceration of mind* in such a conversion, that it can hardly be sincere and lasting.' The truth of this reflection may be confirmed by many and eminent instances, some of which will occur to most of my readers.ₓ   10

ₐWhen we were aloneₓ I introduced the subject of death and endeavoured to maintain that the fear of it might be got over. I told him that David Hume said he was no more uneasy to think he should [*not be* than that he *had not been*⟩] *not be* after this life, than that he *had not been* before he began to exist. ₐ*Johnson.*ₓ 'Sir if [a man⟩] he really thinks so his perceptions are disturbed; he is mad. If he does not   15
think so he lies. Hume knows he lies.[5] He may tell you *[RC 16]* he holds his finger in the flame of a candle, without feeling pain. Would you believe him? When he dies he at least gives up all he has.' — 'Foote[6] Sir told me that when he was very ill he was not affraid to die.' ₐ*Johnson.*ₓ 'It is not true Sir. Hold a pistol to Foote's breast or to Hume's breast and threaten to kill them, and you'll see how they   20
behave.' ₐ*Boswell.*ₓ 'But may we not [calm⟩] fortify our minds for the approach of death?' — Here ₐI am sensibleₓ I was in the wrong to bring before his view what he ever looked upon with horrour; for although when in a celestial frame in his 'Vanity of Human Wishes' he [can suppose/has figured⟩] has supposed Death to be 'kind Nature's signal for retreat' from this state of being to 'a happier seat' [the general   25
state of *del*] his thoughts upon this *[RC 17]* aweful [transition/change was dismally apprehensive⟩] change were in general full of dismal apprehensions. [Garrick told me that he beleived him to be harrassed with doubts. I agreed, and said *del*] His mind resembled the vast amphitheatre the Collosseum at Rome. In the center [stands his Judgement like a mighty gladiator which combats doubts which like the   30
wild beasts are all arround in cells/cages⟩] stood his Judgement which like a mighty gladiator combated those apprehensions that like the wild beasts of the *Arena,* were all arround in cells ready to be let out upon him.   [He grumbles and growls while they foam and roar. They fight and he drives them into their dens, but never kills them, so that they are allways coming out again upon him.⟩] After a conflict   35
he drove them back into their dens, but not killing them, they were still assailing him. To my question [if we might not calm our minds for the approach of death he answered in passion/in haste /angrily⟩] whether we might not fortify our minds for the approach of death he answered in passion 'No, Sir — let it alone. It matters not

---

[5] Presumably this sentence, which does not appear in the revises, had been deleted in first proof. The reason may be a simple wish to eliminate repetition, but JB's own complicated attitude toward Hume's cheerful atheism, as manifested in his interview with the dying philosopher, may also help to explain the change. See Bruce Redford, 'Boswell's Fear of Death', *Studies in Scottish Literature* 21 (1986), pp. 99–118.

[6] In the revises '*Boswell*' was inserted immediately before 'Foote' to clarify the change in speaker.

how a man dies [RC 18] but how he lives. [It>] The act of dying is not of importance, it lasts so short a time.' ₍He added (with an earnest look),₎ 'A man knows it must be, and submits. It will do him no good to whine.'[7]

    I attempted to continue the conversation. He was [provoked said>] so pro-
5 voked that he said, 'Give us no more of this' and was thrown into such a state of agitation that he expressed himself in a way that alarmed and distressed me; shewed an impatience [to have me leave him, and when I was going away said>] that I should leave him, and when I was going away called to me sternly 'Dont let us meet tomorrow.'

10   I went home exceedingly uneasy. All the harsh observations which I had ever heard made upon his character crowded into my mind and I seemed to myself [RC 19] like the man who had put his head into the Lyon's mouth a great many times with perfect safety, but at last had it bit off.

    Next morning I sent him a note [₍acknowledging₎ del] stating that I might have
15 been in the wrong, but it was not intentionally; he was therefore I could not help thinking, too severe upon me. That notwithstanding our agreement not to meet that day I would call in my way to the City and stay five minutes by my watch. 'You are' said I 'in my mind since last night surrounded with cloud and storm. Let me have a glimpse of sunshine and go about my affairs in serenity and cheerfulness.'

20   Upon entering his study, I was glad that he was not alone which would have made our meeting more awkward. There were with him Mr. Steevens and Mr. Tyers, both [RC 20] of whom I now saw for the first time. My note or his own reflection had softened him[8] for he received me very complacently ₍so that I unexpectedly found myself at ease and joined in the conversation₎.

25   He said the Criticks had done too much honour to Sir Richard Blackmore by writing so much against him. That his Creation had been helped by various wits, a line by Philips and a line by Tickel, so that by their aid and that of others the Poem had been made out. I defended Blackmore's lines which have been celebrated for absolute nonsense

30   A painted vest Prince Voltiger had on
      Which from a naked Pict his grandsire won.[9]
I maintained it to be a poetical conceit. A Pict being painted, if he is slain in battel and a vest is made of his skin it is a painted vest won from him though he was naked.

---

[7] When correcting the revises, EM 'could not help writing to Mr. Plympsel, if possible to add the following note — to the words — "it will do him no good to whine."' EM's note, never incorporated into the text, would have read as follows: 'Bacon in his admirable *Essays* has delivered a congenial sentiment, which may serve to place Dr. Johnson's notion on this subject in its true light: "Certainly the contemplation of death, as *the wages of sin*, and passage to another world, is holy and religious; but the fear of it, as a tribute due unto nature, is weak."' As EM explained in a letter to JB, 8 July 1790, he had happened to be reading 'Of Death' 'when the printers boy called' and was struck by the fact that Bacon's words seemed 'admirably to express and *justify* Johnson's notions' (*Corr. 2*, p. 329).

[8] 'My note or his own reflection had softened him' was printed in the revises 'My note had, on his own reflection, softened him'. Led astray by JB's misplaced insertion mark (which appears after 'had') the compositor read 'or' as 'on'. This error went uncorrected.

[9] In the second edition 'Blackmore's lines' has been changed to 'Blackmore's supposed lines', and a footnote explains that the couplet should be attributed (on the authority of Richard Steele) to Edward Howard.

Johnson spoke unfavourably [RC 21] of a certain pretty voluminous Authour saying 'He used to write anonymous books and then other books commending those books, [which/in which>] in which there was something of rascality.

This little incidental quarrel and reconciliation which I may be perhaps thought to have detailed too minutely must be esteemed as one of many proofs which his friends had that [though he might be charged with bad *humour* at times/was at times a bad=humoured>] though he might be charged with bad *humour* at times [RC 22] he was allways a good=*natured* man; and I have heard Sir Joshua Reynolds a nice and delicate observer of manners particularly remark that when upon any occasion Johnson had been rough to any person in company he took the first opportunity of making it up by drinking to him or addressing his discourse to him; but if he found his dignified indirect overtures sullenly neglected he was quite indifferent and considered himself as having done all that he ought to do and that the other was now in the wrong.

[MS 352] Being to set out for Scotland on the 10 of November, I wrote to him at Stretham begging that he would meet me in town on the 9th; but if this should be very inconvenient [for/to him I would come out to him. He answered>] to him I would go thither. His Answer was as follows[1]

. . . .

I was detained in town till it was too late on the 9th so went out to him early in the morning [of/on>] of the 10th October.[2] 'Now' said he 'that you are going to marry, do not expect more from Life than Life [will/can>] will afford. You may often find yourself out of humour, and you may often think your wife not studious enough to please you, and yet you may have reason to consider yourself as upon the whole very [happily/well>] happily married.'

ₐ[MS opp. 353] Talking of marriage in general, he observed 'Our marriage service is too refined. It is calculated only for the best kind of marriages; whereas we should have a form for matches of convenience, of which there are many.' He agreed with me that there was no absolute necessity for having the marriage ceremony performed by a regular clergyman, for this was not commanded in scripture.ₐ

ₐ[MS opp. 352] I was volatile enough to repeat to him a little epigrammatick Song of mine on Matrimony which Mr. Garrick had a few days before procured to be set to Musick.

    A MATRIMONIAL THOUGHT
    In the blythe days of honey=moon,
    With Kate's allurements smitten,
    I lov'd her late, I lov'd her soon,
    And call'd her dearest kitten.
    But now my kitten's grown a cat,
    And cross like other wives,
    O! by my soul, my honest Mat!
    I fear she has nine lives.

---

[1] Direction to the compositor, 'To JAMES BOSWELL Esq. / Dear Sir / Upon balancing / (Take it in)'. This Paper Apart no longer forms part of the *Life* MS.

[2] In the third edition the date was changed from October to November, apparently at the urging of the Rev. John Campbell, who had alerted JB to the mistake in a letter of 19 April 1793 (*Corr.* 2, p. 525).

My illustrious friend said, ['Mighty well Sir; but don't swear'〉] 'It is very well Sir;
but you should not swear' upon which I altered 'O! by my soul' to 'alas! alas!'〉

5   [MS 353] He was [good enough to accompany〉] so good as to accompany me to
London, and [see me into/set me upon〉] see me into the post=chaise which was to
carry me on my road to Scotland. And sure I am, that however inconsiderable
[many/some〉] many of the particulars recorded [at this time/of this year〉] at this time
may appear to some, they will be esteemed by the best part of my readers as genuine
traits of his character, contributing together to give a full fair and distinct view of it.

      In 1770 he published a political pamphlet entitled *The False Alarm*, intended to
10   justify the conduct of Ministry and their majority [of〉] in the House of Commons for
having virtually assumed it as [a proposition〉] an axiom that the expulsion of a
Member of Parliament was equivalent to exclusion, and thus having declared
Colonel Luttrel to be duely elected for the County of Middlesex
[while/notwithstanding that〉] notwithstanding Mr. Wilkes had a great majority of
15   votes. This being justly considered as a gross violation of the right of election, an
alarm for the Constitution extended itself all over the kingdom. To prove this alarm
to be false was the purpose of Johnson's Pamphlet. But even his vast powers were
inadequate [MS 354] to cope with constitutional truth and reason, and his argument
failed of effect, 〈and the House of Commons have since expunged the offensive
20   Resolution from their Journals.〉 That the house of Commons might have expelled
Mr. Wilkes repeatedly and as oft/often[3] as he [should be/was〉] should be rechosen
was not denied. But incapacitation cannot be but by an act of the whole Legislature.
It was wonderful to see how [the prejudice of party or rather the prejudice of
opinion/inclination could〉] a prejudice in favour of Government in general and an
25   aversion to popular clamour could blind and contract such an understanding as
Johnson's 〈in this particular case〉. Yet the wit the sarcasm the [keen vivacity of
eloquence〉] eloquent vivacity which [animated this pamphlet/this pamphlet dis-
played〉] this pamphlet displayed made it be read at that time with great avidity, and
it will ever be read with pleasure for the sake of its composition.[4] That this Pamphlet
30   endeavoured to infuse a narcotick indifference as to publick concerns into the minds
of the people , and that it broke out sometimes into an extreme coarseness of
contemptous abuse is but too evident. Indeed I [am well/was〉] am well informed
that there was struck out from it an expression still more degrading than any that
[now remain/remain/are left〉] now remain 'Had government been
35   [overturned/changed〉] overturned by this faction England had died of a *Thyrasis*'.[5]

---

[3] The alternative is resolved by the printing of 'often' in the revises.

[4] A deleted marginal memorandum in JB's hand suggests, 'Give some short specimens
and put in the compliment to the King'.

40   [5] The final sentence of this paragraph was omitted in the printing of the revises;
presumably, EM had deleted it in first proof. On 8 July he reported to JB that he had taken
a 'liberty ... which, I think, upon reflection you will approve. It was to strike out two lines
in which you mention an expression which you have heard Johnson used originally in *The
False Alarm*, and struck out. "Why raise up against him a host of enemies, by telling a thing
that need not be told, and in which perhaps your information may have been inaccurate?"'
(*Corr. 2*, p. 330). JB's informant was Bennet Langton (*Boswelliana*, p. 274); *thyrasis* is the
same as *phthiriasis* ('a morbid condition of the body in which lice multiply excessively,
causing extreme irritation', *OED*). Marshall Waingrow suggests that the sentence in

It must not however be omitted that when the storm of his violence subsides, he [pays a grateful compliment⟩] takes a fair opportunity to pay a grateful compliment to the King who had [liberally *del*] rewarded his merit 'these low born railers have endeavoured, surely without effect [MS 355] to alienate the affections of the people from the only King who for almost a century has much appeared to desire, or much endeavoured to deserve them.' And 'every honest man must lament that the faction has been regarded with frigid neutrality by the Tories who being long accustomed to signalise their principles by opposition to the Court do not yet consider that they have at last a King who knows not the name of party and who wishes to be the common father of all his people.'

To this Pamphlet which was at once discovered to be Johnson's several Answers came out, in which care was taken to remind the Publick of his former attacks upon government and of his now being a Pensioner, without [considering or *del*] allowing for the honourable terms [of⟩] upon which Johnson's pension ⋏was granted and accepted⋏ or the change of system which the British Court had undergone upon the accession of his present Majesty. He was however soothed in the highest strain of panegyrick in a Poem called [*The Remonstrance*⟩] 'The Remonstrance' by the Reverend Mr. Stockdale to whom he was upon many occasions a kind Protector.

⋏The following admirable minute made by him describes so well his own state and that of numbers to whom self=examination is habitual that I cannot omit it.⋏ [6]

. . . .

Of this year I have obtained the following Letters
To the Rev. Dr. Farmer Cambridge[7]

[Paper Apart] [8] Sir,

As no man ought to keep wholly to himself any possession that may be useful to the publick I hope you will not think me unreasonably intrusive if I have recourse to you for such information as you are more able to give me than any other man.

In support of an opinion which you have already placed above the need of any more support Mr. Steevens a very ingenious Gentleman lately of King's College has collected an account of all the translations which Shakespeare might have seen and used. He wishes his catalogue to be perfect, and therefore intreats that you will favour him by the insertion of such additions as the accuracy of your inquiries has enabled you to make. To this request I take the liberty of adding my own solicitation.

We have no immediate use for this catalogue, and therefore do not desire that it should interrupt or hinder your more important employments. But it will be kind to let us know that you receive it. I am / Sir, etc. [Your most obedient and most humble servant *del*] Sam. Johnson.

5

10

15

20

25

30

35

---

question originally appeared in the sixth paragraph from the end of *The False Alarm* (*Corr. 2*, p. 330 n. 10; *Political Writings*, Yale ed., 1977, p. 343).

[6] Direction to the compositor, '(Take in from Prayers and Meditations p. 101 all that is under the black line and proceed to p. 102 to the word rules, upon which put a mark for a Note Prayers and Medit. p. 101)'. This Paper Apart no longer forms part of the *Life* MS.

[7] Direction to the compositor, '(Take it in)'.

[8] The copy is entirely in the hand of JB.

Johnson's Court Fleet=street
March 21 1770

[MS 356]   To The Reverend Mr. Thomas Warton[9]

[Paper Apart TW][1] Dear Sir,

5   The readiness with which you were pleased to promise me some notes on Shakespeare, was a new instance of your friendship. I shall not hurry you; but am desired by Mr. Steevens, who helps me in this edition,[a] to let you know, that we shall print the tragedies first, and shall therefore want first the notes which belong to them. We think not to incommode the readers with a supplement; and therefore,
10 what we cannot put into its proper place, will do us no good. We shall not begin to print before the end of six weeks, perhaps not so soon. I am, etc., Sam. Johnson. London, June 23, 1770.

       To The Rev. Dr. Joseph Warton[2]

 ·

       To Mr. Francis Barber[3]

 ·

15   To the Same[4]

 ·

[MS 356 resumed][5] During this year there was a total cessation of all correspondence between Dr. Johnson and me, without any coldness on either side, but

  [a] This edition appeared in [1778 *del*] 1773. It has been followed by two more editions.[a1]

---

  [9] Direction to the compositor, '(Take it in from the Parcel p 21)'.

  [1] See *Life* MS i. 195 n. 6.

  [2] Direction to the compositor, '(Take it in)'. This Paper Apart no longer forms part of the *Life* MS.

  [3] Direction to the compositor, '(Take it in)'. This Paper Apart no longer forms part of the *Life* MS.

  [4] Direction to the compositor, '(Take it in)'. This Paper Apart no longer forms part of the *Life* MS.

  [5] JB created two versions of MS page 356. Both begin with the directions to the compositor to take in letters to Thomas Warton, Joseph Warton, and Francis Barber. And both contain the sentence beginning 'During this year ...'. The two versions diverge, however, in the substance of their prefatory remarks. The original MS page 356 introduces Langton's Johnsoniana, the second version the Maxwell 'Collectanea'. JB's marginal comment on the original 356, 'Reserve this for another year when not in London', marks his decision to reposition the Langton material; eventually these Johnsoniana were incorporated into the early part of the year 1780 (see Hill-Powell iv. 1). What is transcribed here is the second version of MS 356; the first version will appear in volume 4 of this edition. All changes that JB made while writing the second version are duly noted. Discrepancies between the first and the second versions are noted only if they constitute significant alterations of tone or meaning.

  [a1] This footnote was omitted from the revises and the printed editions.

merely from procrastination continued from day to day, and as I was not in London [and so *del*] I had no opportunity of enjoying his company and recording his conversation. To supply this blank I shall present my readers with some *Collectanea* obligingly furnished to me by the Reverend Dr. Maxwell of Falkland in Ireland some time assistant preacher at the Temple, and for many years the social friend of Johnson who spoke of him with a very kind regard.[6/7]

. . . .

[MS 357] In 1771 he published another political Pamphlet entitled '*Thoughts on the late Transactions respecting Falkland's Islands*' in which upon [a detail of materials/facts evidently furnished to him by Ministry>] [materials furnished to him by Ministry, but compressed in his own words>] materials furnished to him by Ministry, and upon general topics expanded in his richest style he successfully [endeavoured/laboured>] endeavoured to persuade the nation that it was wise and laudable to [accept of certain limited concessions from the Court of Spain for the violence with which our possession of those Islands had been interrupted/disturbed, but/yet suffering the *del*] suffer the question of right to remain undecided, rather than involve [our/the>] our country in [another/a>] another war. [That he perhaps rated the consequence of/was insensibly led to give a fallacious state of those islands to Great Britain too low/as very inconsiderable I shall not absolutely contradict. But surely every>] It has been suggested by some, with what truth I shall not take upon me to decide, that he rated the consequence of those islands to Great Britain too low. But however this may be every humane mind must ⟨surely⟩ applaud the earnestness with which he averted the Calamity of war a calamity so dreadful that it is astonishing how civilised nay christian [MS 358] nations can still deliberately continue to renew it. His description in this Pamphlet of [the miseries of war>] its miseries is one of the [finest/noblest>] finest pieces of eloquence in the english language[, and I have heard it repeated more than once with warm admiration by Mr. Erskine, whose own powers of Oratory qualify him for judging and relishing that of others. *del*].[8] Upon this occasion [too/also>] too we find Johnson lashing the party in opposition with [unbounded/excessive>] unbounded severity and making the fullest use of [what/contempt which>] what he ever reckoned a most effectual [weapon contempt>] argumentative instrument contempt. His character of their very able mysterious champion JUNIUS is executed with all the force of his genius and

---

[6] Direction to the compositor, '(Take them in) and mark the beginning and end of each paragraph with inverted commas and do not print Italicks'. The Maxwell 'Collectanea' no longer form part of the *Life* MS.

[7] In June 1787 William Maxwell (1732–1818), D.D., supplied JB with several packets of 'genuine highflavored *Johnsoniana*' and granted him permission to use the material as he saw fit (*Corr. 2*, pp. 215–16). Although the MS has not been recovered, we can deduce that JB freely edited Maxwell's anecdotes.

[8] The Hon. Thomas Erskine (1750–1823), later (1806) first Baron Erskine, had given up his military career in 1775 in order to read for the bar. He rose to the position of Attorney General to the Prince of Wales (1783–92) and ultimately Lord Chancellor (1806–07). Famous as a rhetorician, Erskine specialized in cases involving libel and treason; his clients included Thomas Paine (Namier and Brooke ii. 406).

finished with the highest [care/art>] care. He seems to have exulted in sallying forth to single combat against the boasted [/and formidable/>] and formidable hero who bid[9] defiance to 'principalities and powers and the rulers of this world.'

This Pamphlet [we all know>] it is observable was softened in one particular after the first edition for the conclusion of Mr George Grenville's character [stood/ran>] stood thus ‸Let him not however be depreciated in his grave‸ he had powers not universally possessed; could he have enforced payment of the Manilla ransom *he could have counted it* [which was instead] [MS 359] which instead of retaining its sly sharp point was [a flat unmeaning addition/explanation>] reduced to a [mere flat unmeaning/mere unmeaning>] mere flat unmeaning expression or if I may use the word — *truism* 'he had powers not universally possessed, and if he sometimes erred he was likewise sometimes right.'[1/2]

[MS 364][3] [Mr. Strahan the Printer who had been long in intimacy with him in the course of his literary labours who was ‸at once‸ his friendly agent in receiving his pension for him and his banker in supplying him with money when he wanted it, who was himself now a member of Parliament and who loved much to be employed in political negociation, thought he should ‸now‸ do eminent service both to Government and Johnson, if he could be the means of his getting a seat in the House of Commons. With this view>][4]

[Paper Apart] Mr. Strahan the Printer who had been long in intimacy with Johnson in the course of his literary labours, who was at once his friendly agent in receiving his pension for him, and his banker in supplying him with money when he wanted it, who was himself now a member of Parliament and who loved much to be employed in political negociation, thought he should do eminent service both to Government and Johnson, if he could be the means of his getting a seat in the House of Commons. With this[5] [MS 365] view he wrote a letter to one of the Secretaries of the treasury [(he forgot which)>] I believe Sir Grey Cooper[6] of

---

[9] By the stage of the revises 'bid' had been replaced with 'bade', a grammatical change of which SJ would have approved: in his *Dictionary*, he lists 'bid' as the present tense and 'bade' as the preterite.

[1] Direction (a later addition) to the compositor, 'Here take in a parcel dated by mistake in 1772 beginning [about the middle of the p. 364 *del*] "Mr. Strahan the Printer etc.".' The next several paragraphs are taken from this passage, as well as from accompanying Papers Apart.

[2] SJ to Bennet Langton, 20 March 1771, belongs to that group of letters first inserted at the end of the second volume of the second edition, and then moved to their chronologically appropriate places for the third edition. See *ante* p. 10 n. 1.

[3] This passage from MS 364 is accompanied by a marginal note, 'This about March 1771'.

[4] There is nothing in the MS directing the compositor to replace this passage with the revised version found in the Paper Apart. However, JB does note on the Paper Apart itself, 'To be taken in on the back of p. 358'.

[5] The Paper Apart ends abruptly after 'this'. Although there is nothing in the Paper Apart or the MS itself to indicate that the compositor was to complete this paragraph with the original version of it contained on MS 365, such was clearly JB's intention. He may have decided that, because the last sentence on MS 365 can be read without difficulty, it did not need to be copied over.

[6] Compare this deletion of Cooper's name with one that occurred on MS 437, also in first proof. See *post* p. 132 and n. 3.

which he gave me [a copy/the original draught>] a copy in his own hand=writing which is as follows.[7]

[Paper Apart] [8] Sir

You will easily recollect, when I had the Honour of waiting upon you some time ago, I took the Liberty to observe to you, that Dr. Johnson would make an excellent Figure in the House of Commons, and heartily wished he had a Seat there. My reasons are briefly these.

I know his perfect good Affection to his Majesty and his Government, which I am certain he wishes to support by every Means in his Power.

He possesses a great Share of manly, nervous, and ready Eloquence; is quick in discerning the Strength or weakness of an Argument; can express himself with Clearness and Precision, and fears the Face of no Man alive.

His known Character as a Man of extraordinary Sense and unimpeached Virtue, would secure him the Attention of the House, and could not fail to give him a proper Weight there.

He is capable of the greatest Application, and can undergo any Degree of Labour, where he sees it necessary, and where his Heart and Affections are strongly engaged. His Majesty's Ministers might therefore securely depend on his doing, upon every proper Occasion, the utmost that could be expected from him. They would find him ready to vindicate such Measures as tended to promote the Stability of Government, and resolute and steady in carrying them into Execution. Nor is any thing to be apprehended from the supposed Impetuosity of his Temper. To the Friends of the King you will find him a Lamb, to his Enemies a Lion.

For these Reasons I humbly apprehend that he would be a very able and useful Member. And I will venture to say the Employment would not be disagreeable to him; and knowing as I do, his strong Affection to the King, his Ability to serve him in that Capacity, and the extreme Ardor with which I am convinced he would engage in that Service, I must repeat, that I wish most heartily to see him in the House.

If you think this worthy of Attention, you will be pleased to take a convenient Opportunity of mentioning it to Lord North. If his Lordship should happily approve of it, I shall have the Satisfaction of having been, in some Degree, the humble Instrument of doing my Country in my Opinion a very essential Service. I know your Good nature, and your Zeal for the public Welfare will plead my Excuse for giving you this trouble.

I am, with the greatest Respect / Sir / Your most obedient and humble Sevt /
William Strahan
New=Street
March 30, 1771.

[MS 365 resumed] This recommendation we know was not effectual; but how or for what reason can only be conjectured. It is not to be believed that Mr. Strahan would have applied unless Johnson had approved of it. I never heard him mention the subject. But at a later period of his life, when Sir Joshua Reynolds told him that

---

[7] Direction to the compositor, '(Take it in)'.

[8] The following note, in JB's hand, appears at the top of this Paper Apart: 'This Letter in the handwriting of William Strahan Esq. was written out fair and sent by him to one of the Secretaries of the Treasury at the time. He told me he did not recollect which. It produced no effect'.

Mr. Edmund Burke [had said that if he had gone early into parliament he would have made the greatest figure there / enlarged on the great figure he would have made if he had gone early into parliament/ had said that if he had gone early into parliament he would have made a very great figure there, he said 'I should like to try

5   my hand yet'.〉] had said that if he had gone early into parliament he certainly would have been the greatest speaker that ever was there [Johnson cried out/ Johnson['s] words were〉] Johnson exclaimed 'I should like to try my hand now'.

It has been much agitated among his friends and others whether [there was good reason to expect that *del*] he would have been a powerful speaker in Parliament had

10   he been brought in when advanced in life. [I should have supposed that his ready force of mind his strength and richness of expression his wit and humour and above all his sarcastical keeness [MS 366] might have had great effect in a popular assembly; and that the bulkiness of his figure and striking peculiarity of his manner would have aided the effect/ impression〉] I am inclined to think that his 〈extensive

15   knowledge, his〉 quickness and force of mind his vivacity and richness of expression his wit and humour and above all his poignancy of sarcasm [MS 366] would have had great effect in a popular assembly; and that the magnitude of his figure and striking peculiarity of his manner would have aided the effect. But I remember it was observed by Mr. Flood that Johnson having been long used to sententious

20   [brevity/ conciseness/ compression〉] brevity and the short flights of conversation might have failed in that continued and expanded kind of argument which is requisite in stating complicated matters in publick speaking, and as a proof of this he mentioned the supposed speeches in Parliament written by him for the Magazine none of which in his opinion [had much matter in them or *del*] were [〈not〉 *del*] at

25   all like real debates. 〈The opinion of one who is himself so eminent an orator must be allowed to have great weight.〉 [This〉] It was confirmed by Sir William Scott, who mentioned that Johnson had told him that he had several times tried to speak in the Society of arts and sciences, but 'had found he could not get on.' From Mr. William Gerrard Hamilton I have heard that Johnson when [talking how prudent it

30   was〉] observing to him that it was prudent for a man who had not been accustomed to speak in publick to begin [as plainly as possible〉] his speech in as simple a manner as possible, acknowledged that he rose in that Society to deliver a speech which he had prepared 'but' said he 'all my flowers of Oratory forsook me.' [After all [MS 367] I however cannot help wishing that he *had* 'tried his hand'; and I wonder that

35   Ministry did not make the experiment.〉] I however cannot help wishing that he *had* 'tried his hand' and I wonder that Ministry did not make the experiment.[9]

[MS 359 resumed] 〈I at length renewed a correspondence which had been too long discontinued.〉

To Dr. Johnson

40   My Dear Sir   Edinburgh / 18 April 1771
I can now fully understand those intervals of silence in your correspondence with me which have often given me anxiety and uneasiness; for although I am conscious that my veneration and love for Mr. Johnson have never in the least abated, yet I have deferred for almost a year and a half to write to him.

---

[9] Direction to the compositor, 'Pages 365 and 366 have been taken in, as they in fact belonged to 1771'.

I gave him an account of my comfortable life as a married man and a lawyer in practice at the scotch bar — invited him to Scotland and promised to attend him to the highlands and Hebrides.

To JAMES BOSWELL Esq.[1]

· · · · · · · · · · ·

To SIR JOSHUA REYNOLDS, *in Leicester-fields*[2]   5

· · · · · · · · · · ·

To DR. JOHNSON[3]

· · · · · · · · · · ·

[MS 360]   [TO DR. JOHNSON[4]

[My Dear Sir   Auchinleck / 17 October 1771⟩]

Thanking him for his last letter and his obliging reception of Mr. Beattie — that I had been at Alnwick lately and had good accounts of him from Dr. Percy⟩]   10

In October I again wrote to him thanking him for his last letter and his obliging reception of Mr. Beattie — informing him that I had been at Alnwick lately and had good accounts of him from Dr. Percy.

In his religious record of this year we observe that he was better than usual both in body and mind, and better satisfied with the regularity of his conduct. But he   15 is still 'trying [his ways/himself⟩] his ways'[5] too rigorously. He [accuses himself of/charges himself with⟩] charges himself with not rising early [/enough/⟩] enough yet he mentions what was surely a sufficient excuse for this supposing it to be a duty as seriously required as he all his life [long *del*] appears to have thought it. 'One great hindrance is want of rest; my nocturnal complaints grow less troublesome   20 towards morning and I am tempted to repair the deficiencies of the night.'[a] Alas, how hard would it be if this [were not to be permitted/were to be imputed to a sick man as a crime⟩] indulgence were to be imputed to a sick man as a crime. In his retrospect on the following Easter Eve he says, 'When I review the last year I am able to recollect so little done, that shame and sorrow [*though perhaps too weakly*⟩]   25 though perhaps too weakly come upon me'. Had he been judging of any one else

---

[a] Prayers and Medit., p. 105.

---

[1] Direction to the compositor, 'Dear Sir / If you are now able (take it in)'. This Paper Apart no longer forms part of the *Life* MS.

[2] Direction to the compositor, possibly in the hand of EM, 'Take in letter to Sir Joshua Reynolds'. It is clear that the decision to include this letter was taken at a later stage. This Paper Apart no longer forms part of the *Life* MS.

[3] Direction to the compositor, 'My Dear Sir / The Bearer (take it in) / Edinburgh / 27 July 1771'. This Paper Apart no longer forms part of the *Life* MS. In the third edition, SJ to Bennet Langton, 29 August 1771, is inserted immediately following JB to SJ, 27 July 1771. The letter to Langton belongs to that group first inserted at the end of the second volume of the second edition, and then moved to their chronologically appropriate places for the third edition. See *ante* p. 10 n. 1.

[4] JB originally intended to include an edited version of this letter, as his directions to the compositor ('Take in letter with ***') make clear. He changed his mind, however, and instead supplied a brief summary, which was then revised by EM. The next paragraph was marked for deletion, but finally preserved through a series of marginal 'stet' markings.

[5] JB decides to keep his text as close as possible to the biblical passage he has in mind ('Let us search and try our ways', Lamentations 3: 40).

in the same circumstances, how clear would he have been on the favourable side. ₍How very difficult and in my opinion almost constitutionally impossible it was for him to be raised early even by the strongest resolutions appears from a note in one of his little paperbooks (containing words arranged for his Dictionary) written I suppose about 1753. 'I do not remember that since I left Oxford I ever rose early by mere choice, but once or twice at Edial and two or three times for Rambler.' I think he had fair ground enough to have quieted his mind as to this by concluding that he was physically incapable of what is at best but a commodious regulation.₎

₍In 1772 he was altogether quiescent as an Authour; but it will be found from the various evidences which I shall bring together, that his mind was acute lively and vigorous.

> To Sir JOSHUA REYNOLDS
>
> Dear Sir.
> Be pleased to send to Mr. Banks whose place of residence I do not know, this note which I have sent open that if you please you may read it.
> When you send it do not use your own seal.
> Feb. 27. 1772. I am etc. / Sir / Your most humble servant
>
> SAM: JOHNSON

> To JOSEPH BANKS Esq:
> Perpetua ambita bis terra præmia lactis
> Hæc habet altrici Capra secunda Jovis.[a]
> Sir.
> I return thanks to you and to Dr. Solander for the pleasure which I received in yesterday's conversation. I could not recollect a Motto for your Goat, but have given her one. You Sir may perhaps have an epick poem from some happier pen than that of Sir / your most humble servant / Sam: Johnson
> Johnson's Court Fleetstreet
> Feb. 27 1772.₎

> To DR. JOHNSON[6]

. . . .

[MS 361]   To JAMES BOSWELL Esq:[7]

. . . .

> To BENNET LANGTON Esq[8]

. . . .

[a] Thus translated by a friend.
> In fame scarce second to the nurse of Jove,
> This goat who twice the world had travers'd round
> Deserving both her Master's care and love
> Ease and perpetual pasture now has found.[al]

---

[6] Direction to the compositor, 'Take it in'. This Paper Apart no longer forms part of the *Life* MS.

[7] Direction to the compositor, '₍Dear Sir₎ / That you are coming / (Take it in)'. This Paper Apart no longer forms part of the *Life* MS.

[8] Direction to the compositor, 'I congratulate etc. / (Take it in)'. JB's original intent was to insert this letter after SJ's letter to Joseph Banks. He later changed his mind, however. This Paper Apart no longer forms part of the *Life* MS.

[al] Direction to the compositor, 'Take in Paper S'. Paper 'S' itself bears the following marking, 'opposite to p. 360'.

On the 21 March [in the forenoon *del*] I was happy to be again in [his›] Dr. Johnson's study and was glad to see my old acquaintance Mr. Francis Barber who was now returned home to him. [After waiting a short time the sound of his feet upon the timber steps was weighty and well announced his approach. *del*] He received me with a hearty welcome ₍saying₎ 'I am glad you are come, and glad you 5 are come upon such an errand' (meaning to support the Schoolmaster). ₍*Boswell.*₎ 'I hope Sir he will be in no danger. It is a very delicate [matter/thing›] matter to interfere between a Master and his scholars. Nor do I see how you can fix the degree of severity that a master may [use/exercise›] use.' ₍*Johnson.*₎ 'Why Sir till you fix the degree of obstinacy and negligence of the scholars, you cannot 10 fix the degree of severity of the master. Severity must be continued until obstinacy be subdued and negligence be cured.' — He mentioned the severity of Hunter his own Master. 'Sir' said I 'Hunter is a scotch name. So ₍it should seem₎ this schoolmaster who beat you so severely was a scotchman. I can now account for your prejudice against the scotch.' ₍*Johnson.*₎ 'No Sir he was not scotch, and 15 [except for›] abating his brutality he was a very good Master.'[9]

[Journal 32] [We had before this, when by ourselves talked of [J33/RJ 1] his two political Pamphlets›][1] We talked of his two political Pamphlets *The False Alarm*, and [*Thoughts respecting the Transactions concerning Falklands Islands.*›] *Thoughts on Falklands Islands*. Johnson. 'Well Sir which of [em›] them did you think the best?' 20 *Bos*₍*well.*₎ 'I liked the second best.' *Johns*₍*on.*₎ 'Why Sir I liked the first best; and Beattie liked the first best. Sir there is a subtelty of disquisition in the first that is worth all the fire of the second.' *Bos*₍*well.*₎ 'Pray Sir is it true that Lord North paid you a visit, and that you got £200 a year of addition to your pension?' *Johns*₍*on.*₎ 'No Sir. Except what I had from the Bookseller, I did not get a farthing by them. 25 And between you and me, I believe Lord North is no friend to me.' *Bos*₍*well.*₎ 'How so Sir.' *Johns*. 'Why Sir you cannot account for the fancies of men. [*Bos*₍*well.*₎ But Sir [Journal 34/RJ 2] don't you think him an able minister? *Johns*. Yes indeed Sir. *del*] Well how does Lord Elibank? and how does Lord Monboddo?' *Bos*₍*well.*₎ 'Very well Sir. Lord Monboddo still maintains the superiority of the 30 savage life.' *Johns*₍*on.*₎ 'What strange narrowness of mind now is that to think the things we have not [known/seen›] known are better than the things which we

---

[9] Direction to the compositor, '(Go to leaves of a smaller quarto ₍marked RJ₎)'. Paper Apart RJ is made up primarily of leaves removed from JB's London Journal for 1772 (J 24). Most of these have since been returned to their proper places in the Journal. What is transcribed here is a collection of loose leaves — in essence, sub-Papers Apart to the Journal entries — that contain additions to or revisions of the original journal account: only this material was designed specifically for the *Life*. For the convenience of the reader, who may wish to compare JB's various adaptations with the original passages, two aids are provided: cues (in the form of bracketed textual snippets) that guide the reader to the appropriate journal sections whenever the narrative breaks off in the sub-Papers Apart; and JB's pagination, which was originally designed to assist the printer in compiling these materials in the proper order. It should be noted that JB numbered all leaves — both those containing the journal entries and those that adapt them to the *Life* — consecutively from 1 to 79, inadvertently omitting the number 10. The pages numbered 45–63 have not been located. The complete original narrative can be consulted in *Boswell for the Defence*, pp. 41–133.

[1] JB renumbered these journal leaves when he decided to include them in the Papers Apart for the *Life*. This repagination seems to have occurred at the same time that JB made changes to the text itself.

have [known/seen>] known.' *Bos*ʌ*well.*ʌ 'Why Sir that is a common prejudice.' *Johns*ʌ*on.*ʌ 'Yes Sir. But a common prejudice should not be found [in one whose trade it is to rectify errour/in a Judge>] in one whose trade it is to rectify errour.'

5   [Then came in a Mr. _____ who was to go out Mate>] A Gentleman having come in who was to go as a Mate in the ship along with Mr. Banks and Dr. Solander Dr. Johnson asked what were the names of the ships [which were to go upon>] destined for the expedition. [Mr. _____ said>] The Gentleman answered They were once to be called the *Drake* and the *Rawleigh*, but now they were to be called the *Resolution* and the *Adventure*. [Journal 35/RJ 3] *Johns.* 'Much better; for had the *Rawleigh* returned

10   without going round the world it would have been ridiculous. To give them the names of the *Drake* and the *Rawleigh* was laying a trap for satire.' *Bos*ʌ*well.*ʌ 'Had not you some desire to go upon this expedition Sir?' *Johns*ʌ*on.*ʌ 'Why yes; but I soon laid it aside. Sir there is very little ʌofʌ intellectual in the course. Besides, I see but at a [little>] small distance. So it was not worth my while to go to see birds fly which I

15   should not have seen fly; and fishes swim which I should not have seen swim.'

     [Supplemental Paper Apart RJ][2] The Gentleman being gone and Dr. Johnson having left the room for some time a debate arrose between the Reverend Mr. ·Stockdale and Mrs. Desmoulins whether Mr. Banks and Dr. Solander were entitled to any share of glory from their expedition. When Dr. Johnson returned

20   to us I told him the subject of their dispute. [*Johnson.* Why Sir ...]

     [I thanked him ...]

     [He then spoke ...]

     [I gave him an account ...]

     [RJ 9] engaged to dine abroad and asked me to return to him in the evening at nine

25   ʌwhich I accordingly didʌ.

     We drank tea with Mrs. Williams who told us a story of second sight which happened in Wales where she was born. He listened to it very attentively, and said he should be glad to have some instances of that faculty well authenticated. His elevated wish for more and more evidence for spirit in opposition to the grovelling belief of

30   materialism led him to a love of such mysterious disquisitions. He again justly observed that we could have no certainty of the truth of supernatural appearances unless something was told us which we could not know by ordinary means or something done which could not be done but by supernatural power. That Pharaoh in reason and justice required such evidence from Moses nay that [our Saviour said ...]

35   [We talked of the Roman ...]

     [I mentioned the petition ...]

     [I mentioned the motion ...]

     [He disapproved of ...]

     [In the morning we ...]

40   [I gave him an account ...]

     [RJ 18] friend seems to possess. Foote is however very entertaining with a kind of conversation between wit and buffoonery.'

     He [recommended/advised>] recommended to me to go and see Cox's Museum 'which said he for power of mechanism and splendour of shew is a very fine exhibition.'

45   On Monday March 23 I found him busy [with *del*] preparing a fourth edition of his

---

[2] Unlike the other leaves of Paper Apart RJ, this one is unnumbered.

Folio Dictionary. Mr. Peyton one of his [original/ancient>] original Amanuenses was writing for him. I put him in mind of a meaning of the word *side* which he had omitted viz. Relationship as Fathers side Mothers side. He put it in. I asked him if *humiliating* was a good word? he said he had seen it frequently used, but he did not know if it could be allowed to be legitimate english. He would not admit *Civilization*, but only *Civility*. With great deference to him I thought *Civilization* from to *civilize* better in that sense than *civility* as it is better to have a distinct word for each sense [than one word ...]³

[He seemed busy ...]
[I then reminded ...]
[After he had read ...]
[We talked of languages ...]
[He said, he never ...]
[We went to the Mitre ...]

[RJ 22] all left with the full exercise of their corporeal faculties. In our schools in England many boys have been maimed; yet I never heard of an action against a schoolmaster on that account. Puffendorf I think maintains the right of a Schoolmaster to beat his scholars.

On Saturday March 27 I introduced to him Sir Alexander Macdonald with whom he had expressed a wish to be acquainted. He received him very courteously.

Sir [Alexander observed ...]

[Satellite Paper Apart P] ⁴ Upon another occasion I talked to him upon this subject as I had taken a good deal of pains to improve my pronunciation, by the aid of the late Mr. Love of Drury=lane Theatre when he was a Player at Edinburgh, and also of old Mr. Sheridan. Johnson said to me 'Sir, your pronunciation is not offensive.' With this concession I was pretty well satisfied; and let me give my countrymen of North Britain an advice not to aim at absolute perfection in this respect, not to speak high english as we are apt to call what is far removed from Scotch, but which is by no means good english, and makes 'the fools who use it' truly ridiculous. Good english is plain easy and smooth in the mouth of an unaffected english gentleman. The prim prating of a studied and factitious pronunciation for which a man is allways on the watch allways under constraint, and seems not to speak with his natural organs but through some pipe of brass or other metal is exceedingly disgusting. I really think it is agreable to hear a small degree of the provincial varieties as the notes of different birds concur in the harmony of the grove and please more than if they were all exactly alike. I could name some gentlemen of ireland to whom a slight proportion of the accent and recitative of that country is an advantage. The same observation will apply to the gentlemen of Scotland. I do not mean that we should speak as broad as a certain prosperous member of parliament from that country, though Lord Graham once observed to me⁵ that 'it was of no small use to

5

10

15

20

25

30

35

---

³ In correcting the revises, JB changed 'that sense' to 'the sense opposed' and then altered it again for the second edition to 'in the sense opposed to *barbarity*'. The final change may reflect the influence of SJ's *Dictionary*, whose primary definition of 'civility' is 'Freedom from barbarity'.

⁴ Satellite Paper Apart 'P' is an unnumbered, later addition to the numbered packet RJ. It bears the following direction to the compositor, 'For p. 94 of Leaves R.J to be taken in on page 361'.

⁵ This section contains an ambiguity that is resolved by the time of the revises, which substitute 'it has been well observed' for 'Lord Graham once observed to me'. It is just possible that JB originally had in mind two Scottish M.P.'s: the unnamed 'prosperous member' (plausibly

him; it roused the attention of the house by its uncommoness; it was equal to tropes and figures in a good english speaker.' I would give as an instance of what I mean to recommend to my countrymen the pronunciation of the late Sir Gilbert Elliot and may I presume to add that of the present Earl of Marchmont who told me with great good humour that one day the master of a shop in London where he was not known said to him 'I suppose Sir, you are an American.' 'Why so' said his Lordship? 'Because Sir' (replied the shopkeeper) 'you speak neither english nor scotch, but something different from both which I conclude is the language of America.'

[Boswell. 'It may ...]
[I again visited ...]
[Boswell. 'I do not ...]
[We went down ...]
[I mentioned Elwal ...]

[RJ 31] Elwal failed in his scheme of making himself a man of great consequence.

On tuesday March 31 He and I dined at General Paoli's[; nobody else there but Count Gentili del].[6] A question was started whether the state of marriage was natural to man. *Johnson.* Sir It is so far [from being natural ...]

[We then fell ...]
[We talked of ...]
[Dr. Johnson went ...]
[He said, 'Goldsmith's ...]
[I said, that ...]
[He censured ...]
[We talked of ...]
[I asked him how ...]

[RJ 35] before others; you must ask some people how they like their wine, oftener than others. You therefore offend [as many as⟩] more people than you please. You are like the French statesman who said when he granted a favour '*J'ai fait dix mecontens et un ingrat*'. Besides Sir being entertained ever so well at a man's table impresses no lasting regard or esteem. No Sir [(speaking with/in a low and earnest voice/tone) del] [You will make sure of power and influence by lending privately sums of money to your neighbours at a small interest or perhaps at no interest at all⟩] the way to make sure of power and influence is by lending money confidentially to your neighbours at a [small/low⟩] small interest or perhaps at no interest at all and having their bonds in your possession. ⟨Boswell.⟩ 'May not a man ⟨Sir⟩ employ his riches to advantage in educating young men of merit?' — ⟨Johnson.⟩ 'Yes Sir, [if/provided⟩] if they fall in your way; but if [you once have it⟩] it is understood that [you patronise young men ...]

---

identified in Hill-Powell as Henry Dundas) and James Graham (1755–1836), Marquis of Graham, M.P. for Richmond (1780–84) and Great Bedwyn (1784–90), later (1790) third Duke of Montrose (Namier and Brooke ii. 526). The interpretation of the sentence turns on the antecedent of 'him': is Graham referring to himself or to Dundas? There are no memoranda or journal entries to clarify this question.

[6] JB describes Count Gentili, whom he had met through Pasquale Paoli, as 'a Corsican count long in the Austrian service, and who gave up his commission to go home and fight along with his countrymen, and then accompanied the General to England' (Journ. 19 March 1772). Gentili had been awarded a British pension of £200 p.a.; he lived in London until 1776, when he left on a voyage that led to his mysterious disappearance in Surinam (Joseph Foladare, *Boswell's Paoli*, 1979, p. 102).

['Were I a ...]
[The conversation now ...]
[We then walked ...]
[I said there ...]
[Happening to meet ...]   5
[Sir Adam suggested ...]
[Sir Adam was ...]

[RJ 41] On Sunday April 5 after attending divine service at St. Paul's Church I
found him alone. Of a Schoolmaster of his acquaintance a native of Scotland he said,
'He has a great deal of good about him; but he is also very defective in some respects.   10
His inner part is good but his outer part is mighty awkward. You in Scotland do not
[arrive at/reach/acquire>] attain to that nice critical skill in languages which we get
in our schools in England. I would not put a boy to him whom I intended [for a
man/[undeciphered word]>] for a man of learning. But for the sons of citizens who are
to learn a little, get good morals, and then go to trade, he may do very well.'   15
I mentioned a cause in which I had [RJ 42] appeared as counsel at the bar of The
General Assembly of the Church of Scotland, where a *Probationer* as one licensed to
preach but not yet ordained is called was [opposed from/hindered in being
induced/refused induction>] opposed in his application to be inducted because it
was alledged that he had been guilty of fornication five years before. ⟨Johnson.⟩   20
'Why Sir, [if he has repented of it it should not be an insurmountable/sufficient
objection.>] if he has repented it is not a sufficient objection. A man who is good
enough to go to heaven is good enough to be a Clergyman.' — This was a humane
and liberal sentiment. But the character of a Clergyman is more sacred than that of
an ordinary Christian [man *del*]. As he is to instruct with authority he should be   25
regarded [RJ 43] with reverence, as one upon whom divine truth has had the effect
to set him above such transgressions as men less exalted by spiritual habits, and yet
upon the whole not to be excluded from heaven have been betrayed by the
predominance of passion. That Clergymen may be considered as sinners in general
as all men are cannot be denied; But this reflection will not counteract their good   30
precepts so much, as the absolute knowledge of their having been guilty of certain
specifick immoral acts. I told him that by the rules [of the Church ...]
[I spoke of ...]
[He said, he ...]
[On Monday, April 6, ...]   35
[Fielding being ...]
[A book of travels, ...]
[We talked of gaming ...]
[Mr. Erskine told ...]
[After Mr. Erskine ...]   40
[I talked of ...]
[I argued warmly ...]
[On Thursday, April 9 ...]
[He observed, ...]
[Talking of ghosts, ...]   45
[I mentioned witches, ...]
[On Friday, April 10, ...]

[Armorial bearings ...]
[I started the question ...]
[Let it be remembered, ...]
[The General told us, ...]
5   [Dr. Johnson said, ...]
[A question was started, ...]
[Goldsmith told us, ...]
[The subject of ghosts ...]
[[Here the date]]
10   [On Saturday, April 11, ...]
['The charge is, ...]
['This, Sir, ...]
[Of our friend ...]

[RJ 64] often does to keep you in mind of him lest you should forget that he is in the company.
15   *Boswell.* 'Yes, he stands forward.' *Johnson.* 'True Sir; but if a man is to stand forward, he should
[chuse⟩] wish to do it, not in an awkward posture, not in rags; not so as that he shall only be
exposed to ridicule.' *Boswell.* '⟨For my part⟩ I like very well to hear honest Goldsmith talk
away carelessly.' *Johnson.* 'Why yes Sir; but he should not like to hear himself.'
        On Tuesday April 14 the Decree of the Court of Session in the Schoolmaster's Cause
20   was reversed in the House of Lords, upon a very eloquent speech by Lord [RJ 65] Mansfield
who [shewed himself quite an adept in school discipline,/seemed quite at home when
expatiating upon school discipline,⟩] shewed himself an adept in school discipline, but I
thought was too rigorous towards my Client. On the evening of the next day [I met Dr.
Johnson at the Crown and Anchor tavern in the Strand, with Mr. Langton his brother in
25   law Lord Binning and three/some other gentlemen⟩] I supt with Dr. Johnson at the
Crown and Anchor tavern in the Strand in company with Mr. Langton and his brother
in law Lord Binning. I repeated a sentence of Lord Mansfield's speech of which by the
obliging aid of Mr. Longlands the Solicitor ⟨who compared notes with me⟩ I have a full
copy 'My Lords severity is not the way to govern either boys or men.' 'Nay' said Johnson
30   'it is the way to *govern* them. I know not if it be the way to *mend* them.'
        I talked of the recent expulsion of six students from the University [RJ 66] of Oxford who
were Methodists, and would not desist from publickly praying and exhorting. *Johnson.* 'Sir,
that expulsion was extremely just and proper. What have they to do at an University who
are not willing to be taught but will presume to teach. Where is Religion to be learnt but
35   in/at⁷ an University? Sir they were examined, and found to be mighty ignorant fellows.'
Boswell. 'But was it not hard, Sir to expell them for I am told they were good beings.'
Johnson. 'Sir I believe they might be good beings; but they were not fit to be in the
University of Oxford. A Cow is a very good animal in the/a⁸ field; but we turn her [RJ 67]
out of a garden.' Lord Elibank used to repeat this as an illustration uncommonly happy.
        Desireous of calling Johnson forth to talk and exercise his wit though I should
40   myself be the object of it, I resolutely ventured to undertake the defence of convivial
indulgence in wine, though he was not tonight in the most genial humour. After
urging the common plausible topicks, I at last had recourse to the maxim *in vino veritas*;
a man who is well warmed with wine will speak truth. *Johnson.* 'Why Sir that may be

---

⁷ The alternative is resolved by the printing of 'at' in the revises.
⁸ The alternative is resolved by the printing of 'the' in the revises.

an argument for drinking, if you suppose men ₍in general₎ to be [all *del*] liars. But Sir I would not keep company with a fellow who lyes as long as he is sober, [RJ 68] and whom you must make drunk, before you can get a word of truth out of him.'ᵃ

Mr. Langton [said he was establishing>] [told us he was establishing>] told us he was about to establish a school upon his estate but [he expressed doubts which had>] it had   5 been suggested to him, that it might have a tendency to make the people less industrious. *Johnson.* 'No Sir. While learning to read and write is a distinction, the few who have that distinction may be the less inclined to work. But when every body learns to read and write it is no longer a distinction. A man who has a laced waistcoat is too fine a man to work. But if every body [RJ 69] had laced waistcoats, we should   10 have people work in laced waistcoats. There are no people whatever more industrious none who work more than our manufacturers. Yet they have all learnt to read and write. Sir you must not [omit/neglect/abstain from>] neglect doing a thing immediately good for fear of remote consequential evil — for fear of its being abused. A man who has candles may sit up too late, which he would not do if he had not candles, but   15 nobody will deny that the art of making candles by which light is continued to us beyond the time that the sun gives us light, is a valuable art and ought to be preserved.' *Boswell.* 'But Sir would it not be better to follow nature, and [RJ 70] go to bed and rise just as nature gives us light or withholds it?' *Johnson.* 'No Sir, for then, we should have no kind of equality in the partition of our time between sleeping and waking. It would   20 be very different in different seasons, and in different places. In some of the northern parts of Scotland how little light is there in the depth of winter.'

We talked of Tacitus, and I hazarded an opinion that with all his merit for penetration shrewdness of judgement and terseness of expression he was too compact, too much broken into hints as it were and therefore too difficult to be easily under-   25 stood. — To my great satisfaction Dr. Johnson sanctioned this opinion, [RJ 71] 'Tacitus [rather appears to have put down/rather seems as if he had put down notes for writing a History than to have written a history>], Sir seems to me rather to have made notes for an historical work than to have written a history.'ᵇ [Though we did not part till past twelve I attended him home, and we drank tea with Mrs. Williams. *del*]   30

ᵃ [Mrs. Piozzi in her Anecdotes has given a very erroneous Account of this incident, as if she had been present. She had it from me, but has remembered it indistinctly and brewed it up with her own fancy.>] Mrs. Piozzi in her Anecdotes p. 261 has given [a very erroneous>] an erroneous account of this incident as [she has done as>] [she has done>] of many others. She pretends to relate it from recollection as if she herself had   35 been present; when the fact is that she had it from me. She has represented it as a personality, and the true point has escaped her.ᵃˡ

ᵇ It is remarkable that Lord Monboddo whom on account of his resembling Dr. Johnson in some particulars Foote called an Elzevir edition of him has by coincidence made the very same remark. Origin and Progress of Language Vol 3 Edit 2 p ____.ᵇˡ   40

ᵃˡ JB's original version of this note was placed at the foot of the page. When he deleted it, he wrote his revised version of the note on the verso and cued the compositor with the direction, 'Go to the back'.

ᵇˡ JB left the page number blank, to be filled in later. The number 219 was supplied when the revises were corrected.

At this time it appears from his Prayers and Meditations that he had been more than commonly diligent in religious duties; particularly in reading the Holy Scriptures. It was Passion Week, that solemn season which the Christian World has [appropriated/consecrated>] appropriated to the commemoration of the mysteries of our

5   Redemption, and during which, whatever embers of Religions are in our breasts will be kindled into pious [flame/heat>] warmth. [One [RJ 72] of his papers in the Rambler[9] published in Passion Week is a most valuable religious discourse which may be read with great advantage again and again. *del*] I paid him short visits both on friday and saturday, and seeing his large folio Greek Testament before him, beheld him with a reverential awe

10   and would not intrude upon [his time/him>] his time. While he was thus employed to such good purpose and while his friends in their intercourse with him [could find/perceive no marks/traces but of a vigorous intellect/understanding and a lively imagination, how painful/pathetick is it to read in his private register>] constantly found a vigorous intellect and a lively imagination, it is melancholy to read in his private register 'My mind is

15   unsettled and my memory confused. I have of late turned my thoughts with a very useless earnestness upon past incidents. I have yet got [RJ 73] no command over my thoughts; an unpleasing incident is almost certain to hinder my rest.'[a] [How heroick>] What philosophick heroism was it in him to appear with such manly fortitude to the world, while he was inwardly so distressed. We may surely believe that the mysterious principle of being

20   made perfect through suffering was to be strongly exemplified in him.

On sunday 19 being Easter=day General Paoli and I paid him a visit [in the forenoon/morning>] before dinner. We talked of the notion that blind persons can distinguish colours by the touch. Johnson said that the great Sanderson mentions his having attempted to do it; but that he found he was aiming at an impossibility; that to

25   be sure a difference in the surface makes the difference of colours, but that difference is so fine that it is *[RJ 74]* not sensible to the touch. The General mentioned Juglers and fraudulent gamesters who could know cards by the touch. Dr. Johnson said those cards must not have been so well polished as ours commonly are.

We talked of sounds. The General said no simple sound was pretty but only a harmonious

30   composition of sounds. I presumed to differ from this opinion, and mentioned the soft and sweet sound of a fine woman's voice. *Johnson.* 'No Sir, if a serpent or a toad uttered it you would think it ugly.' *Boswell.* 'So you would [think/presume>] think Sir, were a beautiful tune to be uttered by one of those animals.' *Johnson.* 'No Sir; [they'd say 'twas well>] it would be admired. We have seen fine fidlers whom we liked as ill as toads' (laughing). *[RJ 75]* [He

35   said difference of Taste with respect to its being a good or bad was just>]

Talking on the subject of Taste in the arts, he said that difference of taste was in truth difference of skill. [But said I is>] *Boswell.* 'But Sir, is there not a quality called taste which consists merely in perception or in liking. For instance we find people differ much as to what is the best [style of english composition/english style of

40   composition in writing>] style of english composition. [Some tell you Swift's is the best; others that a fuller and grander way of writing is the best.>] Some think Swift's is the best; others prefer a fuller and grander way of writing.' *Johnson.* 'Sir you must first define what you mean by style before you can judge who has a good taste in style, and

---

[a] Prayers and Medit. p. 111.

[9] It is likely that JB refers to *Rambler* No. 110 (6 Apr. 1751).

who has a bad. Those of the two tastes whom you have mentioned dont differ as to good and bad. They both agree that Swift has a good neat style; but one loves a *[RJ 76]* neat style, another loves a style of more splendour. ‹In like manner,› one loves a plain coat, another loves a laced coat but neither will deny that [each coat is good of its kind/both are good of their kind›] each coat is good of its kind.'   5

While I remained in London this spring I was with him at several other times both by himself and in company [with others *del*]. I dined with him ‹one day at the Crown and Anchor tavern in the Strand with Lord Elibank Mr. Langton and Dr. Vansittart of Oxford.› [It would be too minute to specify what was said each particular day. Upon the whole I have›] Without specifying each particular day, I have preserved the following memorable things.[10]   10

I regretted the reflection in his Preface to Shakespeare against Garrick to whom we cannot but apply the following passage 'I collated such copies as I could procure and wished for more, but have not found the collectors of these rarities very communicative.' *[RJ 77]* I told him that Garrick had complained to me of it, and had vindicated himself by assuring me that Johnson was made welcome to the full use of his collection, and that he   15 left the key of it with a servant with orders to have a fire and every convenience for him. I found Johnson's notion was that Garrick wanted to be courted for them, and that on the contrary Garrick should have courted him, and sent him the Plays of his own accord. [The unhappy jealousy or indignant pique which I have formerly supposed, need not be again mentioned.›] But indeed considering the slovenly and careless manner in which   20 Books were treated by Johnson it could not be expected that scarce and valuable editions should have been lent to him.

A Gentleman having to some of the usual arguments for drinking added this, 'you know Sir drinking drives away *[RJ 78]* care and makes us forget whatever is disagreable. Would not you allow a man to drink for that reason.' *Johnson.* 'Yes Sir, if he sat next *you*.'   25

I expressed a liking for Mr. Francis Osborn's Works and asked him [what he thought/his opinion›] what he thought of that Writer? He answered 'A conceited fellow. Were a man to write so now, the boys would throw stones at him.' He however did not alter my opinion of a favourite Authour to whom I was first directed by his being quoted in the *Spectator* and in whom I have found much shrewd and lively sense   30 expressed indeed in a style somewhat quaint which, however, I do not dislike. His book has an air of originality. We figure to ourselves an ancient *[RJ 79]* gentleman talking to us [; I have figured this in a more lively manner since I have been a visitor of the Representative of that respectable family at his noble/fine seat at/of Chicksand *del*].[1]

When one of his friends endeavoured to maintain that a Country gentleman might   35 contrive to pass his life very agreably [Why Sir said he/*Johnson*. Why Sir›] 'Sir' said he, 'you cannot give me an instance of any man who is permitted to lay out his own time,

---

[10] From this point until he begins his account of the legal case involving 'vitious intromission' (MS 367), JB was dependent on 'rough notes, highly condensed and obscure'. JB seems not to have found them until after he had written the corresponding portion of the *Life*, and then to have used them with unusual carelessness (*Catalogue* i. 13). For the two significant discrepancies between notes and narrative, see below.

[1] JB was much taken with the *Advice to a Son* (1656) of Francis Osborne (1593–1659). He made reading notes on Osborne's work (M244) and quoted it in *The Hypochondriack* (Nos. 1, 22). On 25 September 1785 he visited Chicksands, the Bedfordshire estate of Sir George Osborne (1742–1818), Bt., which he described in his journal as 'a complete fine old abbacy'.

contriving not to have tedious hours.' This observation however is equally applicable to gentlemen who live in cities and are of no profession.

[MS 362] [On the 21 April I dined with him at the Crown and Anchor tavern in the Strand. *del*] He said 'there [was no permanent national character. It
5   varied⟩] is no permanent national character, it varies according to circumstances. Alexander the Great swept India. Now the Turks sweep Greece.'

A [Gentleman who had no more to tell but that⟩] learned Gentleman who in the course of conversation wished to inform us of this simple fact that the Counsel upon the Circuit at Shrewsbury were much bitten by fleas, took I suppose seven or eight
10   minutes in relating it circumstantially.[2] [How large bales of woolen=cloth were lodged in the Town Hall — how Fleas were nestled there in prodigious numbers — how the lodgings of the Counsel were near to the Town hall — And how wonderfully those little animals moved from place to place.⟩] He in a plenitude of phrase told us that large bales of woolen=cloth were lodged in the Town Hall — that by reason of this Fleas
15   nestled there in prodigious numbers — that the lodgings of the Counsel were near to the Town hall — And that those little animals moved from place to place with wonderful agility. Johnson sat in great impatience till the gentleman had [fairly finished and⟩] finished his tedious narrative and then burst out ['I wish Sir, you had seen a Lion;⟩], 'It is a pity Sir, that you have not seen a Lion; for [a flea/you have⟩] a
20   flea has taken you such a time, that a Lion must have served you a twelvemonth.'[a]

[On the 24 April I found him at home. He would not allow Scotland the credit of/to boast of Lord Mansfield because he was educated in England. Much may be made of/done with a Scotchman said he if he be *caught* young.⟩] He would not allow Scotland to derive any credit from Lord Mansfield; for he was educated in
25   England. 'Much' said he 'may be made of a Scotchman if he be *caught* young.'

[He said there is more thought in Beattie than in Robertson.[3] There is but a shallow stream of reflection in History.⟩] [Talking of an Historian and a Moralist he said there is more thought in the Moralist than in the Historian. There is but a shallow stream of thought in History.⟩] Talking of a modern Historian and a modern Moralist he said there
30   is more thought in the Moralist than in the Historian. There is but a shallow stream of thought in History. ₍Boswell.₎ 'But surely Sir, an Historian has reflection?' *Johnson.* 'Why yes Sir, and so has a cat when she [catches/gets⟩] catches a mouse for her kitten; but she cannot write like [Beattie⟩] the moralist. Neither can [Robertson⟩] the Historian.'

He said, 'I am [MS 363] very unwilling to read the Manuscripts of Authours and
35   give them my opinion. If the Authours who apply to me have money I bid them ₍boldly₎ print without a name; if they have written in order to get money I

---

[a] Mrs. Piozzi to whom I told this Anecdote has related it as if the Gentleman had given 'the *natural history* of the Mouse.'[a1]

---

[2] JB's notes for 22 August make it very likely that the 'learned Gentleman' is Robert Vansittart (1728–89), D.C.L., Regius Professor of Civil Law at Oxford.

[3] The original MS readings confirm what Croker and Hill-Powell surmised, on the basis of context and the asterisks (seven for Beattie and nine for Robertson) that were supplied in the second edition.

[a1] By the stage of the revises, the page reference to Mrs. Piozzi's *Anecdotes* had been supplied.

tell them to go to the Booksellers and make the best bargain they can.' ['But if〉] *Boswell*. 'But Sir if a Bookseller should bring you a Manuscript to [look at/consider〉] look at' — ['Why I〉] *Johnson*. 'Why Sir, I would desire the Bookseller to take it away.'

[I mentioned a Gentleman who was unwilling to leave Spain and return home to Britain.〉] I mentioned a friend of mine who had resided long in Spain and was unwilling to return home to Britain.[4] [Sir he〉] *Johnson*. 'Sir, he [has got/is in love with〉] is attached to some woman.' 〈*Boswell*.〉 'I rather believe Sir it is the fine climate which keeps him there.' 〈*Johnson*.〉 'Nay Sir how can you talk so [/foolishly/ *del*]? What is *climate* to happiness? [Put〉] Place me in the heart of Asia should I not be exiled. [What is climate to the complex system of life/living — 〉] What proportion does climate bear [to/in〉] to the complex system of human life — You may advise me to go and live at Bologna to eat sausages. The sausages there are [very fine〉] the best in the world, and they lose much by being carried.'[5]

[I spent some very pleasant days with him this spring at Mr. Thrale's where I enjoyed what he called with high relish 'the full flow of London talk' but my notes are so miserably short, that nothing can be perfectly recovered. *del*][6]

On Saturday [9 May〉] May 9 Mr. Dempster and I had agreed to dine by ourselves at [MS 364] the British Coffeehouse. Johnson on whom I happened to call in the [forenoon〉] morning said he would join us [and I could not object; and though his presence changed altogether the nature of the party from its original intention we were not disatisfied〉] which he did and we spent a very pleasant day though I recollect but little of what passed.

He said Walpole was a Minister given by the King to the People. Pitt was a Minister given by the People to the King — as an Adjunct.

'The misfortune of Goldsmith in conversation is this; he goes on without knowing how he is to get off. His genius is great,[7] but his knowledge is small. As they say of a generous man it is a pity but he were rich, we may say of Goldsmith it is a pity but he were knowing. He would not keep his knowledge to himself.'

[MS 367] [8] Before leaving London this year I consulted him upon a question purely of scotch law. It was held of old and continued for a long period to be an

5

10

15

20

25

30

---

[4] JB refers to his brother, Thomas David (1748–1826), who had been living in Spain since 1767 (Notes 24 Apr.; *Earlier Years*, p. 341).

[5] This conversational passage derives from JB's notes, which record a franker, more staccato exchange: 'Told my brother unwilling to leave Spain. Johns. Then he has got some woman. B. No Sir I believe it is the fine climate. *Johns*. How can you talk so [much *del*] like an ass. What is climate to happiness. I can go to the finest climates But put me in the heart of Asia would I not be exiled. What is climate [upon〉] in the complex system of living. [You may as well *del*] *Bos*. Sir it is a fine thing 〈Johns〉 Why Sir you may bid me go and live at Bologna to 〈eat s〉ausages. Sausages are fine; & they lose much by being carried' (Notes 24 April 1772/J25).

[6] These notes cover the period from 22 April to 15 May (J25). JB may have decided to delete this sentence because he had been expanding the notes quite successfully in the preceding paragraphs.

[7] The notes for 9 May read, 'His merit great'.

[8] Direction to the compositor, 'Pages 365 and 366 have been taken in, as they in fact belonged to 1771'.

established principle in that law that whoever intermeddled with the effects of a person deceased without the interposition of legal authority to guard against imbezzlement should be subjected to pay all the debts of the deceased as having been guilty of what was technically called *Vitious intromission*. The Court of
5   Session had gradually relaxed the strictness of this principle where the interference proved had been inconsiderable. I had laboured the winter before in a case *Wilson* against *Smith and Armour* to persuade the Judges to return to the ancient law. It was my own sincere opinion that they ought to adhere to it; but I had exhausted all my powers of reasoning in vain.   [Johnson was of my opinion, and
10 in order to assist me in my petitioning the Court for a revision and alteration of the Decree he>] Johnson thought as I did; and in order to assist me in my application to the Court for a revision and alteration of the Judgement he dictated to me the following Argument.⁹

[*Paper Apart*]¹ This [it is urged>] we are told is a law which has its force only
15 from the long practice of the court; and may therefore be suspended or modified as the Court shall think proper.

Concerning the power of the Court to make or to suspend a law we have no intention² to inquire. It is sufficient for our purpose that every just law is dictated by reason and that the practice of every legal court is regulated by equity. It is the
20 quality of reason to be invariable and constant, and of equity, to give to one man what in the same case is given to another. The advantage which humanity derives from law is this that the law gives every man a rule of action, and prescribes a mode of conduct which shall entitle him to the support and protection of Society. That the law may be a rule of action it is necessary that it be known and that it may be
25 known it is necessary that it be permanent and stable. The law is the measure of civil right; but if the measure be changeable, the extent of the thing measured never can be settled.

To permit a law to be modified at discretion is to leave the community without law. It is to withdraw the direction of that publick wisdom by which the
30 deficiencies of private understanding are to be supplied. It is to suffer the rash and ignorant to act at discretion and then to depend for the legality of that action on the sentence of the Judge. He that is thus governed lives not by law but by opinion; nor by a certain rule to which he can apply his intention before he acts but by an uncertain and variable opinion which he can never know, but after he has
35 committed the act on which that opinion shall be passed. He lives by a Law (if a law it be) which he can never know before he has offended it. To this case may be justly applied that important principle *misera est servitus ubi jus est aut incognitum aut vagum*. If Intromission be not criminal till it exceeds a certain point and that

---

⁹ Direction to the compositor, '(Take it in)'.
¹ This Paper Apart bears the following heading in the hand of JB: 'This was dictated to me by Mr. Samuel Johnson at London, in Spring 1772 in the Cause Wilson Smith and Armour which he took the trouble to read. J.B.'
² In the revises, 'intention' was changed to 'intent,' an alteration that accurately reflects the hierarchy of definitions in SJ's *Dictionary*. For 'intent,' SJ lists as the first meaning 'A design; a purpose'; this sense, which is also JB's above, is, according to SJ, merely a secondary definition for 'intention,' after 'Eagerness of desire'.

point be unsettled and consequently different in different minds the right of Intromission and the right of the Creditor arising from it are all *jura vaga* and by consequence are *jura incognita*, and the result can be no other than a *misera servitus* an uncertainty concerning the event of action, a servile dependance on private opinion.

It may be urged, and with great plausibility, that there may be Intromission   5
without fraud which however true, will by no means justify an occasional and arbitrary relaxation of the law. The end of law is protection as well as vengeance. Indeed vengeance is never used but to strengthen protection. That society only is well governed where life is freed from danger and from suspicion where possession is so sheltered by salutary prohibitions that violation is prevented more frequently   10
than punished. Such a Prohibition was this while it operated with its original force. The Creditor of the deceased was not only without loss but without fear. He was not to seek a remedy for an injury suffered; for injury was warded off.

As the law [now stands,⟩] has been sometimes administered, it lays us open to wounds because it is imagined to have the power of healing. To punish fraud when it   15
is detected is the proper act of vindictive justice; but to prevent fraud and make punishment unecessary is the great employment of legislative wisdom. To permit intromission and to punish fraud is to make law no better than a pitfal. To tread upon the brink is safe; but to come a step further is destruction. But surely it is better to enclose the gulf and hinder all access, than by encouraging us to advance a little to   20
entice us afterwards a little further, and let us perceive our folly only by our destruction.

As law supplies the weak with adventitious strength, it likewise enlightens the ignorant with extrinsick understanding. Law teaches us to know when we commit injury and when we suffer it. It fixes certain marks upon actions by which we are admonished to do or to forbear them. *Qui sibi bene temperat in licitis*, says one of the   25
Fathers, *numquam cadit in illicta*. He who never intromits at all will never intromit with fraudulent intentions.

The relaxation of the law against vicious intromission has been very favourably represented by a great Master of Jurisprudence[3] whose words have been exhibited with unecessary pomp and seem to be considered as irresistibly decisive. The great   30
moment of his authority makes it necessary [for me *del*] to examine his position. [Satellite Paper Apart K][4] 'Some ages ago, before the ferocity of the inhabitants of this part of the Island was subdued, the utmost severity of the civil law was necessary, to restrain individuals from plundering each other. Thus the man who intermeddled irregularly with the moveables of a person deceased was subjected to all the debts of   35
the deceased without limitation. This makes a branch of the law of Scotland known by the names of *Vitious Intromission*: and so rigidly was this regulation applied in our

---

[3] The revises include a footnote ('Lord Kames, in his "Historical Law Tracts"') that had apparently been added in first proof. In the revises, this note was printed at the foot of the page, but with the superscript missing. JB noted in the margin: 'There is no reference to the *Note* that I can perceive. It should be on Jurisprudence'.

[4] Direction to the compositor, 'See Paper marked K'. This supplementary Paper Apart in turn bears the following heading in JB's hand, 'For Paper which is taken in on p. 367'. The body of Paper Apart K is in an unidentified hand. JB cues the compositor with an abbreviated version of the first sentence: 'Some ages ago say he before the feroc of the inhabs of this part of the ile was subdued etc. (take in the whole)'.

Courts of law that the most trifling moveable abstracted *mala fide* subjected the intermeddler to the foregoing consequences which proved in many instances a most rigorous punishment — But this severity was necessary, in order to subdue the undisciplined nature of our people. It is extremely remarkable that in proportion to
5   our improvement in manners this regulation has been gradually softned, and applied by our sovereign Court with a sparing hand.' [Main Paper Apart resumed][5] I find myself under a necess of observ that this learnd and [judic>] judicious writer has not accurately distingd the [defic>] deficiencies and demands of the diff condits of human life, wc from a degree of savagness and independance in wc all laws are vain, passes or
10   may pass by innumerable gradations to a state of reciprocal benignity in wc laws shall be no longer [necess>] necessary. Men are first wild and unsocial living each man to himself, taking from the weak and losing to the strong. In their first coalitions of society much of this original savageness is retained. Of general happiness the product of general confidence there is yet no thought. [Many>] Men continue to prosec their
15   own advant by the nearest way and the utmost sever of the civ law is necess to restrain Individs from plund each other. The restraints then necess are restraints from plunder from acts of publick violence and undisguised oppression. The ferocity of our ancestors as of all othr nations produced not fraud but rapine. They had not yet learnd to cheat, and attempted only to rob. As manners grow more polished with the
20   knowledge of good, men attain likewise dexterity in evil. Open rapine becomes less frequent, and violence gives way to cunning. Those who before invaded pastures and stormed houses now begin to enrich themselves by unequal contracts and [fraudul>] fraudulent intromissions. It is not against the violence of ferocity but the circumventions of deceit that the law was framed and I am afraid the increase of commerce and
25   the incessant [strug>] strugle for riches wc commerce excites give us no prospect of an end speedily to be expected of artifice and fraud. It therefore seems to be no very conclusive reasoning wc connects those two propositions 'the nation is become less ferocious and therefore the laws agt fraud and *coven* shall be relaxed.'
      Whatever reason may have influenced the judges to a relaxation of the law, it
30   was not that the nation was grown less feroc and I am afraid it cannot be affirmed that it is grown less fraudulent.
      Since this law has been represented as rigourously and unreasonably penal it seems not improper to consider what are the conditions and qualities that make the justice or propriety of a penal law.
35   To make a [pen>] penal law [reas>] reasonable and just two conditions are necessary and two are proper. It is [necess>] necessary that the law shd be adequate to its end that if it be observed it shall prevent the evil agt wc it is directed. It is 2dly necessary that the end of the law be of such importance as to deserve the security of a penal sanction. The othr condits of a pen law wc tho not absolutely

---

[5] From this point onward in the main Paper Apart, JB relies heavily upon abbreviations, some of which he expands in a later draft. By the stage of the revises, all of the abbreviations had been expanded. Apparently impressed by the compositor's skill at deciphering his shorthand — or perhaps responding to an earlier query — JB wrote an encouraging note (about the printing of 'conditions' for 'condits') in the margin of the revises: 'You are right as to the word *conditions*'. In the transcription above, both JB's shorthand and his occasional later-draft expansions have been recorded as they appear in the MS.

necess are to a very high degree fit are that to the moral violation of the law there are many temptations and that of the physical observance there is great facility.

All these [condits>] conditions apparently concur to justify the law wc we are now considering. Its end is the security of property; and property very often of great value. The method by wc it effects the security is efficacious because it   5
admits in its [origi>] original rigour no gradations of injury but keeps guilt and inocence apart, by a distinct and definite limitation. He that intromits is [crim>] criminal; he that intromits not is [inoc>] inocent. Of the two [2dry>] secondary considerations it cannot be denied that both are in our favour. The [temptat>] temptation to intromiss is [freq>] frequent and strong so strong and so frequent as   10
to require the utmost activity of justice and vigilance of caution to withstand it's prevalence and the method by wc a man may entitle himself to legal intromission is so open and so facile that to neglect it is in itself a proof of [fraud intent>] fraudulent intention for why shd a man omit to do but for reasons wc he will not confess that wc he can do so easily, and that wc he knows to be required by the law.   15
If the temptation were rare, a penal law might be deemed [unecess>] unecessary. If the duty enjoined by the law were of [diffic>] difficult performance [an omission tho it cd not/*undeciphered word*>] omission though it could not be justified might be pitied. But in the [pres>] present case neither equity nor [compass>] compassion can [oper>] operate agt it. A useful a [necess>] necessary law is broken not only   20
without a [reason>] reasonable motive but [wt>] with all the inducements to [obed>] obedience that can be derived from safety and facility.

I therefore return to my orig position that a law to have its effect must be permanent and stable. It may be said in the lang of the schools Lex non recepit] majus et minus. We may have a law or we have no law but we cannot have half a   25
law. We must either have a rule of action or be permitted to act by discretion and by chance. Deviations from the law must be uniformly punished or no man can be certain when he shall be safe.

That from the rigour of the [orig Institut>] original Institution this court has sometimes departed cannot be denied. But as it is evident that such deviations as they   30
make law uncertain make life unsafe I hope that of departing from it there will now be an end that the wisdom of our Ancestors will be treated wt due reverence and that consistent and steady Decisions will furnish the people wt a rule of action and leave fraud and fraudulent intromission no future hope of impunity or escape.

[MS 368] It is astonishing with what comprehension of mind and clearness of   35
penetration [he thus treated a subject altogether new to him and how superiour his intellectual powers appeared when tried>] he thus treated a subject altogether new to him without any other preparation than my having stated to him the arguments which had been used on each side of the question. His intellectual powers appeared with peculiar lustre when tried against those of one [by no means inconsiderable>] of no   40
mean fame Lord Kames and that too in his Lordships own department; for the Opinion which Johnson so ably refutes though in the most courteous terms towards its Authour may be found in his Lordship's [*Historical Law Tracts*] 'Historical Law Tracts.'

This Masterly Argument after being prefaced and concluded with some sentences of my own and garnished with the usual formularies was actually printed and   45
[laid before/considered by>] laid before the Lords of Session, but without success.

Sir David Dalrymple Lord Hailes one of their number had critical sagacity enough to [discover/discern>] discover a more than ordinary hand in the *Petition*. I told him that Dr. Johnson had honoured me with his pen. His Lordship pointed out exactly where his composition began and where it ended. ₍But that I may do impartial justice and

5   conform to the great rule of all Courts *Suum cuique tribuito*⁶ I must add that their Lordships in general though they [thought this '*a very well drawn paper*'>] were pleased to call this '*a well drawn paper*' preferred the former very inferiour Petition which I had written, thus confirming the truth of an observation made by one of their number to me in a merry mood, 'My dear Sir, give yourself no trouble in the composition of the

10   papers you present to us. For indeed it is casting pearls before swine.'₎
[To Dr. SAMUEL *Johnson*>] [MR. BOSWELL To Dr. *Johnson*   Edinburgh
                                                        16 July 1772

My Dear Sir
It is now time to remind>]

15   (Renewed my solicitations that he would this year accomplish his long in-tended visit to Scotland.)⁷
To JAMES BOSWELL Esq:⁸

. . . .

[MS 369] To Dr. Samuel Johnson⁹

. . . .

[₍* * * * *

20   I was much disappointed that you did not come to Scotland last autumn. However I must own that your letter prevents me from complaining not only₎ *del*]¹

In 1773 he [made no appearances as an original Writer/Authour by himself>] published nothing except in giving an edition of his Folio Dictionary with additions and corrections, nor did he so far as is known furnish any productions of

25   his fertile pen to [any one of his numerous friends and I may well add dependants. But his Shakspeare having succeeded so well, that two editions of it were sold, he this year had the satisfaction to see a third edition of it, but with such additions and improvements as greatly augmented/increased it's value in a very high degree. So well had he acquitted himself as a Commentator, that>] any of his numerous

---

⁶ This tag is adapted from Cicero's *De Officiis*: 'in hominum societate tuenda tribuendoque suum cuique et rerum contractarum fide': 'with the conservation of organized society, with rendering to every man his due, and with the faithful exchange of obligations assumed' (Loeb ed., trans. Walter Miller, I. v. 15).

⁷ Deleted direction to the compositor, 'Take it in'.

⁸ Direction to the compositor, '"The regret" (Take it in)'. This note is followed by an asterisk that refers the compositor to a marginal note: 'N.B. In Dr. Johnson's letter here to be taken in on line 6 after esteem put a few asterisks, and leave out all between *esteem* and *But*'. This Paper Apart no longer forms part of the *Life* MS.

⁹ Direction to the compositor, '(Take in ₍what is unscored of₎ letter 25 Decr. 1772)'. 'What' is written over an undeciphered word. This Paper Apart no longer forms part of the *Life* MS.

¹ Written on the verso of MS 368, this extract from the letter to Dr. Johnson of 25 December 1772 breaks off unexpectedly. This Paper Apart no longer forms part of the *Life* MS.

friends or dependants.[2] His Shakspeare indeed which had been received with high approbation by the Publick and gone through several editions [with great accessions and valuable improvements by>] was this year republished by George Steevens Esq: a Gentleman not only deeply skilled in ancient learning but of [most>] very extensive [reading/acquaintance>] reading in english literature especially the early writers and at the same time of [a most acute and penetrating discernment and elegant taste instead of depreciating Johnson's Shakespeare, and publishing one of his own, thought it an honour to be joined with/to him and share his glory>] acute discernment and elegant taste and who by his great and valuable additions to Dr. Johnson's work justly obtained considerable reputation
> *Divisum imperium cum Jove Cæsar habet.*
> To James Boswell Esq.[3/4]

[MS 370][5] On Saturday 3 April the day after my[6] arrival in London this year I went to his house [at night>] late in the evening and sat with Mrs. Williams till he came home. I found in the London Chronicle Dr. Goldsmith's apology to the Publick for beating Evans [the Bookseller/Publisher on account of a newspaper paragraph which>] a Bookseller on account of a paragraph in a newspaper published by him which Goldsmith thought impertinent to him and to a Lady of his acquaintance. The Apology was written so much in [Mr.>] Dr. Johnson's manner that both Mrs. Williams and I supposed it to be his. [But he soon undeceived us.>] But when he came home he soon undeceived us. When he said to Mrs. Williams 'Well, Dr. Goldsmith's *manifesto* has got into your paper' — I asked him if [*Goldsmith*>] Goldsmith [writ it?>] had written it? with an air that [made/let>] made him see I suspected [he had done it.>] it was his though subscribed by Goldsmith. ['Sir' said he>] *Johnson*. 'Sir Dr. Goldsmith would no more have asked me to write such a thing as that for him, than [he'd>] he would have asked me to feed him with a spoon or to do any thing else that argued [his del] imbecillity. I as much believe

---

[2] By the stage of the revises, this passage had been amplified to read 'dependants, except the Preface to his old amanuensis Macbean's 'System of ancient Geography'. When JB read through the revises, he changed 'System' to 'Dictionary'. In the second edition, further changes were made in the form of a footnote keyed to 'Preface': 'He, however, wrote, or partly wrote, an Epitaph on Mrs. Bell, wife of his friend John Bell, Esq. brother of the Reverend Dr. Bell, Prebendary of Westminster, which is printed in his Works. It is in English prose, and has so little of his manner, that I did not believe he had any hand in it, till I was satisfied of the fact by the authority of Mr. Bell.'

[3] Direction to the compositor, 'I have read your kind (take it in)'. This Paper Apart no longer forms part of the *Life* MS.

[4] While the second edition was in press, JB received from James Abercrombie (1758–1841), an American businessman, copies of letters from SJ to Phineas Bond and William White (*Corr. 2*, pp. 462–65; *Letters of Johnson* ed. Redford, ii. 11–14). These he inserted at the end of the portion of text devoted to the year 1773, including an apology for disrupting the chronological sequence. Only in the third edition did the two letters appear in their proper position, after SJ's letter to JB of 24 February 1773.

[5] At the head of MS 370 is a marginal note by JB, apparently to himself: 'Two letters from me to him. See if anything in them'. This note was later deleted.

[6] Direction to the compositor, 'Stet this line'. When JB deleted the marginalia at the head of this page, he also — presumably inadvertently — crossed out the first line of text: 'On Saturday 3 April the day after my'.

that he wrote it, as if I had seen him do it. Sir, had he shewn it to any one friend he would not have been allowed to publish it. He has indeed done it very well; but [it is/'tis>] it is a foolish thing well done. I suppose he has been so much elated with the success of his new Comedy that he has thought every thing that concerned

5   him must be of importance to the Publick.' [ʌGoldsmithʌ del] Boswell. 'I [suppose>] fancy, Sir, this is the first time that he has been engaged in such an adventure.' [MS 371] Johnson. 'Why Sir I believe it is the first time he has beat. He may have been beaten before. [No, Sir, 'tis>] This, Sir, is a new plume to him.'

  I mentioned Sir John Dalrymple's 'Memoirs' ʌof Great Britain and Ireland'ʌ

10 and his discoveries [against>] to the prejudice of Lord Russel and Algernon Sydney. Johnson. 'Why Sir Every body who had just notions of government thought them rascals before. It is well that all [mankind/the world>] mankind now [sees>] see them to be rascals.' Boswell. 'But Sir may not those discoveries be true without their being rascals.' Johnson. 'Consider Sir, would any of them [have been

15 willing to have had these things/circumstances known>] [have been willing to have had these things/circumstances which he has told known>] have been willing to have had it known that they intrigued with France. Depend upon it Sir he who does what he is affraid should be known has something rotten about him. This Dalrymple seems to be an honest fellow; for he tells equally what makes against

20 both sides. But nothing can be poorer than his ʌmode ofʌ writing[; tis the>]. It is the mere bouncing of a schoolboy. Great He! but greater She! and such stuff.'

  I could not agree with him in this criticism, for though Sir John Dalrymple's style is not regularly formed in any respect, and one cannot help smiling sometimes at [sallies which seem affected>] [some of his sallies which seem affected>]

25 his affected *grandiloquence*, there is [much clearness and precision>] in his writing a pointed vivacity and much of a gentlemanly spirit.[7]

  At Mr. Thrale's [on the evening of Wednesday April 7>] in the evening he repeated his usual paradoxical [Argument>] declamation against Action in publick Speaking. 'Action [said he del] [MS 372] can have no effect upon

30 reasonable minds. It may [enforce>] augment noise; but it never can enforce argument. If you speak to a dog, you use action — You hold up your hand thus — because he is a brute, and in proportion as men are removed from brutes action will have the less influence upon them.' Mrs. Thrale. 'What then, ʌSirʌ becomes of Demosthenes's saying "Action, Action, Action."' Johnson. 'Demosthenes

35 ʌMadamʌ spoke to an assembly of brutes, to a barbarous people.'

  I thought it [amazing>] extraordinary that he should deny the [power/influence>] power of rhetorical action upon human nature when it is proved by innumerable facts in all stages of society. Reasonable beings are not solely reasonable. They have fancies which may be pleased, passions which may be roused. [I could not help

40 supposing some defect in his perceptions/perceptive faculty del]

  ʌLord Chesterfield being mentioned, Johnson remarked that almost all of that celebrated Nobleman's witty sayings were pun. He however allowed the merit of good wit to his Lordships saying of Lord Tyrawley and himself when both very old and failed: 'Tyrawley and I have been dead these two years; but we [dont chuse to

45 let it be known/chuse to keep it a secret>] dont chuse to let it be known.'ʌ

---

[7] Deleted direction to the compositor, 'Take in Paper D'. Paper Apart D is actually taken in on MS 376, *post* p. 89.

He talked with [satisfaction›] approbation of an intended edition of *The Spectator* with notes, two volumes of which had been prepared by a gentleman eminent in the literary world and [his assistance given/promised to a Continuator›] the materials which he had collected for the remainder had been transferred to another hand. He observed that all works which describe manners require notes in sixty or seventy years or less, and   5 [he had told all he knew that›] told us he had communicated all he knew that could throw light upon the *Spectator*. He said Addison had [made/drawn›] made his Sir Andrew Freeport a true Whig arguing against giving charity to beggars and throwing out other such ungracious sentiments; but that he had thought better, and made amends, by making him found an hospital for decayed farmers. *[MS 373]* He called for the Volume   10 of the Spectator in which that account is contained and read it aloud to us. He read so well, that every thing acquired additional weight and grace from his utterance.

[He repeated to us a correct edition of a stanza which he had composed in ridicule of a modern imitation of the simplicity of Ancient English Poetry which was as follows/runs thus   15
        I put ›]
The conversation having turned on modern imitations of Ancient Ballads and some one having praised their simplicity he treated them with that ridicule which he allways displayed when this subject was mentioned [and repeated to us a stanza which he had composed in that style/in ridicule of them which was as follows   20
        I put my hat upon my head
        And walk'd into the Strand
        And there I met another man
        Who's hat was in his hand. *del*]⁸
[I mentioned a distinguished Orator having a custom of introducing scripture   25 phrases in his speeches in the House of Commons.⁹ *Johnson.* 'I am affraid Sir he sacrifices every thing to his wit. It is very wrong to introduce scripture thus ludicrously.›] He disapproved of introducing scripture phrases into secular discourse. This seemed to me a question of some difficulty. A Scripture expression may be used like a highly classical phrase to produce an instantaneous strong impression; and it may be   30 done without being at all ludicrous. Yet I own there is danger that applying the language of our sacred book to ordinary subjects may tend to lessen our reverence for it. ₍If therefore it be introduced at all it should be with very great caution.₎

On thursday April 8 I sat a good part of the evening with him but he was very silent. He said, '*Burnetts History* ₍of his own times₎' is very entertaining; the style indeed is   35 mere *[MS 374]* chit chat. I do not believe that Burnett intentionally lyed; but he was so much prejudiced, that he took no pains to find out the truth. He was like a man who resolves to regulate his time by a certain watch; but will not inquire whether the watch is right or not.'

---

⁸After deleting this passage, JB made a marginal note to himself to reinsert the material elsewhere in the MS: 'NB This comes in among Mr. Steevens's Johnsoniana'. The anecdotes from George Steevens that JB positions late in the biography (MS 966, Paper Apart 'Varia', sub-paper apart; Hill-Powell iv. 324–25) do not include this parody. See also *Corr. 2*, pp. 146–52.

⁹ This 'distinguished Orator' is almost certainly Edmund Burke: JB elsewhere calls him 'a celebrated orator,' while persistently criticizing his speeches for their 'oratorical sallies' (Journ. 17 Feb. 1786).

Though he was not disposed to talk, he was unwilling that I should leave him, and when I [/looked at my watch and/>] looked at my watch and told him it was twelve o'clock, he cried 'Whats that to you and me?' and ordered Frank to tell Mrs. Williams that we were coming to drink tea with her, which we did. [I was very
5   desireous of seeing him at church; and thinking I could not have a better opportunity than passion/holy week I proposed/offered to attend him next day, which he allowed.>] It was settled that we should go to church together next day.

On the 9 of April being Good Friday I breakfasted on tea and Cross Buns, *Doctor* Levet, as Frank called him making the tea. He carried me with him to the Church
10   of St. Clement Daines where he had his seat, and his behaviour was as I had imaged to myself, solemnly devout. I never shall forget the tremulous earnestness with which he pronounced the aweful petition in the Litany '*In the hour of death and at the day of judgement Good Lord deliver us.*'[1]

We went to church both [forenoon and afternoon>] in the morning and evening.
15   In the interval between ⟨the two services⟩ we did not dine but he read in the Greek New=testament and I turned over several of his books. [MS 374 verso] In Arch=Bishop Laud's Diary I found the following passage which I read to Dr. Johnson.[2]

[Paper Apart L][3] 1623 Februar 1 Sunday I stood by the most illustrious Prince Charles[a] at dinner. He was then very merry; and talked occasionally of many
20   things with his attendants. Among other things he said that if he were necessitated to take any particular profession of life, he could not be a lawyer, adding his reasons I *cannot* (saith he) *defend a bad, nor yield in a good cause.*' [Laud seems to approve of this; for he adds 'May you ever hold this resolution, and succeed (most serene Prince) in matters of greater moment, for ever prosperous *del*] [MS 375
25   resumed] *Johnson*. 'Sir, this is false reasoning; because every cause has a bad side, and a lawyer is not overcome though the Cause which he has [pleaded is/supported be>] endeavoured to support be determined against him.'

I told him that Goldsmith had said to me [the other day>] a few days before, 'As I take my shoes from the shoemaker, and my coat from the taylor, so I take my
30   religion from the Priest.' I regretted this loose way of talking. Johnson, 'Sir, he knows nothing, he has made up his mind about nothing.'

To my great surprise he asked me to dine with him on Easter=day. I never supposed that he had a dinner at his house, [and was not a little curious to see how it would be served up *del*] for I had not ⟨then⟩ heard of any one of his friends
35   having been entertained at his table. He told me 'I generally have a meat pye on

---

[a] afterwards Charles I.

---

[1] Next to this paragraph in the margin of the revises appears a note in JB's hand: 'I have attended to all the Qu[erie]s. I am obliged to you for the [attention *del*] suggestions. On this page there are two good corrections.'
[2] Direction to the compositor, '(Take in Paper ⟨L⟩)'. In this Paper Apart, JB quotes from Henry Wharton's *History of the Troubles and Tryal of the Most Reverend Father in God, and Blessed Martyr, William Laud* (1695), which begins with a selection from Laud's diary. Though it is clear that SJ owned this book in 1773, the *History* was not in his library at the time of his death.
[3] At the top of this Paper Apart, JB wrote and then deleted the following heading: 'Diary of Arch=Bishop Laud'. Lest there be any confusion as to where this Paper Apart ought to be inserted into the main manuscript, JB also wrote, 'Opposite to p 375'.

sunday. It is baked at a publick oven which is very properly allowed, because one man can attend it [where for⟩], so there is the advantage of not keeping servants from church to dress dinners.'

April 11 being Easter Sunday, after having attended ⟨divine service⟩ at St. Pauls, I repaired to Dr. Johnson's. I had gratified my curiosity much in dining with ⟨JEAN JACQUES⟩ ROUSSEAU while he lived in the wilds of Neufchatel. I had as great a curiosity to dine with DR. SAMUEL JOHNSON [in the gloomy recess of Bolt Court⟩] in the dusky recess of a Court in Fleetstreet.[4] I supposed we should hardly have knives and forks, and only some strange uncouth ⟨illdrest⟩ dish. But I found every=thing in [very/exceedingly⟩] very good order. [There was nobody with us [MS 376] but Mrs. Williams and a young woman whom I did not know. We had a very good soup,⟩] We had no other company [MS 376] but Mrs. Williams and a young woman whom I did not know. [We had a very good soup, a boiled leg of lamb and spinnage, a veal pye and a rice pudding, pickled walnuts and onions, porter and port wine. One of his dishes reminded him of a joke which he told me A Lady Lade Mr. Thrale's sister when she saw Sir George Colebrooke/a certain Baronet in a white waistcoat and green coat,[5] said he was like a leg of lamb and spinnage.⟩][6] As a dinner here was considered as a singular Phænomenon, and I was frequently interrogated on the subject my readers may perhaps be curious to know our bill of fare. Foote I remember in allusion to Francis the *negro* was willing to suppose that our repast was *black broth*. But the fact was that we had a very good soup, a boiled leg of lamb and spinnage, a veal pye and a rice pudding.

Of Dr. John Campbell the Authour [of the Lives of the Admirals *del*] he said 'He is a very inquisitive and a very able man and a man of good ⟨religious⟩ principles, though I am affraid he has been deficient in practice. Campbell [I suppose has not been within a church for many years; but he never passes by a church but he pulls/without pulling off his hat. This shews him to be/that he is⟩] is radically right, and we may hope that in time there will be good practice.'[7]

He owned that he thought Hawkesworth [his imitator/imitated him⟩] was one of his imitators but he did not think Goldsmith [was/did⟩] was. Goldsmith [he said/said he⟩], he said, [had/has⟩] had great merit. ⟨*Boswell.*⟩ 'But Sir, he is [much indebted/obliged to you/owes much to you⟩] much indebted to you for his getting so [far up/high⟩] high in the publick estimation.' ⟨*Johnson.*⟩ 'Why Sir, he has perhaps got *sooner* to it by [that/his intimacy with me⟩] his intimacy with me.'[8]

---

[4] JB's change reflects his uncertainty about the date of SJ's move from Johnson's Court to Bolt Court. The move took place in 1776 (Hill-Powell iii. 535–36).

[5] Interlined above 'waistcoat', JB has written 'Qu vice versa', meaning that the waistcoat could have been green and the coat white.

[6] SJ met Sir George Colebrooke (1729–1809), Bt., a banker and director of the East India Company, through Henry Thrale: the two men had been 'Contemporary *gay* Fellows, & *Play* Fellows' (*Thraliana* ii. 1067). This 'joke' was obviously a favourite in the Streatham Park circle: Hester Thrale records the anecdote twice in *Thraliana* (i. 26, 335).

[7] This paragraph is based on the same journal entry (11 Apr. 1773) that JB had mined for his comments on Campbell under 1763: see *Life* MS i. 289. EM noted the repetition of material in a marginal note in the revises ('In p. 226 this is said before'), to which JB responded, also in the margin of the revises, 'But in different phrase so stet'.

[8] Direction to the compositor, 'Paper D'.

[Paper Apart D] [9] Goldsmith though his [very allowable *del*] vanity often excited him to occasional competition had a very high regard [for Johnson. He inscribed to him his favourite Comedy 'She Stoops to conquer' and in the Dedication pays him this handsome and just compliment>] for Johnson which he

5   expresses in the strongest manner in the Dedication of his Comedy entitled 'She Stoops to Conquer.'[a]

[MS 376 resumed] He [said>] observed that there were very few books printed in Scotland before the Union. He had seen a complete Collection of [them all/the whole of them *del*] them in the possession of the Honourable Archibald Campbell

10   a nonjuring Bishop.[b] I wish this collection had been kept entire. [A number of that venerable gentleman's books as appears from a plate with his name and arms pasted on the inside [MS 377] of the boards, were purchased for the Library>] Many of them [MS 377] are in the Library of the Faculty of Advocates at Edinburgh. I told [him>] Dr. Johnson that I had some intention to write the life of

15   the learned and worthy Thomas Ruddiman. He said 'I should take pleasure in helping you to do honour to him. But his farewell letter to the Faculty of Advocates when he resigned the office of their Librarian should have been in latin.'

 ᴧI put a question to him upon a fact in common life which he could not answer

20   nor have I found any one else who could. 'What is the reason that women servants though obliged to be at the expence of purchasing their own clothes have much lower wages than men servants to whom a great proportion of that article is furnished?, and when in fact our female house servants work much harder than the male.'ᴧ

25   He told me that he had twelve or fourteen times attempted to keep a journal of his life, but never could persevere. He advised me to do it. 'The great thing,' said he 'to be recorded is the state of your own mind; and you should write down every thing that you remember, for you cannot judge at first what is good or bad; and write immediately while the impression is fresh; for it will not be the same a week

30   afterwards.'

I again solicited him to communicate to me the particulars of his early years. He said 'You shall have them all for twopence. I hope you shall know a great deal

[a] [Dear Sir *del*] "By inscribing this slight performance to you, I do not mean so [your *del*] much to compliment[al] you as myself. It may do me some honour to

35   inform the publick that I have lived many years in intimacy with you. It may serve the interests of mankind also to inform them that the greatest wit maybe found in a character, without impairing the most unaffected piety."

[b] See an Account of this learned and respectable Gentleman and of his curious [Book upon>] work on the *Middle State* Journal of a Tour to the Hebrides, 3 Edit.

40   p 371.

---

[9] The heading of this Paper Apart reads, 'To be taken in on p. 376'.

[al] After 'compliment', the hand switches from that of JB to that of EM.

more of me before you write my Life.'[1] [He gave me a good deal this day, which I wrote down and have melted into the Narrative, which I am now pursuing/continuing⟩] He mentioned to me this day many circumstances, which I wrote down when I went home and have interwoven in the former part of this Narrative.　　　　　　　　　　　　　　　　　　　　　　　　　　　　　　　5

On April 13 he and Dr. Goldsmith and I dined at General Oglethorpe's.[2]

. . . .

On thursday [15 April⟩] April 15 I dined with him [MS 378] and Dr. Goldsmith at General Paoli's. We found here Signor Martinelli of Florence Authour of a History of England in Italian printed in London.

I spoke of Allan Ramsays Gentle Shephered in the scottish dialect as the best　10
pastoral that had ever been written, [not only filled with ⁄not only full of⁄as abounding not only with⟩] not only abounding with beautiful rural imagery and just and pleasing sentiments but being [the truest⟩] a real picture of manners, and I offered to teach Dr. Johnson to understand it. 'No Sir' said he, 'I wont learn it. You shall retain your superiority by my not knowing it.'　　　　　　　　　15

This brought on [an argument if one was lessened by another's knowing⟩] a question whether one man is lessened by another's acquiring an equal degree of knowledge with him. Johnson asserted the affirmative. I maintained that [it might be so in matters of⁄with respect to knowledge which produces⟩] the position might be true in those kinds of knowledge which produce wisdom power and force　20
[by which one man can in so far govern others.⟩] so as to enable one man to have the government of others. But that [one⟩] a man is not in any degree lessened by others knowing as well as he what ends in mere pleasure. Eating fine fruits drinking delicious wines, reading exquisite poetry.

The General [observed⁄said⟩] observed that Martinelli was a Whig. *Johnson.* 'I　25
am sorry for it. It shews the spirit of the [times⁄age⟩] times. He is obliged to temporise.' [— I said I thought Toryism prevailed⟩] *Boswell.* 'I rather think Sir that Toryism prevails in this reign.' *Johnson.* 'Do you think so, Sir? You see [MS 379] your friend Lord Littleton⁄Littelton[3] [⁄a nobleman/⟩] a nobleman is obliged ⟨in his History⟩λ to write the [lowest⟩] most vulgar Whiggism.'　　　　　　　30

An animated debate took place whether Martinelli should continue his History of England to the present day. *Goldsmith.* 'To be sure he should.' *Johnson.* 'No Sir. He would give great offence. He would have to tell of almost all the living great what they do not wish [told⁄to have told⁄to be told⁄should be told⟩] told.' *Goldsmith.* [A native may be more cautious⟩] 'It may perhaps be necessary for a　35
native to be more cautious, but a foreigner who comes among us without prejudice [stands like a Judge⟩] [is like a Judge⟩] may be considered as holding the place of a

---

[1] In the revises (i. 395) EM has bracketed the section that runs from 'He told me' through 'write my Life' and noted in the left-hand margin, 'This almost verbatim.' JB responds 'Qu It is much varied so Stet.' The parallel passage under discussion appears under 1763 (*Life* MS i. 302). Cf. also p. 88 n. 7, above.

[2] Direction to the compositor, '(Here take in three smaller quarto leaves)'. The leaves to which JB refers come from the Journal (J 28), and are not transcribed here. See *Boswell for the Defence*, pp. 180–82.

[3] The alternative is resolved by the printing of 'Lyttelton' in the revises.

Judge and may speak his mind freely.[4] *Johnson*. 'Sir, a foreigner [/when he issues
a work from the press/>] when he sends a work from the press [is/ought>] ought to
be on his guard [/against errour and mistaken enthusiasm/>] against catching the
errour and mistaken enthusiasm ⟨of the people among whom he happens to be.'⟩
Goldsmith. '/Sir/[5] he wants only to sell his history, and tell truth one an honest the
other a laudable motive.' *Johnson*. '⟨Sir⟩ They are both laudable motives. It is
laudable in a man to wish to *live* by his labours; but he should ⟨write⟩ so as he may
live [/by them/>] by them not so as he may be knocked on the head. I would advise
him to be at Calais before he publishes his history of the present age. A foreigner
who attaches himself to a political party in this country is in the worst state that
can be imagined. He is looked upon as a mere intermeddler. A native may do it
from interest.' *Boswell*. 'Or principle.' *Goldsmith*. 'There are people who tell a
hundred ⟨political⟩ lies every day and [MS 380] are not hurt [/by it/>] by it. [Far
more may one>] Surely then one may tell truth with safety.' *Johnson*. 'Why Sir, in
the first place, he who tells a hundred lies, has disarmed the force of his lies. But
besides, a man had rather have a hundred lies told of him than one truth which he
[does not wish should be told/wishes should not be told>] does not wish should be
told.' *Goldsmith*. 'For my part, I'd tell truth and shame the devil.' *Johnson*. 'Yes
⟨Sir⟩; but the devil will be angry. I wish to shame the devil as much as you
[/do/>] do but I should chuse to be out of the reach of his claws.' *Goldsmith*. 'His
claws can do you [little>] no harm when you have the shield of truth.'

It having been observed that there was little hospitality in London *Johnson*.
'Nay Sir [any/a>] any man who has [a/any>] a name or who has [the/any general>]
the power of pleasing will be very generally invited in London. The man Sterne
I have been told has had engagements for three months.' *Goldsmith*. '[/And/>] And
a very dull fellow.' *Johnson*. 'Why no Sir.'

Martinelli told us that for several years he lived much with Charles
Townshend, and that he ventured to tell him he was a bad joker. *Johnson*. ⟨'Why
Sir thus much I can say upon the subject.⟩ One day he and a few more agreed to go
and dine in the country and each of them was to bring a friend in [MS 381] his
carriage with him. Charles Townshend [who was to take Fitzherbert with him but
said>] asked Fitzherbert to go with him but told him,
"You must find somebody to bring you back. I can only carry you there."
[Fitzherbert did not much like this, and answered 'It will do very well, for then the
same jokes will serve in returning as in going.' — Meaning to say/which meant that
his jokes were not extemporaneous, but that he bottled up wit.>] Fitzherbert did not
much like this arrangement. He however consented, observing sarcastically, "It
will do very well, for then the same jokes will serve you in returning as in going."'

An eminent publick character being mentioned — *Johnson*. 'I remember being
present when he shewed himself to be so corrupted or at least something so
different from what I think right, as to maintain that [you must/should go along
with>] a member of parliament should go along with [your>] his party right or

---

[4] JB's notes reveal that the 'foreigner' in question is Giuseppe Baretti (15 Apr. 1773/
J30).
[5] The optional word, which JB left unresolved, is printed in the revises.

wrong. Now Sir this is so [different›] remote from native virtue, from scholastick virtue that [a man/he›] a good man must have undergone a great change ∧before he can reconcile himself to such a doctrine.λ It is maintaining that you may lie to the publick, [/for you lie when you call that/support as right which you think wrong, or the reverse/›] for you lie when you call that right which you think wrong, or the reverse. A friend of ours who is too much an echo of that gentleman observed that [a man/the one›] a man who does not stick uniformly to a party is only waiting to be bought.' 'Why then,' said I 'he is only waiting to be what that gentleman *[MS 382]* is allready.'[6]

We talked of the King's coming to see Goldsmith's new Play. — 'I wish he would' said Goldsmith — [but with an affected indifference added:›] adding however with an affected indifference 'not that it would do me the least good.' *Johnson.* [We shall say›] 'Well then Sir let us say it would do *him* good ∧(laughing)λ. No Sir ['tis so erroneous in such a state as ours not to wish to please the Chief Magistrate.›] this affectation will not pass; it is mighty idle. In such a state as ours who would not wish to please the Chief Magistrate?' *Goldsmith.* 'I do wish to please him. I remember a line in Dryden.

And ev'ry poet is the Monarch's friend.
It ought to be reversed.' *Johnson.* 'Nay, there are finer lines [in Dryden.

[Colleges
No rebel ever was a friend to arts.›] in Dryden on this subject.
For colleges on bounteous Kings depend
And never rebel was to arts a friend.'[7]

∧General Paoli observed that successful rebels might. MARTINELLI. 'Happy Rebellions.' GOLDSMITH. 'We have no such phrase.' GENERAL PAOLI. 'But have you not the *thing*?' GOLDSMITH. 'Yes. All our happy Revolutions. They have hurt our constitution, and will hurt it, till we mend it by another happy Revolution.' — I never before discovered that my friend Goldsmith had so much of the old prejudice in him.

General Paoli talking of Goldsmith's new Play said 'Il a fait un compliment tres gracieux á une certaine grande dame', meaning a duchess of the first rank.

I expressed a doubt whether Goldsmith intended it in order that I might hear [it›] the truth from himself. It perhaps was not quite fair to endeavour to bring him to a confession, as he might not wish to avow, positively his taking part against the Court. He smiled and hesitated. The General at once relieved him by this beautiful image 'Monsieur Goldsmith est comme la mer qui jette des perles et beaucoup d'autres belles choses, sans s'en appercevoir.' GOLDSMITH. 'Tres bien dit, et tres elegament.'λ

A person was mentioned who it was said could take down in short hand the speeches in parliament with perfect exactness.[8] *Johnson.* 'Sir it is impossible. I

---

[6] JB's notes reveal that the 'eminent publick character' is Edmund Burke, and the 'friend of ours' Joshua Reynolds (15 Apr. 1773/J30).

[7] In the first draft, JB sketched in the gist of the quotation from *Absalom and Achitophel* that he later supplied in full.

[8] JB's notes reveal that the reporter is Sir Henry Cavendish (1732–1804), Bt., who took shorthand notes of parliamentary debates from 1768 to 1774.

remember one *Angel* who came to me to write him a Preface or Dedication to a Book upon short hand, and he professed to write as [quick as the living voice⟩] fast as a man could speak. In order to try him I took down a Book, and read while he wrote, and I favoured him for I read more deliberately than usual. I had
5 [read/gone⟩] proceeded but a very little way, when he [MS 383] begged I would desist, for he could not follow me.' — Hearing now for the first time of this Preface or Dedication, I said 'What an expence Sir do you put us to in buying Books to which you have written Prefaces or Dedications.' *Johnson.* 'Why I have dedicated to the Royal Family all round, that is to say to the last Royal Family.' [*Boswell.* I
10 would have them all. *del*] *Goldsmith.* 'And perhaps Sir not one sentence of wit in a whole Dedication.' *Johnson.* [Perhaps/Probably⟩] 'Perhaps not Sir.' — *Boswell.* 'What then is the [reason for/meaning of⟩] reason for coming to a particular person to do that which any one may do as well?' *Johnson.* 'Why Sir One man has greater readiness at/in⁹ doing it than another.'
15 I spoke of Mr. Harris of Salisbury as being a very learned man [/and in particular/⟩] and in particular [a great⟩] an eminent grecian. *Johnson.* 'I am not sure of that. His friends give him out as such, but I know not who of his friends are able to judge of it.' *Goldsmith.* 'He is what is much better. He is a worthy humane man.' *Johnson.* 'Nay Sir, that is not to the purpose of our argument. That will as
20 much prove that he can play upon the [MS 384]¹ fiddle as well as Giardini as that [he's/he is a great⟩] he is an eminent Grecian.' [Goldsmith observed that the⟩] *Goldsmith.* 'The greatest musical performers [make/get⟩] have but small [gains⟩] emoluments. Giardini I am told does not get above £700 a year.' *Johnson.* 'That is ₍indeed but₎ little for a man to get who does best that which so many endeavour
25 to do. There is nothing ₍I think₎ in which the power of art is shewn so much as in playing on the fiddle. In all other things we can do something at first. Any man will forge a bar of iron if you give him a hammer — not so well as a smith, but tolerably. A man will saw a piece of wood and make a box [/though not a very neat one/⟩] though a clumsy one but give him a fiddle and a fiddlestick and he can do
30 nothing.'
On Monday [19 April⟩] April 19 He [came⟩] called on me with Mrs. Williams in Mr. Strahans coach and carried me out to dine with Mr. Elphinston at his Academy at Kensington. A Printer having acquired a fortune sufficient to enable him to keep his coach was a good topick for the credit of literature. Mrs. Williams
35 said that another printer Mr. Hamilton had not waited so long as Mr. Strahan but had kept his coach several years sooner. *Johnson.* 'He was in the right. Life is short. The sooner that a man [begins to enjoy/takes the enjoyment of⟩] begins to enjoy his wealth the better.'
Mr. Elphinston talked [to him *del*] of a New Book that [MS 385]² was much
40 admired and asked Dr. Johnson if he had read it. ₍*Johnson.*₎ 'I have looked into it.' — 'What,' said Mr. Elphinston, 'have you not read it through?' Johnson, offended at being thus pressed, and so obliged to own his cursory mode of reading answered

---

⁹ The alternative is resolved by the printing of 'at' in the revises.
¹ MS 384: private collection; location undetermined (transcribed from a photostat at Yale).
² MS 385: Hyde Collection.

[with an angry and contemptous look⟩] tartly 'No, Sir. Do *you* read books *through?*'

[The subject of duelling being introduced he again defended it, and put his argument upon what I have ever thought the most solid/firmest basis, that if publick war be allowed to be lawful private war must be equally so/lawful.⟩] He this day again defended duelling, and put his argument upon what I have ever thought the most solid basis, that if publick war be allowed to be consistent with morality private war must be equally so. — Indeed, we may observe what strained arguments are used to reconcile war with the Christian Religion. But in my opinion it is exceedingly clear that duelling having better reasons for its barbarous violence is more justifiable than War in which thousands go forth without any cause of ₍personal₎ quarrel and massacre each other.

On Wednesday [21 April⟩] April 21 I dined with him at Mr. Thrale's. A Gentleman attacked Garrick for being vain. *Johnson.* 'No wonder ₍Sir₎ that he is vain. A man who is perpetually flattered in every mode that [you can conceive⟩] [it can be conceived/done⟩] it can be conceived. So many bellows have blown the fire that one [*MS 386*] wonders he is not ₍by this time become₎ a cinder.' *Boswell.* 'And such bellows too. Lord Mansfield with his cheeks like to burst Lord Chatham like an Eolus. I have read such notes from them to him as were enough to turn his head.' *Johnson.* [True. He⟩] 'True. When he whom every body else flatters flatters me I then am truly happy.' Mrs. Thrale. 'The sentiment is in Congreve I think.' *Johnson.* 'Yes Madam, in "The Way of the World"

₍"If there's delight in love, 'tis when I see
That heart which others bleed for, bleed for me."₎ [3]
No Sir I should not be surprised though Garrick chained the ocean and lashed the winds.' [Somebody asked if it should not be lashed the ocean and chained the winds?⟩] ₍*Boswell.*₎ 'Should it not be lashed the ocean and chained the winds?' *Johnson.* 'No Sir.[4] ₍Recollect the original [in Juvenal *del*]

In Corum atque Eurum solitus sævire flagellis
Barbarus, Æolio nunquam hoc in carcere passos,
Ipsum compedibus qui vinxerat Ennosigæum.

This does very well when both the winds and the sea are personified and mentioned by their mythological names as in Juvenal; but when mentioning them in plain language, [my⟩] the application of the epithets suggested by me is the most obvious; and accordingly my friend himself in his imitation of the passage which describes Xerxes has

The waves he lashes, and enchains the wind.'₎ [5]
We talked of the [melancholy/sad⟩] melancholy end of a Gentleman who had [made away with/killed⟩] destroyed himself. *Johnson.* 'It was owing to [imaginary/imagined difficulties which had he talked with any friend/any friend if

---

[3] This quotation (in JB's hand) is superimposed upon the direction, 'Take in the passage'.

[4] Direction to the compositor, '(he repeated the latin, which take in)'. The passage that JB indicates is to be taken in appears on the verso of MS 385.

[5] At some stage between MS and revises, JB inserted here a paragraph in which 'a learned gentleman' expatiates on 'the happiness of a savage life' and is roughly handled by SJ (Hill-Powell ii. 228). As JB's notes reveal, the gentleman was William Weller Pepys, and the conversation took place on 28 April 1772 (J25, *Cat.* i. 14).

he had talked with him he could have been shewn were easily remedied. — I asked him if he thought all who killed themselves/committed suicide were mad.>] imaginary difficulties ˏin his affairsˏ which had he talked with any friend would soon have vanished.' *Boswell.* 'Do you think Sir that all who commit suicide are
5 mad?' [Sir, said he,>] *Johnson.* 'Sir, they are often not universally disordered in their intellect but one passion presses so upon them ˏthatˏ they yield to it and destroy themselves as a passionate man will stab another.'   [MS 387] [After a man>] He added 'I have often thought that after a man has taken the resolution to kill himself, it is not courage in him to do any thing however desperate because he
10 has nothing to fear.' *Goldsmith.* 'I dont see that.' *Johnson.* 'Nay but My Dear Sir why should not you see what every one else sees?' *Goldsmith.* 'It is for fear of something that he has resolved to kill himself. And will not that disposition to fear restrain him?' *Johnson.* 'It does not signify that the fear of something made him resolve. It is upon the state of his mind after the resolution is taken that I argue.
15 Suppose a man either from fear, or pride or conscience [has taken a resolution to kill himself, once that resolution is taken he has nothing to fear.>] or whatever motive has resolved to kill himself. When once the resolution is taken he has nothing to fear.   He may then go and take the King of Prussia by the nose, at the head of his army. He cannot fear the rack who is resolved to kill himself. When
20 Eustace Budgel was walking down to the Thames determined to drown himself, he might if he pleased without any [apprehension of danger/difficulty>] apprehension of danger have turned aside, and first set fire to St. James's Palace.'

ˏDR. JOHNSON to JOHN HOOLE Esq.ˏ [6]

. . . .
On [Wednesday 29 April>] [Tuesday 27 April>] Tuesday April 27 Mr.
25 Beauclerk [MS 388] and I [/after having paid a number of other visits/ called on him in the forenoon>] called on him in the morning. As we walked up Johnson's Court, I said 'I have a veneration for this Court' ['So have I', said Beauclerk.>] and was glad to find that Beauclerk had the same reverential enthusiasm. We found him alone. We talked of [a Book which had been lately circulated in presents.>]
30 Mr. Andrew Stuarts ˏelegant and plausibleˏ Letters to Lord Mansfield. *Johnson.* [They have/It has>] 'They have not answered the end. [They have/It has>] They have not been talked of. I have never heard of [it>] them. This is owing to [its>] their not being sold. People seldom read a book which is given to them; and few [get it>] are given. The way to spread a work is to sell it at a low price. No man will
35 send to buy a thing that costs even sixpence, [without an intention/unless he is>] without an intention to read it.'   ˏ*Boswell.* [It appears to me to be wrong/Was it not wrong>] 'May it not be doubted Sir whether it be proper to publish [such *del*] letters arraigning the ultimate Decision of an important Cause [by/in>] by the Supreme Judicature of the Nation?' *Johnson.* 'No Sir I do not think it was wrong
40 to publish [such>] these letters. If they are thought to do harm, why not answer

---

[6] Because it lacks the customary cues to the compositor, this insertion appears to be a note from JB to himself concerning the earlier of two letters from SJ to John Hoole (19 December 1774). This letter appears at the end of the narrative for 1774 (Hill-Powell ii. 289).

them? But they will do no harm. If Mr. Douglas [be the son/is truly/is indeed/is really the son>] be indeed the son of Lady Jane, he cannot be hurt. If he [be/is>] be not her son and yet has the great estate of the family of Douglas, he may well submit to have a pamphlet against him by Andrew Stuart. Sir I think such a publication does good as it does good to shew us the possibilities of human life. And Sir you will   5
not say that [the Douglas cause/it>] the Douglas cause was a cause of easy decision, when it divided your court as much as it could do, to be determined at all. When your Judges were seven and seven, the casting vote of the President must be given on one side or other, no matter for my argument on which, one or the other *must* be taken; as when I am to move, there is no matter which leg. And then Sir it was   10
otherwise determined here. No Sir a more dubious determination of any question cannot be figured.' [*Beauclerk*.[7] Then Sir he had but half an/the acknowledgement of Parents for that of the Father must go for nothing as he was clearly a forger of letters.' ₍*Boswell*. 'You must not mind Sir John Stewart. He was a strange lively rattling man. He never could tell truth exactly.' *Johnson*. 'Then Sir he is not to be   15
believed.'₎ *Johnson*. 'And as to Lady Jane she must be made so pious and holy — Sir were we sure of this and that she had an enlightened piety it might have much weight. But some people when they have made a vow, though it be wrong, think they must/ought to persevere.[8] del][9/a

                                                                                                                                        20

[a] I regretted that Dr. Johnson [would never g>] never took the trouble to study a question which interested nations. He would not even read a pamphlet which I wrote upon it entitled 'The Essence of the Douglas Cause' which I have reason to flatter myself had considerable effect *in favour of* Mr. *Douglas*; [I own that my zeal for Mr. Douglas was very warm so that he is indebted to me for exertions in his favour which can hardly be repaid, and therefore ₍some₎ allowance must be made   25
for my enthusiasm. *del*] [But as I do not like to look on an old friend with>] [I am

---

[7] This deleted exchange is based on JB's notes for 27 April 1773: 'Then Sir says Beauc he had by half acknowl of Pars as one clearly forger. This Mr. Johns & he made out somehow between 'em. Said I you must not mind Sr. J. He could never tell truth. Well then Sir he is not to be believed & as to Lady J. She must be made so pious & holy. Sir if we were sure of that & that was enlightened piety much. But many people when they have made vow think must persevere' (J29).

[8] These deleted comments reflect the question at the heart of the Douglas controversy: did the inconsistencies in the claims made by Sir John and Lady Jane provide evidence of deceit, or, as F. A. Pottle puts it, did these 'very gaps and discrepancies in the story ... [testify] to its essential truth'? (*Earlier Years*, p. 314). Beauclerk's description of Sir John as 'a forger of letters' reflects the widely held Hamiltonian belief that Sir John had falsified crucial testimony — four letters from a French surgeon certifying that Lady Jane had been delivered of twin sons. JB's defence of Sir John — that 'he was a strange lively rattling fellow' whose deviations from the truth should not be held against him — echoes his *Essence of the Douglas Cause* (1767), in which he portrayed Sir John as a harmless but eccentric old man 'of vivacity and dissipation ... particularly remarkable for a strange incorrect memory' (73). Like Beauclerk, SJ casts doubt on a key document in the case: the *Letters of Lady Jane Douglas*, which portrayed her as an innocent and long-suffering victim.

[9] Direction to the compositor, 'Take in paper D as a note'. This Paper Apart represents JB's final version of the many additions and deletions with which he had experimented on the verso of MS 387.

He said 'Goldsmith should not be for ever attempting [to shine/victory>] to shine in conversation. He has not temper for it, he is so much [hurt if>] mortified when he fails. [/Sir/>] Sir a game of jokes is composed partly of skill, partly of chance. A man may be beat at times by one who has not the tenth part of his wit.
5 Now Goldsmith's putting himself against another is like a man laying a hundred to one [who/when he>] who cannot spare the hundred. [It is not worth a man's while to lay>] It is not worth a man's while. A man should not lay a hundred to one unless he can [MS 389] easily spare it though he [has/should have>] has a hundred chances for him. He can get but a guinea and he may lose a hundred. Goldsmith
10 is in this state. When he contends — if he gets the better it is a very little addition to [one who has his reputation.>] a man of his literary reputation. If he does not get the better, he is [hurt>] miserably vexed.'

ʌJohnsons own superlative power of wit set him above any risk of such uneasiness. Garrick had [remarked/said>] remarked to me of him a few days
15 before, 'Rabelais and all other wits are nothing compared with Him. You may be diverted by them. But Johnson gives you a forcible hug and shakes laughter out of you [/whether you will or no/>] whether you will or no.'ʌ [1]

[Paper Apart G] [2] ʌGoldsmith however was often very fortunate in his witty contests even when he entered the lists with Johnson himself. Sir Joshua
20 Reynolds was in company with them one day when Goldsmith said that he thought he could write a good fable, mentioned the simplicity which [is required for that species of composition, and remarked the want of propriety of making animals talk in character>] that kind of composition requires, and observed that in most fables the animals introduced seldom talk in character. [For instance, said
25 he>] [He particularly gave as an instance>] 'For instance' said he 'the fable of the little fishes [ʌ(said he)ʌ del] who [seeing>] saw birds fly over their heads and envying them petitioned Jupiter to be changed into birds, [Now said he>] the skill continued he [the skill del] consists in making [those little fishes>] them talk like little fishes.' While he indulged himself in this fanciful [and ingenious del] reverie,
30 he observed Johnson [scratching>] shaking his sides, and laughing [at him del].

———

not one of those who desert>] [But as I am one of those who remain steady to what they have once fairly espoused, I will now after more than twenty years renew my declaration of belief in the truth of his legal filiation, and shall only add>] *of whose legitimate filiation I was then and am still firmly convinced.* Let *me* add that [no
35 proposition>] no *fact* can be more respectably ascertained than by a Judgement of the most august tribunal in the world, a Judgement in which Lord Mansfield and Lord Camden united in 1769 and [against>] from which only five of a numerous body entered a [dissent>] Protest.[a1]

---

[1] Direction to the compositor, 'Take in paper G'.
[2] This Paper Apart bears the heading, 'To be taken in on page opposite to p. 389'.

[a1] Words in italics are revisions in the hand of EM.

Upon which [suddenly turning he smartly proceeded, 'Why Dr. Johnson, if you were to make little fishes talk you would make them talk like whales.'>] he smartly proceeded, 'Why Dr. Johnson, this is not so easy as you seem to think, for if you were to make those little fishes talk they would talk like whales.'

Johnson [in>] though remarkable for his great variety of composition never   5
exercised his talents in fable [unless we admit his Tale>] [except in his beautiful Tale/except we allow his beautiful>], except we allow his beautiful Tale published in Mrs. Williams's Miscellanies to be of that species. I have [indeed/also>] however found among his manuscript collections the following sketch of one: 'Glowworm lying in the garden saw a candle in a neighbouring palace, — and   10
complained of the littleness of his own light — another observed — wait a little — soon dark — have outlasted poll [many] of these glaring lights which only are brighter as they haste to nothing.'$_\lambda$[3]

[MS 389 resumed] On thursday [29 April I found him remarkably well and he proposed that he would walk with me to General Oglethorpe's in Lower   15
Grosvenor Street where we were to dine. As we were walking through Berkeley Square, Sir Joshua Reynolds and Dr. Goldsmith hailed us from Sir Joshua's coach and made us come in/up and take a seat. They told us they were at some loss for they did not perfectly recollect where the General's house was. 'So' said I 'you have taken us up as guides.' Said Johnson very pleasantly, 'I wondered indeed at   20
their great civility.' At the General's we/*undeciphered word* found one Lady Miss Lockwood[4] Mr. Thrale, and Mr. Langton in company with Dr. Goldsmith.>] April 29 I dined with him at General Oglethorpe's where were Sir Joshua Reynolds Mr. Langton Dr. Goldsmith and Mr. Thrale. I was very desireous to get Dr. Johnson absolutely fixed in his resolution to go with me to the Hebrides this year,   25
and I told him that I had [just received a letter from Principal/Dr. Robertson [MS 390] upon the subject/wishing he would come. 'Let us hear it,' said he. I read it and he was much pleased and I was satisfied that he was now absolutely resolved that he would this year make out his long intended Tour.>] received a letter[5] from Dr. Robertson the historian [MS 390] upon the subject with which he was much   30
pleased and now talked in such a manner of his long intended Tour that I was satisfied he meant to visit Scotland this year.

The custom of [the people of Otaheite to eat dogs>] eating dogs at Otaheite being mentioned Goldsmith observed that this was also a custom in China [(*Johnson*. I did not know that.) and *del*] that a dog=butcher is as common there as   35

---

[3] In the third edition, EM inserts a note on SJ's poem, the text of which has not been recovered (*Poems* 1964, p. 394). See also *Poems* 1974, p. 471.

[4] The 'Miss Lockwood' present at Oglethorpe's on 29 April had also dined there with JB, SJ, and Goldsmith on 13 April (J28). She had been invited as part of a matchmaking scheme designed by JB and Oglethorpe to put the financially troubled Goldsmith 'in a comfortable situation for life' (JB to Oglethorpe, 14 August 1773/MS L995). By autumn, however, the plan had come to nothing. Writing to JB in the Hebrides, Oglethorpe lamented that 'Goldsmith was by cruel Fates deny'd ... [from] ... complying with my frequent Invitations' (16 September 1773/MS C2113). During the summer and autumn of 1773, Goldsmith was suffering from a disease of the urinary tract (Ralph Wardle, *Oliver Goldsmith*, 1957, pp. 264, 266).

[5] Deleted query in the margin: 'Shd it not be quoted here?'

any other butcher, and that when he walks [out/out of his quarter>] abroad all the
dogs fall on him. *Johnson*. ₍'That is not owing to his killing dogs Sir.₎ I remember
a Butcher at Lichfield whom a dog that was in the house where I lived allways
attacked. It is the smell of carnage which provokes this, no matter what animals
5 he has killed.' *Goldsmith*. [/Yes/>] 'Yes there is a general abhorrence in animals at
the signs of massacre. If you put a tub full of blood into a stable, [the horses are/a
horse is>] the horses are like to [go/run>] go mad.' *Johnson*. 'I doubt that.'
Goldsmith. [/Nay/>] 'Nay 'tis a fact well authenticated.' *Thrale*. 'You had better
[try/prove>] prove it before you put it into your Book on Natural History. You may
10 do it in my stable if you will.' *Johnson*. 'Nay Sir, I would not have him [prove it/do
that>] prove it. If he [takes>] is content to take his information from others, he
may get through his book with little trouble [MS 391] and without [/much/>] much
endangering his reputation. But if he makes experiments for so comprehensive a
Book as his, there would be no end ₍to them₎. His [credit might/wo suffer on
15 account of erroneous>] erroneous assertions would then fall upon himself, and he
might be blamed for not having made experiments as to every particular.'

₍The character of Mallet having been introduced and spoken of slightingly by
Goldsmith, *Johnson*. 'Why Sir, Mallet had talents enough to keep his literary
reputation alive as long as he himself lived, and that let me tell you is doing a good
20 deal.' *Goldsmith*. 'But I cannot agree that it was so. His literary reputation was
[dead/cold>] dead long before his natural death. I consider [a man's/an
Authour's>] an Authour's literary reputation to be alive only while his name will
ensure him a good price for his copy from the Booksellers. I will get you (to
Johnson) a hundred guineas for any thing whatever that you shall write if you put
25 your name to it.'₎

[Of Dr. Goldsmith's new Play/Comedy *She Stoops to Conquer* he said 'I>] Dr.
Goldsmith's new Play 'She Stoops to Conquer' being mentioned *Johnson*. 'I know
of no Comedy for many years that has so much exhilarated an audience, that has
answered so much the great end of Comedy, making an audience merry.'

30 Goldsmith having said that Garrick's Compliment to the Queen which he
introduced into the Play of [*The Chances*>] 'The Chances' which he had altered
and revised this year was mean and gross flattery. *Johnson*. ₍'Why Sir₎ I would not
write, I would not give solemnly under my hand a Character beyond what I
thought really true; but a speech on the stage let it flatter ever so extravagantly is
35 formular. It has [allways been/been so long>] always been formular [MS 392] to
flatter Kings and Queens, so much so, that even in our church service we have our
most religious King" used indiscriminately whoever is King. Nay they even flatter
themselves "we have been graciously pleased." No modern flattery however is so
gross as that of the Augustan Age where the Emperour was deified *Presens Divus
40 habebitur Augustus*. And as to meaness (rising into warmth) how is it mean in a
player — a Showman — a fellow who exhibits himself for a shilling to flatter his
Queen. The Attempt indeed was dangerous; for if it had missed, what became of
Garrick and ₍what became of₎ the Queen? As Sir William Temple says of a Great
General [it is necessary not only/it is not only necessary>] it is necessary not only
45 that [he design in a great manner/well, but that he have success.>] his designs
should be formed in a masterly manner, but that they should be attended with

success. Sir, it was right [in an age/at a time›] at a time when the Royal family is
not generally liked, to let it [be seen/appear›] be seen that [the people like at least
one of them/at least one of them is liked›] the people like at least one of them.' *Sir
Joshua Reynolds*. 'I do not [see›] perceive why the profession of a Player should be
[MS 393] despised, [for the purpose of all the employments of mankind is surely/is   5
ultimately to produce amusement/for all the employments of mankind are subser-
vient to the great end of producing pleasure›] for the great and ultimate end of all
the employments of mankind is to produce amusement. Garrick produces more
[amusement/entertainment›] amusement than any body.' *Boswell*. [Garrick is not
so bad as a Lawyer who shews himself for two guineas, and will speak/maintain any   10
nonsense.›] 'You say Dr. Johnson that Garrick exhibits himself for a shilling. In
this respect he is only on a footing with the lawyer who exhibits himself for his fee
and even will maintain any nonsense or absurdity if the Case requires it. Garrick
refuses a play or a part which he does not like. A Lawyer never refuses.' *Johnson*.
'Why ₍Sir₎ what does this prove? Only that a Lawyer is worse. Boswell is now like   15
Jack in the Tale of a tub who when he is puzzled [in/with/by›] by an argument
hangs himself. He thinks [I'll/I shall›] I shall cut him down but [I'll/I shall›] I'll
let him hang' (laughing ₍vociferously₎). *Sir Joshua Reynolds*. 'Mr Boswell thinks
that [a lawyers being an acknowledged honourable profession if he proves the
Player's to be more honourable, he proves his argument.›] the profession of a   20
lawyer being unquestionably honourable if he can shew the profession of a Player
to be more honourable, he proves his argument.'

On friday [30 April›] April 30 I dined with him at Mr. Beauclerk's where were
Lord Charlemont Sir Joshua Reynolds and some more [company.›] members of
the Literary Club whom he had obligingly invited to meet me, as I was this evening   25
to be balloted for as candidate for admission into that [very *del*] distinguished
society. Johnson had done me the honour to propose me, and Beauclerk was very
zealous for me.

Goldsmith being mentioned — *Johnson*. 'It is amazing how little Goldsmith
knows. He seldom comes where he is not more ignorant than any one else.' [MS   30
394] *Sir Joshua Reynolds*. 'Yet there is no man whose company is more liked.'
Johnson. 'To be sure Sir. When people find a man of the most distinguished
abilities as a Writer, their inferiour while he is with them it must be [very
pleasing/highly gratifying›] highly gratifying ₍to them₎. What Goldsmith
[/comically/›] comically says of himself is very true he allways gets the better when   35
he argues alone; meaning that he is master of a subject in his study and can write
well upon it, but when he [is in company›] [gets into company›] comes into
company grows confused and unable to talk. Take him as a Poet, his [*Traveller*›]
Traveller is a very [Capital work/performance›] fine performance ay and so is his
[*Deserted Village*] Deserted Village were it not sometimes too much [the/an›] the   40
echo of his Traveller. [Take him as a Poet — as a Comick Writer — as an
Historian — he is very able.›] Whether indeed we take him as a Poet — as a
Comick Writer — or as an Historian — he stands in the first class.' *Boswell*.
'Historian! My Dear Sir! you surely will not [call his short little compilation of the
Roman History equal to the Works of other historians›] rank his compilation of   45
the Roman History with the Works of other historians [now living/of this age›] of

this age.' *Johnson.* 'Why who are before him?' *Boswell.* 'Hume — Robertson —
Lord Lyttleton.' *Johnson.* [(growing warm and jealous of the scotch)>] (his
antipathy to the scotch beginning to rise) 'I have not read Hume.　But
[surely/doubtless>] doubtless Goldsmiths History is better than the *verbiage* of
5　Robertson or the foppery of Dalrymple.'　*Boswell.* 'Will you not admit the
superiority of Robertson, in [whom we/whose history we>] whose history we *[MS
395]* find such penetration — such painting!' *Johnson.* 'Sir you must consider how
that penetration and that painting are [exerted/employed>] employed. It is not
History, it is imagination. He who describes what he never saw draws from fancy.
10　Robertson [paints/draws>] paints minds as Sir Joshua paints faces in a
history=piece. [He>] [The Painter>] He imagines an heroick countenance. You
must look upon [his>] Robertson's work as Romance and try it by [another>] that
standard. History it is not. ‸Besides‸ Sir it is [the/a>] the great excellence [of/in>]
of a writer to put into his book as much as his Book will hold. Goldsmith has done
15　this in his History. Now Robertson might have put twice as much into his Book.
Robertson is like a man who has packed [up money>] gold in wool. The wool takes
up more room than the [money>] gold. No Sir I allways thought Robertson would
be crushed by his own weight, — would be buried [under/by>] under his own
ornaments. Goldsmith tells you [shortly/in a short space>] shortly all you want to
20　know. Robertson [detains you/keeps you>] detains you a great deal too long. No
man will read [Robertson>] [Robertson's cumbrous narrative>] Robertson's cumbrous detail a second time; but Goldsmiths plain narrative will please again and
again. I would say to Robertson what an old tutor of a College said to one of *[MS
396]* his pupils — "Read over your [compositions/sermons>] compositions, and
25　wherever you [find/see/meet with>] meet with a passage which you think [very>]
particularly fine, strike it out." Goldsmith's abridgement is better than that of
Lucius Florus or Eutropius and I will venture to say that if you compare him with
Vertot in the same [places/parts>] places [as to Rome>] of the Roman history you
will find him better. Sir He has the art of compiling, and of [writing>] [writing
30　every thing he has to say>] saying every thing he has to say in a pleasing manner.
He is now writing a Natural History, and will make it as entertaining as a Persian
Tale.'

　　‸I cannot dismiss the present topick without observing that it is probable that
Dr. Johnson who often owned that he 'talked for victory' rather urged plausible
35　objections to Dr. Robertson's excellent historical Works in the ardour of contest,
than expressed his real and decided opinion for it is not easy to suppose that he
should so widely differ from the rest of the Literary World.‸

　　‸*Johnson.*‸ I remember once [walking/being>] being with Goldsmith in Westminster Abbey. While we surveyed the Poet's Corner I said to him,
40　　　　　Forsitan et nostrum nomen miscebitur illis.[6]

---

　　[6] By the stage of the revises, a footnote had been added identifying the source of the
quotation: 'Ovid. de Art. Amand. l. iii. v. 13'.

When we got to Temple=bar, he stopped me pointed to the heads upon it[7] and
slyly whispered me

    Forsitan et nostrum nomen miscebitur *illis*.[8/a]

Johnson praised John Bunyan highly. 'His [*Pilgrim's Progress*⟩] "Pilgrim's
Progress" [/said he/ *del*] has great merit both for invention imagination and the   5
conduct of the [story/work⟩] story ⟨and it has had the best evidence of its merit
the general and continued approbation of mankind. Few books I believe have had
a more extensive sale.⟩ It is remarkable that it begins very much like the Poem of
Dante yet there was no translation of [it.⟩] Dante when Bunyan wrote. There [MS
397] is reason to believe that he had read Spencer'.   10

    [A plan for having monuments⟩] [A proposition which had been in agitation
for having monuments erected to eminent⟩] A Proposition which had been
agitated that monuments to eminent persons should for the time to come be
erected in St. Paul's Church as well as in Westminster Abbey was mentioned, and
it was asked who should [have the honour of having his monument first erected.⟩]   15
be honoured by having his monument first erected there. Some=body suggested
Pope. *Johnson*, 'Why Sir as Pope was a Roman Catholick I would not have his
[come/erected⟩] come first. I think Milton's rather should have the precedence.[9]
I think more highly of him now than I did at twenty. There is more thinking in
him and in Butler than in any of our poets.'   20

    Some of the company expressed a wonder why the Authour of so excellent a
Book as [*The Whole Duty of Man*⟩] 'The Whole Duty of Man' should conceal
himself. *Johnson*. 'There may be different reasons figured for this, any one of
which would be very sufficient. He may have been a Clergyman, and may have
thought that his religious counsels would have less weight when known to come   25
from a man whose profession was Theology. He may have been a man whose
practice was not suitable to his principles so that his character [might/would⟩]
might injure the effect of his Book, which he had written in a season [MS 398] of

---

    [a] In allusion to Dr. Johnson's supposed political principles.[a1]

---

    [7] The annotation in Hill-Powell (ii. 238 n. 3) is misleading: the heads on Temple Bar
were those of Francis Townley and George Fletcher, officers of the Manchester regiment
that had fought in the '45 (*Corres. Walpole*, ix. 46 n. 2). They had been executed on 30 July
1746, along with seven other officers of the regiment; the heads of three of these were
exposed in Manchester (GM 16, 1746, p. 437; *A Genuine Account of the Behaviour,
Confession, and Dying Words of Francis Townly ... for High Treason*, 1746). The fact that
Goldsmith is pointing not to Scots but to English Jacobites gives the political import of his
gesture added significance.

    [8] This line is followed by a series of asterisks that have been deleted. At one stage, JB
apparently considered inserting a passage here.

    [9] In the second edition, a footnote is keyed to 'precedence': 'Here is another instance of
his high admiration of Milton as a Poet, notwithstanding his just abhorrence of that sour
Republican's political principles. His candour and discrimination are equally conspicuous.
Let us hear no more of his "injustice to Milton"'.

    [a1] The note in the revises reads, 'In allusion to Dr. Johnson's supposed political
principles, and perhaps his own.'

penitence. Or he may have been a man of rigid self=denial so that he would have no reward for his pious labours, while in this world, but refer it all to a future state.'

[The Gentlemen went away to their Club, and as one blackball could exclude I sat in such anxious suspence as even the charms of Lady Diana Beauclerk's
5   conversation could hardly/not quite relieve. Mr. Beauclerk's coach returned for me in less than half an hour with a note from him that I was chosen/elected. I question if any election now could give me a higher sensation.>] [The Gentlemen went away to their Club, and in a short time I received the agreable intelligence that I was chosen.>] The Gentlemen went away to their Club, and I was left at
10   Beauclerks till the fate of my election should be announced to me.[1] In a short time I received the agreable intelligence that I was chosen. I hastened to the [Turk's=head in Gerard Street Soho>] place of meeting, and was introduced to such a Society as can seldom be found. [Mr. Edmund Burke — Dr. Nugent — Mr. (now Sir William) Jones. There were also present I remember Mr. Garrick Dr.
15   Goldsmith and the company with whom I had dined.>] Mr. Edmund Burke, whom I then saw for the first time,[2] and whose splendid talents had long made me ardently wish for his acquaintance, Dr. Nugent, Mr. Garrick Dr. Goldsmith Mr. (now[3] Sir William) Jones and the company with whom I had dined. ₍Upon my entrance Johnson [who had proposed me as a Member *del*] placed himself behind
20   a chair on which he leant as on a desk or pulpit, and with humourous formality gave me a *Charge*, pointing out the [duties incumbent upon me>] conduct expected from me as a good member of this Club.₎

Goldsmith produced some very absurd verses which had been publickly rehearsed to an audience for money.[4] [Mr. Burke read them aloud to the Club, and
25   made us laugh heartily. *del*] *Johnson*. 'I can match this nonsense. There was a Poem called [*Eugenio*>] 'Eugenio' which came out some years ago and concluded [MS 399] thus

> And now ye trifling self=assuming elves
> Brimful of pride, of nothing, of yourselves,
30   > Survey Eugenio, view him o'er and o'er
> Then sink into yourselves and be no more.[5]

---

[1] In the second edition, a sentence is inserted here that reflects the sentiment of the deleted MS passage: 'I sat in a state of anxiety which even the charming conversation of Lady Di Beauclerk could not entirely dissipate'.

[2] The rough notes for JB's London jaunt of the previous year show that he had met Burke at a dinner given by Sir Joshua Reynolds on 6 May 1772 (J25).

[3] Since Jones had died in 1794, the third edition substitutes 'afterwards' for 'now'.

[4] JB's notes suggest that Goldsmith 'produced' *The Jesuit* (1773), an ode by the Rev. George Marriott. The same episode is included in the anecdotes from Bennet Langton that JB inserted at the beginning of 1780 (Hill-Powell iv. 13; MS Paper Apart Langtoniana).

[5] In the second edition, a footnote is inserted and keyed to 'more': 'Dr. Johnson's memory here was not perfectly accurate: "Eugenio" does not conclude thus. There are eight more lines after the last of these quoted by him; and the passage which he meant to recite is as follows:

"Say now ye fluttering, poor assuming elves,
"Stark full of pride, of folly, of — yourselves;

Nay Dryden in his Poem on the Royal Society has these lines
> Then we upon our globe's last verge shall go
> And see the ocean leaning on the sky
> From thence our rolling neighbours we shall know
> And on the lunar world securely pry.   5

Talking of [puns/that species of wit called a pun›] puns, Johnson ‚who had a great contempt for that species of wit₎ deigned to allow that there was one good pun in [Menagiana›] 'Menagiana.'

    [cor de fier del][6]

Much pleasant conversation passed which Johnson [relished/seemed to rel‑   10
ish›] relished with great good humour. But [his conversation alone/only his sayings›] his conversation alone or what led to [it/them›] it or was interwoven with it [that del] is the business of this [record›] work.

On saturday [1 May›] May 1 we dined by ourselves at our old rendesvous the Mitre tavern. He was placid but not much disposed to talk. He observed that [the   15
irish mixed more/better with the english than the scotch did; their language was nearer to english as a proof of which they did/do very well as Players which Scotchmen could/do not›] 'The irish mix better with the english than the scotch do; their language is nearer to english as a proof of which they succeed very well as Players which Scotchmen do not. Then Sir they have not that extreme national‑   20
ity which we find in the Scotch. [Sir I will do you the justice›] I will do you Boswell, the justice to say that you [MS 400] are the most unscottified of your countrymen. You are almost the only instance of a Scotchman that I have known who did not at every other [word/sentence›] sentence bring in some other scotchman.' [Upon this subject he once said with exquisite wit to Dr. Barnard now   25

    "Say where's the wretch of all your impious crew
    "Who dares confront his character to view?
    "Behold Eugenio, view him o'er and o'er,
    "Then sink into yourselves, and be no more.
Mr. Reed informs me that the authour of Eugenio, a Wine Merchant at Wrexham in the Denbighshire, soon after its publication, viz. 17th May, 1737, cut his own throat, and that it appears by Swift's Works, that the poem had been shewn to him and received some of his corrections. Johnson had read "Eugenio" on his first coming to town, for we see it mentioned in one of his letters to Mr. Cave, which has been inserted in this work.'

[6] This deleted reference, which functioned as a cryptic memorandum, was replaced in proof by an explanatory final clause, 'I think on the word corps.' For the second edition, JB inserted a note keyed to 'corps' that overturned this supposition: 'Probably I have mistaken the word, and imagined it to be Corps, from its similarity of sound to the real one. For an accurate and shrewd unknown gentleman, to whom I am indebted for some remarks on my work, observes on this passage — "Q. if not on the word Fort? A vociferous French preacher said of Bourdaloue, "Il preche fort bien, et moi bien fort." — Menagiana. See also Anecdotes Litteraires Article Bourdaloue.' The 'shrewd unknown gentleman' behind this note had anonymously sent JB a list of 'Queries? arising from the Life of Dr. Johnson' together with suggestions for revisions (Corr. 2, pp. 591–93). By the stage of the third edition, however, JB had acquired additional information from James Abercrombie of Philadelphia, who disputed what the anonymous correspondent had suggested and supported JB's original conjecture (Corr. 2, pp. 532–39). Accordingly, the note keyed to 'corps' was rewritten; it appears in the third edition as it does in Hill-Powell.

Bishop of Kilaloe who expressed an apprehension that, were he to visit Ireland he might be as severe upon the irish as upon the Scotch. 'No Sir; the irish are a fair people; they never speak well of one another.' *del*]

5   We drank tea with Mrs. Williams. [I consulted him as to/on the Question⟩] I introduced a Question [of Patronage *del*] which [is/has been⟩] has been so much agitated in the Church of Scotland ⟨whether the claim of Lay Patrons to present Ministers to parishes be well=founded, and supposing it to be well=founded, whether it ought to be exercised without the concurrence of the people. That Church is composed of a series of judicatures: a Presbytery — a Synod and finally
10   a General Assembly before all of which this matter may be contended; [those who constitute the lower judicatures *del*] and in some cases the Presbytery having refused to induct or *settle* as they call it the person presented by the Patron it has been found necessary to appeal to the General Assembly.⟩ He said I might see the Subject [well=handled⟩] well treated in the 'Defence of Pluralities'; and although
15   he thought that a Patron should exercise his right with tenderness to the inclinations of the people of a parish, he was very clear as to [the⟩] his right. [At my request he did me the favour to dictate to me the following Argument upon the subject.⟩] Then supposing the question to be pleaded before the General Assembly, he dictated to me what follows.[7]

. . . .

20   On friday [7 May⟩] May 7 I breakfasted with him at Mr. Thrales ⟨in the Borough⟩. [I attempted to defend a Lady against whom her husband had obtained a sentence of divorce.⟩] While we were alone I endeavoured as well as I could to apologise for a Lady who had been divorced from her husband by Act of Parliament. I said that he had used her very ill, had behaved brutally to her, and that she
25   could not continue to live with him without having her delicacy contaminated, that all affection for him was thus destroyed [MS 401] that the essence of [conjugal/matrimonial⟩] conjugal union being gone there remained only a cold form a mere civil obligation; that she was in the prime of life with [qualities/every quality⟩] qualities to produce happiness [which it would be a great pity should be
30   lost/which ought not to be lost⟩] [that it was a great pity should be lost⟩] that these ought not to be lost, and that the gentleman on whose account she was divorced had gained her heart [in these circumstances⟩] while thus unhappily situated. Seduced perhaps by the charms of the Lady in question I thus attempted to palliate what I was sensible could not be justified for when I had finished my harangue, my
35   venerable friend gave me a proper check. [*Johnson.* My⟩] 'My Dear Sir never [accustom your mind/allow yourself⟩] accustom your mind to mingle virtue and vice. The woman's a whore and there's an end on't.'[8]
He described the Father of one of [our/his⟩] his friends thus 'Sir he was so [affluent⟩] exuberant a talker at [County/publick⟩] publick meetings that the
40   Gentlemen of his county were affraid of him. No business could be done for his declamation.'

---

[7] Direction to the compositor, 'Take [it in⟩] in Paper marked P. and put inverted commas to the beginning of each paragraph'. This Paper Apart no longer forms part of the *Life* MS.

[8] JB's notes read: 'Good break. Angry at me for defend Lady Di. Go to Scot. Go to Scot! I never heard talk so foolishly' (J29).

He would not give me ∧full∧ credit when I [told them how⟩] mentioned that I had carried on [some conversation/a little time⟩] a short conversation by signs with some Esquimaux who were [now/then⟩] then in London particularly ∧with∧ one of them who was a Priest. He thought I could not make them understand ∧me∧. No man was more incredulous as to [particulars⟩] particular facts which were at all extraordinary and therefore no man was more [scrupulously/nicely⟩] scrupulously inquisitive in order to [sift⟩] discover the truth. [His faith in Revelation was founded upon a strict inquiry. *del*]

I dined with him this day at the house of my friends, Messieurs Edward and Charles Dilly *[MS 402]* Booksellers in the [Poultry with their elder brother Squire Dilly, Dr. Goldsmith Mr. Langton Mr. Claxton Rev. Dr. Mayo a steady calvinist teacher, Rev. Mr. Toplady, Rev. Mr. Temple who wrote the character of Gray adopted first by Mr. Mason and afterwards/then by Dr. Johnson.⟩][9] Poultry; there were present their elder brother Mr. Dilly of Bedfordshire, Dr. Goldsmith Mr. Langton Mr. Claxton Rev. Dr. Mayo a dissenting Minister, Rev. Mr. Toplady, and my friend the Rev. Mr. Temple.

Hawkesworth's Compilation of the voyage/s/[1] to the south sea being mentioned *Johnson.* 'Sir if you talk of it as a subject of commerce it will be gainful if as a Book that is to increase human knowledge I believe there will not be much of that. Hawkesworth can tell only what [the Voyagers have/Banks has told him and they have/he has not found much/found very little, only/but one animal I think⟩] the Voyagers have told him and they have found very little, only one new animal I think.' *Boswell.* 'But many insects ∧Sir∧.' *Johnson.* ∧'Why Sir, as to insects,∧ Ray reckons of british insects twenty thousand species. [They/Banks⟩] They might have staid at home and discovered enough in that way.'

Talking of birds I mentioned Mr. Daines Barrington's ingenious [Essay/Paper⟩] Essay against the [system/notion⟩] received notion of their migration. *Johnson.* [Supposing the migration of certain birds to be true, we have as good evidence for it as it can admit.⟩] 'I think we have as good evidence for the migration of woodcocks as can be desired. [We see them disappear⟩] [They disappear⟩] We find they disappear at a certain time of the year and appear again at a certain time of the year, *[MS 403]* and some of them when weary in their flight, [have been known to alight/lighted⟩] have been known to alight on the rigging of ships far out at sea.' — One of the company observed that there had been instances of some of them found in summer in Essex. *Johnson.* Sir that strengthens our/the[2] argument. [*Exceptio firmat/probat regulam*⟩] *Exceptio probat regulam.* [Some being found/From instances of only some being found⟩] Some being found [shews/we may infer⟩] shews that if all remained many would be found. A few sick or lame ones may remain.'

---

[9] In a letter to JB, 3 September 1771, W. J. Temple included an epitaphic description of Thomas Gray, who had died on 30 July (*Corr.* 6, p. 297). JB sent this 'character' to the *Lond. Mag.* (March 1772, xli. 140); it was then adopted by William Mason in his *Poems of Mr. Gray; to which are prefixed Memoirs of his Life and Writings* (1775, pp. 402–04). At JB's urging, SJ included the character in his 'Life' of Gray (*Lives* iii. 429–31). See *ante Life MS* i. 10 n. 9.

[1] The alternative is resolved by the printing of 'voyages' in the revises.

[2] The alternative is resolved by the printing of 'our' in the revises.

Goldsmith. 'There is a partial migration of the Swallows, the stronger ones migrate, the [others/rest>] others do not [/migrate/ *del*].'

    Boswell. 'I am well assured that the people of Otaheite who have the bread=tree, the fruit of which serves them readily for bread laughed heartily when

5   they [heard all>] were informed of the tedious process necessary [with/among>] with us to have bread: [as sowing reaping threshing grinding baking.>] plowing sowing harrowing reaping threshing grinding baking.' *Johnson.* 'Why Sir, all ignorant savages will laugh when they are told of the advantages of civilised life. Were you to tell men who live without houses, how we pile brick upon brick and

10   rafter upon rafter, and that after a house is [up>] raised to a certain heigth, a man tumbles [off/down>] off /a scaffold/[3] and breaks his neck, he would laugh heartily at [the folly of/us for>] our folly in building; but it does not follow that men are better without houses. No Sir, ([lifting>] holding up a slice *[MS 404]* of a good loaf). This is better than the bread=tree.'

15   He repeated an argument [against the reason of animals/the notion of animals having reason>] which is to be found in his Rambler against the notion that the brute creation is endowed with the faculty of reason. 'Birds build by instinct; they never improve. They build their first nest as well as any one [after>] that they ever build.' *Goldsmith.* 'Yet we see if you take away a bird's nest with the eggs in it [she

20   will make a slighter nest and lay again/when she is to lay again she will make a slighter nest.>] she will make a slighter nest and lay again.' *Johnson.* 'Sir that is because at first she has full time and makes her nest deliberately. In the case you mention she is pressed to lay and must therefore make her nest quickly and consequently it will be slight.' *Goldsmith.* 'The nidification of birds is what is least

25   known in natural history, though one of the most curious things in it.'

    I introduced the subject of Toleration. *Johnson.* 'Every society has a right to preserve publick peace and order, and therefore has a good right to prohibit the propagation of opinions which have a dangerous tendency. To say the *Magistrate* has this right is using an inadequate word. It is the *Society* for which the Magistrate

30   is Agent. He may be morally or theologically wrong in restraining the propagation of opinions which he *[MS 405]* thinks dangerous, but he is politically right.' *Mayo.* 'I am of opinion Sir that every man [has a right>] is entitled to liberty of conscience in religion, and that the Magistrate cannot restrain that ⟨right⟩.' *Johnson.* 'Yes Sir—I agree with you. Every man has a right to liberty of conscience,

35   and with that the Magistrate cannot interfere. People confound liberty of thinking with liberty of talking, [and with>] nay with liberty of preaching. Every man has a physical right to think as he pleases; for it cannot be discovered how he thinks. He has not a moral right, for he ought to inform himself. But Sir no member of a society has a right to *teach* any doctrine contrary to what that society

40   [holds/hold>] holds to be [right>] true. The Magistrate I say may be wrong in what he thinks, but while he thinks himself right he may and ought to enforce what he thinks.' *Mayo.* 'Then Sir we are to remain allways in errour and truth never can prevail, and the Magistrate was right in persecuting the first Christians.' *Johnson.* 'Sir the only method by which ⟨religious⟩ truth can be established is by martyr-

---

[3] The optional word, which JB left unresolved, is printed in the revises.

dom. The Magistrate has a right to enforce what he thinks, and he who is conscious of the truth has a right to suffer. I am affraid there is *[MS 406]* no other [way/test>] way [/of ascertaining the truth/>] of ascertaining the truth but by persecution on the one hand and enduring it on the other.' *Goldsmith*. 'But how is a man to [do?>] act, Sir? ⋏Though firmly convinced of the truth of his doctrine,⋌ 5 may he not think it wrong to expose himself to persecution? [Has he a right to occasion voluntary suicide/Is it not like committing voluntary suicide?>] Has he a right to do so? Is it not as it were committing voluntary suicide?' *Johnson*. 'Sir, as to voluntary suicide as you call it, there are twenty thousand men in an army who will go without scruple to be shot at and mount a breach for five=pence a day.' 10 *Goldsmith*. 'But have they a moral right to do [this/so>] this?' *Johnson*. 'Nay Sir, if you [wont/will not>] will not take the [universal/general>] universal opinion of mankind I have nothing to say. If Mankind cannot defend their own way of thinking I cannot defend it. Sir if a man is in doubt whether it would be better for him to expose himself to martyrdom or not, he should not do it. He must be 15 convinced that he has a delegation from heaven.' *Goldsmith*. 'I would consider whether there is the greater chance of good or evil [on/upon>] upon the whole. If I see a man who has fallen into a well I would wish to help him out; but if there is a greater probability that he shall pull me in than that I shall pull him out I would not attempt it. So were I to go to Turkey I might wish to convert the Grand Signor 20 to the Christian faith. *[MS 407]* But when I considered that I should probably be put to death without effectuating my purpose in any degree, I should keep myself quiet.' *Johnson*. 'Sir you must consider that we have perfect and imperfect obligations. Perfect obligations which are generally not to do something, are clear and positive, as "thou shalt not kill." But charity for instance is not defineable by 25 limits. It is [a/our>] a duty to give to the poor; but no man can say how much another should give to the poor, or when [one>] a man has given too little to save his soul. In the same manner, it is [a/our>] a duty to instruct the ignorant, and of consequence to convert infidels to Christianity. But no [/ordinary/ man//man in the common course of things/>] man in the common course of things is obliged to 30 carry this to [the/such a>] such a degree [of incurring/as to incur>] as to incur the danger of martyrdom, as no man is obliged to strip himself to the shirt in order to give charity. I have said that a man must be persuaded [of his having/that he has>] that he has a particular delegation from heaven.' *Goldsmith*. 'How is this to be known? Our first Reformers [who were>] [were>] who were burnt for not believing 35 bread and wine to be Christ.' *Johnson*. ⋏(interrupting him)⋌ 'Sir they were not burnt for not believing bread and wine to be Christ but for insulting those who [believed/did believe>] did believe it. And Sir, when the first Reformers began, they did *[MS 408]* not intend to be martyred. As many of them ran away as could.' *Boswell*. 'But Sir there was your countryman Elwal who you told me challenged 40 King George with his black=guards and his red=guards.' *Johnson*. 'My countryman Elwal Sir should have been put in the stocks a [good>] proper pulpit for him and he'd have had [audience enough>] a numerous audience. A man who preaches in the stocks will allways [have hearers enough/have plenty of hearers>] have hearers enough'. *Boswell*. 'But Elwal thought himself in the right.' *Johnson*. 'We are not 45 providing for mad people. There are places for them in the neighbourhood' (meaning Moorfields). [ᴧ*Dr.*ᴧ *del*] *Mayo* 'But Sir is it not very hard that I should not be allowed to teach my children what I really believe to be the truth.' *Johnson*. 'Why Sir you might contrive to teach your children *extra scandalum*; but Sir the Magistrate if he knows it has a right to restrain you. Suppose you teach your

5   children to be thieves.' [ᴧ*Dr.*ᴧ *del*] *Mayo* 'This is making a joke of the subject.' *Johnson*. 'Nay Sir, take it thus — that you teach them the community of goods, for which there are as many plausible arguments as for most erroneous doctrines. You teach them that all things at first were in common *[MS 409]* and that no man had a right to any thing but as he laid his hands upon it; and this [is still⟩] still is or

10   ought to be the rule amongst mankind. Here, ᴧSirᴧ, you sap the great principle in society: Property. And don't you think the Magistrate would have a right to [stop you /from teaching this/⟩] prevent you? Or suppose you should teach your children the [notions/doctrine⟩] notions of the [Preadamites⟩] Adamites, and they should [get/go⟩] run naked into the streets, would not the magistrate have a right to flog

15   'em into their doublets?' [ᴧ*Dr.*ᴧ *del*] *Mayo* 'I think the Magistrate has no right to interfere till there is some ouvert act.' *Boswell*. 'So, though he sees [a Blunderbuss charging⟩] an ennemy to the state charging a blunderbuss, he is not to interfere till it is fired off.' ᴧ*Dr.*ᴧ *Mayo* 'He must be sure of its direction against the State.' *Johnson*. 'The Magistrate is to judge of that. He has no right to restrain your

20   thinking, because the evil centers in yourself. If a man were sitting at this table and chopping off his fingers the Magistrate as guardian of the community has no authority to restrain him however he might do it from kindness as a parent. Though indeed [/upon more consideration I think/⟩] upon more consideration I think he may, as it is probable that he who is chopping off his own fingers may soon

25   proceed to chop off [other peoples⟩] those of other people. If I think it right to steal Mr. Dilly's Plate, I am a bad man, but he can say nothing to me. If I make an open declaration that I think so, he will keep me *[MS 410]* out of his house. If I put to my hand, I shall be sent to Newgate. This is the [gradation/rate⟩] gradation of thinking, preaching, and acting. If a man thinks [wrong/errour/pernicious

30   doctrine⟩] erroneously, he may keep [it⟩] his thoughts to himself and [not be troubled/nobody will trouble him⟩] nobody will trouble him. If he preaches [it⟩] erroneous doctrine, society may expell him. If he acts in consequence of it, the law takes place and he is hanged.' [ᴧ*Dr.*ᴧ *del*] *Mayo* 'But Sir ought not Christians to have liberty of conscience?' *Johnson*. 'I have allready told you so Sir. You are

35   coming back to where you were.'[4] *Boswell*. 'Dr. Mayo [is allways taking/allways takes⟩] is allways taking a [retour⟩] return post=chaise and [going/goes⟩] going the stage [over/back⟩] over again. He has it at half=price.' *Johnson*. 'Dr. Mayo ᴧlike other champions for unlimited tolerationᴧ has got a set of words.[a] Sir [it/there⟩] it is no matter politically whether the Magistrate be right or wrong. Suppose a

40   [a] Dr. Mayo's [unruffled⟩] calm temper and steady perseverance rendered him an [excellent opponent⟩] admirable subject for the exercise of Dr. Johnson's [vigorous⟩] powerful abilities. He never flinched, but after [repeated⟩] reiterated blows remained ᴧseeminglyᴧ unmoved as at the first. The scintillations of

---

[4] There appears to be a deleted asterisk after 'were'. Presumably, JB originally intended to place the footnote (which appears three sentences on) here.

Club were to be formed to drink confusion to King George the Third and a happy restoration to Charles the Third; this would be very bad with respect to the State; but every member of that Club must either conform to its [regulations/rules›] rules or be turned out [/of it/›] of it. Old Baxter I remember maintains that the Magistrate should tolerate all things that are tolerable. This is no good definition 5 of toleration upon any principle; but it shews that he thought [some things not tolerable/that some things were not tolerable›] some things were not tolerable.' *Toplady.* 'Sir you have untwisted this difficult subject with great [MS 411] dexterity.'

During this Argument Goldsmith sat in great agitation from a wish to get in and 10 shine. Finding himself excluded he had taken his hat to go ‹away›; but remained for some time with it in his hand, like a gamester who at the close of a long night [waits›] lingers for a little while to see if he can have a favourable opening ‹to finish with success›. Once when he was beginning to speak he found himself overpowered by the loud voice of Johnson who was at the opposite end of the table 15 and did not perceive Goldsmith's attempt. Thus disappointed ‹of his wish to obtain the attention of the company,› Goldsmith in a passion threw down his hat ‹looking angrily at Johnson and› crying in a bitter tone '*take* it'. When Toplady was going to speak Johnson uttered some sound which Goldsmith supposed to be beginning again and taking the word from Toplady. Upon which he seised this 20 opportunity of venting his own envy and spleen under ‹the› pretext of supporting another person. 'Sir' said he to Johnson, 'the Gentleman has heard you patiently for an hour. Pray allow [him to speak/us to hear him›] us now to hear him.' *Johnson.* [(angrily)›] (sternly) 'Sir I was not interrupting the Gentleman. I was only giving him a signal of my attention. Sir you are [very impertinent to me›] 25 impertinent.' *Goldsmith* made no reply, but continued in the company [MS 412] for some time.

A gentleman present ventured to ask Dr. Johnson if there was not a material difference as to toleration of opinions which lead to action and opinions merely speculative; for instance [might not the magistrate tolerate›] would it be wrong in 30 the magistrate to tolerate those who preach against the doctrine of the Trinity.[5] Johnson was highly offended and said 'I wonder Sir how a Gentleman of your piety can introduce this subject [here›] in a mixed company.' He told me afterwards that the impropriety was, that perhaps some of the company might have [declared sentiments›] talked on the subject in such terms as would have shocked him, or he 35 might have been forced to appear in their eyes a narrowminded man. The Gentleman with submissive deference said he had only hinted at the question

Johnson's genius flashed every time he was struck, without his receiving any injury. Hence he obtained the epithet of THE LITERARY ANVIL.[a1]

---

[5] JB's notes read: '*Langton* who was so quiet and so prudent Said Is there not a difference between opinions that lead to action & opinions merely specul for inst doct of trin' (J29).

[a1] This note, written on the verso of MS 409, bears the deleted heading 'Literary Anvil'. This may have functioned as a temporary aide-mémoire as JB continued with the composition of the main text.

from a desire to hear Dr. Johnson's opinion upon it.[6] *Johnson.* 'Why then Sir I think that permitting men to preach any opinion contrary to the doctrine of the established church [is so far/tends to>] tends in a certain degree to lessen [the force of *del*] the authority of the Church and [therefore/consequently>] consequently to

5   [lessen/weaken>] lessen *[MS 413]* the influence of Religion.' 'It may be considered' said the Gentleman 'whether it ⟨may not⟩ be politick to tolerate in such a case.' *Johnson.* ⟨'Sir⟩ We have been talking of *right*. This is another question. I think it is *not* politick to tolerate in such a case.'

    ⟨Though he did not think it fit that so aweful a subject should be introduced in

10   a mixed company, and therefore at this time waved the theological question, yet his own orthodox belief in the sacred mystery of the T\ʀɪɴɪᴛʏ is evinced beyond doubt by the following passage in his private devotions: 'O Lord hear my prayers for Jesus Christs sake, to whom with Thee and the Holy Ghost, *three persons and one* G\ᴏᴅ, be all honour and glory world without end. Amen'.[a] ⟩

15   [Dr. Leland's 'History of Ireland' being mentioned — >] [*Boswell*. Mr. Dilly how does Dr. Leland's 'History of Ireland' sell?>] *Boswell*. Pray Mr. Dilly how does Dr. Leland's "History of Ireland" sell?' — *Johnson* (bursting forth with a generous indignation). 'The irish are in a most unnatural state; for we see there the minority [prevail/prevailing>] prevailing over the Majority. There is no instance ⟨even⟩ in

20   the ten persecutions of [any thing so severe as the protestants of Ireland have exercised>] [such severity as that with which the protestants of Ireland have treated>] such severity as that which the protestants of Ireland have exercised against the Catholicks. Did we tell them we have conquered them it would be above board. To punish them by confiscation and other penalties as Rebels is

25   monstrous injustice. King William was not their lawful Sovereign. He had not been acknowledged by [the parliament of Ireland>] [their parliament>] the parliament of Ireland, when they appeared in arms [for>] against him.'

    I [spoke favourably of the Catholicks/Romish Religion>] here suggested something favourable of the Roman Catholicks. *Toplady*. 'Does not their invocation of

30   Saints suppose omnipresence in the Saints?' *Johnson*. 'No Sir. It supposes only pluripresence and when spirits are divested of matter it seems *[MS 414]* probable that they should see with more extent than when in an embodied state. There is therefore no approach to an invasion of any of the divine attributes, in the invocation of Saints. But I think it is will=worship and presumption. I [see no/do

35   not see a>] see no command for it, and therefore think it is safer not to practise it.'

    He and Mr. Langton and I [took a coach>] went together to the Club, where we found Mr. Burke Mr. Garrick and some other members and amongst them our friend Goldsmith who sat silently brooding over Johnson's [having called him impertinent>] reprimand to him after dinner. Johnson perceived this, and said

40   [aside/low>] aside to some of us 'I'll make Goldsmith forgive me,' and then called to him in a loud voice, 'Dr. Goldsmith something passed today where you and I dined. I ask your pardon.' Goldsmith answered placidly 'It must be much from you

---

[a] Prayers and Meditations p. 40.

---

[6] JB's notes read: '*Langton* timorous like ghost I only hinted etc' (J29).

that I take ill.' And so at once the difference was over, and they were on as easy terms as usual, and Goldsmith [rattled/dashed>] rattled away.

In our way to the Club tonight when I regretted that Goldsmith would upon every occasion endeavour to shine, by which he often exposed himself Mr. Langton observed that he was not like Addison who was content with the fame of his writings, and did not aim also at excelling in conversation for which he found himself unfit; and that he said to a Lady who complained of his having [said>] talked little in company, 'Madam I have but ninepence in ready money; but I can draw for a thousand pounds.' I [said>] observed that Goldsmith had *[MS 415]* a great deal of gold in his [drawers/cabinet>] cabinet at home[7] but [not content he would be>] not content with that was allways taking out his purse. *Johnson.* 'Yes Sir and that so often an empty purse!' [I went home with him and drank tea with Mrs. Williams *del*][8]

[Paper Apart G] Goldsmith's incessant desire of [shining or *del*] being conspicuous in company, was the occasion of his sometimes appearing to such disadvantage as one should hardly have supposed possible in a man of his genius. When his literary reputation had risen deservedly high and his society was much courted, he [was>] became very jealous of the extraordinary attention which was every where paid to Johnson. One evening in a circle of the wits, he found fault with me for talking of Johnson as entitled to the honour of unquestionable superiority. 'Sir' said he 'you are for making a monarchy of what should be a republick.'

But he was exceedingly mortified when [he was *del*] talking in a company with fluent vivacity and as he flattered himself to the admiration of all who were present, a german who sat next him, and perceived Johnson rolling himself as if about to speak, suddenly stopped him saying, 'Stay stay, Toctor Shonson is going to say something.' This was no doubt very provoking, especially to one so irritable as Goldsmith who frequently mentioned it with strong expressions of indignation.

[The truth is that sometimes>] It may also be observed that Goldsmith was sometimes content to be treated with an easy familiarity, but upon occasions would be consequential and important. An instance of this occurred in a small particular. Johnson had a way of contracting the names of his friends as Beauclerk Beau Langton Lanky Murphy Mur Boswell Bozzy. I remember one day when Tom Davies was telling that Dr. Johnson said 'We are all in labour for a name to *Goldy's* play,' Goldsmith seemed displeased that such a liberty should be taken with his name, and said 'I have often desired him not to call me *Goldy*.' ⌜Tom was remarkably attentive to the most minute circumstance about Johnson. I recollect his telling me once on my arrival in London, 'Sir our great friend has made an improvement on his appellation of old Mr. Sheridan. He calls him now *Sherry derry*.'⌝

---

[7] JB's first draft of 'at home' reads 'in the Inn'—presumably a reference to the Middle Temple, where Goldsmith lodged in the late 1760s and early 1770s (Ralph Wardle, *Oliver Goldsmith*, 1957, p. 276; Henry B. Wheatley and Peter Cunningham, *London Past and Present*, 1891, i. 236–37, ii. 85, 343).

[8] Direction to the compositor, 'Take in paper G'.

$\overset{\displaystyle 9}{\overset{\displaystyle \wedge\text{———————————}\lambda}{}}$

To The Reverend Mr. Bagshaw ⟨at Bromley⟩_λ ^{a/1}

[PA opp. 415][2] Sir,

I return you my sincere thanks for your additions to my dictionary, but the new
5   Edition has been published some time, and therefore I cannot now make use of
them. Whether I shall ever revise it more I know not. If many readers had been
as judicious, as diligent, and as communicative as yourself, my Work had been
better. The World must at present take it as it is.

I am, Sir, Your most obliged and most humble Servant,
10   Sam. Johnson

May 8, 1773.

[MS 415 resumed] On sunday [9 May⟩] May 8 I dined with him at Mr. Langton's
with Dr. Beattie and some other company. He [was ?violent in defence
of/eloquent on the subject of⟩] descanted on the subject of Literary Property. [He
15   said there seemed⟩] 'There seems,' said he, 'to be in Authours ⟨a stronger right of
property than that by occupancy,⟩ a metaphysical right, ⟨a right as it were⟩ of
Creation, which should from its nature be perpetual but [that the consent of
nations was⟩] the consent of nations is against it, and indeed reason and the
interests of learning [were⟩] are against it, for were it to be perpetual [no Book
20   could be generally diffused amongst mankind however useful it might be⟩] no
Book, however useful, could be universally diffused amongst mankind, should the
[Authour or *added and del*] proprietor take it into his head to restrain its circulation.
No Book could have the advantage of being edited with notes, however necessary
to its elucidation, should the [Authour or *added and del*] proprietor perversely
25   oppose it. For the general good of the World, therefore, whatever valuable Work
has once been created by an Authour and issued ⟨out⟩ by him

[a] The Reverend Thomas Bagshaw M.A. who died Nov. 20 1787 in the 77th year
of his age, Chaplain of Bromley College in Kent and Rector of Southflete. He had
resigned the cure of Bromley parish [for *del*] some time before his death. [This⟩] For
30   this and another letter ⟨from Dr. Johnson in 1784⟩ to the same truly respectable
man I am indebted to Dr. John Loveday of the Commons who has obligingly
transcribed them for me from the originals in his possession.[a1]

———————

[9] Direction to the compositor, 'Put a short line'.

[1] Direction to the compositor, 'Take in the letter "I return you my sincere thanks etc."
and send me the copy as it contains another letter to come in 1784'.

[2] This Paper Apart, in the hand of John Loveday, is headed: 'Transcribed from the
Originals in the possession of Dr. John Loveday, one of the Executors of the Revd. Thomas
Bagshaw, M.A., who died on Nov. 20, 1787, in the 77th year of his age, Chaplain of
Bromley College in Kent, and Rector of Southflete. He had resigned the Cure of Bromley
Parish some time before his death. This truly respectable man, in conjunction with a
learned freind, constantly furnished Dr. Johnson with corrections and improvements of his
Dictionary.' This Paper Apart contains not only SJ to Bagshaw, 8 May 1773, but also SJ to
Bagshaw, 12 July 1784 (Hill-Powell iv. 351–52; *post* MS Papers Apart 917–18).

[a1] JB's addition to this note, which described Loveday's retirement from business and his
work as an editor of Townson, first appeared in the third edition.

should be understood as no longer in his power, but as belonging to the [Publick. At>] Publick; at the same time the Authour [was>] is entitled to *[MS 416]* [a suitable>] an adequate reward. This he should have by an exclusive right to his Work for a considerable number of years.'

ʎHe attacked Lord Monboddo's curious [speculations>] speculation on the   5
primitive state of human nature observing 'Sir, it is all conjecture about a thing useless if known to be true. Knowledge of all kinds is good. Conjecture as to things useful is good but conjecture as to what it would be useless to know, such as whether men ever went upon all four is very idle.'ʎ

On Monday [9 May>] May 9 as I was to set out on my return for Scotland next   10
morning I was desireous to see as much of Dr. Johnson as I could. But I first called on Goldsmith to take leave of him. The jealousy and envy which, though possessed of many most amiable qualities, he [fairly>] frankly avowed [broke out violently/displayed itself>] broke out violently at this interview. [I argued with Johnson upon Goldsmith's declaring his envy upon another occasion, that we   15
should forgive him on account of his openess/could not be angry with him, he was so open.>] Upon another occasion when Goldsmith confessed himself to be of an envious disposition, I contended with Johnson that we ought not to be angry with him, he was so open. 'Nay Sir,' said Johnson 'we must be angry that a man has such a superabundance of an odious quality that he cannot keep it within his own breast   20
but it boils over.' [But in my opinion Goldsmith>] In my opinion however Goldsmith had not more of it than other people [/have/>] have, but only talked of it freely.

He now seemed very angry that Johnson was going to be a Traveller, said 'he would be a dead weight for me to carry, and that I [should/would>] should never be   25
able to [lug/carry>] lug him along through the Highlands and Hebrides.' Nor [would he patiently allow me/could he bear to hear me>] would he patiently allow me to enlarge upon Johnson's wonderful [talents>] abilities, but called out 'Is he like *[MS 417]* [Burke>] _____³ who winds into a subject like a serpent?' — 'But' said I 'Johnson is the Hercules who [strangles serpents/can strangle a/that   30
serpent>] strangled serpents in his cradle.'

I dined with ʎDr.ʎ Johnson at General Paoli's. He [grew/was so ill with some violent internal complaint that he could stay but a very short while, and went home in a coach.>] [was obliged by illness to leave the company early.>] was obliged by indisposition to leave the company early. He appointed me however to   35
meet him in the evening at [Mr. Chambers's/a friend's>] Mr. (now Sir Robert) Chambers's in the Temple where he accordingly came though he continued to be very ill. [Chambers/Our friend>] Chambers, as is common on such occasions [would needs prescribe>] prescribed various remedies to him. *Johnson* (fretted by pain). 'Prithee don't tease me. Stay till I am well, and then you shall tell me how   40
to cure myself.' He grew better and talked with a noble enthusiasm of keeping up the representation of [respectable families, a particular in his character>] respect-able families. His zeal on this subject was a circumstance in his character

---

³ The revises print 'Burke' in spite of JB's deletion and replacement of the name with a blank space, perhaps because he left 'Burke' as the catchword at the bottom of MS 416.

exceedingly remarkable when it is considered that he himself had no pretensions to blood. I heard him once say 'I have great merit in being zealous for subordination and the honours of birth for, I can hardly tell who was my Grandfather.' He maintained the dignity and propriety of male succession in opposition to [Langton/another freind>] the opinion of one of our friends,[4] who had that day [with/under Chambers's advice/direction made his will>] employed Mr. Chambers to draw his will devising his estate to his three sisters in preference to a [remoter heir male/male heir>] remote heir male. *[MS 418]* He called them [/the/ *del*] three *dowdies* [. He said>] and said with as [stately>] high a spirit as the boldest baron in the most perfect days of the feudal system, 'An ancient estate should [/allways/>] allways go to males. It is mighty foolish to let a stranger have it [who>] because he marries your daughter [and takes/on condition of taking>] and takes your name. [I would not let/have a rascal take my name. *del*] As for an estate newly [got/acquired>] acquired by trade you may give it if you will to the dog *Towser*, and let him keep his *own* name.'

I have known him at times exceedingly diverted at what seemed to others a very small sport. He now laughed immoderately ⟨without any reason that we could perceive⟩ at [Langton's/our friends>] our friends making his will, called him '[Langton>] _____ the *testator*' and added 'I dare say he thinks he has done a thing, a mighty thing. He won't stay till he gets home to produce this wonderful deed. He'll call up the Landlord of the first Inn on the road, and after a suitable preface upon mortality and the uncertainty of life will tell him that he should not delay making his will; and here Sir will he say is my will which I have just made with the assistance of one of the ablest lawyers in the kingdom and he will read it to him' [(*laughing all the time*)>] (laughing all the time). 'He believes he has made this will; but he did not make it. You' ⟨(to Chambers)⟩ 'made it for him. I hope you ⟨have⟩ had more conscience than to make him say "being of sound understanding" ha ha ha. I hope *[MS 419]* he has left me a legacy. [He should leave hatbands and gloves to all the Club. *del*] I'd have his Will turned into verse like a Ballad.' In this ⟨playful⟩ manner did he run on [as full of/overflowing with drollery as a man could be, but surely such drollery as we should never expect it from the Authour of 'The Rambler'. Yet it must be very amusing and please us in a high degree to find that our mighty Moralist and Philologist could be so playful.>] exulting in his own pleasantry which certainly was not such as might be expected from the Authour of 'The Rambler', but which is here preserved that [my *del*] readers may be acquainted even with the slightest occasional characteristicks of so eminent a man.

[Chambers/Our friend>] Mr. Chambers did not by any means relish this jocularity upon a matter of which *pars magna fuit*, and seemed impatient till he [got us out of his Chambers/turned us away>] got rid of us. Johnson could not stop his merriment, but continued laughing all the way till we [got/were>] got without the Temple Gate. [I cherished it calling out 'Langton the testator Langton Longshanks.' This tickled his fancy so much that he roared out 'I wonder to whom

---

[4] The deleted reference to Langton in the MS confirms Hill-Powell's hypothesis that he was the subject of this paragraph.

he'll leave his legs?'[5] and then burst into such a fit of laughter, that he seemed almost in a convulsion; then in order to support himself he laid hold of one of the posts which were then at the side of the foot pavement, and bellowed forth such peals that in the dark silence of the night his voice resounded from⟩] He then burst into such a fit of laughter, that he appeared to be almost in a convulsion; and in order to support himself laid hold of one of the posts which were at that time at the side of the foot pavement and sent forth peals so loud that in the silence of the night his voice seemed to resound from Temple=bar [MS 420] to Fleet=ditch.[6]

This most ludicrous [scene/exhibition⟩] exhibition of the [aweful and melancholy/grave, melancholy and aweful⟩] aweful, melancholy and venerable Johnson happened well to counteract the feelings of sadness which I used to experience when parting with him for a considerable time. I accompanied him to his door, where he gave me his blessing.

ₐHe records of himself this year: 'Between Easter and Whitsuntide, having always considered that time as propitious to study, I attempted to learn the low=dutch language.'ᵃ It is to be observed that he here admits an opinion of the human mind being influenced by seasons, which he ridicules in his [Rambler⟩] writings. His progress he says 'was interrupted by a fever which by the imprudent use of a small print left an inflammation in his useful eye.' We cannot but admire his spirit when we know that amidst a complication of bodily and mental distress he was still animated with the desire of intellectual improvement.[7] Various notes of his studies appear on different days in his Manuscript Diary of this year, such as 'Inchoavi lectionem Pentateuchi — Finivi lectionem Conf. Fab. Burdonum — Legi primum actum Troadum — Legi Dissertationem Clerici postremam de Pent. — 2 of Clark's Sermons — L. Appolonii pugnam Bebryciam[8] — L. centum versus Homeri.' Let this serve as a specimen of what accessions of literature he was perpetually infusing into his mind, while he charged himself with idleness.⟩

ₐThis year died Mrs. Salusbury mother of Mrs. Thrale a Lady whom he appears to have esteemed much, and whose memory he honoured with an epitaph.⟩[9]

ᵃ Prayers and Meditations p 129.

[5] Langton's remarkable height provided a running source of merriment: his friends delighted in comparing him to a stork and a maypole (Corr. 3, p. lxxv).

[6] This passage derives from JB's notes: 'He laughed immoderately at Langt. Langt the testator. I dare say he thinks he has done thing a mighty thing. He wont stay till he gets home. He'll read his will to ye Landlord of the first Inn on the road. Chambers you helped him. Did you put in being of sound understanding ha ha ha. I hope he has left me a Legacy. He shd leave hatbands & gloves to all the Club. Id have his will turned into verse like a Ballad. In this manner did he run on. Chambers accompanied us to the Temple Gate. Mr. Johns cd not stop his merriment. I cherished it crying Testator Langt Longshanks. Johns. I wonder to whom he'll leave his legs? Ha ha ha making all Fleetstreet resound at the silent midnight hour' (J29).

[7] The footnote supplying Burney's illustration of SJ's intellectual curiosity first appears in the third edition.

[8] 'Bebryciam' was printed in the revises 'Betriciam'. 'Bebryciam' is the correct reading, but it was never restored — yet another piece of evidence that proof was not read against the MS.

[9] In the revises, a footnote is keyed to this sentence: 'Mrs. Piozzi's Anecdotes of Johnson, p. 131'.

[To Dr. Samuel Johnson⟩] Mr. BOSWELL to DR. JOHNSON
Edinburgh, 29 May 1773
[(See if any thing can be excerpted out of it)⟩] (Pressing him to persevere in his projected visit to the Hebrides)[1]

5   To James Boswell Esq.[2]

. . . .

[See if anything should be excerpted from my letters of 20 and 29 July⟩] [I wrote to him two other⟩] I again wrote to him informing him that the Court of Session rose on the twelfth of August, hoping to see him before that time, and expressing perhaps in too extravagant terms my admiration of him, and my expectation of
10 pleasure from our intended tour.
           To *James Boswell Esq.*[3]

. . . .

           To James Boswell Esq.[4]

. . . .

           To James Boswell Esq.[5]

. . . .

           To James Boswell Esq.[6]

. . . .

15 His stay in Scotland was from the 18 of August on which he arrived till the 22 of November on which he set out on his return to London; and I suppose [MS 421] ninety four days were never passed by any man in a more vigorous exertion.

He came by Berwick upon Tweed to Edinburgh, where he remained a few days, and then went by St. Andrews Aberdeen Inverness and Fort Augustus to the
20 Hebrides to visit which was the principal object he had in view. He visited the Isles of Sky Rasay Col Mull and Icolmkill.[7] He travelled through Argyleshire by Inverary and from thence by Lochlomond and Dumbarton to Glasgow by Loudon,

---

[1] JB originally intended to include excerpts from his letter of 29 July 1773, but by the stage of the revises he had substituted a brief summary as an introduction to SJ's letter of 5 July: 'In a letter from Edinburgh, dated the 29th of May, I pressed him to persevere in his resolution to make this year the projected visit to the Hebrides, of which he and I had talked for many years, and which I was confident would afford us much entertainment.'

[2] Direction to the compositor, 'When your letter (take it in)'. This Paper Apart no longer forms part of the *Life* MS.

[3] Direction to the compositor, 'I shall set out (take it in)'. This Paper Apart no longer forms part of the *Life* MS.

[4] Direction to the compositor, 'Not being (take it in)'. This Paper Apart no longer forms part of the *Life* MS.

[5] Direction to the compositor, 'I came hither (take it in)'. This Paper Apart no longer forms part of the *Life* MS.

[6] Direction to the compositor, 'Mr. Johnson's compliments (take it in)'. This Paper Apart no longer forms part of the *Life* MS.

[7] In the revises, JB changed 'Mull and Icolmkill' to 'Mull, Inchkenneth and Icolmkill', and reinforced the alteration with a marginal note about spelling: 'Pray Observe that in Inchkenneth there is first an H and then a K; As these letters are apt to be mistaken in MS I mention this. The first syllable of the word is the same with the measure *Inch*'. For a discussion of JB's approach to orthography, see *Earlier Years*, pp. 358–59. Two pages before, JB had noted, 'By revising this sheet I have catched an Island which I had omitted'.

then to Auchinleck in Ayrshire, the seat of my Family [as I had the honour to attend him during the whole of his journey *del*] and then by Hamilton back to Edinburgh where he [spent some more time⟩] again spent some time. He thus saw the four Universities of Scotland [and *del*] its three principal Cities, and as much of the highland and insular life as was sufficient for his philosophical contempla-   5
tion. ⟨I had the pleasure of accompanying him during the whole of this Journey.⟩ [That he was entertained as he strongly expressed it 'like Princes in their course'⟩] He was respectfully entertained by the great the learned and the elegant wherever he went, nor was he less delighted with the [respectful *del*] hospitality which he [experienced/*undeciphered word*⟩] experienced in [wild districts/situations⟩] hum-   10
bler life. [MS 422] [How he was considered and with what dispositions he travelled I shall insert the following letters.⁸ *del*]⁹

[MS 424]¹ [The force and⟩] His various adventures and the force and vivacity of his mind, as exercised during this Peregrination upon innumerable topicks [had been faithfully recorded by me⟩] have been faithfully and to the best of my abilities   15
displayed in my 'Journal of a Tour to the Hebrides' to which as the Publick has been pleased to honour it by a very extensive circulation I beg leave to refer, as to a separate and remarkable [period/part/portion⟩] portion of his Life² which may be there [viewed⟩] seen in detail and which exhibits as striking [a view of his mind/a specimen of his powers⟩] a view of his powers in conversation as his works   20
do of his excellence in writing. [To embody it here would render this publication/the present compilation too bulky; besides that it would justly be [MS 425] thought unbecoming in me to load a great many of my readers with the purchase of that/a Book/a Collection of which they are allready in possession.⟩] [MS opp. 424] Nor can I deny to myself the very flattering gratification of inserting   25
here the character which my friend Mr. Courtenay has been pleased to give of my Journal.³

[MS opp. 425] ⟨During his stay at Edinburgh after his return from the Hebrides, he was at great pains to obtain [every kind/species of *del*] information concerning

---

⁸ Deleted direction to the compositor, '(Take in Lord Elibank's correspondence, the Duke of Argyle's)'. This direction was superseded by one reading, 'Go to page 424 "His various etc."' The effect of this direction is to delay the commentary on SJ's *Journey* so that it appears in 1775 rather than in 1773.

⁹ Next to this sentence appears a deleted query in JB's hand, 'should I insert other references to them?'

¹ JB has drawn a hand in the margin to reinforce his direction to the compositor, which indicates where on MS 424 the narrative is to be taken up. The cutting and splicing involved in JB's rearrangement is repeatedly indicated by the presence of hands drawn in the margin. See *post* p. 126, nn. 4, 6.

² EM's note quoting SJ to Hester Thrale, 3 November 1773, first appeared in the third edition.

³ Direction to the compositor, '(Take it in) p. 22 "With Reynold's pencil" down to "shall have his ain"'. Now JB instructs the compositor to excerpt fourteen lines from John Courtenay's *Poetical Review of the Literary and Moral Character of Dr. Johnson* (1786). This extract stops short of the final couplet, 'Two Georges in his loyal zeal are slur'd, /A gracious pension only saves the third!' (2nd ed., 1786, p. 22).

Scotland, and it will appear from his subsequent letters that he was not less solicitous for intelligence on this subject after his return to London.λ

[MS 425] To James Boswell Esq.[4]

. . . .

[To James Boswell del]

5   His humane forgiving disposition was put to a pretty strong test on his return to London by a liberty which Mr. Thomas Davies had taken with him in his absence, which was to publish two volumes [under/with the title of>] entitled 'Miscellane-ous ﹏and Fugitive﹏ Pieces' ﹏which he advertised in the Newspapers﹏ by the Authour of the "Rambler"'. In this Collection several of [his>] Dr. Johnson's

10   acknowledged writings and several of his anonymous performances and some which he had written for others were inserted; but there were also some in which he had no [concern/hand>] concern whatever. He was at first very angry as he had good reason to be. But upon consideration of his poor friend's narrow circumstances and that he ﹏had only a little profit in view and﹏ meant no harm,

15   [but only his own good del], he soon relented, and continued his kindness to him as formerly.

    [In 1774 he seems in/at the time>] In the course of his [MS 426] self=examination [he reviewed del] this year he seems to have been much dejected, for he says, January 1, 1774: 'This year has past with so little improvement, that

20   I doubt whether I have not rather impaired than increased my learning.'[a] And yet we have seen how he *read* and we know how he *talked* during that period.

    ﹏He was now heartily engaged in writing an Account of our Travels in the Hebrides in consequence of which [he became a more frequent correspondent with me.>] I had the pleasure of a more frequent correspondence with him.λ [5]

25   To James Boswell Esq.[6]

. . . .

To James Boswell Esq.[7]

. . . .

[a] Prayers and Meditations, p.   .[al]

---

[4] Direction to the compositor, "'I came home (take it in) / (Take in what is proper of my letters of 2 and 18 Decr.)'". These Papers Apart no longer form part of the *Life* MS.

[5] See *ante* p. 84 n. 4. In the second edition, JB prefaced the eleventh-hour insertion of these letters — both of which were dated 4 March 1773, but both of which were placed after letters from December of that year — with a paragraph apologizing for any disruption to the chronological sequence of events in the *Life*: 'Though the first part of my narrative of this year was printed off before I received them, they will now come in with very little deviation from chronological order.' This paragraph was not included in the third edition, for by that time the letters had been repositioned.

[6] Direction to the compositor, "'My operations (take it in)'". This Paper Apart no longer forms part of the *Life* MS.

[7] Direction to the compositor, "'In a day or two (take it in)'". This Paper Apart no longer forms part of the *Life* MS.

al The page number (129) had been supplied by the time of the revises.

To James Boswell Esq.[8]

. . . .

ᴧ[Here or by and by he wrote>] He wrote the following letters to [George *del*] Steevens, his able associate in editing Shakspeare.ᴧ[9]

. . . .

ᴧOn the 5 of March[1] I wrote to him requesting his counsel whether I should this spring come to London. I stated to him on the one hand some pecuniary embarrassments which together with my wife's [situation>] state of health at the time made me hesitate, and on the other the pleasure and improvement which my annual visit to the Metropolis allways afforded me; and particularly mentioning a peculiar satisfaction which I experienced in celebrating [Easter>] the festival of Easter in St. Paul's Cathedral: that to my fancy it appeared like going up to Jerusalem at the feast of the passover, and that the strong devotion which I felt on that occasion diffused its influence through the rest of the year.ᴧ

To James Boswell Esq.[2]

. . . .

To James Boswell Esq.[3]

. . . .

To James Boswell Esq.[4]

[MS 427] To James Boswell Esq.[5]

. . . .

---

[8] Direction to the compositor, 'Dr. Webster's information (take it in)'. This Paper Apart no longer forms part of the *Life* MS.

[9] In the revises, this sentence — and the three letters accompanying it — have been inserted between the second and the third of SJ's letters to JB (those of 7 February and 5 March).

[1] This added passage superseded a direction to the compositor which read, '(Take in what is proper of my letter of 5 March)'.

[2] Direction to the compositor, 'I am ashamed (take it in)', followed by a deleted direction, '(Take in what is proper of my letter of 6 April)'. This Paper Apart no longer forms part of the *Life* MS.

[3] Direction to the compositor, '"The Lady" (take it in)'. This Paper Apart is no longer part of the *Life* MS. This direction to the compositor is followed by a second, 'Take in what is proper of my letters 12 and 19 May) ᴧfrom Paper LL1ᴧ'. In the revises, JB to SJ, 12 May 1774, was inserted here, but not JB to SJ, 19 May 1774. Paper Apart LL1 no longer forms part of the *Life* MS.

[4] Direction to the compositor, '"Yesterday I sent" (take it in)'. This Paper Apart no longer forms part of the *Life* MS. This direction to the compositor is followed by another, '(Take in what is proper of my letter of 25 June ᴧfrom Paper LL2ᴧ)'. Although Paper Apart LL2 no longer forms part of the *Life* MS, the text of it may be found in Hill-Powell ii. 279 (where it is erroneously dated 24 June, as is the case in the second and third editions).

[5] Direction to the compositor, '"I wish you could have looked" (take it in)'. This Paper Apart no longer forms part of the *Life* MS. This direction to the compositor is followed by another, '(Take in what is proper of my Letters 30 Aug. and 16 Septr.)'. Additional letters were inserted into the text at a later date: SJ to Robert Levet, 16 Aug. 1774, in the second edition, and SJ to Bennet Langton, 5 July, in the third edition. The letter to Langton belongs to that group first inserted at the end of the second volume of the second edition, and then moved to their chronologically appropriate places for the third edition. See *ante* p 10 n. 1.

To James Boswell Esq.[6]

. . . .

[To James Boswell Esq. *del*][7]

His Tour to Wales which was made in company with Mr. and Mrs. Thrale,
though it no doubt contributed to his health and amusement, [was by no means

5   the source/foundation of⟩] did not give occasion to such a discursive exercise of
his mind as our Tour to the Hebrides. I do not find that he kept any Journal or
notes of what he saw there. All that I heard him say of it was that instead of bleak
and barren mountains there were green and fertile ones and that one of the Castles
in Wales would contain all the castles that he had seen in Scotland.

10   [ᴧMrs. Thrale mentions an anecdote during this Tour in a manner much to his
disadvantage.ᴧ *del*][8]

Parliament having been dissolved and his friend Mr. Thrale who was a steady
supporter of government having again to encounter the storm of a contested
election he wrote a short political *[MS 428]* Pamphlet entitled [*the Patriot*] 'The

15   Patriot,' addressed to the Electors of Great Britain, a title which [they who are
accustomed to interpret that word as denoting an abettor of popular and tumultu-
ous resistance will say was denominated/given from contradiction, as *lucus a non
lucendo*⟩][9] to factious men who consider a patriot only as an opposer of the
measures of government will appear strangely misapplied. [But it was⟩] It was

20   however written with energetick vivacity and [I think without a single hard word
or abstruse expression/idiom, but abstracting from his defence/except its still
defending⟩] except those passages in which it endeavours to vindicate the glaring
outrage of the House of Commons in the case of the Middlesex election, and
[hinting his approbation of⟩] [hinted his approbation of⟩] to justify the attempt to

25   reduce our fellow subjects in America to unconditional submission it contained an
admirable display of the properties of a real Patriot in the original and genuine
sense, a sincere steady rational and unbiassed friend to the interests and prosperity
of his country. ᴧIt must be acknowledged however that both in this and his two
former pamphlets there wasᴧ [1/2]

---

[6] Direction to the compositor, '"Yesterday I returned" (take it in)'. The text of this letter
may be found in Hill-Powell ii. 284–85.

[7] Deleted direction to the compositor, '"There has appeared lately" (take it in)'.

[8] In her *Anecdotes of the Late Samuel Johnson LL.D.* (1786), Hester Piozzi attributed to SJ
an acerbic comment on 'a lady of quality, since dead, who received us at her husband's seat
in Wales with less attention than he had long been accustomed to': '"That woman (cries
Johnson) is like sour small-beer, the beverage of her table, and produce of the wretched
country she lives in: like that, she could never have been a good thing, and even that bad
thing is spoiled"' (*Johnsonian Miscellanies*, ed. G. B. Hill, i. 264). According to Hill, Mrs
Piozzi identified the object of SJ's abuse as Lady Catherine Wynne. For Lady Catherine
(*née* Perceval), see Hill-Powell v. 449, n. 1.

[9] The OED defines *'lucus a non lucendo'* as 'a paradoxical or otherwise absurd derivation;
something of which the essence or qualities are the opposite of what its name suggests'.

[1] This sentence is completed in the revises, 'amidst many powerful arguments, not only
a considerable portion of sophistry, but a contemptuous ridicule of his opponents, which
was very provoking'.

[2] At this point the second edition inserts a letter from SJ to John Perkins, 25 Oct. 1774,
as well as a footnote that identifies Perkins.

To James Boswell Esq.[3]

This letter shews his tender concern for an amiable young gentleman to whom
we had been very much obliged in the Hebrides. I [insert/have>] insert it
according to its date, though before receiving it I had written an answer to his
letter of October 1st and [had in that informed him of [MS 429] the affecting   5
misfortune/unhappy event which he apprehended. Our letters had crossed one
another upon the road>] informed him of the melancholy event [MS 429] that the
young Laird of Col was unfortunately drowned.[4]

To James Boswell Esq.[5]

In his manuscript Diary of this year, there is the following entry: 10
'Nov. 27. Advent Sunday. I considered that this day being the beginning of the
eclesiastical year was a proper time for a new course of life. I began to read the
Greek Testament regularly at 160 verses every Sunday. This day I began the Acts.
'In this week I read Virgil's Pastorals. I learned to repeat the Pollio and Gallus.
I read carelessly the first Georgick.'   15
Such evidences of his unceasing ardour both for 'divine and human lore' when
advanced in to his sixty fourth year, and notwithstanding his many disturbances
from disease must make us at once honour his Spirit and lament that it should be
so grievously clogged by its material tegument. It is remarkable that he was
[very/always>] always fond of the precision which[6] [MS 430] [numbers produce/is   20
produced by calculation>] calculation produces. Thus we find ₍in one of his
manuscript diaries: '12 pages in 4to Gr. Test. and 30 pages in Beza's folio comprise
the whole in 40 days'.₎ [7]
    DR. JOHNSON to Mr. HOOLE[8]

[In 1775 the first production of his pen>] The first effort of his pen in 1775 was   25
'Proposals for Publishing the Works of Mrs. Charlotte Lennox' ₍in three volumes
quarto₎. [His Diary Jan. 2 bears/bears Jan. 2 'wrote Charlotte's>] [His Diary Jan.
2 mentions 'wrote Charlotte's>] In his Diary Jan. 2, I find this entry, 'wrote

---

[3] Direction to the compositor, '"There has appeared" (take it in)'. This Paper Apart no
longer forms part of the *Life* MS.
    [4] Deleted direction to the compositor, '(Take in what is proper of mine 29 Octr and ?26
Novr)'.
    [5] Direction to the compositor, '"Last night I corrected" (take it in)'. This Paper Apart
no longer forms part of the *Life* MS.
    [6] JB deleted the phrase 'It is remarkable that he was always fond of the precision which',
then reinstated it with four 'stet' markings.
    [7] Ink and spacing alike make it clear that JB broke off after 'There we find,' for reasons
that a marginal note helps to explain: 'Mark instances of his calculating how many verses
a day to read the Bible etc. etc.' This note, together with the presence of several lines'
worth of blank space between '40 days' and 'DR. JOHNSON', suggest that JB gathered the
illustrative detail and then completed the sentence at some later date.
    [8] Direction to the compositor, '"I have [received>] returned your Play"'. This Paper
Apart no longer forms part of the *Life* MS.

Charlotte's proposals,' but indeed the internal evidence would have been quite
sufficient. ₍Her claim to the favour of the Publick was thus enforced.₎[9]

[*Paper Apart*][1] Most of the Pieces, as they appeared singly, have been read with
Approbation, perhaps above their Merit, but of no great Advantage to the Writer.
5   She hopes, therefore, that she shall not be considered as too indulgent to Vanity,
or too studious of Interest, if, from that Labour which has hitherto been chiefly
gainful to others, she endeavours to obtain at last some Profit for herself and her
Children. She cannot decently enforce her Claim by the Praise of her own
Performances; nor can she suppose, that, by the most artful and laboured Address,
10   any additional Notice could be procured to a Publication, of which HER MAJ-
ESTY has condescended to be the PATRONESS.[2]

[₍3 Janry 1775 I wrote to him again when₎ *del*]
[₍To DR. SAMUEL JOHNSON
Dear Sir   3 Janry 1775
15   The charms₎ *del*]
To James Boswell Esq.[3]

. . . .

To James Boswell Esq.[4]

. . . .

To James Boswell Esq.[5]

. . . .

[*MS 431*] *To Dr. Lawrence*[6/7]
20   [*Paper Apart*]
Sir,   Feby 7, 1775
One of the Scotch Physicians is now prosecuting a Corporation that in some
publick instrument have stiled him *Doctor of Medicine* instead of *Physician*.

---

[9] Direction to the compositor, '(Take in from the Asterisks)'. This superseded a deleted
direction that read, '(Take them in)'.

[1] JB quotes from *Proposals for Printing by Subscription*, *dedicated to the Queen*, *a new and
elegant Edition*, *enlarged and corrected*, *of the Original Works of Mrs. Charlotte Lennox*, which
he annotated for use in the *Life* (P77).

[2] The second edition inserts a sentence here: 'He this year also wrote the Preface to
Baretti's "Easy Lessons in Italian and English"'.

[3] Direction to the compositor, '"You never did ask" (take it in)'. This direction to the
compositor is followed by another, '(Mine of 19 Janry)', which originally read, '(Excerpt
mine of 19 Janry)'. Neither of these Papers Apart forms part of the *Life* MS.

[4] Direction to the compositor, '"I long to hear" (take it in) ₍But N.B. *omit the verses*₎',
which is dated 21 January. This direction is immediately followed by a second, '(Excerpt
mine of 27 Janry)'. These Papers Apart no longer form part of the *Life* MS.

[5] Direction to the compositor, '"You sent me" (take it in)'. This Paper Apart no longer
forms part of the *Life* MS. This direction to the compositor is immediately followed by a
deleted one, reading '(Excerpt mine of 30 Janry)'. Yet another direction follows, this one
reading, '(Excerpt mine of [30 Janry⟩] 2 Febry)'. That Paper Apart no longer forms part of
the *Life* MS.

[6] Direction to the compositor, '₍"One of the Scotch Physicians"₎ (Take it in from
——)'.

[7] In the revises, a footnote is keyed to 'Dr. Lawrence': 'The learned and worthy Dr.
Lawrence, whom Dr. Johnson respected and loved as his physician and friend'.

Boswell desires, being advocate for the Corporation to know whether *Doctr. of Medicine* is not a legitimate title, and whether it may be considered as a disadvantageous distinction. I am to write tonight be pleased to tell me. I am, Sir,

Yr Most Etc.

Sam. Johnson   5

[MS 431 resumed]   To James Boswell Esq.[8]

. . . .

[What were the words which Mr. McPherson a robust highlander in the vigor/prime of life wrote to the venerable Sage I have never heard, but I do not find that any person connected with him has denied the general report that they were of a very different nature from words of literary contest which should have   10 met the bold argumentative attack of so illustrious a writer. But Dr. Johnson's Answer I can give as dictated to me by himself and written down⟩] What words were used by Mr. McPherson in his letter to the venerable Sage I have never heard, but they are generally said to have been of a nature very different from the language of literary contest. Dr. Johnson's Answer appeared in the newspapers of   15 the day and has since been frequently republished. I give it as dictated to me by himself written down in his presence and authenticated by a note in his own hand=writing '*This, I think, is a true copy*'.[9]

. . . .

ₐMr. MacPherson little knew the character of Dr. Johnson if he supposed that he could be easily intimidated; for no man was ever more remarkable for personal   20 courage. He had indeed an aweful dread of death, or rather 'of something after death' and what rational man who seriously thinks of quitting all that he has ever known can be without that dread. But his fear was [artificial⟩] from reflection his courage natural. His fear in that one [instance/respect⟩] instance was the result of philosophical and religious consideration. He feared death, but he feared nothing   25 else, not even what might occasion death. Many instances of his resolution may be mentioned. [Mr. Beauclerk told me that one day at his house in the country when two large dogs were fighting/worrying, He went up to them and cuffed them asunder and at another time when cautioned not to put too many balls into a gun/charge a gun with too many balls lest it should burst, he put in six or seven,   30 and fired it off against a wall.⟩] One day at Mr. Beauclerks house in the country when two large dogs were fighting, He went up to them and beat them till they separated, and at another time when told of the danger there was that a gun might burst if charged with many balls he put in six or seven, and fired it off against a wall.

[Mr. Langton told me that once at Oxford when they were swimming together,   35 Mr. Langton shewed him a pool which was reckoned particularly dangerous; upon

---

[8] Direction to the compositor, '"I am surprised" (take it in)'. This Paper Apart no longer forms part of the *Life* MS.

[9] Direction to the compositor, '⟨Take it in)'. This Paper Apart no longer forms part of the *Life* MS. In the second edition, JB asserted that he had 'deposited it in the British Museum'. As late as 1808, however, EM could not locate the dictated version, which remains untraced (*Corr. 2*, p. 607; SJ's *Journey*, ed. J. D. Fleeman, 1985, p. xxx n. 1). The text printed by JB differs in several respects from the holograph (*Letters of Johnson* ed. Redford, ii. 168–69).

which he went/made for/plunged directly into it. And he himself confirmed to me a story which I was told how he was attacked in the street by four men, to whom he would not yield, but fought them fairly till the watch came up›] [When Mr. Langton and he were swimming together near Oxford, Mr. Langton cautioned

5   him about/against a pool which was reckoned particularly dangerous; upon which he directly swam in it. He told me that he was attacked in the street by four men, to whom he would not yield, but kept them all at bay till the watch came up and carried them all to the round=house. Mr. Garrick told me that one evening at the Play/in the Theatre at Lichfield a gentleman took possession of a chair which was

10   placed for him between the side=scenes when he had quitted it for a moment. When he returned, he civilly demanded his seat, and the gentleman having refused it, he laid hold of him and tossed him chair and all/and the chair he sat on in to the pit. When Foote threatened to mimick him upon the stage he purchased a large oak cudgel declaring his resolution to beat him, which effectually checked

15   the wantoness of the Wit.[1] McPherson's menaces made him provide himself with the same implement of defence; and had he been assaulted, old as he was, I have no doubt that he would have made his material/corporeal prowess be felt as much as he did his intellectual.›] [Paper Apart C][2] Mr. Langton told me that when they were swiming together near Oxford, he cautioned Dr. Johnson against a pool

20   which was reckoned particularly dangerous upon which Johnson directly swam into it. He told me himself that one night he was attacked in the street by four Men, to whom he would not yield, but kept them all at bay, till the Watch came up and carried both him and them to the Round=house. Mr. Garrick told me, that at the play=house at Litchfield Johnson had a chair placed for him between the

25   side scenes. Having quited it for a moment, a Gentleman took possession of it, and when Johnson on his return civilly demanded his seat, rudely refused to quit it ; upon which Johnson laid hold of him and tossed him and the chair he sat on into the pit. Foote who so successfully revived the old comedy by exhibiting living characters had resolved to mimick Johnson on the stage expecting great profits

30   from his ridicule of so celebrated a man. Johnson being informed of his intention, and being at dinner at Mr. Thomas Davies', the bookseller's, from whom I had the story, he asked Mr. Davies 'What was the common price of an oak stick' and being answered sixpence, 'Why then Sir' said he 'give me leave to send your Servant to purchase me a shilling one. I'll have a double quantity for I am told Foote means

35   to *take me off*, as he calls it and I am determined the fellow shall not do it with impunity.' Davies took care to acquaint Foote of this, which effectually checked the wantoness of the wit. Mr. Macpherson's menaces made Johnson provide himself with the same implement of defence and had he been attacked I have no

---

[1] At one stage JB considered adding a cross-reference to the first mention of this episode: in the margin are two deleted notes, 'and we have ment[ioned]' followed by 'How he intended to treat Mr. Foote has been allready mentioned in this work'. See MS 347, *ante* p. 49.

[2] Direction to the compositor, 'Paper C', 'To be taken in on page opposite to p. 431 at the word "*wall*" instead of what is delete as being almost illegible'. Although the direction to the compositor is in JB's hand, the majority of the letter is in the hand of Veronica Boswell. The significant additions and changes made by JB are noted below.

doubt that Old as he was he would have made his corporal prowess be felt as much [as he did *del*] his intellectual.

[MS 431 resumed] His 'Journey to the Western Islands of Scotland' is [one of the best books that this eminent Writer ever gave to the world as it abounds›] a most valuable performance. It abounds in extensive philosophical views of   5 [various situations of human society and painted in rich and glowing colours, and teems with philosophical sentiments›] society and abounds in ingenious sentiments and [MS 432] lively description. A [great deal indeed of the Book was/is drawn evidently/made out of speculations which he might have formed//and probably did form//had formed chiefly in London long before he saw the wild   10 regions which we visited together, but which the actual sight of them certainly quickened. Mr. Orme one of the ablest historians of this/the age is/was of that opinion which he expressed to me in that grand and beautiful figurative manner which his original genius and long residence in Asia have concurred to produce. 'There are›] considerable part of it indeed consists of speculations, which many   15 years before he saw the wild regions which we visited together, probably had employed his attention, though the actual sight of these scenes undoubtedly quickened and augmented them. Mr. Orme, a very able historian, agreed with me in this opinion, which he thus strongly expressed: 'There are in that Book thoughts which by long revolution in the great mind of Johnson have been formed   20 and polished like pebbles rolled in the Ocean!'[3/4/5]

[MS 422 resumed][6] That he was [to/in›] to some degree of excess a *true=born englishman* so as to have ever entertained an undue prejudice against both the country and the people of Scotland must be allowed. But it was a prejudice of the [head/opinion›] head and not of the [heart/disposition›] heart. He had no   25 ill=will to the Scotch, for if he had been conscious of that, he would never have thrown himself into the bosom of their country [and/nor] and trusted to the protection of its remote inhabitants with a fearless confidence. [The Account which he published of his 'Journey,' though almost universally admired for its profound research upon many curious topicks, its perspicuous observations, and   30 strong as well as beautiful language has been ignorantly and virulently attacked by

---

[3] A marginal directive to the compositor instructs him to 'Take in *Note* from Critical Review'. By the time of the revises, JB had changed his mind: no such note appears in the printed text.

[4] Direction to the compositor, 'Return to p. 422'. JB has then drawn a hand, which corresponds to marginal directions on MS 422. See *ante* p. 188 n. 1 and n. 6 below.

[5] JB quotes the version of Orme's account that he had included in a footnote to his *Tour to the Hebrides* (1785, p. 515). He had reworked this from his journal entry: 'Mr Orme the East Indian Historian to whom Dempster once introduced me, knew me again, & accosted me. We talked together a good while of Mr J's Journey, which he admired much. He said he had more fancy than any man in this country; & that there were in his Journey, great thoughts which had been rolled & rolled in his mind, as in the sea. The image appeared very good at the time. I doubt if I have taken it well down' (7 Apr. 1775/J40).

[6] At the point at which MS 422 is resumed, JB has drawn a hand in the margin and written beneath it, 'N.B. Should not what is between the above *hand* and that on p. 424 be taken in rather in 1774 after his "Journey" was published'. The response to this query was written at a later stage, also in the margin: 'Yes. It comes in page 432'.

some/individuals. *del*] His remark upon the nakedness of the Country from its being denuded of trees was made after having travelled two hundred miles along the eastern coast where certainly trees are not to be found [near the road/by the way=side>] near the road and he said it was 'a map of the road' that he gave. His
5 [doubts/opinion>] disbelief of the authenticity of the Poems published as the compositions of Ossian a highland Bard was confirmed [by a very strict inquiry/examination>] in the course of his Journey by a very strict examination of the evidence offered for it, and although [*MS 423*] [I am sorry to be forced to own/say that *del*] their authenticity was made too much a national point [by the
10 scotch/in Scotland>] by the scotch, there were certainly many respectable [exceptions>] persons in that country who did not concur in this, so that his [able *del*] Judgement upon the question [ought/should>] ought not be decried even by those who differ from him [in whole or in part/altogether *del*]. ⟨As to myself I can only say upon a subject now become very uninteresting, that when the Fragments of
15 Highland Poetry first came out, I was much pleased with their wild peculiarity, and [I was one of the many/a number who subscribed so/as much as was sufficient/half a guinea a piece to bear the expence of Mr. James McPherson the translator/editor, then an obscure young man making a search through the highlands for a long Poem, which we were told/it was said was preserved some-
20 where in those regions.>] was one of those who subscribed to enable their editor Mr. McPherson then a young man to make a search in the highlands and Hebrides for a long Poem in the Earse language which was reported to be preserved somewhere in those regions. But when [there came forth/he produced>] there came forth an Epick Poem in Six Books with all the common circumstances of
25 former Compositions of that nature, and when upon an attentive examination of it there was found such a recurrence of the same images that were in the fragments, and when no ancient manuscript to authenticate the work was deposited in any publick library, though that was insisted on as a reasonable proof, *who* could forbear to doubt? [Had even one of the most potent Chieftains produced it he
30 could scarcely have taken it amiss that his word was not to have implicit authority. But Mr. James McPherson surely could not arrogate to himself such supreme consequence. *del*]⟨ And certainly the grateful acknowledgements which [he>] Johnson has made of kindnesses received must completely refute the brutal reflections which have been made against him as if he had made a thankless
35 return.[7] His candour and amiable disposition is conspicuous from his conduct when informed by Mr. MacLeod of Rasay that he had committed a mistake which gave that Gentleman some uneasiness. ⟨He wrote him a courteous and kind letter and inserted in the newspapers an advertisement correcting the mistake.⟩ [a/8]

---

[a] See Journal of a Tour to the Hebrides Edit. 3 p. 520.

---

[7] This sentence was extensively reworked in proof. It is printed in the revises as follows: 'Johnson's grateful acknowledgments of kindness received in the course of this tour, completely refute the brutal reflections which have been thrown out against him, as if he had made an ungrateful return; and his delicacy in sparing in his book those who we find from his letters to Mrs. Thrale were just objects of censure, is much to be admired.'

[8] Deleted direction to the compositor, '⟨Take in his Letter to the Laird of Rasay and the Advertisement ⟨as a Note⟩)'.

But I cannot do any thing so well myself upon this [subject as inserting/subject. For the honour of Scotland I shall insert⟩] subject as inserting some extracts of [the/a⟩] a letter which Mr. Dempster wrote to me after having read Dr. Johnson's Book/Journey.[9]

. . . .

And ₍Mr. Knox₎ another native of Scotland who has since made the same   5
Tour and published his Account of it says:[1]

. . . .

[MS 424] His private letters to Mrs. Thrale written during the course of his Journey which therefore may be supposed to convey his genuine feelings at the time abound in such benignant sentiments towards the people who shewed him civilities that no man whose temper is not very rugged and sour can retain a doubt of the goodness of his   10
heart. [₍Nay, so delicate was he that he suppressed in his own Account of his Journey the parsimony of one of the highland chiefs which that Lady has thought fit to expose to the world by publishing Johnson's letters to her and with the affectation of leaving out the *name* giving the *place* so as not to be misunderstood.₎ del][2/3]

[MS 432 resumed] It is [wonderful to think/recollect⟩] painful to recollect with   15
what virulence he was assailed by numbers of [shallow/superficial⟩] shallow irritable North=Britons on account of his supposed injurious treatment of their country and countrymen in his 'Journey'. Had there been any just ground for such a [suspicion/charge⟩] charge would [a/Mr.⟩] the virtuous and candid Dempster have given his opinion of the Book in the terms which I have quoted? Would [a   20
Knox⟩] the patriotick Knox[4] have spoken of it as he has done?[5] [For surely if

---

[9] Direction to the compositor, '(Take them in from ₍Paper marked D₎)'. This Paper Apart no longer forms part of the *Life* MS.

[1] Direction to the compositor, '(take in Paper Apart)'. This Paper Apart no longer forms part of the *Life* MS.

[2] The grudging hospitality of Sir Alexander (later Lord) Macdonald during their Hebridean trip was a source of abusive banter between JB and SJ, who also criticized Sir Alexander to Hester Thrale (*Letters of Johnson* ed. Redford, ii. 70, 77, 114). However, SJ's references in his *Journey* are studiously neutral. As JB observes, Hester Piozzi's excisions in her *Letters to and from the Late Samuel Johnson, LL.D.* (1788) do little to disguise the original frank criticisms. Nevertheless, JB's own injudicious reference in his *Tour*, only partially veiled, had almost provoked a duel with Macdonald (*Later Years*, pp. 306–11).

[3] At this point JB originally intended to add a note defending himself from the charge — levelled by John Wolcot ('Peter Pindar') in his *Poetical Congratulatory Epistle to James Boswell, Esq., On his Journal of a Tour to the Hebrides* — that threats from Lord Macdonald had compelled alterations in the *Tour*. After struggling with the note, JB abandoned it in mid-sentence: 'A scribler of infamous character having [falsely *del*] ₍in some of his black=guard publications₎ repeatedly asserted that [I struck out some part⟩] my leaving out a small part of my Journal was *in consequence of a requisition from Lord Macdonald*, I think it necessary [thus *del*] explicitly to declare that it is a *falshood*, and I am sure that the noble Lord will confirm what I thus [publickly *del*] ...'.

[4] A footnote keyed to Knox's name appears in the revises, apparently having been added in first proof: 'I observe with much regret, while this work is passing through the press, (August, 1790,) that this ingenious gentleman is dead'. In the second and subsequent editions, the footnote was couched in the past tense.

[5] The second edition inserts a new sentence here: 'Would Mr. Tytler, surely " — a *Scot*, if ever *Scot* there were" have expressed himself thus?'

scottish Patriots can be imaged in perfection these gentlemen are examples. *del*]
[MS 433] And let me add, that Citizen of the World as I [hold myself to be/am⟩]
hold myself to be, I have that degree of predilection for my *natale solum* nay I have
that [fair conviction/sense/impression of the merit of an ancient nation⟩] just
5   sense of the merit of an ancient nation which in old times was renowned for its
valour and maintained its independence against a powerful neighbour, and in
modern times has [excelled in all the arts of civilization⟩] been equally distinguished for its ingenuity and industry in civilised life, that I should have felt a
generous indignation at any injustice done to it. Johnson treated Scotland no
10   worse than he did [even his best friends/all his friends⟩] even his best friends,
whose characters he used to give as they appeared to him both in light and shade,
[nothing neither extenuating nor setting down aught in malice. *del*].[6] Some people
who had not exercised their minds sufficiently [found fault with/complained⟩]
condemned him for censuring his friends. But Sir Joshua Reynolds whose
15   philosophical penetration and justness of thinking are not less known to those
who live with him than his genius in his art is admired by the world explained his
conduct thus: 'He [loved/prided himself on⟩] was fond of discrimination which he
could not shew without [pointing out/marking⟩] pointing out both the [bad and
the good/bad as well as the good⟩] bad as well as the good in every character, and
20   as his friends were those [MS 434] [whose/the⟩] whose characters he knew best,
they afforded him the best opportunity for [nicely discriminating/separating⟩]
shewing the acuteness of his judgement.'
   ₐHe expressed to his friend Mr. Windham of Norfolk his wonder at the extreme
jealousy of the Scotch, and their resentment at having their country described by
25   him as it really [is/was⟩] was, when to say that it was a country as good as England
would have been a gross falshood. 'None of us' said he 'would be offended that/if[7]
a foreigner who has travelled here should say that Vines and Olives don't grow in
[Britain⟩] England', and as to his prejudice against the Scotch which I allways
ascribed to that nationality which he observed in *them*, he said to the same
30   gentleman 'When I find a scotchman to whom an englishman is as a scotchman,
[that scotchman/he⟩] that scotchman shall be as an englishman to me.' His
intimacy with many gentlemen of Scotland and his employing so many natives of
that country as his amanuenses prove that his prejudice was not virulent, and I
have deposited in the British Museum amongst other pieces of his writing, the
35   following note in answer to one from me asking if he would meet me at dinner at
the Mitre though a friend of mine a scotchman was to be there: 'Mr. Johnson does
not see why Mr. Boswell should suppose a scotchman less acceptable than any
other man. He will be at the Mitre.'
   My much valued friend Dr. Barnard now Bishop of Kilaloe having once
40   expressed to him an apprehension, that if he should visit Ireland he might treat the
people of that country more unfavourably than he had even done the scotch, he
answered with strong pointed double=edged wit, 'Sir you have no reason to be

---

[6] JB alludes to Othello's final speech: 'When you shall these many deeds relate, / Speak
of me as I am; nothing extenuate, / Nor set down aught in malice' (V. ii. 342–44).
  [7] The alternative is resolved by the printing of 'if' in the revises.

affraid of me. The Irish are not in a conspiracy to cheat the World by false representations of the merits of their countrymen. No Sir the Irish are a fair people. [I never heard them>] They never speak well of one another.'[8]

He told me an instance of scottish nationality which made a very unfavourable impression upon his mind. A scotchman of some consideration in London solicited him to recommend by the weight of his learned authority to the office of master of an english school a person of whom he who recommended him confessed he knew no more but that he was [connected to him as *del*] his Countryman. Johnson was shocked at this unconscientious attempt.ᴧ

All the miserable [cavillings/*undeciphered word*>] cavillings against his Journey in newspapers magazines and other fugitive publications I can speak from certain knowledge only furnished him with sport. At last there came out a [blackguard Book>] scurrilous volume larger than [his 'Journey'>] Johnson's own, filled with rancorous[9] abuse, [and bearing a/the name>] under a name real or fictitious of some [/low/>] low man in an obscure corner ᴧof Scotlandᴧ though supposed to be [chiefly composed by one/a person once as low and obscure as can almost be supposed but now loaded with wealth, it is said raised by purse pride/and swollen with purse pride>] the work of a man better known in both countries. The effect which it had upon [him>] Johnson was to produce this pleasant observation to Mr. Seward ᴧto whom he lent the book:ᴧ '[The>] This fellow must be a Blockhead. ᴧThey don't know how to go about their abuse.ᴧ Who [will/should>] will read a five shilling Book against me? No, Sir if they had wit, they should have kept pelting me with [/sixpenny/ *del*] pamphlets.'[1]

. . . .

To James Boswell Esq.[2]

. . . .

On tuesday 21 March I arrived in London [in the forenoon and found>] [and in repairing to Bolt Court before dinner found>] and in repairing to Dr. Johnson before dinner found him in his study sitting with Mr. Peter Garrick the elder

5

10

15

20

25

---

[8] This anecdote originally appeared on MS 400 (*ante* p. 105–05). There, SJ's comparison was placed in the context of a dinner at the Mitre, 1 May 1773, at which SJ praised JB for being so '*unscottified*' that he need 'not at every other sentence bring in some other Scotchman.' JB's decision to transfer Barnard's anecdote to 1775 may well reflect a desire to place it *after* the account of SJ's comments on Scotland and the Scots occasioned by the Hebridean tour. This rearrangement of material not only gave Barnard's anecdote more narrative force, but it also preserved the chronological sequence: as the Bishop informed JB, 15 October 1785, SJ's comment on the Irish had been made 'above ten years ago, soon after the Publication of his Tour to Scotland' (*Corr. 2*, p. 122). It should be noted that Barnard, in supplying JB with this material for the *Life*, expressed reservations about printing it: 'These were as nearly his words as I can recollect. But how pleasing it may be to either Nation to publish them, I leave to your Judgement' (*Corr. 2*, p. 122).

[9] In the revises, JB altered 'rancorous' to 'scurrilous' then back to 'rancorous' before finally settling on 'malignant'.

[1] Direction to the compositor, '([Excerpt mine of 11 and 18>] Take in mine of 18 febry)'. This Paper Apart no longer forms part of the *Life* MS.

[2] Direction to the compositor, '"I am sorry" (take it in)'. This Paper Apart no longer forms part of the *Life* MS.

brother of David, strongly resembling [MS 435] him in his countenance and voice but of more sedate and placid manners. Johnson [told>] informed me that though ⱉMr.ⱊ Beauclerk was in great pain, it was hoped he was not in danger, and that he now [wished/was>] wished to consult Dr. Heberden to try the effect of a *new*

5   *understanding*. Both at this interview and in the evening at Mr. Thrales where he and Mr. Peter Garrick and I met again he was violent upon the Ossian Controversy, [saying>] observing 'We do not know that there are any ancient ⱉearseⱊ manuscripts and we have no other reason to disbelieve that there are men with three heads but that we do not know that there are any such ⱉmenⱊ.' He also was

10   outrageous upon his supposition that my countrymen loved Scotland better than truth saying 'All of them — nay not all, — but *droves* of them would come up and attest what they think for the honour of Scotland.' He also persevered in his wild allegation that he questioned if there was a tree between Edinburgh and the english border [ⱉthat wasⱊ *del*] older than himself. I assured him [of his

15   mistake/errour>] he was mistaken, and [said that>] suggested that the proper punishment would be that he should receive a stripe [at/for>] at every tree [above/of>] above a hundred years old that was found within that space. He laughed and said 'I believe I might submit to it for a *bawbee*.'

     The doubts which ⱉin my correspondence with himⱊ I had ventured to state as

20   to the justice and [propriety>] wisdom of the conduct of Great Britain towards the [MS 436] American colonies, while I at the same time requested that he would enable me to [inform/instruct>] inform myself upon that momentous subject, he had altogether disregarded; and had [now>] recently published a Pamphlet entitled 'Taxation no Tyranny an Answer to the Resolutions and Address of the American

25   Congress.'

     ⱉHe had long before indulged most unfavourable sentiments of our fellow subjects in America. For, as early as 1769 I was told by Dr. John Campbell that he had said of them 'Sir they are a [parcel/race>] race of convicts and ought to be thankful for anything [they get/we allow/grant them>] we allow them short of

30   hanging.'ⱊ

     Of this [publication/performance>] performance I avoided to talk with him; for I [came to have a>] had now formed a clear and settled opinion that [the people of America/our american colonies were well warranted/had a full constitutional right to resist>] the people of America were well warranted to resist a claim that

35   their fellow subjects in the Mother Country should have the ⱉentireⱊ command of their fortunes by taxing them without their own consent, and the extreme violence which it breathed, appeared to me so inconsistent with the mildness of [an abstract christian Sage>] a christian philosopher, and so [directly/very>] directly opposite to the principles of peace which he had so beautifully recommended in his Pamphlet

40   respecting Falklands Islands, that I was sorry to see him appear in so unfavourable a light. Besides I could not perceive in it that ability of argument or that felicity of expression for which he was upon other occasions so eminent. Positive Assertion, sarcastical rage and extravagant ridicule which he himself reprobated as a test of truth, ⱉwereⱊ united in this Ministerial Rhapsody. [He seemed to me instead of a

45   dexterous Champion to be a furious Bull turned [MS 437] loose to trample down and toss and gore the Colonists and all their friends. *del*]

That this Pamplet was written at the desire of [those/some⟩] those who were then in power I have no doubt and indeed he owned to me that it had been revised and curtailed by [some/one⟩] some of them: he supposed /in particular/ [Mr. Charles Jenkinson⟩] Sir Grey Cooper — /how humiliating to the great Johnson./[3] He told me that they had struck out one passage, which was to this effect 'that the Colonists could with no solidity argue from their not having been taxed while in their infancy that they should not now be taxed. We do not put a calf into the plow. We wait till he is an Ox.' ₍He said 'They struck it out either critically as too ludicrous, or politically as too exasperating. I care not which. It was their business. If an Architect says "I will build five stories", and the man who employs him says "I will have only three", the employer is to decide.' 'Yes Sir' said I 'in ordinary Cases. But should it be so [when the Architect gives his skill and labour gratis/if it is a gratis⟩] when the Architect gives his skill and labour gratis?'₎

Unfavourable as I am [very sorry/constrained⟩] constrained to say my Opinion of this Pamphlet was, [as it⟩] yet since it was congenial with the sentiments of numbers at that time, and as every thing relating to the writings of Johnson is [of importance/interesting⟩] of importance in literary history I shall here[4] insert some passages which were struck out [/either by himself or those who revised it/⟩] either by himself or those who revised it. They appear printed in a few proof leaves of it in my possession marked with corrections in his own hand writing. ₍I shall distinguish them by *Italicks*.₎

In the paragraph where he says the Americans were incited to resistance by European intelligence from 'men whom they thought their friends but who were friends only to themselves' there followed '*and made by their selfishness the enemies of their country.*'

[MS 438] And the next paragraph ran thus 'On the original contrivers of mischief *rather than on those whom they have deluded* let an insulted Nation pour out its vengeance.'

The paragraph which came next was in these words: '*Unhappy is that country in which men can hope for advancement by favouring its enemies. The tranquillity of stable government is not always easily preserved against the machinations of single innovators; but what can be the hope of quiet when factions hostile to the legislature can be openly formed and openly avowed?*'

After the paragraph which now concludes the Pamphlet there followed this in which he certainly means the [great/renowned⟩] great Earl of Chatham, and glances at a certain popular Lord Chancellor.

---

[3] The final clause ('he supposed /in particular/ Sir Grey Cooper — /how humiliating to the great Johnson./') was deleted by JB in the revises, perhaps because the former Secretary of the Treasury still wielded considerable influence (*Works*, Yale ed., x. 401). In 1775, Cooper had served as go-between during the Ministry's negotiations with SJ; he had then, acting on behalf of the government, censored 'Taxation no Tyranny' in proof. As Donald Greene points out, William Strahan appears to have assisted 'in watering down Johnson's bold language to the milder terms the government wished to employ' (*Works*, Yale ed., x. 401). Cooper is also mentioned by name on MS 365, but in the first edition he appears as 'one of the Secretaries of the treasury'. See *ante* p. 63 and n. 6.

[4] The compositor misread 'here' as 'there', and this error went uncorrected.

ʎ'If[5] by the fortune of war they drive us utterly away, what they will do next can only be conjectured. If a new monarchy is erected they will want a KING. He who first takes into his hand the scepter of America, should have a name of good omen. WILLIAM has been known both as conqueror and deliverer, and perhaps England however contemned might yet supply them with ANOTHER WILLIAM. Whigs indeed are not willing to be governed, and it is possible that KING WILLIAM may be strongly inclined to guide their measures; but Whigs have been cheated like other mortals and suffered their leader to become their tyrant under the name of their Protector. What more they will receive from England no man can tell. In their rudiments of empire they may want a CHANCELLOR.'ʎ

Then [came/stood>] came this paragraph:

'*Their numbers*[6] ʎare at present not quite sufficient for the greatness which in some form of government or other is to rival the ancient monarchies; but by Dr. Franklin's rule of progression they will in a century and a quarter be more than equal to the inhabitants of Europe. When the Whigs of America are thus multiplied let the princes of the earth tremble in their palaces. If they should continue to double and to double, their own hemisphere will not long contain them. But let not the boldest oppugners of authority look forward with delight to this futurity of whiggism.'ʎ

How it ended I know not, as it is cut off abruptly at the [foot/bottom>] foot of the last of these proof pages.

[The False Alarm — Thoughts on *del*]

[Here ended his labours for Government which notwithstanding the brilliant rays which shine through some of them it were to be wished had never existed. *del*]

[MS opp. 439] [ʎThis unlucky pamphlet/publication/performance drew upon him various attacks. Against the common weapons of literary warfare he was hardened. But there were two instances of animadversion which I communicated to him and from which I could judge both from his silence and his looks appeared to me to impress him much. One was a 'A Letter to Samuel Johnson LLD' published [in Octavo *del*] without a name, but written by the Reverend Dr. Joseph Towers[7] which treated him with all the respect due to his general character but expostulated with him in a strain of able and affecting argument thus.[8] The other was a paragraph of a letter to me from my friend the Reverend Mr. Temple Authour of/who wrote/who furnished the character of Gray which has had the honour to be adopted both by Mr. Mason and Dr. Johnson.[9] The words were 'How can your

---

[5] Direction to the compositor, 'Print all on this page in Italicks and small Caps'. This succeeded an earlier direction which read, 'Print these paragraphs in *Italicks*'.

[6] Deleted direction to the compositor, '(take it in)' This direction was replaced by a '†', which in turn cued the compositor to turn to the verso of MS 437. Thus, the text of this paragraph comes under the heading attached to that leaf, 'Print all on this page in Italicks and small Caps'.

[7] The full title of Towers's work was *A Letter to Dr. Samuel Johnson: occasioned by his Late Political Publications*; it appeared in January 1775 (Helen McGuffie, *Samuel Johnson in the British Press, 1749–1784*, 1976, p. 137).

[8] JB left several blank lines between 'thus' and 'The other...', intending to enter the quotation that was eventually inserted via Paper Apart TT. See *post* p. 134.

[9] This material originally appeared in MS 402. See *ante* p. 106.

great I will not say your *pious* but your *moral* friend support the barbarous measures of administration which they had/have not the face to ask even their infidel pensioner Hume to defend?[1]   Confident as Johnson may have been/as we may believe Johnson to have been in the rectitude of his own mind, he may have felt/it may have given him sincere uneasiness that his conduct should be erroneously imputed to unworthy motives by good men, and the usefulness/influence/effect of his valuable writings be obstructed or lessened.ₓ[2] *del*]

[MS 439] His Pamphlets in [support/favour>] support of the measures of Administration were published on his own account, and he afterwards collected them into a Volume with the title of 'Political Tracts by the Authour of the Rambler' with this motto.[3/4]

. . . .

[Paper Apart TT][5] These pamphlets drew upon him numerous attacks. Against the common weapons of literary warfare he was hardened; but there were two instances of animadversion which I communicated to him, and from what I could judge, both from his silence and his looks appeared to me to impress him much.

[The other was 'A Letter to Dr. Samuel Johnson occasioned by his late political publications' without a name but written by Dr. Joseph Towers.>] One[6] was a Pamphlet entitled 'A Letter to Dr. Samuel Johnson occasioned by his late political publications.'   It appeared [before/previous to>] previous to his 'Taxation no Tyranny' and was written by Dr. Joseph Towers. In that performance Dr. Johnson was treated with the respect due to so eminent a man[7] while his conduct as a political writer was boldly and pointedly [arraigned.

5

10

15

20

---

[1] JB refers to a passage in a letter from Temple, 26 March 1775: 'When we have the pleasure of seeing you, American affairs will be better known to you; but I hope you will receive your information from Mr Burke rather than Dr Johnson. Is it inconsistent in your pious friend, I should have added *moral* too, to commence in his old age a writer in support of at least unpopular and violent measures?   They dare not require such a return from another of their Pensioners, even the infidel D. Hume' (*Corr.* 6, p. 361). JB did not consult the original when composing this passage for the *Life* but paraphrased from memory.

[2] JB reinstated this deleted passage on Temple below, at the end of Paper Apart TT. See *post* p. 135.

[3] Direction to the compositor, '(Take in Paper marked TT)'.

[4] The quotation from Claudianus, missing in the MS, had been supplied by the stage of the revises.

[5] At the head of this leaf, JB wrote, 'TT for page 439 at top' and then deleted 'at top'.

[6] JB originally placed the paragraph devoted to Temple before the discussion of Towers. When he decided to reverse the order of these 'two instances of animadversion,' he revised the opening sentences and directed the compositor to transpose the two sections.   The transcription reflects this revised sequence.

[7] Keyed to this passage is the deleted draft for a note in Plymsell's hand at the bottom of p. 460 of the revises: 'Since [Dr. Johnson's>] my great friend's death, Dr. Towers has published "An Essay on the Life, Character, and Writings of Dr. Samuel Johnson," [in which though a dissenting minister, he has in several passages given ₓhimₓ liberal praise.'>] in which he has given him liberal praise.'

It began thus: 'When a man who has rendered himself eminent by his productions in morals and in polite literature engages in political contentions, and in those which are apprehended to be of great national importance, it may reasonably be expected of such a Writer that he should distinguish himself, not by
5   party violence and rancour, but by moderation and by wisdom, and that at least he should not wholly lose sight of that liberality of sentiment which should characterise the scholar, nor of that decency and politeness which should adorn the gentleman. But unhappily your political productions have been chiefly remarkable for bitterness of invective unjust and uncandid representations, the most
10   bigotted prejudices against them whom you oppose, and the highest strains of contemptuous insolence.'>] arraigned as inconsistent with [that of>] the character of one who if he did employ his pen upon that subject 'it might reasonably be expected should distinguish himself not by party violence and rancour but by moderation and by wisdom.'

15   It concluded thus 'I would however wish you to remember, should you again address the publick under the character of a political writer, that luxuriance of imagination or energy of language will ill compensate for the want of candour, of justice, and of truth. And I shall only add that should I hereafter be disposed to read as I heretofore have done, the most excellent of all your performances THE
20   RAMBLER, the pleasure which I have been accustomed to find in it will be much diminished by the reflection that the writer of so moral, so elegant, and so valuable a work, was capable of prostituting his talents in such productions as the *False Alarm*, the *Thoughts on the Transactions respecting Falklands' Islands*, and the *Patriot*.'

25   I am very ready to do justice to the merit of Dr. Towers, of whom I will say that although I abhor his whiggish democratical notions and propensities (for I will not call them principles) I esteem him as an ingenious [well *del*] knowing and very convivial man.

[One>] The other instance was a paragraph of a letter to me from my old and
30   most intimate friend the Reverend Mr. Temple who wrote the character of Gray which has had the honour to be adopted both by Mr. Mason and Dr. Johnson in their accounts of that poet. The words were 'How can your great, I will not say your *pious* but your *moral* friend support the barbarous measures of administration which they have not the face to ask even their infidel pensioner Hume to
35   defend.'[8]

ʌConfident as Johnson may have been of the rectitude of his own mind, he may have felt sincere uneasiness that his conduct should be erroneously imputed to unworthy motives by good men, and the influence of his valuable writings be on that account, in any degree obstructed or lessened.ʌ

40   [MS 439 resumed] He complained to a Right Honourable friend of [the first abilities and most elegant manners with whom he maintained a long intimacy that as his pension>] distinguished talents and very elegant manners with whom he maintained a long intimacy and whose generosity towards him will afterwards

---

[8] At this point JB reinforced his decision to transpose the discussion of Temple and Towers by instructing the compositor to 'see back of the sheet' for the final paragraph.

appear, that his pension having been given to him as a literary character he had been applied to by Administration to write political pamphlets and he was even so much irritated that he declared his resolution to resign his pension. His friend shewed him the impropriety of this, and he afterwards expressed his gratitude and said he had received good advice. To that friend he [expressed⟩] signified a wish to have his pension secured to him for his life.

On friday [24 March⟩] March 24 I met him at the LITERARY CLUB [where were/with⟩] where were Mr. Beauclerk, Mr. Langton Mr. Colman Dr. Percy Mr. Vesey Sir Charles Bunbury Dr. George Fordyce Mr. Steevens Mr. Charles Fox. Before he came in we talked of his Journey to [MS 440] the Western Islands and of his coming away 'willing to believe the second sight' which seemed to excite some ridicule. I was then so impressed with the truth of many of the stories of it which I had been told that I avowed my conviction, saying 'He is only willing to believe I do believe. The evidence is enough for me, /though not for his great mind/.[9] What will not fill a quart bottle will fill a pint bottle. I am filled with belief.' 'Are you?' said Colman. 'Then cork it up.'

ₐI found his 'Journey' the common topick of conversation in London at this time wherever I happened to be. At one of Lord Mansfield's [formal Sunday evening conversations/Sunday evening formal conversations⟩] formal Sunday evening conversations ₐstrangelyₐ called *Levées*, his Lordship addressed me 'We have all been reading your travels Mr. Boswell.' I answered 'I was [but/only⟩] but the humble attendant of Dr. Johnson, my Lord.' [His Lordship with that air and manner which none who ever heard him speak can forget replied⟩] The Chief Justice replied with that air and manner which none who ever heard him speak can forget, 'He speaks ill of nobody but Ossian.'ₐ

Johnson was in great [spirits/glee⟩] spirits this evening ₐat the Clubₐ and [talked away/harangued⟩] talked with [high success⟩] great animation and success. He attacked Swift as he used to do upon all occasions. [He said '"the tale of the Tub"⟩] '"The Tale of a Tub" is so much superiour to his other writings that one can hardly believe he was the Authour of it.[1] There is in it such a vigour of mind, such a swarm of thoughts, so much of nature and art and life.' I wondered to hear him say of 'Gulliver's Travels', 'When once you have thought of big men and little men, it is very easy to do all the rest.' I endeavoured to make a stand for Swift [MS 441] and tried to rouse those who were much more able to defend him; but in vain. Johnson at last of his own accord allowed very great merit to the Inventory of Articles found in the pockets of the Man Mountain, particularly the description of his Watch which it was conjectured was his God as he consulted it upon all occasions. He observed that 'Swift put his name [to but/but to⟩] to but two things (after he had a name to put): The Plan for the Improvement of the english language, and the last Drapier's letter.'

From Swift there was an easy transition to [old Mr. Sheridan⟩] Mr. Thomas Sheridan. —*Johnson.* 'Sheridan is a wonderful admirer of the Tragedy of Douglas

---

[9] The optional phrase, which JB left unresolved, is printed in the revises.

[1] In the second edition JB inserts a footnote devoted to a defence of Swift's 'learning as well as his acuteness in logick and metaphysicks'.

and presented its Authour with a gold medal. Some years ago at a Coffee=house
in Oxford I called to him "Mr. Sheridan, Mr. Sheridan, how came you to give a
gold medal to Home for writing that foolish play?" This you see was wanton and
insolent. But I *meant* to be wanton and insolent. A medal has no value but as a
5   stamp of merit. And was Sheridan to assume to himself the right of giving that
stamp? If Sheridan was magnificent [MS 442] enough [to give/offered›] to bestow
a gold medal as [a premium for dramatick excellence/an honorary reward to
dramatic genius›] an honorary reward of dramatick excellence he should have
requested one of the Universities to [confer it/chuse the person.›] chuse the
10 person on whom it should be conferred. But Sheridan had no right to give a stamp
of merit. It was counterfeiting Apollo's coin.'
   On Monday [27 March›] March 27 I breakfasted with him at Mr. Strahan's.
He told us that he was engaged to go [at night/that evening›] that evening to Mrs.
Abington's benefit. 'She was visiting some Ladies whom I was visiting, and begged
15 that I would come to her benefit. I told her I could not hear. But she insisted so
much on my coming, that it would have been brutal to have refused her.' This was
a speech quite characteristical. [He did not mention the Ladies whom he was
visiting. He loved to be mysterious in little matters. He used to say 'I am to dine
at the other end of the town. I am to dine near Grosvenor Square,' so that we
20 might suppose that it was with a Duke. And he was vain of a fine actress's
solicitations. He said the Play was to be the Hypocrite, altered from Cibber's
Nonjuror. He said›] He loved to bring forward his having been in the gay circles
of life. And he was perhaps a little vain of the solicitations of this elegant and
fashionable actress. He told us the Play was to be the Hypocrite altered from
25 Cibber's Nonjuror so as to satyrise the Methodists. He said 'I do not think the
character of the Hypocrite [just as/justly applicable to›] justly applicable to the
Methodists [MS 443] but it was [very just as/very justly applicable›] very applicable to the Nonjurors. I once said to Dr. Madan a Clergyman of Ireland who was a
great Whig, that I believed a Nonjuror would have been less criminal in taking the
30 oaths [/imposed by the ruling power/›] imposed by the ruling power than refusing
them; because refusing them necessarily laid him under almost an irresistible
temptation to be more criminal; for, a man *must* live and if he precludes himself
from the [supports of the›] support furnished by the establishment will probably be
reduced to very wicked shifts to [get a support›] maintain himself.'[a]   [*Boswell. A*

35   [a] His opinion however upon the subject appears to have been fixed for in his
'Life of Fenton' he observes 'with many other wise and virtuous men who at that
time of discord and debate ‸[about the [*undeciphered word del*] year]‸ consulted
conscience well or ill-formed more than interest, he doubted the legality of the
government, and refusing to qualify himself for publick employment by taking the
40 oaths required left the university [of›] without a degree' which he calls 'this
perverseness of integrity.'
   The question concerning the morality of taking oaths ‸of whatever kind‸
imposed by the prevailing power at the time rather than be excluded from all
consequence or ‸even‸ any considerable usefulness in Society has been agitated
45 with all the acuteness of casuistry. It is [a well-known story›] related that he who

man who took/I said that I should think that>] *Boswell.* 'I should think Sir that a
man who took the oaths contrary to his principles was a determined wicked man,
because he was sure he was committing perjury. Whereas a Nonjuror might be
insensibly led to do what was wrong, without being so directly conscious of it.'
Johnson. 'Why Sir a man who goes to bed to his Patron's Wife is pretty sure that he   5
is committing wickedness.' [/*Boswell*/>] *Boswell.* 'Did the nonjuring clergymen do
so, Sir?' *Johnson.* 'I am affraid many of them did.'

    I was startled at [his/this proposition; and after all am by no means clear that it
is just.>] his argument; and could by no means think it convincing. Had not his
own Father taken the oaths, [MS 444] (as to which he once observed to me when   10
I pressed him upon it, '*that* Sir he was to settle with himself') he would probably
have been more violent against a swearing Jacobite.

    'Had he not resembled my Father as he *swore*'.

    Mr. Strahan talked of launching into the great Ocean of London ˄in order˄ to
have a chance for rising to eminence and observing that many men were kept back   15
from trying their fortune there because they were born to a competency said,
'Small certainties are the bane of men of [genius and abilities>] talents,' which
Johnson confirmed. He put Johnson in mind of a remark which he had made to
Mr. Strahan 'There are few ways in which a man can be more innocently employed
than in getting money.' 'The more one thinks of this' said Strahan 'the juster will   20
it/it will² appear.'

    Mr. Strahan had taken a poor boy from the country as an apprentice upon [his>]
Johnson's recommendation. [He desired/asked>] Johnson desired Mr. Strahan to
let him have five guineas [to>] on account; and [speaking of the boy said *del*]: 'I'll
give [him>] this boy one. Nay, if [one/a man>] a man recommends a boy and does   25
nothing for him it is [not well/sad work>] sad work. Call him down.'

    I followed him into the Court=yard [MS 445] behind Mr. Strahan's house; and
there I had [an example/a proof>] a proof of what I had heard him profess, that he

---

devised the oath of Abjuration profligately boasted that he had framed a test
which should damn one half of the nation and starve the other. [To minds>] Upon   30
minds not [lofty enough>] exalted to inflexible integrity or minds in whom zeal for
a party is predominant to excess, taking [oaths to government inconsistent with or
[against>] that oath against conviction may have been [appl>] palliated under the
plea of necessity, or ventured upon in heat, as upon the whole producing more
good than evil ˄also˄.   35

    At a county election in Scotland many years ago when there was a warm
contest between the friends of the Hannoverian succession and [its>] those against
it, the oath of abjuration having been [unhandsomely *del*] demanded, the
freeholders upon one side rose to [go away. A hearty gentleman>] go away, upon
which a hearty gentleman one of their number ran to the door to stop them,   40
calling out with much earnestness, 'Stay stay my friends and let us swear the rogues
out of it.' [Happily we now live at a time period when *del*]

---

² The alternative is resolved by the printing of 'it will' in the revises.

talked alike to all. 'Some people' said he 'tell you that they let themselves down to the capacity of their hearers. I never do that. I speak uniformly [in as intelligible a manner/and intelligibly>] in as intelligible a manner as I can.'

'Well my boy how do you go on?' — 'Pretty well Sir. But they are affraid I an't
5   strong enough for some parts of the [work/business>] business.' — /Johnson/ [3]
'Why I shall be sorry for it; for when you consider with how little mental power and corporeal labour a printer can get a guinea a week, it is a very desireable [occupation/business>] occupation for you. Do you hear — take all the pains you can; and if this does not do, we must think of some other way of life for you.
10   There's a guinea.'

Here was one of the many many instances of his [effectual>] active benevolence. At the same time the slow and [loud>] sonorous solemnity with which [he leant down/stooped and harangued/talked to>] while he bent himself down he addressed a little thick short=legged boy, [and/contrasted with>] contrasted with
15   the boy's awkwardness and awe could not but excite some ludicrous emotions.

I met him at Drury=lane Playhouse in the evening. [Sir Joshua Reynolds had secured forty places in the front boxes, and had>] Sir Joshua Reynolds at Mrs. Abington's request had promised to bring [me *del*] a body of wits to her benefit, and having secured forty places in the front boxes, had done [MS 446] me the honour
20   [to let me have/assign me one>] however slight my title, to put me in the groupe. Johnson sat [/on the seat/>] on the seat directly behind me; [but/and>] and as he could neither see nor hear at such a distance from the stage he was wrapped up in grave abstraction and [was/seemed>] seemed quite a cloud amidst all the sunshine of glitter and gayety. I wondered at his patience in sitting out a Play of five acts,
25   and a Farce [*Bon Ton del*] of two.[4] He spoke very little. But after the prologue to *Bon Ton* had been spoken which he could hear pretty well from the more slow and distinct utterance, he [said>] observed 'Dryden has written prologues superiour to any that [/David/>] David Garrick has written; but [/David/>] David Garrick has written more good prologues than Dryden has done. It is wonderful [how he has
30   written such a variety of them/what a variety of them he has written>] that he has been able to write such a variety of them.'

[I half persuaded him to go with me ⟨after the Play⟩ to sup at Beauclerk's. He went a part of the way. But suddenly stopped short and took a resolution to go home. He said with a placid look 'But I don't love Beauclerk the less.' Such little
35   circumstances may to some appear too slight/may by some be thought too small. But I draw the portrait of Johnson in the style of a flemish painter. I am not satisfied with hitting the large features. I must be exact as to every line in his countenance every hair, every mole. But I am chiefly [MS 447] anxious not to

---

[3] The optional word, which JB left unresolved, is printed in the revises.

[4] According to Frances Burney's account, SJ had been 'ordered' to the theatre by 'Mrs. Abington, or Mrs. Somebody … but I placed myself in the middle of the first row of the front boxes, to show that when I was called I came' (*Diary and Letters of Madame D'Arblay*, ed. Charlotte Barrett, rev. Austin Dobson, 1904, ii. 143). The performance (27 March 1775) was a highly successful benefit for Mrs. Abington, who played Charlotte in *The Hypocrite* as well as Miss Titup in the abbreviated, two-act version of *Bon Ton* (*Lond. Stage*, 4. iii. 1838, 1876, 1879). See *post* p. 144 (MS 451).

omit any trait however slight that evinces/illustrates the philanthropy of his disposition which has been so grossly misunderstood. There was an affectionate caveat in his 'But I don't love Beauclerk the less' which indicated a tenderness more than common. *del*]⁵

At Mr. Beauclerk's was Mr. Garrick whom I made happy with Johnson's praise   5
of his Prologues; and I suppose in gratitude to him he took up one of his favourite topicks the nationality of the Scotch which he maintained [with⟩] in his pleasant manner with the aid of a little poetical fiction. 'Come come don't deny it. They are really national. Why now the Adams are as liberal=minded men as in [the world/England⟩] the world. But I don't know how, all their workmen are scotch.   10
You are to be sure [very/wonderfully⟩] wonderfully free from that nationality. But so it [is/happens⟩] happens that you employ the only ∧scotch∧ shoeblack in London.' He took off his old Master very ludicrously repeating
    Os homini sublime dedit, cælumque tueri
    Jussit, et erectos ad sidera tollere vultus   15
looking downwards all the time and while pronouncing the four last words, absolutely touching the ground with a kind of contorted gesticulation.

∧I have been considered by those who knew Johnson best as being able to imitate most exactly his manner in all respects which now that he is gone affords sometimes no small gratification to myself as well as to others of his friends; and   20
indeed I cannot too frequently request of my readers while perusing his conversation to endeavour to keep in mind his deliberate and strong utterance with the other particulars which I have been careful to mention. His tone in speaking was indeed very impressive,[a] and I wish it could be preserved as musick is written,

[a] My noble friend Lord Pembroke said once to me at Wilton with a happy   25
pleasantry and some truth that 'Dr. Johnson's sayings would not appear so extraordinary were it not for his "*bow-ow way*"'. The sayings themselves are generally of sterling merit; but doubtless his *manner* [is⟩] was an addition to their effect and therefore should be attended to as much as may be.[a1]

---

⁵ This deleted passage originates in JB's journal: 'I half persuaded him to go with me to Beauclerk's. But he suddenly took a resolution to go home, saying, "But I don't love Beauclerk the less"; or something quite to that effect, for I am so nice in recording him that every trifle must be authentic. I draw him in the style of a Flemish painter. I am not satisfied with hitting the large features. I must be exact as to every hair, or even every spot on his countenance'. JB reintroduced the metaphor of the 'Flemish painter', which is central to his biographical method, in the account of SJ at Ashbourne, 22 September 1777 (Hill-Powell iii. 191). The original context suggests that visual portraiture prompted JB's verbal conceit: on 27 March SJ appears to have been sitting to Frances Reynolds at Sir Joshua's (Journ. 27 Mar. 1775; *Ominous Years*, p. 101 and n. 2).

[a1] In the revises, the footnote continues: 'It is necessary, however, to guard those who were not acquainted with him, against overcharged imitations or caricatures of his manner, which are frequently attempted, and many of which are secondhand copies from the late Mr. Henderson the actor, who, though a good mimick of some persons, did not hit the likeness of Johnson.' This addition appears to have been made in first proof. At the stage of the revises, EM altered 'hit the likeness of Johnson' to 'represent Johnson correctly'. He

according to the very ingenious method of Mr. Steele in his 'System of intonation as applied to language' in which that of Mr. Garrick and other eminent speakers is if I may use the expression put *in score*._λ ⁶/⁷

    [MS 448] Next day I dined with Johnson at Mr. Thrale's. He attacked Gray,
5 [calling him/and called him›] calling him 'a dull fellow'. [I said›] BOSWELL. 'I understood he was reserved and might appear dull in company. But surely he was not dull in his poetry.' JOHNSON. '[/No/ *del*] Sir he was dull in company, dull in his closet, dull every where. He was dull in a new way, and that made many people think him GREAT. He was a mechanical Poet.' He then repeated some ludicrous
10 lines which [I lost/have lost›] escaped my memory and said 'Is not that GREAT like his Odes?' Mrs. Thrale [said they›] maintained that his Odes were melodious upon which he exclaimed [contemptuously *del*]:
        'Weave the warp and weave the woof.'
I added in a solemn tone,
15   'The winding sheet of Edward's Race.
There is a good line.' 'Ay' said he 'and the next line is a good one,' pronouncing it Contemptously:
        'Give ample verge/room⁸ and room enough.'
    No [said he›] Sir, There are but two good stanzas in Gray's poetry which are in
20 his "Church=Yard."' He then repeated the Stanza:

---

⁶ In the revises, EM underlined '*in score*' and wrote in the margin a potential replacement for that phrase, 'not correct — better "by peculiar symbols"'. This alternative is deleted. But in the second edition JB adds a note to justify his use of '*in score*'. A contribution from Charles Burney appears in the third edition.

⁷ In the revises, this paragraph becomes two. First, a paragraph in praise of Garrick's powers as a mimic is substituted for JB's tribute to himself: 'Garrick, however, when he pleased, could imitate Johnson very exactly; for that great actor, with his distinguished powers of expression which were so universally admired, possessed also an admirable talent of mimickry. He was always jealous that Johnson spoke lightly of him. I recollect his exhibiting him to me one day, as if saying, "Davy is futile," which he uttered perfectly with the tone and air of Johnson.' The second paragraph in the revises reworks the second half of the paragraph in the MS: 'I cannot too frequently request of my readers while they peruse my account of Johnson's conversation, to endeavour to keep in mind his deliberate and strong utterance. His mode of speaking was indeed very impressive; and I wish it could be preserved as musick is written, according to the very ingenious method of Mr. Steele, who has shewn how the recitation of Mr. Garrick, and other eminent speakers, may be transmitted to posterity *in score*.' In the margin of the revises, EM changes 'may be transmitted' to 'might be transmitted'. A footnote (not in the MS) is keyed to 'Mr Steele': 'See "*Prosodia Rationalis*; or, an Essay towards establishing the Melody and Measure of Speech, to be expressed and perpetuated by peculiar Symbols." London, 1779.' Presumably these various changes to the MS text occurred in first proof.

⁸ The alternative is resolved by the printing of 'verge' in the revises.

---

also underlined 'Dr. Johnson's sayings would not appear so extraordinary, were it not for his *bow-ow way*' and queried in the margin 'Qu before'. JB crossed out EM's query and responded, 'No It is in my Tour to the Hebrides'. EM was wary of JB's use of '*bow-ow*', as he was of 'colloquialisms and vulgarisms of all sorts' (see To JB, 23 Dec. 1790, *Corr.* 2, p. 375). In a letter dated 5 March 1791, he urged JB, 'Pray omit ... your *bow wough* entirely' (*Corr.* 2, pp. 390–91).

'For who to dumb forgetfulness a prey'
mistaking one word for, instead of *precincts*, he said *confines*. [He added 'The other Stanza I forget'/'The other Stanza' said he 'I forget'.⟩] He added 'The other Stanza I forget.'

A young Lady who had married a man [MS 449] much her inferiour in rank being mentioned,[9] a question arose how a woman's relations should [behave to/treat her⟩] behave to her in such a situation; and ₍I cannot but be struck in a manner that [delicacy/politeness⟩] delicacy forbids me to express, while/when[1] I [resume/recapitulate⟩] recapitulate the debate.₎ It is not a little remarkable that while I [was for⟩] contended that she ought to be treated with the utmost violence and steadiness of displeasure, so as to have her [if possible totally obliterated/totally obliterated if possible⟩] if possible totally obliterated from the recollection of her family, Mrs. Thrale was all for mildness and forgiveness; and according to the [common/vulgar⟩] vulgar phrase, making the best of a bad bargain. JOHNSON. 'Madam we must distinguish. Were I a man of rank, I would not let [my/a⟩] a daughter starve who had made a mean marriage; but [as she has/had⟩] having voluntarily degraded herself from the [state⟩] rank which she was originally entitled to hold, I would support her only in the [state⟩] rank which she herself has chosen, and would not put her on a [footing/level⟩] level with my other daughters. You are to consider Madam that it is our duty to maintain the [subordination/various orders⟩] subordination of civilised society, and when [there is/one is guilty of⟩] there is a gross and shameful deviation from Rank it should be punished so as to deter others from the same perversion.'

₍After [considering this subject over and over again⟩] frequently considering this subject I am [more and more/still⟩] more and more confirmed in the opinion which I then expressed and which was sanctioned by the authority and illustrated by the wisdom of Johnson. And I think it of the utmost consequence to the [essential good/happiness⟩] happiness of Society, to which subordination is absolutely necessary. It is weak and pitiful and unworthy to relax in such cases. It is sacrificing general advantage to [personal/private⟩] private feelings and those too of a fantastical kind if there [is to be no distinction of rank.⟩] be no value in distinction of rank. If there is, let it be steadily maintained. If there is not, what does a degraded sister or daughter suffer by being kept in the situation to which she has descended? If indulgence be shewn to such conduct and the offenders know that in a shorter or longer time they shall be received as well as if they had not [contaminated/disgraced⟩] contaminated their [blood/birth⟩] blood by a base

5

10

15

20

25

30

35

---

[9] JB's journal makes it clear that the 'young Lady' in question was Susan Fox-Strangways (1744–1827), daughter of the first Earl of Ilchester. In 1764 Lady Susan had secretly married the actor William O'Brien (d. 1815), much to the dismay of her father, whose reaction Horace Walpole vividly described: 'Poor Lord Ilchester is almost distracted; indeed, it is the completion of disgrace — even a footman were preferable; the publicity of the hero's profession perpetuates the mortification. ... I could not have believed that Lady Susan would have stooped so low' (*Corres. Walpole*, xxxviii. 367). JB had met O'Brien at the theatre the previous evening (*Journ*. 27 March 1775).

₍ [1] The alternative is resolved by the printing of 'while' in the revises. See end notes, p. 262, for further details of the changes made to this passage in printing.

alliance the great check upon that inordinate [and perverse *del*] caprice which generally occasions low marriages will be removed and the fair and comfortable order of improved life will be miserably [impaired/disturbed>] disturbed.ᵧ

[Sir Joshua Reynolds had told me>] I had been told that Johnson was [of
5　opinion/positive>] of opinion that the character of the 'respectable hottentot' in Lord Chesterfield's [MS 450] Letters was not meant for him, but for George Lord Lyttelton who [was to be sure/certainly was>] it must be acknowledged was very awkward.　One reason which [he>] Johnson gave was that Lord Chesterfield had never seen him eat or drink.　But this circumstance of the Caricature might easily
10　have been added from fancy; and none of his friends could doubt that he was the person meant, though [I contrived now to bring him upon the subject and found/when I contrived now to bring him upon the subject I found>] I contrived now to bring him upon the subject and found him fully persuaded of the contrary. He told me that he did say these Letters 'taught the Morals of a Whore and the
15　manners of a dancing=master.' I always endeavoured to get as many of his sayings as I could authenticated by himself.　He said there was no wonder that Lord Chesterfield's letters had so [great/rapid>] great a sale, considering that they were the letters of a Statesman a Wit one who had been so much in the mouths of mankind one long accustomed *volitare per ora virûm*.[2]
20　[On friday March 31 having dined with Lord Mountstuart who took a wicked fancy to disable me from going to the Literary Club or at least to send me to it in the state of Copernicus in the tippling Philosophers,[3] I was not rigid enough to resist his [MS 451] Lordship's social gayety/convivial cordiality and generous wine; and in short I went to our Club in exuberant spirits. I found Dr. Johnson Dr.
25　Percy Mr. Fox Mr. Langton and some more members whom I did not recollect/have not marked down.　I would needs encounter the great man.　So I went and stood by his chair and rated/rallied him thus.>] [MS opp 450] [I supped with him and some other friends at a tavern.　One of the company attempted with too much forwardness to rally him on his late appearance at the theatre, but had
30　reason to repent of his temerity.>] [MS 451 attachment][4] On Friday March 31 I supped with him and some friends at a tavern.　One of the company attempted with too much forwardness to rally him on his late appearance at the Theatre; but

---

[2]Although JB did not mark this paragraph for deletion, he realized at some later stage that it substantially repeated material appearing under 1754 (see *Life* MS i. 193, and n. 8). He therefore substituted — probably in first proof, as the changes appear in the revises — a severely abbreviated version: 'Lord Chesterfield's letters being mentioned, Johnson said, "It was not to be wondered at that they had so great a sale, considering that they were the letters of a statesman, a wit, one who had been so much in the mouths of mankind, one accustomed *virum volitare per ora*."'

[3] JB alludes to *The Tipling Philosophers*, a poem by Edward Ward (1667–1731).　It describes the effects of alcohol on no fewer than fifty-one great thinkers, including Copernicus: 'With Wine he replenish'd his Veins, / And made his Philosophy reel, / Then fancy'd the World, like his Brains. / Run round like a Chariot-Wheel' (London, 1710, p. 39).

[4] The third and final version of this material appears on a small leaf attached to MS 451; this attachment bears the heading in JB's hand 'Top of p. 451'.

had reason to repent of his temerity. *[MS 451 resumed]* 'Why, Sir, did you go to Mrs. Abington's Benefit? Did you see?' *Johnson.* 'No.' 'Did you hear?' *Johnson.* 'No.' – 'Why then did you go?' *Johnson.* 'Because she is a favourite of the Publick; and when the Publick cares the thousandth part [about>] for you that it does [about you>] for her I will go to your benefit too.' [This quieted/composed me. *del*]   5

[Next day I expected/was affraid that he would give me/administer a severe reprimand; but he was very gentle, and gave me a most judicious advice which was whenever I had drunk wine, not to go into a new company, because it would then be perceived and I would not be in unison with them. Mr. Colman told me that when somebody with no good intention asked Dr. Johnson 'Well Sir did you see   10 your friend Boswell the /next/ day after coming to the Club in such a state/as he did?' — 'Yes Sir.' — 'And what did he say?' — 'Sir he said all that man should say. He said he was sorry.' *del*][5]

ʌ[He made me so easy/put me so much at ease that I now won a bet /of five shillings//of a crown>] Next morning I won a small bet from Lady Diana Beauclerk   15 by asking him as to one of his particularities, which her Ladyship [laid/wagered>] laid I durst not do. It seems he had been frequently observed at the club to put into his pocket the peel of the seville oranges which he squeesed into the drink which he made for himself. Beauclerk and Garrick told me of it, and seemed to think that he had a strange unwillingness to be discovered. We could not divine what he did   20 with them; and this was the bold question to be put.[6] I saw on his table the spoils of the preceeding night, some fresh peels with all the pulp taken out and nicely scraped and cut into pieces. 'O Sir' said I 'I now see so far what you do with the orange peels which you put into your pocket at the club.' *Johnson.* 'I have a great love for them.' ʌ*Boswell.*ʌ 'And pray Sir what do you do with them? You scrape   25 them it seems very neatly and what next.' *Johnson.* 'I let them dry Sir.' ʌ*Boswell.*ʌ 'And what next?' ʌ*Johnson.*ʌ 'Nay Sir you shall know their fate no farther.' ʌ*Boswell.*ʌ 'The World then must be left in the dark. ʌIt must be said (assuming a mock solemnity)ʌ "He scraped them and let them dry, but what he did with them next he never could be prevailed with to tell."' ʌ*Johnson.*ʌ 'Nay Sir, you   30 should say it more emphatically; "he could not be prevailed with even by his dearest friends to tell."'ʌ

He had this morning received his Diploma [of>] as Doctor of Laws from the University of Oxford. He did not vaunt of his new dignity but I understood he was highly pleased with it. I shall here *[MS 452]* insert the progress and completion of   35 that high academical honour in the same manner as I have traced his obtaining that of Master of Arts.[7]

---

[5] This anecdote was reworked and repositioned. See *post* p. 190 (MS 505).

[6] It is likely that SJ used the orange peel to counteract what he termed, writing to Hill   40 Boothby on 31 December 1755, 'indigestion and lubricity of the bowels': 'Take an ounce of dried orange peel finely powdered, divide it into scruples, and take one Scruple at a time in any manner; the best way is perhaps to drink it in a glass of hot red port, or to eat it first and drink the wine after it. If you mix cinnamon or nutmeg with the powder it were not worse, but it will be more bulky and so more troublesome. This is a medicine not disgusting, not costly, easily tried, and if not found useful easily left off' (*Letters of Johnson* ed. Redford, i.   45 120).

[7] Direction to the compositor, '(Take in the Letter Diploma etc.)'.

[Paper Apart O][8] To the Revd. Dr. Fothergill Vice Chancellor of the University of Oxford to be communicated to the Heads of Houses and proposed in Convocation.

Mr. Vice Chancellor and Gentlemen

The Honour of the degree of M.A. by Diploma formerly conferred upon Mr.
5 Samuel Johnson in consequence of his having eminently distinguished himself by the publication of a series of Essays excellently calculated to form the manners of the People and in which the Cause of Religion and Morality has been maintained and recommended by the strongest powers of argument and elegance of language reflected an equal degree of lustre upon the University itself.
10 The many learned Labours which have since that time employed the attention and displayed the abilities of that Great Man so much to the advancement of Literature and the benefit of the Community render him worthy of more distinguished honours in the Republic of Letters: and I persuade myself that I shall act agreably to the sentiments of the whole University, in desiring that it may be
15 proposed in Convocation to confer on him the degree of Doctor in Civil Law by Diploma. To which I readily give my consent and am,

Mr. Vice Chancellor and Gentlemen,
Your affectionate Friend and Servant,
North[a]
20 Downing Street
March 23, 1775[9]

. . . .

Viro[1] *reverendo Thomæ Fothergil, S.T.P. Universitatis Oxoniensis Vicecancellario, S.P.D.*
Sam: Johnson.
25 *Multis non est opus, ut Testimonium quo, Te præside, Oxonienses Nomen meum posteris commendarunt, quali animo acceperim compertum faciam. Nemo sibi placens non lætatur; nemo sibi non placet qui Vobis, literarum Arbitris, placere potuit. Hoc tamen habet incommodi tantum Beneficium, quod mihi nunquam posthac sine vestræ Famæ detrimento vel labi liceat vel cessare; semperque sit timendum, ne quod mihi tam*
30 *eximiæ Laudi est, Vobis aliquando fiat Opprobrio.*
Vale.[b]
7 Id. Apr. 1775[2]

[MS 452 resumed] He revised some sheets of Lord Hailes's Annals of Scotland, and wrote some [notes/corrections>] notes [/on the margin/>] on the margin

35   [a] Extracted from the Convocation Register Oxford.[a1]
   [b] The Original is in the Hands of Dr. Fothergill, then Vice-Chancellor, who made this transcript. - T. Warton'.

---

[8] Direction to the compositor, 'This comes in upon page 452'.
[9] SJ's diploma no longer forms part of the *Life* MS.
[1] This Paper Apart bears the heading, 'Print this in italicks'.
[2] For a translation of this letter of acknowledgment, see *Letters of Johnson* ed. Redford, v. 49.

[a1] This note may have been intended as a replacement for the following, which appears deleted at the end of the transcript: 'Compared with the Original in the University Register — James Boswell'.

[in/with a›] with red ink which he bid[3] me tell his Lordship did not sink into the paper and might be wiped off with a wet spunge, so that he did not [spoil/deface›] spoil his Manuscript. [An attention to a small particular like this when its use or convenience appears was not unworthy of him. *del*] I told him there were very few of his friends so accurate as that I could venture to [put/take›] put down in writing what   5 they told me as his sayings. —*Johnson*. 'Why should you [put/write/take down›] write down my sayings?' —*Boswell*. 'When they are good.'[4] *Johnson*. 'Nay you may as well [put/write›] put down the sayings of any one else that are good.' ⟨'But where' I might with great propriety have added 'can I find such?'⟩

I returned to him by appointment in the evening and we drank tea with Mrs.   10 Williams. He was just returned from dining at Mr. William Gerrard Hamilton's, and had been [brought home/set down at home›] set down at home by Mr. Jackson [(called the all knowing)›] (called the omniscient) in his coach. [So it had been a high day with him. But he was silent/disposed to taciturnity and not in very good humour. *del*] He had seen ⟨at Mr. Hamilton's⟩ a Gentleman *[MS 453]* who he was   15 told was a very great traveller. But I found that neither he nor Mr. Jackson gave him that ⟨full⟩ credit without which there is no pleasure in the [society/hearing›] society of travellers.[5] I was curious to [hear/learn›] hear what opinion so able a Judge ⟨as Johnson⟩ had formed of his abilities and I asked if he was not a man of sense? *Johnson*. 'Why Sir he is not a distinct relater; and I should say he is neither abounding nor   20 deficient in sense. I did not perceive any [superiour sense/superiourity of understanding›] superiority of understanding.' *Boswell*. 'But will you not allow him a nobleness of resolution?' *Johnson*. 'That ⟨Sir⟩ is not to the present purpose. We are talking of his sense. A fighting cock has a nobleness of resolution.'

Next day Sunday [2 April›] April 2 I dined with him at Mr. Hoole's the   25 Translator of Tasso.[6] There was a very good pudding. Mr. Hoole ordered another which came; upon which Johnson repeated,

'And lo two puddings smoak'd upon the board.'[7]

---

[3] Here, as elsewhere, 'bid' was changed to 'bade' by the stage of the revises, perhaps in accordance with SJ's prescription in his *Dictionary* that 'bade' is the appropriate preterite form.

[4] In the revises, EM notes in the margin that this 'answer does not correspond with the question' and proposes 'I only write them down when etc.'. In response, JB changes 'When they are good' to 'I write them when they are good'.

[5] The revises omit all references to William Gerrard Hamilton and to Richard Jackson: 'I visited him by appointment in the evening, and we drank tea with Mrs. Williams. He told me that he had been in the company of a gentleman whose extraordinary travels had been much the subject of conversation. But I found that he had not listened to him with that full confidence ...'. Though Hamilton, whom JB termed in a letter to EM '[t]hat *nervous* mortal' (*Corr. 2*, p. 387), insisted that two leaves in vol. 2 be cancelled, simply because he was named as an informant, there is no evidence that he put pressure on JB to alter this passage (Hill-Powell iv. 556–57). JB's journal as well as SJ's letter to Hester Thrale, 1 April 1775, make it clear that the 'very great traveller' under discussion was James Bruce (1730–94), who had recently returned from an expedition in search of the source of the Nile (*Letters of Johnson* ed. Redford, ii. 193 and n. 1).

[6] The revises omit the rest of this paragraph entirely, moving directly to the discussion of Pope: 'Next day, Sunday, April 2, I dined with him at Mr. Hoole's. We talked of Pope.'

[7] '"Live like yourself," was soon my Lady's word; / And lo! two puddings smoak'd upon the board' (Pope, *Epistle to Bathurst* [Twickenham edition], *ll*. 359–60).

He rose from table soon after dinner and walked in the garden. We conjectured that this was to avoid being reminded to go to church, a duty which he almost ever performed with a sluggish reluctance. Mrs. Hoole said he would loiter away the time and then find out that it was too late to go. A message was sent to him to
5 know if he would have tea [soon/in good time>] soon so as to go/get to church. He answered [hastily>] shortly 'I shall not go to church this afternoon, and I am in no haste for tea.' [MS 454] After this there was no more to be said.

 When he joined us, he talked of Pope [and He said *del*], 'He wrote his Dunciad for fame. That was his primary motive. Had it not been for that the dunces might
10 have railed against him [enough>] till they were weary, without his troubling himself [with/about>] about them. He delighted to vex them, [no doubt. But>] no doubt; but he had more delight in seeing how well he could vex them.'

 [He mentioned the Odes to Obscurity and Oblivion in ridicule of 'cool Mason and warm Gray' and said, 'They are'>] The Odes to Obscurity and Oblivion in
15 ridicule of 'cool Mason and warm Gray' being mentioned, Johnson said, 'they are Colman's best things.' [Upon its being observed/I said>] Upon its being observed that it was believed these Odes were made by Colman and Lloyd [together/jointly>] jointly, *Johnson.* 'Nay [man>] Sir, how can two People make an Ode? [Perhaps/It is possible>] Perhaps one made one of them and one the other.'
20 I observed that two People had made a Play and quoted the Anecdote of Beaumont and Fletcher who were brought under suspicion of treason because while concerting the plan of a Tragedy when sitting together at a tavern, one of them was overheard saying to the other 'I'll kill the King.' *Johnson.* 'The first of these Odes is the best. But [they are both good/I love them both>] they are both good. They
25 exposed a very bad kind of writing.' *Boswell.* 'Surely Sir Mr. Mason's Elfrida is a fine Poem. At least you will allow there are some good passages in it.' *Johnson.* 'There are now and then [MS 455] some good imitations of Milton's bad manner.'

 I often wondered at the little taste which he had for [the writings either of Gray or Mason>] [his low estimation both of the writings of Gray and Mason>] his low
30 estimation of the writings of Gray and Mason. Of [Gray>] Gray's poetry I have in a former part of this Work expressed my high opinion. And for [ₓthat ofₓ *del*] Mr.[8] Mason I have ever entertained a warm admiration. His 'Elfrida' is exquisite both in poetical [description/expression>] description and moral sentiment; and his 'Caractacus' is a noble Drama [teeming with grand strains of/in various styles.
35 Who among us can read without a proud emotion this passage

            and called it Britain. *del*][9]
 Nor can I [omit/neglect>] omit paying my tribute of praise to some of his [other/smaller>] smaller Poems which I have read with [delight>] pleasure and

---

 [8] The compositor having ignored JB's deletion of 'that of', the revises read, 'and for that of Mr. Mason'.

 [9] JB left a blank in the MS at this point to accommodate a quotation from William Mason's *Caractacus, A Dramatic Poem* (1759). As a reminder to himself, he jotted down the end of the penultimate line, 'Girt it with silver cliffs, and call'd it Britain' (1st ed., 1759, p. 37). As JB later decided to delete the entire passage, the blank remained unfilled.

which no criticism shall persuade me not to [admire〉] like. If I wondered at
Johnson's not tasting the works of Mason and Gray still more have I wondered at
their not tasting [him/his works.〉] his works that they should be insensible to his
energy of diction, to his splendour of images, and comprehension of thought.
Tastes may differ as to the violin the lute¹ the hautboy in short [as to all the   5
lesser/ordinary instruments〉] all the lesser instruments. But who [MS 456] [ever
was insensible to/could suppose one insensible to〉] ever was insensible to the
powerful impressions of the Majestick Organ?

His [*Taxation no Tyranny*〉] 'Taxation no Tyranny' being mentioned, he said 'I
think I have not been attacked enough for it. Attack is the reaction. I never   10
[think/believe〉] think I have hit hard unless it rebounds.' *Boswell*. 'I don't know
Sir, what you would be at. Five or six shots of small arms in every Newspaper and
repeated cannonading in Pamphlets might I think satisfy you. — But Sir you'll
never make out this match of which we have talked, with [Mrs. Macaulay/a certain
political Lady〉] a certain political Lady,² since you are so severe against her   15
principles.' *Johnson*. 'Nay Sir. ₍I have the better chance for that.₎ She is like the
Amazons /of old/;³ she must be courted by the sword. But I have not been severe
upon *her*.' *Boswell*. 'Yes Sir, you have made her ridiculous.' *Johnson*. 'That was
already done ₍Sir₎. [To make Mrs. Macaulay ridiculous is like blacking the
chimney.〉] To endeavour to make _____⁴ ridiculous is like blacking the chimney.'   20

I put him in mind [how〉] that the Landlord at Ellon in Scotland said that he
heard he was the greatest man in England — next to Lord Mansfield. 'Ay Sir' said
he 'the exception defined the idea. A Scotchman could go no farther
        "The force of nature could no farther go."'

Lady Miller's Collection of Verses by [MS 457] [the fore/first people〉] fashion-   25
able people which were put into her Vase at Batheaston Villa near Bath in
competition for honorary prizes being mentioned, he held [all this/the whole〉]
them very cheap, [and said del] '*Bouts rimés* is a mere conceit, and an *old* conceit
now; and I wonder how people were persuaded to write in that manner for this
Lady.' I said Captain [_____/Phipps〉] _____wrote for the vase. *Johnson*. 'He   30
was a Blockhead for his pains.' *Boswell*. 'The Duchess of Northumberland wrote.'
Johnson. 'Sir, The Duchess of Northumberland may do what she pleases. Nobody
will say anything to a Lady of her high rank. But I should be apt to throw [/
Phipps's/〉] _____'s⁵ verses in his face.'⁶

---

¹ The compositor misread 'lute' as 'flute', and this error went uncorrected.

² The deleted MS reference to Mrs. Macaulay confirms Croker's suspicion, quoted in
Hill-Powell, that she was the 'political Lady' in question. To judge from Capel Lofft's letter
to JB, 20 May 1791, the reference was transparent: 'I suppose all your readers will understand
alike who is the political Lady whom your Friend represents as impossible to be made
ridiculous for a reason expressed by an allusion very vehemently sarcastic' (*Corr. 2*, pp. 409–
10). Despite pressure from Lofft to suppress this passage, JB insisted upon retaining it.

³ The optional phrase, which JB left unresolved, is printed in the revises.

⁴ JB originally wrote 'Mrs. Macaulay', then deleted her name and substituted a blank,
which by the stage of revises had been replaced with '*her*'.

⁵ This blank in the revises is filled with six asterisks.

⁶ Constantine John Phipps (1744–92), R.N., later (1790) 1st Baron Mulgrave, M.P. for
Lincoln (1768–74), Huntingdon (1776–84), and Newark-upon-Trent (1784–90)

ₓI talked of the cheerfulness of Fleetstreet owing to the constant quick succession of people which we perceive [continually *del*] passing through it. JOHNSON. 'Why Sir Fleetstreet has a very animated appearance. But I think the full tide of human existence is at Charing Cross.'

5   He made the common remark on the unhappiness which men who have led a busy life experience when they retire in expectation of enjoying themselves at ease, and that they generally languish for want of their habitual occupation and wish to return to it. He mentioned as strong an instance of this as can well be figured. 'An eminent tallow chandler in London who had acquired a considerable

10   fortune gave up the trade in favour of his foreman, and went to live at a country house in the vicinity. He soon grew weary, and paid frequent visits to his old shop where he desired they might let him know their *melting days,* and he would come and assist them which he accordingly did. Here Sir was a man to whom the most disgusting circumstance in the business to which he had been used, was a relief

15   from idleness.'ₓ

     On Wednesday [5 April⟩] April 5, I dined with him at Mr. Dilly's with Mr. John Scott ₓof Amwellₓ the Quaker, Mr. Langton, Mr. Miller (now Sir John), and Dr. [John⟩] Thomas Campbell, an irish Clergyman whom I [invited to my friend's table⟩] took the liberty of inviting to Mr. Dilly's table, having seen him at Mr.

20   Thrale's and [understood/been told⟩] been told that he had come to England, chiefly with a view to see Dr. Johnson, [of/for⟩] for whom he entertained the highest veneration. [I was much pleased with his good humour and simplicity of manner, which though a tall, stately, comely man made us have a kind of fondness/liking for him as for a favourite/pleasing child.[7] [MS 458] I[8] ....

(Namier and Brooke iii. 277–78). Phipps's contribution to Anna Miller's *Poetical Amusements at a Villa near Bath* (1775) was a six line *bout rimé* for the opening page:

> Hard to my muse it is, I must confess,
> In six fix'd rhymes aught witty to express;
> Why did I mix with Wits? who must detest
> And crush my follies which their sense molest
> Thus the poor mole, who rises into light,
> Dies when he meets the sun's refulgent might.

The Duchess of Northumberland's contribution included comparable couplets, such as one in praise of her hostess: 'A muffin, Jove himself might feast on, / If eat with Miller at Batheaston' (11). Lady Miller made a half-hearted effort to conceal the identities of her authors, printing Phipps's name as 'Hon. Mr. Ph — ps' and the Duchess of Northumberland's as 'Her Gr — e the D — — ss of N — m — r — d'.

In the revises, JB's 'I said Captain _____ wrote for the vase' was replaced by the ambiguous 'I named a gentleman of his acquaintance, who wrote for the Vase'. This alteration led Croker to suggest Richard Graves, while Hill proposed William Seward (Hill-Powell ii. 337).

[7] On 1 April JB had met Thomas Campbell at the Thrales' home in Southwark (Journ.). Campbell confirms that he dined on 5 April 'with Dilly in the Poultry, as guest to Mr. Boswell' (*Dr. Campbell's Diary of a Visit to England in 1775*, ed. James L. Clifford, 1947, p. 72).

[8] This reading can be established because 'I' appears as a catchword at the bottom of MS 457.

... ever a man of knowledge and talents, and he *del*][9] He has since published 'A Philosophical Survey of the South of Ireland' a very entertaining Book which has however one fault that it assumes the fictitious character of an Englishman. [I was happy in giving him a large bunch of clover by introducing him to/letting him enjoy the conversation of Johnson. *del*]   5

We talked of speaking in publick. JOHNSON. [/'Speaking in publick/Publick speaking Sir is not allways a test of abilities./>] 'We must not estimate a man's [abilities>] powers by his being able or not able to deliver his sentiments in publick. Isaac Hawkins Browne [(one of the first wits of this country)>] one of the first wits of this country got into [this *del*] Parliament and never opened his mouth. For my   10 own part I think it is more disgraceful [not/never>] never to try to speak, than to try it and fail, as it is more disgraceful not to fight, than to fight and be beat.' This argument appeared to me fallacious; for if a man has not spoken it may be said that he would have done [MS 459] very well had he tried, whereas if he has tried and failed, there is nothing to be said for him. 'Why then,' said I, 'is it thought   15 disgraceful [for/in>] for a man not to fight,[1] and not disgraceful not to speak in publick?' *Johnson.* 'Because there may be other reasons for a man's not speaking in publick than want of resolution. [/He may have nothing to say (laughing)/ /Whereas/ you know>] He may have nothing to say (laughing). Whereas ₍Sir₎ you know courage is reckoned the greatest of all virtues because/for[2] unless a man   20 has that virtue he has no security for preserving [the others/any others>] any others.'

He observed that the statutes against bribery were intended to prevent upstarts with money from getting into [Parliament. He said that>] Parliament adding that if he were a Gentleman of [estate>] landed property, he would turn out all his   25 tenants who did not vote for the Candidate whom he supported. *Langton.* 'Would not that Sir be checking the freedom of election?' *Johnson.* 'Sir, [the Law /Legislature>] the Law does not mean that the privilege of voting should be independent of old family interest — of [/the/>] the permanent property [/of the/a Country/>] of the/a[3] Country.'   30

On thursday [6 April>] April 6 I dined with him at [Tom Davies's/Mr. Thomas Davies's>] Mr. Thomas Davies's, with Mr. Hicky a Painter [MS 460] and my old acquaintance Mr. Moody the [Actor/Player>] Player.[4]

---

[9] Approximately the top third of the leaf has been torn away — a section corresponding to a block of deleted material that begins at the bottom of MS 457. The surviving traces suggest that JB may originally have incorporated a conceit from his journal: 'I told her [Hester Thrale] that I had asked Dr. Campbell the irish clergyman to dine today at Dilly's .... That he was quite like a *pet* sheep (Mrs. Thrale gave me the English phrase, a *cayed* sheep) went with the cows, walked about the house, and every body even the children, gave him clover or a handful of corn or a piece of bread out of their pockets' (Journ. 5 Apr. 1775).

[1] Interlined above 'disgraceful for/in a man not to fight' is an alternative phrase which JB deleted before he had even completed it: 'is disgrace attached to'.

[2] The alternative is resolved by the printing of 'because' in the revises.

[3] The alternative is resolved by the printing of 'the' in the revises.

[4] Direction to the compositor, '(Take in six small leaves)'. These six leaves come from JB's London Journal, 1775 (J40, pp. 15–26); see *Ominous Years*, pp. 125–30, and Hill-

[Next day friday 7 April I dined with him at the LITERARY CLUB, which had now undergone a change to the better that on the first friday of every month we should dine together instead of meeting in the evening.>] [Next day Friday 7 April I dined with him at the LITERARY CLUB, which had now undergone a change to the better,

5　　it having been determined that on the first friday of every month we should dine together instead of meeting in the evening.>] [Next day Friday 7 April I dined with him at the LITERARY CLUB which had now made a good and sensible regulation, it having been determined that on the first friday of every month we should dine together instead of meeting in the evening.>] Friday April 7 I dined with him at a

10　　tavern with a numerous company. [He said>] JOHNSON. 'I have been reading Twiss's Travels ⋏in Spain,⋌ which are just come out. They are as good as the first Book of Travels that you will take up. They are as good as those of Keysler or Blainville [or/nay of Addison>] nay as Addison's[5] if you take out the learning. [(Beauclerk said they are nothing without the learning.) del] They are not so good

15　　as Brydone but they are better than Pokoke's. I have not indeed cut [them up>] the leaves yet; but I have read in them where the pages are open, and I do not suppose that what is on the pages which are closed is worse than what is on the open pages.' It would seem that Addison had not acquired [the/much>] much Italian learning; for, we do not find it introduced into his writings. The only instance that I

20　　recollect is his quoting 'Stavo bene. Per star meglio sto qui.'

　　　I mentioned Addison's having borrowed many of [MS 461] his [learned/classical>] classical remarks from *Leandro Alberti*. Mr. Beauclerk said 'It was alledged that he had borrowed also from another Italian Authour.' *Johnson*. 'Why Sir all who go to look for what the Classicks have said of Italy must find the

25　　same passages;[6] and I should think it would be one of the first things the Italians would do on the revival of learning to collect all that the Roman Authours had said of their country.'

　　　Ossian being mentioned, *Johnson*. 'Supposing the irish and erse languages to be the same which I do not believe yet as there is no reason [to believe/suppose that

30　　they ever wrote their native language in the highlands and isles/the inhabitants of the highlands and isles ever wrote their native language>] to suppose that the inhabitants of the highlands and hebrides ever wrote their native language, it is not to be credited that a long Poem was preserved among them. If we had no evidence of the art of writing being [practised/known>] practised in one of the

35　　counties of England we should not believe that a long Poem was preserved *there*, though in the neighbouring counties where the same language is/was[7] spoken,

---

[5] The third edition introduces a note keyed to 'Addison's' that quotes from a similar passage in JB's *Tour*: 'Speaking of Addison's *Remarks on Italy* in "The Journal of a Tour to the Hebrides," (p. 320, 3rd edit.) he says, "it is a tedious book, and if it were not attached to Addison's previous reputation, one would not think much of it. Had he written nothing else, his name would not have lived. Addison does not seem to have gone deep in Italian literature: he shews nothing of it in his subsequent writings. — He shews a great deal of French learning."' This note is not included in Hill-Powell.

[6] The third edition prints a note (keyed to 'passages') that quotes from JB's *Tour*: '"But if you find the same *applications* in another book, then Addison's learning falls to the ground." Journal of a Tour to the Hebrides, *ut supra*'. This note is not included in Hill-Powell.

[7] The alternative is resolved by the printing of 'was' in the revises.

the inhabitants could write.' [BEAUCLERK. 'The Ballad of Lullabalero/Mr. Beauclerk observed that the ballad of Lullabalero>] MR. BEAUCLERK. 'The Ballad of Lullabalero was once in the mouths of all the people of this country and [is/was>] is said to have had a great effect in bringing about the Revolution. Yet I [question/doubt>] question [if>] whether any body can repeat it now, which shews   5
how improbable it [is/was>] is [MS 462] that much poetry should be preserved by tradition.'

[Dr. Percy/A Gentleman mentioned>] One of the company suggested an internal objection to the antiquity of the Poetry said to be Ossian's that we do not find the Wolf in it, which must have been the case had it been of that age.   10

The mention of the Wolf had led Johnson to think of other wild beasts; and while Sir Joshua Reynolds and Mr. Langton were carrying on a dialogue about something which engaged them earnestly, he in the midst of it broke out 'Pennant tells of Bears' (I forget what). They went on; while he being dull of hearing did not perceive it, or if he did, [was/being>] was not willing to [hear/mind>] mind them.   15
So he continued to roar out his remarks and Bear ('like a word in a Catch' as Beauclerk said) was [allways/repeatedly>] repeatedly heard at intervals, which coming from him who ⟨by those who did not know him⟩ had been so often [assimilated to/denominated by>] assimilated to that ferocious animal while we who were sitting arround could hardly stifle laughter, produced a very ludicrous   20
effect. Silence having ensued he proceeded: 'We are told that the black Bear is inocent; but I should not like to [engage/trust myself>] trust myself with him.' [Said Gibbon/Gibbon muttered>] Mr. Gibbon muttered (in a low voice) 'I should not like to [engage/trust myself>] trust myself with you.' [This though I suppose ironically meant was a judicious truth if applied to a competition of   25
powers/abilities whether mental or corporeal.>] This piece of sarcastick pleasantry was a judicious truth if applied to a competition of abilities.[8]

Patriotism having [occurred as/become>] become one of our topicks Johnson ⟨suddenly⟩ uttered in a strong determined [MS 463] tone an apothegm at which many will start: 'Patriotism is the last refuge of a scoundrel.' But let it be   30
considered that he did not mean a real and [generous love of/genuine zeal for>] generous love of our country, but that pretended Patriotism [of which Great Britain has seen/He had seen too much.>] which so many in all ages and countries have made a cloak for self=interest. Some of us maintained that all Patriots were not [scoundrels, and a gentleman/Mr. Steevens having desired us to name one, Sir   35
Joshua Reynolds mentioned an eminent person/one whom we greatly admired.>] scoundrels. Being urged (not by Johnson) to name one, an eminent person whom we all greatly admired ⟨was mentioned⟩.[9] *Johnson.* 'Sir I do not say that he is not honest. But we have no reason to conclude from his political conduct that he *is* honest. Were he to accept of a place from this Ministry, he would lose that   40

---

[8]At one point JB had marked this entire paragraph for deletion; he later reinstated it, however, by writing 'Stet' four times in the left margin.

[9] In the revises 'one, an eminent person whom we all greatly admired was mentioned' is printed 'one exception, I mentioned an eminent person, whom we all greatly admired'. In JB's journal account it is Sir Joshua Reynolds, not JB, who names the 'eminent person' (Edmund Burke).

character [for/of>] for firmness which he has, and might be turned out of his place in a year. This Ministry is neither stable, nor grateful to their friends as Sir Robert Walpole was. So that he[1] may think it more for his interest to take his chance of his party coming in.'

5   Mrs. Pritchard being mentioned he said 'Her playing was quite mechanical. It is wonderful how little mind [she had/there was in it.>] she had. Sir, she had never read the Tragedy of Macbeth all [/through/>] through. She no more thought of the Play out of which her part was taken, than a shoemaker thinks of the skin, out of which the piece of leather of which he is making a pair *[MS 464]* of shoes, is cut.'

10   On saturday [8 April>] April 8 I dined with him at Mr. Thrale's ⟨where was the irish Dr. Campbell⟩. He had supt the night before [/with Sir Joshua Reynolds/ *del*] at Mrs. Abington's with some [very fine>] fashionable people whom he named,[2] and he seemed much pleased with having made one in so elegant a circle.

       Mrs. Thrale who frequently practised a [very fair/obvious>] trite mode of
15   flattery by repeating his *Bon mots* in his hearing told us that he ⟨had⟩ said a certain celebrated Actor was just fit to stand at the door of an auction=room with a long pole, and cry 'Pray Gentlemen walk in'; and that a certain [Wit/Authour>] Authour ⟨upon hearing this⟩ had said that another still more celebrated Actor was fit for nothing better than that, and would pick your pocket after you came
20   out.[3] *Johnson.* 'Nay [Madam/My Dear Lady>] My Dear Lady there is no wit in [that>] what our friend added; there is only abuse. You may [/as well/>] as well say of any man that he will pick a pocket. Besides the man at the door does not pick peoples pockets. That is to be done within by the auctioneer.'

       Mrs. Thrale told us that Tom Davies repeated in a very bald manner the story of
25   Dr. Johnson's first repartee to me, which I have related exactly.[a] He made me say 'I *was born* in Scotland' instead of 'I *come from* Scotland' *[MS 465]* so that Johnson's saying 'That ⟨Sir⟩ is what a great many of your countrymen cannot help' had no point or even [meaning. Upon this>] meaning and that upon this Mr. Fitzherbert had observed 'It is not every [man/body/one>] man that can *carry* a *bon mot*.'

30   On Monday [10 April>] April 10 I dined with him at General Oglethorpe's with Mr. Langton and the irish Dr. Campbell whom the General had obligingly given me leave to [bring that he might have a very>] bring. I thus had it in my power to gratify him with a very high intellectual feast by not only being with Dr. Johnson, but with General Oglethorpe who had been so long a celebrated name
35   both at home and abroad.[b]

---

[a] P.   [a1]

[b] Let me here be allowed to pay my tribute of most sincere gratitude to the memory of that excellent person [whose intimacy was>] my intimacy with whom

---

[1] JB originally left a blank in the MS here and only later filled it in with 'he'.
[2] These 'fashionable people' included Elizabeth Cosby Fitzroy (d. 1788), and Maj.-Gen. Sir John Irwin (?1728–?88), K.B. (Journ. 8 Apr. 1775).
[3] JB's Journal and Thomas Campbell's *Diary* concur in identifying the actor as Spranger Barry, the author as Arthur Murphy, and the 'still more celebrated Actor' as David Garrick.

[a1] The cross-reference to Volume I (211) appears in the revises, apparently having been supplied at the stage of first proof.

I must again and again intreat of my readers not to suppose that my imperfect record of [the conversations which I give›] conversation contains the half of what was said by Johnson or other eminent persons who lived with him. What [they get›] I have preserved has the value of the most perfect [authenticity; and little as it may be compared with the original/what actually passed, I may without arrogance challenge my Criticks to shew in any Biographical Writer as great a proportion of what the Ancients and most judicious of the moderns have estimated at the highest rate in that most interesting species of composition/writing. *del*] authenticity.

Johnson this day enlarged upon [MS 466] Pope's [sad›] melancholy remark   10
    'Man never *is*, but allways *to be* blest.'
[He›] Johnson asserted that the present was never a happy state to any human being; but that as every part of life ˏof which we are consciousˎ was at some [time future›] [point of time yet to come›] point of time a period yet to come in which felicity was expected, there was some [enjoyment/happiness in hope›] happiness   15
produced by hope. [Upon being›] Being pressed upon this subject and asked if he really was of opinion that though in general happiness was very rare in [the life of man, a man was/we are not sometimes happy in the moment that was present he answered 'Never but when he's drunk.'›] human life, a man was not sometimes happy in the moment that was present he answered, 'Never but when he is drunk.'   20

He [was earnest with›] urged General Oglethorpe to [give the World/write his Life, saying›] give the World his Life. He said, 'I know no man [alive del] whose Life would be more [entertaining/interesting›] interesting. If I were furnished with [ˏtheˎ del] materials I should be very glad to write it.'ᶜ

___

was the more valuable to me that it was unexpectedly and spontaneously con-   25
ferred. Soon after the publication of my Account of Corsica, he did me the honour to call on me, and approaching me wih a ˏfrankˎ courteous air said 'My name Sir is Oglethorpe and I wish to be acquainted with you.' ˏI was not a little flattered to be thus addressed by [so celebrated a character›] an eminent man of whom I had read in Pope from my early years   30
    'Or driven by strong benevolence of soul
    Will fly like Oɢʟᴇᴛʜᴏʀᴘᴇ from pole to pole.'ˎ
I was fortunate enough to be found worthy of his good opinion, in so much that I not only was invited to make one in the many respectable companies whom he entertained at his table, but had a cover at his hospitable board every day when I   35
happened to be disengaged, and in his society I never failed to enjoy learned and animated conversation seasoned with [the del] genuine sentiments of [honour del] virute and [piety›] religion.

    ᶜ The General seemed unwilling to enter upon it at this time. But upon other occasions he communicated to me a [series/number›] number of [parts/facts›]   40
parts which I have committed to writing; but I was not sufficiently diligent in collecting not apprehending that he was to die so soon as he did; for notwithstanding his great age he was very healthy and vigorous, and was at last carried off by a violent [disorder which is often fatal to the young and the vigorous/people in the full vigour of life›] disorder which is often fatal [to men *del*] at any period of life.ᶜ¹   45

154

Mr. Scott of [Amwell's/the Quaker's>] Amwell's Elegies were lying in the room. Dr. Johnson [said>] observed, 'They are very well, [MS 467] but [such as/as good as>] such as twenty people might write.' Upon this I took occasion to contravert Horace's Maxim:

5   '_____mediocribus esse Poetis
              Non di non homines non concessere columnæ'
for here was a very middle rate Poet who pleased a number of people, and therefore poetry of a middle sort was entitled to some esteem, nor could I see why Poetry should not like everything else have different gradations of excellence and
10   consequently of value. [He>] Johnson repeated the common remark that as there is no necessity for our having poetry at all it being merely a luxury, an instrument of pleasure, it [should>] can have no value [at all del] unless when exquisite in its kind. I declared myself not satisfied. 'Why then Sir', said he, 'Horace and you must settle it.' He was not ₍much₎ in the humour of talking.

15   No more of his conversation for some days appears in my Journal except that when a Gentleman told him he had bought a suit of laces for his Lady [Johnson/he>] he said 'Well ₍Sir₎ you have done a good thing and a wise thing.'[4] 'I have done a good thing' [(said the Gentleman) 'but>] (said the Gentleman). 'But, I do not know that I have done a wise thing.' [/Johnson/>] Johnson. 'Yes Sir.
20   No money is better spent than [MS 468] what is laid out for domestick satisfaction. A man is pleased that his Wife is drest as well as other people, and a Wife is [pleased that she is drest.>] [also pleased.>] pleased that she is drest.'

       On friday [14 April>] April 14 being Good Friday I repaired to him in the morning according to [solemn custom and breakfasted with him. Mr. Levet made
25   tea to us.>] my usual custom on this day and breakfasted with him. I observed that he fasted so very strictly that he did not even taste bread, and took no milk to his tea, I suppose because it is a kind of animal food.

       He entered upon the state of the Nation and thus discoursed 'Sir the great [misfortune/loss>] misfortune now is that Government has too little power. All
30   that it has to bestow must of neccessity be given to support itself; so that it cannot reward merit. No man for instance can now be made a Bishop for his learning and piety[5] [but because he is connected>]; his only chance for promotion is his being connected with somebody who has parliamentary interest. Our several ministries in this reign have outbid each other in concessions to the people. Lord Bute
35   though a very honourable man — a man who meant well — a man [who had his blood full/a man whose blood was full>] who had his blood full of prerogative was ₍a theoretical [Politician>] Statesman₎, a [Book-man>] Book-Minister, and

---

[4] The 'Gentleman' and 'his Lady' are JB and Margaret Boswell (Journ. 13 Apr. 1775; *Ominous Years*, pp. 140–41).

[5] Printed in the revises is a footnote that reads, 'From this observation there are some eminent exceptions.' In correcting the revises, JB inserted 'too just' before 'observation'.

[c1]The material contained in this footnote originally appeared in the main text as the conclusion of the paragraph beginning 'He urged General Oglethorpe.' JB deleted the passage, and then reinserted it by writing twice in the left margin 'Stet' as well as 'All this in a note'.

thought this Country could be governed by the influence [MS 469] of the Crown
alone. Then Sir he [/foolishly/ del] gave up a great deal. He advised the King to
agree that the Judges should hold their places for life, instead of [losing them
at/their falling on›] losing them at the acccession of a new King. Lord Bute I
suppose thought to make the King popular by this concession, but the People   5
never minded it, and it was a most impolitick measure. [There is no reason why a
Judge should be for life more than any one else.›] [There is no reason why a Judge
should be for life more than any other person.›] There is no reason why a Judge
should hold his office for life more than any other person in publick trust. A Judge
may be partial otherwise than to the Crown. We have seen Judges partial to the   10
populace. A Judge may become [corrupt/corrupted›] corrupt and yet there may
not be legal evidence against him. A Judge may become froward from age. A
Judge may grow unfit for his office in many ways. It was desireable that [a
possibility of being delivered from him by a new King should be in contemplation.›] there should be a possibility of being delivered from him by a new King.   15
That is now gone by an Act of Parliament *ex gratia* of the Crown. Lord Bute
[advised the King to give up the hereditary revenues of the Crown, and accept
instead of them of the limited sum of £800,000 a year for which nobody thanked
him. When›] advised the King to give up a very large sum of [money arrising from
the property of the prizes taken before the declaration of War which were given to   20
his Majesty by the peace of Paris and amounted to upwards of £700,000 and from
the lands in the ceded Islands which were estimated at £200,000 more. Surely
there was a noble munificence in this gift from a monarch to his People and let it
be remembered that during the Earl of Bute's administration the King was
graciously pleased to give up the hereditary revenues of the Crown and to accept   25
instead of them of the limited sum of £800,000 a year›] money,[6] for which nobody
thanked him. It was of consequence to the King, but nothing to [most of those›]
the Publick among whom it was divided.[a] When I say Lord Bute advised I mean
that such acts were done when he was Minister, and we are to suppose that he
advised them.[7] Lord Bute shewed an [improper›] undue partiality to Scotchmen.   30
He turned out Dr. Nichols a very [great/capital›] eminent man from being

[a] Blackstone however observes that the hereditary revenues being put under
the same management as the other branches of the publick patrimony will produce
more, and be better collected than heretofore; and the Publick is a gainer of £
upwards of £100,000 per annum by this disinterested bounty of his Majesty. Book   35
1 Chap   p. 330.[al]

[6] JB originally intended the material within brackets ('money ... £800,000 a year') for
the main text. He later decided to relegate it to a note, and to amalgamate it with the
footnote that quotes Blackstone. The result is a single long note (keyed to 'a very large sum
of money') that begins, 'The money arrising,' and that alters 'Blackstone however observes'
to 'upon which Blackstone observes'.
[7] This sentence originally followed the second version of the sentence beginning 'Lord
Bute advised the King'.

[al] The chapter number (8) is printed in the revises, apparently having been supplied at
the stage of first proof.

Physician to the King [MS 470] to make room for one of his countrymen a man very low in his profession [who had cured him *del*]. He had [_____/Wedderburne and _____/Home>] _____and _____[8] to go errands for him. He had occasion for people to go errands for him; but he should not have had scotchmen. And certainly he should not have suffered them to have access to him before the first people in England.'

I told [them>] him that the admission of one of them before the first people in England, which had given the greatest offence was no more than what happens at every Minister's levee where those who attend are admitted in the order that they have come, which is better than admitting them according to their rank, for if that were to be the rule, a man who has waited all the morning might have the mortification to see a Peer newly come, go in before him and keep him waiting still.[9] *Johnson.* 'True Sir. But _____[1] should not have come to the Levee to be in the way of people of consequence. He saw Lord Bute at all times; and could have said what he had to say, at any time as well as at the Levee. There is now no Prime Minister. [Lord North is>] There is only an Agent for Government [MS 471] in the House of Commons. We are governed by the [Privy Council>] Cabinet. But there is no one Head there, as in Sir Robert Walpole's time. ₍Boswell.[2] 'What then Sir is the use of Parliament?' Johnson. 'Why Sir,₎ Parliament is a larger Council to the King, and the [benefit/advantage>] advantage of [such a/that>] such a Council is having a [greater>] great number of men of property concerned in the legislature, who for their own interest will not consent to bad laws. ₍And you must have observed Sir that Administration is feeble and timid and cannot act with that authority and resolution which is necessary. Were I in power I would turn out every man who dared to oppose me. Government has the distribution of offices that it may be enabled to support itself.₎

[He said, 'Lord>] [He added, 'Lord>] 'Lord Bute' (he added) 'took down too fast, without building up something [else/new>] new.' ['Because' said I>] Boswell. 'Because Sir, he found a rotten building. — The political coach was drawn by a set of bad horses. It was necessary to change them.' Johnson. 'But he should have changed them one by one.'

I told him that I had been informed by Mr. Orme that many parts of the East Indies were better mapped than the highlands of Scotland. *Johnson.* 'That a country may be mapped it must be travelled over.' 'Nay' said I ₍(meaning to laugh with him at one of his prejudices)₎ 'Can't you say it is not *worth* mapping?'

As we walked to St. Clements Church and saw several shops open upon this most solemn fast=day of the Christian World, [MS 472] I [observed/remarked>] remarked that one disadvantage [of>] arrising from the [greatness/immensity>]

---

[8] In the revises, the first blank was replaced by eleven asterisks and the second by four asterisks.

[9] JB reworks a sentence from his journal so as to avoid mentioning his informant (Lord Mountstuart) and the name of the Scottish favourite (John Home). See *Ominous Years*, pp. 143–44.

[1] In the revises JB's blank space is replaced with four asterisks (designating 'Home').

[2] JB considered making this addition the beginning of a new paragraph. Although he wrote 'NP' in the margin, he later deleted it.

immensity of London was that as nobody was [attended to/minded by their neighbours>] heeded by his neighbour, there was no fear of censure for not [observing/keeping>] observing Good Friday as it ought to be kept and as it is kept in country towns. He said it was upon the whole very well [kept>] observed even in London. He however owned that London was too [big>] large but [said>] added 'It is nonsense to say the head is too big for the body. It would be as much too big though the body were ever so large that is to say though the country were ever so extensive. It has no similarity to a head connected with a body.'

Dr. Wetherell Master of University College Oxford accompanied us home from Church; and after he was gone there came two other gentlemen one of whom uttered the common=place complaints that by the increase of taxes labour would be dear, other nations would undersell us and our commerce would be ruined. [*Johnson* (smiling) said>] JOHNSON (smiling). 'Never fear Sir our commerce is in a very good state; and suppose we had no commerce at all, we could live very well on the produce of our own country.' I cannot omit [MS 473] to mention that I never knew [a>] any man [in my life *del*] who was less disposed to be querulous than Johnson. Whether the subject was his own situation, or the state of the Publick, or the state of human nature in general, though he saw the evils, his mind was turned to resolution, and never to whining ⟨or complaint⟩.

We went again to St. Clements in the afternoon. He had found fault with the Preacher in the [forenoon>] morning for not chusing a text [adapted/appropriated>] adapted to the day. The Preacher in the afternoon had chosen [a very suitable one>] one singularly proper, 'It is finished.'

After the evening service he said 'Come you shall go home with me, and sit just an hour.' But he was better than his word; for, after we had drunk tea with Mrs. Williams, he asked me to go up to his study with him where we sat a long while together in a calm undisturbed frame sometimes in silence, and sometimes conversing as we felt ourselves inclined, or more properly speaking, as *he* [was inclined/appeared>] was inclined; for, during all the course of my long intimacy with him my respectful attention never abated, and my wish to hear him was [MS 474] such that I [constantly watched/was ever on the watch for>] constantly watched every dawning of communication from that great and illuminated mind.

He observed 'All knowledge is of itself of some value. There is nothing [so minute/inconsiderable>] so minute or inconsiderable that I would not rather know it than not. In the same manner, ⟨all⟩ power of whatever sort is of itself desireable. A man would not submit to learn to hem a ruffle of his wife or of his wife's maid. But if a mere wish could [do/attain>] attain it he would rather wish to be able to hem a ruffle.'

He ⟨again⟩ advised me to keep a Journal fully and minutely [⟨as a history of my mind⟩ *del*] but [not so as to mention/I should not mention that>] not to mention such trifles as that meat was too much or too little done, or that [it was fair or rained/the weather was fair or rainy.>] the weather was fair or rainy. He had till very near his death a contempt for [attention to the weather as supposing it to affect the spirits and consequently the temper and disposition. One of his papers in the Idler laughs at it

---

[3] Ironically enough, this passage does not appear in JB's journal or memoranda. The deleted reference is to SJ's *Idler* No. 11.

with great vivacity.>] the notion that the weather affects the human frame.[3]

I told him that our friend Goldsmith had said to me, that he had come too late ⟨into the world⟩ for that Pope and other Poets had taken up the places of fame, so that a man [/of poetical genius/>] of poetical genius could hardly get [MS 475]
5 reputation now, as but a few can have it. JOHNSON. 'That is one of the most sensible things I have ever heard of Goldsmith. It is difficult to get literary fame, and it is every day growing more difficult. Ah Sir that should make a man think of securing happiness in [another/the other>] another World, which all who try sincerely for it may attain. In comparrison of that how little are all other things.
10 The belief of immortality is impressed upon all men, and all men act under an impression of it, however they may talk [or however they may perhaps be>], and though perhaps they may be scarcely sensible of it.' I said it appeared to me that some people had not the least [notion/impression>] notion of Immortality, and I mentioned a distinguished [gentleman/statesman>] gentleman of our acquaint-
15 ance.[4] *Johnson*. 'Sir if it were not for [an impression>] the notion of immortality [_____/He>] He would cut a throat to fill his pockets.' When I quoted this to Beauclerk who knew much more of the gentleman than we did, he said ['He/My friend>] 'He would cut a throat to fill his pockets if it were not for fear of being hanged.'
20 Dr. Johnson proceeded 'Sir, there is a great cry about infidelity; but there are in reality very few infidels. I have heard a [person/Physician>] person originally [a Quaker/of strict education>] a Quaker but now [of loose notions/loose in his notions>] I am affraid a deist say that he did not believe there [MS 476] were in ⟨all⟩ England above two hundred infidels.'[5]
25 He [said>] was pleased to say 'If you come to settle here, we will have one day in the week on which we will meet by ourselves. That is the happiest conversation where there is no competition no vanity, but a [quiet/calm/fair>] calm quiet interchange of sentiments.' In his private Register, this evening is thus marked 'Boswell sat with me till night; we had some serious talk.'[a] It [also appears/appears
30 also>] also appears ⟨[from it>] from the same record⟩ that after I left him he was occupied in religious [duties/employment>] duties, in 'giving Francis his servant some directions for preparation to communicate, [and *del*] in reviewing his life, and resolving on better conduct.' The humility and [devotion/piety>] piety which he discovers on [these/such>] such occasions is truly edifying. ⟨No Saint however
35 in the course of his religious warfare was more sensible of the unhappy failure of pious resolves than Johnson. He said one day to an acquaintance 'Sir, Hell is paved with good intentions.'⟩

[a] Prayers and Meditations p. 138.

---

[4] JB's journal entry for 14 April 1775 identifies this 'distinguished gentleman' as Charles James Fox.
[5] JB's journal entry identifies this deistical physician as Richard Brocklesby, whom SJ, on his deathbed, tried repeatedly to dissuade from 'loose speculative notions' (Hill-Powell iv. 414; MS 1029). SJ's efforts to win over Brocklesby to orthodox Christianity included a recommendation to read Samuel Clarke on 'the expiating Sacrifice' and various 'dicta on the Subject and Importance of Faith' (*Corr. 2*, pp. 32, 94–95; John Wiltshire, *Samuel Johnson in the Medical World*, 1991, pp. 229–30).

On Sunday [16 April⟩] April 15, being Easter day, after having attended the solemn service at St. Paul's, I dined with Dr. Johnson and Mrs. Williams. [We had Soup, Beef-a-la-mode boiled pork, pease pudding, potatoes, roasted lamb and spinnage, porter and port wine. *del*] I maintained that Horace was wrong in placing happiness in *Nil admirari*, for that I thought admiration one of the most   5
agreable of all our feelings, and I regretted that I had lost much of my disposition to admire [as/which⟩] which people generally do [as/when⟩] as they [grow up⟩] advance in life. [*MS 477*] *Johnson*. ['We get a better thing than admiration⟩] 'Sir as a man advances in life, he gets what is better than admiration — judgement — to estimate things at their true value.' I still insisted that admiration was more   10
pleasing than judgement, as love is more pleasing than friendship. The feeling of friendship is like that of being comfortably filled with roast beef; Love like being enlivened with champagne. *Johnson*. 'No Sir, Admiration and love are like being intoxicated with champagne. Judgement and friendship like being enlivened. Waller has hit upon the same thought with you.[a] But I don't believe you have   15
borrowed from Waller. ₍I wish you would enable yourself to borrow more.'₎

[Upon this occasion he enlarged/He took occasion to enlarge⟩] He then took occasion to enlarge on the advantage/s/[6] of reading and combated the idle superficial notion that knowledge enough may be acquired in conversation. 'The foundation' (said he) 'must be laid by reading. General principles must be had   20
from books [which however must be brought to/though no doubt they must be proved by⟩] which however must be brought to the test of real life. In conversation you never get a system. What is [said/talked⟩] said upon a subject is to be gathered from a hundred people. The parts of a truth which [one/a man⟩] a man gets thus, are [*MS 478*] at such a distance from each other, that [one/he⟩] he never   25
[gets/attains to⟩] attains to a full view.'[7]

On tuesday [18 April⟩] April 18 He and I were engaged to go with Sir Joshua Reynolds to dine with Mr. Cambridge at his [delightful/beautiful seat⟩] beautiful villa on the banks of the Thames near Twittenham. Dr. Johnson's tardiness was such that Sir Joshua who had an appointment at Richmond early in the   30
[forenoon/day⟩] day was obliged to go by himself on horseback, leaving his coach

> [a] Amoret's as sweet and good
> As the most delicious food
> Which but tasted does impart
> Life and gladness to the heart.   35
> Sacharissa's beauty's wine
> Which to madness does incline
> Such a liquor as no brain
> That is mortal can sustain.[a1]

---

[6] The alternative is resolved by the printing of 'advantages' in the revises.

[7] SJ to Bennet Langton, 17 April 1775, belongs to that group of letters first inserted at the end of the second volume of the second edition, and then moved to their chronologically appropriate places for the third edition. See *ante* p. 10 n. 1.

[a1] The lines from Waller, a later addition, appear on the verso of MS 476: JB left insufficient space on MS 477 recto to insert them after 'thought with you'.

to Johnson and me. [He>] Johnson was in such good [temper/spirits>] spirits that
every thing seemed [cheerful to him>] to please him as we drove along [and I was
uncommonly easy with him del].

    ₍Our conversation turned on a variety of subjects.₎ He thought portrait
5   painting an improper employment for a Woman. 'Publick practise [said he of
staring in mens faces is very indelicate for a Lady>] of any art' he observed 'and
staring in mens faces is very indelicate in a female.' I happened to start a question
of propriety whether when [one>] a man knows that some of his intimate friends
are invited to the house of another friend with whom they are all equally intimate
10   he may join them without an invitation. JOHNSON. 'No Sir. He is not to go when
he is not invited. They may be invited to abuse him.'
    As a curious instance how little a man knows or wishes to know his own
character in [MS 479] the World, or perhaps as a convincing proof that Johnson's
roughness was only external and did not at all proceed from his heart, I give[8] the
15   following conversation. *Johnson*. 'It is wonderful Sir how rare a quality good
humour is in life. We meet with very few good humoured men.' I mentioned four
of our friends none of whom he would allow to be good=humoured. One was *acid*
another was *muddy* and to the others he had [objections/exceptions>] objections
which have escaped me.[9] Then shaking his head and stretching himself ₍at his
20   ease₎ in the coach and smiling with much complacency he ₍turned to me and₎
said 'I look upon *myself* as a good=humoured fellow.' The epithet *fellow* applied to
the great Lexicographer, the stately Moralist the Masterly Critick, as if he had
been *Sam* Johnson a mere pleasant companion was highly diverting and this light
notion of himself struck me with wonder. I answered also smiling 'No no Sir that
25   will [not/never>] *not* do. You are good=natured but not good=humoured. You are
irascible you have not patience with folly and absurdity. I believe [you/your
mercy>] you would pardon them, if there were time to deprecate your
[vengeance/wrath>] vengeance; but punishment [MS 480] follows so quick after
sentence, that they cannot escape.'
30   I had ₍brought₎ with me a great bundle of scotch Magazines and Newspapers in
which his 'Journey to the Western Islands' was attacked [with all the weapons
which could be got together>] in every mode, and ₍knowing they would afford him
entertainment₎ I read ₍a great part of₎ them to him [almost the whole of/on the
way to Richmond. del]. I wish the writers of them had been present. They would
35   have been sufficiently [mortified>] vexed. One ludicrous imitation of his [man-
ner>] style by Mr. McLaurin ₍now one of the scotch Judges with the title of Lord
Dreghorn₎ was distinguished by him from the rude mass. 'This' said he 'is the best.
But I could caricature my own style much better myself.' He defended his remark
upon the general insufficiency of education in Scotland. He confirmed ₍to me₎

----

[8] In the revises 'give' was erroneously printed 'owe' and then changed by JB to 'insert'.
[9] The four friends were Reynolds, Burke, Beauclerk, and Langton. This passage is
derived from JB's notes for 18 April: 'Sr Jos good hum — No Burke no — I look on myself
as good hum Bos. No no. Youre good natured but not good humd. You are irascible you
have not patience with folly & absurdity. I believe you wd pardon if there were time to
deprecate but punishment follows so quick after senten ... On road Beauc acid Langton
muddy' (18 April 1775/J42).

the authenticity of his witty saying [on/of>] on the learning of the Scotch: 'Their learning is like bread in a besieged town. Every man gets a little, but no man gets a full meal.' 'There is' said he 'in Scotland a [certain diffusion/portion of learning>] [certain portion of learning>] diffusion of learning, a certain portion of it widely and thinly spread.   A Merchant there has as much learning [as one of   5 their Ministers/priests/as a clergyman>] as one of their clergy.'

He [spoke>] talked of Isaac Walton's Lives which was one of his most favourite Books. Dr. Donne's Life he said was the most perfect of them.   [He said it>] [MS 481] He observed that it was wonderful that Walton who was in a very low situation in life [was>] should have been familiarly received by so many [great   10 Men/of the great People>] great Men and that [at a time/in an age>] at a time when the ranks of [men>] society were kept more separate than they are now. He supposed [he>] that Walton had then given up his business [as/of>] as a _____[1] and was only [a Writer/an Authour>] an Authour, and ₍added₎ that [Walton>] he was a great panegyrist. *Boswell.* 'No quality will get a man more   15 friends than a disposition to admire the qualities of others. I do not mean flattery but a sincere admiration.' *Johnson.* 'Nay Sir, Flattery pleases very generally. In the first place the flatterer may think what he says. But in the second place whether he thinks so or not, he certainly thinks [us>] those whom he flatters of consequence enough to be flattered'.   20

No sooner had we made our bow to Mr. Cambridge in his [Library/room>] Library than Johnson ran eagerly to one side of the room intent on poring over the backs of the Books. ₍Said Sir Joshua (aside) 'He runs to [/examine/ the *del*] Books as I do to the pictures. But I have the advantage. I can see /much/[2] more of the pictures than he can of the Books.'₎ [Mr. Cambridge/A Gentleman>] Mr.   25 Cambridge upon this politely said 'Dr. Johnson I am going with your pardon to accuse myself for I have the same custom which I perceive you have. But it seems odd that one should have such a desire to look at the backs of Books.'[3] Johnson ever ready for contest instantly started from his [abstraction/reverie>] reverie, wheeled [about/round>] about and answered 'Sir, the reason is very plain. Knowl-   30 edge is of two kinds. [We can know a subject ourselves [MS 482] or we can know, where we can be informed upon it./We can know how a thing is or where [MS 482] it is or we can know, where it is treated>] We know a subject ourselves or we know, where [MS 482] we can find information upon it. When we inquire into any subject the first thing we have to do is to know what books [there are upon it>] have   35 treated of it. This leads us to look at Catalogues, and at the [/backs of books/>] backs of books [/in libraries/>] in libraries.' Sir Joshua observed to me the extraordinary promptitude with which [Johnson flew upon/our great friend took up>] Johnson flew upon an argument. 'Yes' said I 'He has no formal preparation, no flourishing with his sword. He is through your body in [an instant/a moment>] an instant.'   40

Johnson was here solaced with an elegant entertainment [an accomplished family>] a very accomplished family and [/much/>] much good company, amongst

---

[1] Presumably this phrase was inserted in first proof.
[2] The optional word, which JB left unresolved, is printed in the revises.
[3] When SJ first dined with Charles Burney he examined his host's books in a similar fashion. Burney's note on this incident appeared in the third edition.

whom was Mr. Harris of Salisbury who paid him many compliments on his Journey to the Western Islands.

The common remark as to the utility of reading History having been made JOHNSON. 'We must consider how very little History there is. I mean real
5 authentick history. That certain Kings reigned and certain battles were fought we can depend upon as [true/truth>] true. But all the colouring all the Philosophy of History [is/are>] is conjecture.' ['Then Sir' said I>] BOSWELL. 'Then Sir you [think all History no better than/no more than/only an>] would reduce all History to no better than an Almanack a mere Chronological series of remarkable events.' Mr.
10 Gibbon [who has since published several large volumes under the title of History/of that sort of composition which is generally received as History>] who must at that time have been employed upon his history of which he published the first volume the following year was [MS 483] present, but did not step forth in defence of that [species of writing/?projected Creation>] species of writing.
15 [Perhaps he had/felt the same unwillingness to engage which he expressed on an occasion which I have formerly mentioned. del]⁴

[He said>] Johnson observed that the [force/power>] force of our early habits was [such/so great>] so great that though reason nay though our senses approved of a different course almost every man returned to them.' I do not [suppose that>]
20 believe there is any observation upon human nature better founded than this; and in many cases it is a very painful truth; for where early habits have been mean and wretched, the joy and elevation [of>] resulting from better modes of life must be damped by the/a⁵ gloomy consciousness of being under an almost inevitable doom [to sink/of sinking/of falling>] to sink back into a situation which we
25 recollect with disgust. It surely may be prevented by constant attention and unremitting exertion to establish contrary habits of superiour [force/power>] efficacy.

'The Beggar's Opera' and the common question whether it was pernicious in its effects having been introduced. Johnson. 'As to this matter which has been very
30 much contested I myself am of opinion that more [MS 484] influence has been [ascribed/imputed>] ascribed to the Beggar's Opera than it in reality ever had; for I do not believe that any man was ever made a rogue by being present at its representation. At the same time I do not deny that it may have some influence by making the character of a rogue familiar and in some degree pleasing.ᵃ (Then

35 ᵃ [I have heard it remarked by a very eminent physician [who is>] whose observations on the human character are>] A very eminent physician whose discernment of the human character is acute and penetrating as in his own profession, remarked once at a Club where I was [present del], that a lively young man fond of pleasure and without money would hardly resisit a solicitation from

---

⁴ The revises print an entirely new sentence at the end of this paragraph: 'He probably did not like to *trust* himself with Johnson.' JB handles the deleted cross-reference through a footnote also added in the revises, which directs the reader back to Gibbon's comparison of SJ to a black bear (MS 462). See *ante* p. 152.
⁵ The alternative is resolved by the printing of 'the' in the revises.

collecting himself as it were to give a heavy [and comprehensive *del*] stroke).
There is in it such a *labefactation*[6] of all principles as may be injurious to
Morality.'

While he [delivered/pronounced>] pronounced this Response, we sat in a
comical sort of restraint, smothering a laugh which we were affraid might burst   5
out. In his Life of Gay He has been still more decisive as to the inefficiency of the
Beggars Opera in [corrupting/relaxing>] corrupting society. But I have ever
thought somewhat differently; for indeed, not only are the gayety and heroism of
a Highwayman ⟨as there represented⟩[7] very captivating to a youthful imagination but the arguments for private depredation are so plausible and the allusions   10
and contrasts with other modes of having superiour advantages in society are so
artfully put that it requires a cool and strong judgement to resist so imposing an
aggregate.[8] Yet I own I should be very sorry to have the Beggar's Opera
suppressed for there is in it so much of real London life, so much *[MS 485]* brilliant
wit and such a variety of airs that from early association of ideas engage soothe and   15
enliven the mind that no Performance which the Theatre exhibits delights me
more.

The late 'worthy' Duke of Queensberry as Thomson ⟨in his 'Seasons'⟩ justly
characterises him told me that when Gay first shewed him his/the[1] Beggar's opera
his ⟨Grace's⟩ observation was 'This is a very odd thing Gay. I am satisfied that It   20
is either a very good thing or a very bad thing.' The agreable alternative we know
was in the event conspicuously evident. Mr. Cambridge however confirmed to us
to=day the uncertainty of its success/that the Duke was right in his opinion.[2] He
was told by Quin that during the first night of its appearance it was long in a very
dubious state [of danger *del*] that there was a disposition to damn it and that   25

his mistress to go upon the highway, immediately after [being seen>] being present
at the representation of the Beggars Opera. I have been told of a very ingenious
observation by Mr. Gibbon, that the Beggars Opera may perhaps have [induced>]
sometimes increased the number of highwaymen; but that it has had a beneficial
effect in refining that class of men, making them less ferocious [and *del*] more polite   30
in short more like gentlemen. Upon this Mr. Courtenay said that 'Gay was the
Orpheus of Highwaymen'.

---

[6] In both the notes and *Life* MS, JB began to write *labefaction*. As Geoffrey Scott points
out, 'the hesitancy may cast a shade of doubt on *labefactation*, though this rare form is
justified (OED) by the Latin variant *labefactare*. Neither version of the word is given in
Johnson's Dictionary' (*BP* vi. 45).

[7] JB's later addition of 'as there represented' is omitted in the revises, apparently having
been overlooked by the compositor.

[8] JB's footnote on *The Beggar's Opera* was originally keyed to 'aggregate'.

[1] The alternative is resolved by the printing of 'The' in the revises.

[2] The alternative is resolved by the printing of 'that there was good reason enough to
doubt concerning its success' in the revises.

it was saved by the Song 'Oh ponder well be not severe'.[3] Quin himself had so [poor/bad>] bad an opinion of it, that he refused the part of Captain Macheath and gave it to Walker who acquired [such/the highest>] such celebrity by his grave yet animated performance of it.

5 ₍We talked of a young Gentleman's marriage [with/to>] with an eminent [₍publick₎ *del*] singer and his determination that she should no longer sing in publick, though his Father was very earnest she should, because her talents would be [very *del*] liberally rewarded so as to make her a good fortune.[4] It was questioned whether the ₍young₎ gentleman who had not a shilling in the world but was blest

10 with very [uncommon/distinguished>] uncommon talents, was not foolishly delicate or foolishly proud, and his Father truly rational without being mean. Johnson with all the high spirit of [a/the>] a Roman Senator exclaimed 'He resolved wisely and nobly to be sure. ₍He is a brave man.₎ Would not a gentleman be disgraced by having his Wife [singing publickly/a singing woman>] singing publickly for

15 hire? ₍No Sir₎ There can be no doubt here. I know not [if I should not *prepare*/which would be worse>] if I should not *prepare* myself for a publick singer as [readily/soon>] readily as let my Wife [be one/sing in publick>] be one.₎[5]

Johnson arraigned the modern politicks of this country as entirely devoid of all principle of whatever kind. 'Politicks' said he 'are now nothing more than means

20 of [success in Life/the World>] rising in the World. With this sole view do men engage in politicks, and their whole conduct proceeds upon it. How different [MS 486] in that respect is the state of the Nation now from what it was in the time of Charles the First /during the Usurpation/[6] and after the Restoration in the time of Charles the Second. Hudibras affords a strong proof how much hold political

25 principles had upon the minds of men. There is in Hudibras a great deal of Bullion which will allways last. But to be sure the brightest strokes of his wit owed their force to the impression of the characters which was upon mens minds at the time to their knowing them at table and in the street, in short being familiar with them and above all to his satire being directed against those whom a little while before

30 they had hated and feared. The Nation in general [has ever/at all times been

---

[3] JB's commentary on Polly appears in the third edition: 'the audience being much affected by the innocent looks of Polly, when she came to those two lines, which exhibit at once a painful and ridiculous image, "For on the rope that hangs my Dear, / Depends poor Polly's life"'.

[4] JB's notes confirm what contemporary readers (like Mrs. Piozzi, cited in Hill-Powell ii. 369 n. 2) would have recognized immediately, that the 'young Gentleman' was Richard Brinsley Sheridan and the 'eminent singer' Elizabeth Linley. After their marriage in 1773, Sheridan had refused to let his wife continue her highly successful career; this decision upset Thomas Linley, his daughter's teacher and promoter (*The Letters of Richard Brinsley Sheridan*, ed. Cecil Price, 1966, i. 79–81). It is likely that by 'father' JB means 'father-in-law': Thomas Sheridan, Richard Brinsley's father, strongly disapproved of Elizabeth Linley's 'notoriety', and broke off relations with his son when he married the young singer (ibid. i. 35 n. 1, 81 n. 2).

[5] SJ uses 'prepare' in the specialized sense of 'castrate'. In his bantering about a seraglio, he had agreed to admit JB 'if he were properly prepared; and he'd make a very good eunuch' (Hebridean Journ. 16 Sept. 1773).

[6] The optional phrase, which JB left unresolved, is printed in the revises.

loyal/attached to the Monarch›] has ever been loyal has been at all times ever attached to the Monarch ∧though a few daring rebels have been wonderfully powerful for a time.∧ The murder of Charles the First was undoubtedly not committed with the approbation or consent of the People. Had that been the Case Parliament would not have [quietly given up/ventured to give up›] ventured to consign the Regicides to ∧their∧ deserved punishment. And we [know/see›] know what /exuberance of/[7] joy there was [when Charles the second was restored/upon Charles the second being restored.›] when Charles the second was restored. If Charles the Second had bent all his mind [MS 487] to it had made it his sole object he might have been as absolute as [Lewis›] Louis the Fourteenth.' [*Boswell*. And he would have done›] A Gentleman observed He would have done no harm [/if he had/›] if he had. *Johnson*. 'Why Sir absolute Princes seldom do any harm. But they who are governed by them are governed by chance. There is no security for good government.' [*Cambridge/*A gentleman observed›] *Cambridge*. 'There have been many sad victims to absolute power.' *Johnson*. 'So ∧Sir∧ have there been to popular factions.' *Boswell*. 'The question is [shall we have/be less affraid of›] which is worst, one wild beast or many?' [But let me now observe that happily we are not under a necessity of being under either one or the other/there is not the necessity for our having either one or the other.[8] In our noble constitution as Blackstone has ably illustrated it, there is absolute power neither in one nor in many fallible men/no doubt but it is lodged not in one nor in many fallible beings. It is inherent in the law of the Land. *del*][9]

Johnson praised the Spectator particularly the character of Sir Roger de Coverley. He said 'Sir Roger did not die a violent death as has been generally [said/stated›] fancied. He was not killed. He died only because others were to die, and because his death [afforded/gave›] afforded an opportunity to Addison for some very fine writing. [We have/There is›] We have the example of Cervantes [killing Don Quixote/making Don Quixote die.›] making Don Quixote die. I [MS 488] never could see why Sir Roger is represented as a little cracked. It [appears/seems›] appears to me that the [story/circumstance›] story of the Widow was intended to have something superinduced upon it. But the superstructure did not come.'

Somebody found fault with writing verses in a dead language, maintaining that they were merely arrangements of so many words and laughed at the Universities of Oxford and Cambridge for sending forth Collections of them not only in [Greek and Latin/Latin and Greek›] Greek and Latin, but even in Syriack Arabick and other more unknown tongues.[1] *Johnson*. 'I would have as many of these as

5

10

15

20

25

30

35

---

[7] The optional phrase, which JB left unresolved, is printed in the revises.

[8] In the alternative version of this final clause, JB inadvertently left out the second 'not' and substituted 'having' for 'our being'.

[9] This deleted passage supplements our knowledge of JB's political views, as broadly summarized by Thomas Crawford: 'Boswell hankered after the reign of the Stuarts for a whole complex of reasons, the most compelling being his belief in indefeasible right. His was a monarchism which occasionally led him briefly to adore a despot like Frederick the Great, but his central position was one that accepted Britain's mixed constitution in which the balance of political power was complemented by a balance of property' (*Corr.* 6, p. liv).

[1] JB's notes reveal that this 'somebody' was Sir Joshua Reynolds (J42).

possible; I would have verses in every language that there are the means of acquiring. Nobody imagines that an University is to have at once two hundred Poets; but it [is›] should be able to shew two hundred scholars. [Piresque's death was/At Piresque's death he was›] Piresque's[2] death was lamented I think in forty

5   languages. And I would have at every Coronation and every death of a King every *Gaudium* and every *Luctus* University Verses in [every/all/as many language(s) that/as can be shewn›] every/as many language(s) as can be acquired.[3] I would [MS 489] have [the World to be thus told/it appear to the World thus›] the World to be thus told 'Here is a [Place›] School where every thing may be learnt.'

10   Having [set/gone›] set out next day on a visit to [the Earl of/Lord›] the Earl of Pembroke at Wilton, and to my friend Mr. Temple[4] ‹at Mamhead› in Devonshire and not having returned to town till the second of May, I did not see Dr. Johnson for a considerable time, and during the remaining part of my stay in London kept very imperfect notes of his conversation, which had I according to

15   my usual custom written out at large soon after the time, much might have been preserved which is now irretrievably lost. I can [only now›] now only [record/mention›] record some particular scenes, and a few fragments of his Memorabilia. But to make some amends for my relaxation of diligence in one respect I have to present my readers with arguments upon two Law Cases with

20   which he favoured me.

      On saturday the 6 of May ‹we dined by ourselves at the Mitre and› he dictated to me what follows, to obviate the Complaint formerly mentioned[5] which had been made in the form of an action in the Court of Session by Dr. Memis of Aberdeen that in the same translation of a Charter in which *Physicians* were

25   mentioned, he was called *Doctor of Medecine*.[6]

. . . .

      [MS 490] A few days [thereafter/afterwards›] afterwards I consulted him upon a Cause ‹Paterson etc. against Alexander etc.› which had been decided by a casting vote in the Court of Session [finding the Corporation of Stirling to be›] determining that the Corporation of Stirling was corrupt and setting aside the

30   election of some of their officers, because it was proved that three of the leading men who influenced the majority had entered into an unjustifiable compact, of which however the majority were ignorant.[7] ‹He dictated to me [these few hints›]

---

   [2] JB renders phonetically the name of Nicolas de Peiresc (1580–1637), French philologist and astronomer, a model of humanistic learning whose career SJ is likely to have known through the biography of Pierre Gassendi. The spelling had been corrected by the time of the revises, presumably in first proof.

   [3] The alternative is resolved by the printing of 'as many languages' in the revises.

   [4] Here, the second edition inserts a footnote that refers the reader to JB's first mention of his 'old and most intimate friend' Temple.

   [5] In the revises a footnote keyed to this word directs the reader back to JB's first mention of Dr. Memis (19 January 1775).

   [6] Direction to the compositor, '(Take it in)*'. This Paper Apart no longer forms part of the *Life* MS.

   [7] A deleted marginal note reads, 'See the appeal cases'.

after a little consideration the following sentences upon the subject:$_\lambda$[8]

. . . .

On Monday May 8 we went together and [surveyed/visited>] visited the [affecting mansions/*undeciphered word* scenes>] mansions of Bedlam. I had been informed that he had once been there before with Mr. Wedderburne now Lord Loughborough Mr. Murphy and Mr. Foote, and $_\lambda$I$_\lambda$ had heard Foote give a very   5
entertaining account of Johnson's happening to have his attention arrested by a Man who was very furious and while beating his straw supposed it [was/to be>] to be William Duke of Cumberland $_\lambda$whom he was punishing for his cruelties in Scotland in 1746$_\lambda$.[9] There was nothing peculiarly remarkable this day. But the general contemplation of Insanity was very [affecting/*undeciphered word*>] affect-   10
ing. I accompanied him home and dined and drank tea with him.

Talking of an acquaintance of ours distinguished for knowing an uncommon variety of miscellaneous articles both in antiquities and polite literature he [said>] observed 'You know Sir he [MS 491] runs about with little weight upon his [mind.' On tuesday 9 May I dined with him at General Paoli's. On friday 12 I was with   15
him both in the forenoon and the evening, and>] mind' and talking of another very ingenious gentleman who from the warmth of his temper was at variance with many of his acquaintance, and wished to avoid them, he said 'Sir he leads the life of [a highwayman>] an outlaw.' On friday 12 May as he had been so good as to assign me a room in his house where I might sleep $_\lambda$occasionally$_\lambda$ when [very late   20
with him>] I happened to sit with him to a late hour I took possession/made trial[1] of it this night, [and *del*] found every thing in excellent order, and was attended by honest Francis with a most civil assiduity. [I have however no traces of Johnsonian decision/wisdom except that when *del*] I asked him whether I might attend [a/him>] a Consultation [at/with>] with another Lawyer upon Sunday, as that   25
appeared to me to be [labouring/doing work>] doing work as much in my way as if $_\lambda$[one>] a man of$_\lambda$ any other profession should [labour>] work on the day appropri- ated for [sacred/religious>] religious rest. [He said When>] *Johnson*. 'Why Sir When you are of consequence enough to oppose the practice of consulting upon Sunday you [may/should>] should do it. But you may go now. It is not criminal   30
though it is not what one should do who is anxious for the preservation and increase of piety, to which a [strict/peculiar>] peculiar observance of Sunday [is a great help/tends greatly to help>] is a great help. The distinction is clear between what is of moral and what is of ritual obligation.'

On saturday [13 May>] May 13 I breakfasted [MS 492] with him [by/upon>] by   35
invitation [along with>] accompanied by Mr. $_\lambda$Andrew$_\lambda$ Crosbie Advocate whom he had seen at Edinburgh and the Hon. Col$_\lambda$olonel (now General)$_\lambda$ Edward Stopford brother [to/of>] to Lord Courtown who was desireous of being introduced to him. His [tea and coffee/coffee and tea>] tea and Rolls and Butter and whole

---

[8] Direction to the compositor, '(Take them in from paper marked S)'. The Paper Apart no longer forms part of the *Life* MS.

[9] The second edition adds a footnote, keyed to '1746': 'My very honourable friend General Sir George Howard, who served in the Duke of Cumberland's army, has assured me that the cruelties were not imputable to his Royal Highness'.

[1] The alternative is resolved by the printing of 'took possession' in the revises.

breakfast apparatus were all in such decorum and his behaviour was so [perfectly *del*] courteous, that Colonel Stopford was quite surprised, and wondered how he had heard so much said of Johnson's slovenliness and roughness. I have preserved [no more/little⟩] no more of [this morning's conversation/what passed⟩] what passed [/ except that/⟩] except that Crosbie [won his heart/pleased him much⟩] pleased him much by talking learnedly of Alchymy as to which Johnson was not a positive unbeliever, but rather delighted in considering what progress had actually been made in the transmutation of metals, [∧and mentioned∧ *del*] what near approaches [had been made⟩] there had been to the making of gold, [how it⟩] and told us that it was affirmed that a person in the Prussian² dominions had discovered the secret, but died without revealing it as imagining it would be [injurious/hurtful/prejudicial⟩] prejudicial to [society/mankind⟩] society, and [how⟩] that it was not impossible but it might in time be [found out/generally known⟩] generally known.

    It being asked whether it was reasonable for a man to be angry at another [because a woman preferred him⟩] whom a woman preferred to him *Johnson*. 'I do not see ∧Sir∧ that it is reasonable for [*MS 493*] a man to be angry at another [to whom a woman has given the preference to him/whom a woman preferred to him⟩] whom a woman preferred to him. But Angry he is no doubt, and he is loath to be angry at himself.'

    [On Monday 15 I breakfasted with him with Mrs. Blair a scotch Lady whom he had recommended to me as a client by his letter.³ On tuesday 16 I was with him at Mr. Thrale's at Streatham staid all night and came to town with him next morning, in order to dine at Beauclerk's. He said 'Garrick has not latin enough. He finds out the latin of a passage by the meaning, rather than the meaning by the latin' and he observed that Writers of Travels fail more/are more defective than any others. I passed many hours with him next day of which all my Memorandum/Memorial is 'Much laughing.' It seems/would seem he had that day been in the humour for jocularity and merriment, and upon such occasions I never knew/saw a man in my life laugh more heartily. We may suppose that the high relish of a state so different from his habitual gloom produced more than ordinary exertions of that distinguishing faculty of Man which has puzzled Philosophers so much to explain. I was with him on both the following days, took leave of him and on Monday the 22 set out for Scotland.⟩]

    Before setting out for Scotland on the 23 I was frequently in his company at different places, but during this period have recorded only two remarks. One [of/concerning⟩] concerning Garrick 'He has not latin enough. He finds out the latin by the meaning, rather than the meaning by the latin,' and another concerning Writers of Travels who he observed were 'more defective than any other writers.'⁴ I passed many hours with him on the 17 of which I find all my Memorial

---

² The compositor misread 'Prussian' as 'Russian', and this error went uncorrected.

³ This Mrs. Blair, whom JB saw in London on two other occasions, has not been identified (Journ. 3 May 1781, 21 May 1785).

⁴ Direction to the compositor, "'I passed." See opposite page'. With this note to the compositor, JB reinstates (with revisions) the second half of the paragraph he had deleted previously. The direction is reinforced by JB's marginal note on MS 493 ('NB Stet from *I passed* down to '*explain*'") and by another at the top ('A good part of this Page Stet').

is 'Much laughing.' It would seem he had that day been in the humour for jocularity and merriment, and upon such occasions I never knew a man laugh more heartily. We may suppose that the high relish of a state so different from his habitual gloom produced more than ordinary exertions of that distinguishing faculty of Man which has puzzled Philosophers so much to explain. Johnson's   5
laugh was as remarkable as any circumstance in his manner. It was a kind of good-humoured growl. Tom Davies described it drolly enough. 'He laughs like a Rhinoceros.'[5][6]

To James Boswell Esq.[7]

. . . .

[MS 494][8]   10
[Paper Apart LL][9]   [Of three letters which I wrote to him after my return to Scotland I think it necessary to extract only the following passages:>] After my return to Scotland I [wrote to him three letters>] wrote three letters to him from which I excerpt the following passages:

'I have seen Lord Hailes since I came down. He thinks it wonderful that you are   15
pleased to take so much pains in revising his "Annals." I told him that you said you were well rewarded by the entertainment which you had in reading them.'

'There has been a numerous flight of Hebridians in Edinburgh this summer whom I have been happy to entertain at my house. Mr. Donald McQueen[a] and Lord Monboddo supt with me one evening. They joined in contraverting your   20
proposition that the Gaelick of the highlands and isles of Scotland was not written till of late.'

'My mind has been somewhat dark this summer. I have need of your warming and vivifying rays, and I hope I shall have them frequently. I am going to pass some time with my Father at Auchinleck.'[1]   25

. . . .

[a] A very learned Minister in the Isle of Sky [of *del*] whom both Dr. Johnson and I have mentioned with regard.

---

[5] JB has inserted this detail from his notes for 28 April 1773.

[6] SJ to Bennet Langton, 21 May 1775, belongs to that group of letters first inserted at the end of the second volume of the second edition, and then moved to their chronologically appropriate places for the third edition. See *ante* p. 10 n. 1.

[7] Direction to the compositor, '"I make no doubt" / (Take it in).' This direction is accompanied by a marginal note reading 'N.B. Omit a paragraph marked in page 2 of it'. This Paper Apart (SJ to JB, 27 May) no longer forms part of the *Life* MS.

[8] Deleted direction to the compositor, 'Take in excerpts of mine of 2 June 6 June 22 August. Arrange his of 27 August ⟨to Hoole 28 August⟩ 30 August and mine of 3 September his of 14 Sept. and mine of 19 Septr'. This set of directions was replaced by the following: 'See Paper Apart marked LL'.

[9] Direction to the compositor, 'For p 494'.

[1] Direction to the compositor, 'Take in his of 27 August, leaving ⟨out⟩ last line page first from "You never" to the end of the paragraph and putting three or four stars ****'. This is followed by a second direction, '(Take in his of 30 August)'. A marginal note accompanies these directions to the compositor: 'These two 27 and 30 August are attached to this leaf'. These Papers Apart no longer form part of the *Life* MS.

My Dear Sir[2]

I now write to you, lest in some of your freaks and humours you should fancy yourself neglected. Such fancies I must entreat you never to admit, at least never to indulge for my regard for you is so radicated and fixed that it is become part of
5   my mind, and cannot be effaced but by some cause uncommonly violent. Therfore, whether I write, or not, set your thoughts at rest. I now write to tell you that I shall not very soon write again, for I am to set out to morrow on another journey.

****

Your friends are all well at Streatham and in Leicester fields.[3] Make my
10   compliments to Mrs. Boswell if she is in good humour with me. I am, Sir etc. / Sam Johnson / Septr. 14th 1775

[MS 494 resumed] What he mentions [so slightly/easily⟩] in such light terms as ['I am to set out tomorrow/'Tomorrow I am to set out⟩] 'I am to set out tomorrow on another journey' I soon after discovered was no less than a Tour to France with
15   Mr. and Mrs. Thrale. This was the only time in his life when he went upon the continent.[4/5]

. . . .

To James Boswell Esq.[6]

. . . .

₍To Mrs. Lucy Porter in Lichfield[a/7]

. . . .

To [Mrs. Lucy Porter in Lichfield⟩] The Same₎[8]

. . . .

20   [a] [There can be no⟩] [The daughter of Mrs. Johnson⟩] There can be no doubt that he corresponded with this Lady his step daughter [many years before this⟩] many years previous to 1775 but none of his earlier letters were preserved.

---

[2] Direction to the compositor, 'To the Same'. The transcription of this letter is in the hand of Veronica Boswell, with additions and corrections in JB's hand.

[3] JB explains (in a note for the second edition) that Leicester Fields was the home of Sir Joshua Reynolds.

[4] At this point the third edition prints SJ's two letters to Robert Levet.

[5] Direction to the compositor, '⟨Excerpt mine of 24 Octr.)'. JB temporarily replaced this direction with another, 'Take in Paper O'; ultimately, however, he reverted to the original plan. This Paper Apart no longer forms part of the *Life* MS.

[6] Direction to the compositor, '"I am glad that the young Laird etc." / ⟨Take it in)'. This Paper Apart no longer forms part of the *Life* MS.

[7] Direction to the compositor, '"This week" (Take it in)'. This direction replaced an earlier one reading '(Excerpt mine of 24 Novr.)'. This Paper Apart no longer forms part of the *Life* MS.

[8] Direction to the compositor, '"Some weeks" (take it in)'. This direction is followed by another, 'Take in some Leaves ₍F1₎'. [MS: Rosenbach Museum and Library.] By the stage of the revises, JB had extensively reworked and expanded the section of the *Life* devoted to SJ's trip. The most important change was the inclusion of all the diary entries from the notebook labelled 'France 2'; see Hill-Powell ii. 389–401 and *The French Journals of Mrs. Thrale and Dr. Johnson*, ed. Moses Tyson and Henry Guppy, 1932, pp. 169–88. JB's framing commentary has been collated with the revises and the first three editions.

[Paper Apart F 1st]⁹

It is to be regretted that he did not write an account of his Travels in France, for, as he is reported to have once said that he could write the Life of a broomstick so notwithstanding such a number of former travellers have exhausted almost every thing that can be found in that [Kingdom/country>] great Kingdom, his very accurate [observation, original vigour of thinking/thought and illustrating/description might have>] observation and peculiar vigour of thinking and illustrating would have produced a valuable Work. During his visit to it which lasted but about two months, he wrote notes or minutes of what he saw in two Small paper Books one of which has been lost or perhaps destroyed in that precipitate Burning of his papers [a few days/not long>] a few days before his death which must ever be lamented; but one titled 'France 2.' ₍which consists of Twenty nine pages [uninterrupted *del*]₎ is in my possession. It is a Diurnal Abbreviate of where he was and what he [observed/saw>] observed from the 10 October to the 4 November inclusive being twenty six [days. His whole Tour lasted/was but about two months. It>] days; and shews an extraordinary minute attention to [an infinite>] a variety of particulars of which I shall give a specimen.

Oct. 23 'We went to see the looking glasses wrought. They come from Normandy in cast plates perhaps the third of an inch thick. At Paris they are ground upon a marble table, by rubbing one plate on another with grit between them. The various sands of which there are said to be five, I could not learn. The handle by which the upper Glass is moved has the form of a wheel which may be moved in all directions. The plates are sent up with their surfaces ground but not polished, and so continue till they are bespoken, lest _____ should spoil the surface as we were told. Those that are to be polished are laid on a table covered with several thick cloths hard strained that the resistance may be equal; they are then rubbed with a hard rubber held down hard by a contrivance which I did not well understand. The powder which is used last seemed to me to be iron dissolved in aqua fortis. They called it as Baretti said Mar de l'eau forte which he thought was _____. They mentioned vitriol and saltpetre. The ____ ball swims in the quicksilver. To silver them a leaf of _____ tin is laid, and rubbed with quicksilver to which it unites. The more quicksilver is poured upon it which by its mutual (_____) rises very high. Then a paper is laid at the nearest end of the plate over which the glass is slided till it lies upon the plate, having driven much of the quicksilver before it. It is then I think pressed upon cloaths, and then set sloping to drop the superfluous mercury; the slope is daily heightened towards a perpendicular.'

[The>] His [tender/amiable>] tender affection for his departed Wife of which there are so many undoubted evidences in his 'Prayers and Meditations' appears very feelingly in a slight reflection on viewing this *Palais Bourbon*. Oct. 17. 'The sight of palaces and other great buildings leaves no very distinct images unless to those who talk of them and impress them. As I entered, — my Wife was in my mind. She would have been pleased. Having now nobody to please, I am little pleased.'

_____

⁹ Direction to the compositor, 'To be taken in on p 494'.

When I met him in London the year after, the account of his french Tour which he gave me was 'Sir I have seen all the visibilities of Paris and arround it; but to have formed an acquaintance with the people there would have required more time than I could stay. I was just beginning to creep into acquaintance by means
5 of Colonel Drumgold a very high man Sir head of *L'Ecole Militaire* [and *del*] a most compleat character, for he had first been a professor of Rhetorick, and then became a soldier. And Sir I was very kindly treated by the English Benedictines and have a cell appropriated to me in their convent.' Of his intimacy with them his Diary in France gives testimony. I insert the following [minute>] notice
10 'Oct.31.Tues. I lived at the Benedictines, meagre day, soup meagre, herrings, eels both with sauce. Fryed fish, Lentils tasteless in themselves. In the Library where I found [*blank space*] *de Historia Indica promontorium flectere to double the Cape.* I parted very tenderly from the Prior and Frier Wilkes.' He said, 'The great in France live very magnificently; but the rest very miserably. There is no happy
15 middle [station/state/rank>] station as in England. The shops of Paris are mean; the meat in the markets is such as would be sent to a gaol in England, and Mr. Thrale justly observed that the [french cookery>] cookery of the french was forced upon them by necessity, for they could not eat their meat unless they added some taste to it. The french are an indelicate people; they will spit [in>] upon any place.
20 At Madame [de>] du _____'s a literary Lady of rank the footman [lifted>] took the sugar [with>] in his fingers and [put>] threw it into my coffee. I was going to [put>] [leave>] put it aside, but hearing it was made on purpose for me, I e'en tasted Tom's fingers. [She would make>] The same Lady would needs make tea *a l'angloise.* The spout of the tea pot did not pour freely. She bid the footman blow
25 into it. France is worse than Scotland in every=thing but climate. Nature has done more for the french but they have done less for themselves than the scotch have done.' It happened [curiously>] singularly enough that Foote was at Paris at the same time with Dr. Johnson, and his description of him while there was [sufficiently>] abundantly ludicrous. He [said>] told me that the french were quite
30 astonished at his figure and manner, and at his dress which he [obstinately/resolutely>] obstinately continued, exactly as in London his brown clothes, black stockings and plain shirt. [He>] Johnson told me that an irish gentleman said to him 'Sir you have not seen the best french Players.' Johnson 'Players Sir I look on them as no better than creatures set upon tables and joint
35 stools to make faces and produce laughter [as>] like dancing dogs. But Sir, you will allow that some players are better than others — *Johnson.* 'Yes Sir As some dogs dance better than others.'[1]

While [he>] Johnson was in France, he was generally very resolute in speaking latin. It was a maxim with him that a man should not let himself down, by
40 speaking a language which he speaks imperfectly. Indeed we must have often observed how inferiour, how much like a child a man appears who speaks [broken language>] a broken tongue. When Sir Joshua Reynolds at one of the dinners of the Royal Academy [introduced>] presented him to a frenchman of great distinc-

---

[1] The last three sentences of this paragraph were marked by JB for deletion. He reinstated them at a later stage by writing 'stet' in the margins of the MS.

tion, he would not deign to speak french, but talked latin though his Excellency did not understand it, owing perhaps to Johnson's english [accent⟩] pronuncia- tion. Yet upon another occasion he was observed to speak french to [another⟩] a frenchman of high rank who spoke english, ⟨and being asked the reason with some expression of surprise⟩ [said he⟩] he answered I think my french is as good as his english. Though Johnson understood French perfectly, he could not speak it readily as I have observed at his first interview with General Paoli in 1769. Yet he wrote it I imagine very well as appears from some of his letters in Mrs. Piozzi's Collection, of which I shall transcribe one.[2]

[Paper Apart F 2d] A Madame La Comtesse de _____

May 16. 1771

Oui Madame, le moment est arrivé, et il faut que Je parte. Mais pourquoi faut il partir? est ce que Je m'ennuye? Je m'ennuyerai ailleurs. Est ce que Je cherche ou quelque plaisir, ou quelque soulagement? Je ne cherche rien, je n'espere rien. Aller, voir ce que J'ai vû, etre un peu rejoué un peu degouté, me resouvenir que la vie se passe, et qu'elle se passe en vain, me plaindre de moi, m'enducir aux dehors. Voici le tout de ce qu'on compte pour les delices de l'anné.[3] Que Dieu vous donne, Madame, tous les agrémens de la vie, avec un esprit qui peut enjouir sans s'y livrer trop.

Here let me not forget a curious anecdote as related to me by Mr. Beauclerk which I shall endeavour to exhibit as well as I can in that gentleman's lively manner and in justice to him it is proper to add that Dr. Johnson told me I might rely both on the correctness of his observation and memory, and the fidelity of his narrative. 'When Madame de Boufflers was first in England' (said Beauclerk) 'she was desireous to see Johnson. I accordingly went with her to his chambers in the Temple, where she was entertained with his conversation for some time. When our visit was over she and I left him and were got into Inner Temple lane, when all at once I heard a noise like thunder. This was occasioned by Johnson who it seems upon a little recollection had taken it into his head that he ought to have done the honours of his literary residence to a foreign Lady of Quality, and eager to shew himself a man of gallantry had hurried down the timber staircase in violent agitation. He overtook us before we reached the Temple=gate and brushing in between me and Madame de Boufflers, seised her hand and conducted her to her coach, while he was drest in his [old *del*] rusty brown morning suit ⟨a pair of old shoes by way of slippers, a little shrivelled wig sticking on the top of his head and⟩ the sleeves of his shirt and knees of his breeches hanging loose. A considerable crowd of people gathered round, and were not a little struck by this singular appearance.

[Paper Apart F1 resumed] He spoke Latin with wonderful fluency and eloquence. When Pere Boscovitch was in England, Johnson dined in company with him at Sir

---

[2] Direction to the compositor, 'Take in Paper F2d'.

[3] In the revises Selfe rightly queried the spelling of this word: 'ainé or année — is there any such Fr. word as anné'. This orthographic question was ultimately disregarded: Selfe's marginal query has been crossed out, and the erroneous 'anné' left in place. For the third edition, the spelling was corrected to 'année'.

Joshua Reynolds' and at Dr. Douglas', now Bishop of Carlisle.[4] Upon both occasions that celebrated Foreigner expressed his astonishment at Johnson's latin conversation.[5]

[MS 494 resumed] To Dr. Samuel Johnson[6]

. . . .

5   Mr. MacLean returned with the most agreable accounts of the polite attention with which he was received by Dr. Johnson.[7]

. . . .

[Paper Apart B][8] In the course of this year Dr. Burney ˄informs me that 'he˄ very frequently met Dr. Johnson at Mr. Thrale's at Streatham where they had many long conversations, often sitting up as long as the fire and candles lasted and much longer than the patience of the servants subsisted.'[9]

10   A few of Johnson's sayings which that gentleman recollects shall here be inserted.[1]

'I never take a nap after dinner but when I have had a bad night, and then the nap takes me.'

˄'The writer of an epitaph should not be considered as saying nothing but what is strictly true. Allowance must be made for some degree of exaggerated praise. In

15   lapidary inscriptions a man is not upon oath.'˄

'There is now less flogging in our great schools than formerly, but then less is learned there; so that what the boys get at one end they lose at the other.'

'More is learned in publick than in private schools, from emulation there is the collision of mind with mind or the radiation of many minds pointing to one

20   center. Though few boys make their own exercises, yet if a good exercise is given up, out of a great number of boys, it is made by some body.'

'I hate by=roads in education. Education is as well known, and has long been as well known as ever it can be. Endeavouring to make children prematurely wise is useless labour. Suppose they have more knowledge at five or six years old than

25   other children, what use can be made of it? It will be lost before it is wanted, and the waste of ˄so much˄ time and labour of the teacher can never be repaid. Too much is expected from precocity, and too little performed. Miss _____[2] was an instance of early cultivation; but in what did it terminate? — in marrying a little

---

[4] See *ante* p. 32 n. 3.

[5] The second edition adds a sentence here: 'When at Paris, Johnson thus characterised Voltaire to Freron the Journalist: *"Vir est acerrimi ingenii et paucarum literarum."'*

[6] Direction to the compositor, '"Mr. Alexander MacLean" / (Take it in)'. The Paper Apart no longer forms part of the *Life* MS.

[7] Direction to the compositor, '(Excerpt mine of 18 Decr.)'. This direction was subsequently qualified with 'Go to the back' and was then superseded by a direction reading 'Take in Paper B ˄of Dr. Burney˄'. This Paper Apart no longer forms part of the *Life* MS.

[8] Direction to the compositor, 'To be taken in at [back of *del*] *p. 494'.

[9] See Appendix G in *Life* MS i. 371–77.

[1] Deleted direction to the compositor, 'Take in Paper marked **'.

[2] Just as Capel Lofft had urged JB to delete the unflattering description of Catharine Macaulay (see *ante* p. 148 n. 2), he argued that this 'ridicule' of Anna Letitia Aikin Barbauld should be eliminated from the second edition. One of his points—that 'Dr. Johnson had expressed himself with ... liberal justice' of Mrs. Barbauld in Mrs. Piozzi's *Anecdotes*—was hardly designed to sway JB, who made none of the changes suggested by Lofft (*Corr. 2*, p. 410).

presbyterian parson who keeps an infant boarding school, so that all her employ‑
ment now is "to suckle fools and chronicle small beer." She tells the children, "this
is a cat, and that is a dog, with four legs and a tail; — see there! You are much
better than a cat or a dog, for you can speak." If I had bestowed such an education
on a daughter, and had discovered that she thought of marrying such a fellow, I   5
would have sent her to the *Congress*.'

After[3] having talked [very *del*] slightingly of Musick, he was observed to listen
very attentively while Miss Thrale played on the Harpsichord and with eagerness
he called to her 'Why don't you dash away like Burney.' Dr. Burney upon this said
to him 'I believe Sir we shall make a musician of you at last.' Johnson with   10
[complacent candour/candid complacency>] candid complacency replied 'Sir I
shall be glad to have a new sense given to me.'

He had come down one morning [at Streatham *del*] to the breakfast room and
been a considerable time by himself before any body appeared. When at an after
time he was [upbraided>] twitted by Mrs. Thrale for being very late which he [was   15
very frequently>] generally was he defended himself by alluding to the extraordi‑
nary morning when he had been too early 'Madam I do not like to come down to
vacuity.'

Dr. Burney having remarked that Mr. Garrick was beginning to look old, he
said 'Why Sir no man's face has had more wear and tear.'   20

[MS opp. 495] Not having heard from him for a longer time than I supposed he
would be silent, I wrote to him Decr. 18 not in good spirits. 'Sometimes I have
been affraid that the cold which has gone over Europe this year like a sort of
pestilence has seised you severely. Sometimes my imagination which is upon
occasions prolifick of evil hath figured that you may have some how taken offence   25
at some part of my conduct.'

   [MS 495][4] [To James Boswell Esq. *del*][5]
       [To James Boswell Esq. *del*][6]
       ‚To James Boswell Esq.‚[7]

. . . .

In 1776 [he engaged so far as we know in/can discover in>] Johnson executed   30
so far as I can discover no work of any sort for [the Publick/publication>] the
Publick. [‚He indeed collected his last four Pamphlets in an octavo volume under
the title of 'Political Tracts by the Authour of The Rambler' with this motto.‚ *del*]

---

[3] The rest of the material gathered from Dr. Burney is written on a separate leaf (with the
deleted heading '*Johnsoniana from Dr. Burney*') attached by JB to the original Paper Apart B.
JB appears to have been saving these anecdotes until he found a suitable place to insert them.

[4] Direction to the compositor, 'This page begins Vol. II. It must have a Title (or
whatever it is called) exactly like the first The Life etc.'

[5] Deleted direction to the compositor, '"Never dream" (Take it in)'.

[6] Deleted direction to the compositor, '"I have at last sent" (Take it in)'. This is followed
by a direction to the compositor that was both added and deleted in a later draft: 'Take in
Papers apart B concerning Dr. Burney'.

[7] Direction to the compositor, '(Take in his of Decr. 23 / "Never dream etc.")'. This
Paper Apart no longer forms part of the *Life* manuscript.

But that his mind was still ardent, and fraught with generous wishes [at least *del*] to attain to still higher degrees of literary excellence [appears from his private notes. 'I purposed to apply vigorously to study particularly of the Greek and Italian Tongues.' Such a purpose so expressed at the age of Sixty=seven is admirable and
5   encouraging.>] will by and by be proved by his private notes of this year.
                    To James Boswell Esq.[8]

· ·

[Paper Apart E][9]   At this time was in agitation a matter of great consequence to me and my family which I should not obtrude upon the world were it not that the part which Dr. Johnson's friendship for me made him take in it was the occasion
10 of an [eminent display>] exertion of his abilities which it would be injustice to conceal. [In order to understand what he wrote upon the subject>] That what he wrote upon the subject may be understood it is necessary to give a state of the question which I shall [endeavour to do with brevity and precision>] do as briefly as I can.
15   In the year 1504 the Barony ∧or Manor∧ of Auchinleck in Ayrshire which belonged to a family of the same name with the lands (pronounced *Affleck*) having fallen to the Crown by [the *del*] forfeiture [the most excellent Prince *del*] James the Fourth, King of Scotland [was pleased to grant that Estate/Domain>] granted it to Thomas Boswell a branch of an ancient family in ∧the County of∧ Fife, styling him
20 in the charter '*dilecto familiari nostro*' and assigning as the cause of the grant '*pro bono et fideli servitio nobis prestito.*' [This *del*] Thomas Boswell was slain in battel fighting along with his Sovereign at the fatal field of Floddon in 1513.
        From this very honourable founder of our Family the estate [descended/was conveyed>] was transmitted in a direct series of heirs male, to David Boswell my
25 Father's great grand uncle, who had no sons but four daughters who were all respectably married, the eldest to Lord Cathcart [and from her are descended the present Representatives of that noble family and the heirs of the several alliances which it has formed. *del*][1]

---

[8] Direction to the compositor, '"I have at last sent" (Take it in)'. This Paper Apart no longer forms part of the *Life* MS. This direction to the compositor is followed by another, later deleted: 'Excerpt and take in Mine of 3 Janry My Wife's of ditto His of 15 Janry mine of 30 Janry his of 3 febry mine to Lord Hailes of /20/ Janry — Lord Hailes to me of 23 Janry — Mine to Lord Hailes of Ditto Lord Hailes to me of 24 Janry Lord Hailes to me of 8 febry — Dr. Johns to me of feb 9 and feb 15 mine to him of 20 feb [mine to him/his to me of 29 feb *del*] his to me of 24 feb and to my Wife *being all concerning the important question of our Family Settlement*'. This convoluted direction to the compositor was ultimately replaced with the more succint 'Take in Parcel marked E'.
[9] Direction to the compositor, 'For p. 495'.
[1] JB debated at length whether to include this phrase about his descent from Lady Cathcart. In a single draft, he composed a first version, crossed it out, and then wrote 'stet' several times in the margins. In a later draft, he deleted the 'stets' and clarified the final editorial decision by writing 'Out' in the margin. Perhaps JB was wary of undermining his credibility as proponent of male succession by drawing attention to the importance of the female line in the Boswell family tree.

David Boswell [though much/strongly pressed to give the estate to his eldest daughter was resolute in the military feudal principle of continuing the male succession and therefore settled it on⟩] being resolute in the military feudal principle of continuing the male succession passed by his daughters and settled the estate on his nephew by his next brother who approved of the [devise⟩] deed and renounced any pretensions which he might possibly have ∧in preference to his son∧. But the estate having been burthened with large portions to the daughters and other debts it was necessary for the nephew to sell a considerable part of it and what remained was ∧still∧ much encumbered.

The frugality of the nephew preserved [it and in some degree relieved it⟩] and in some degree relieved the Estate. His son my Grandfather an eminent [Advocate⟩] [Lawyer⟩] Lawyer not only [recovered⟩] repurchased a great part of what had been sold ∧[but added⟩] but acquired other lands∧ and my Father [added considerably to it⟩] who was one of the Judges of Scotland and had added considerably to the Estate [and he *del*] now signified his [inclination/intention⟩] inclination to take [advantage/use of *del*] the privilege allowed by [the⟩] our law[a] [/of Scotland/ *del*] to secure it to his family in perpetuity by an Entail which on account of marriage articles could not be done without my consent.

In the plan of [securing the Estate by an Entail⟩] entailing the Estate I heartily concurred with him though I was the first [to be restrained by it/whom it would restrain⟩] to be restrained by it; but we unhappily differed as to the series of heirs which should be [appointed/established/called to the succession⟩] established or in the language of our law called to the succession. My Father had declared a predilection for heirs general [contracted as I really believe in the course of his laborious and zealous exertions in favour of his Ward the young Countess of Sutherland[2] in the competition concerning her peerage for I think/am pretty confident I can trace my having early derived/imbibed from him a contrary principle. He was willing however to continue/carry on the male succession as far as the descendants of his Grandfather consisting of three families but he insisted that his own heirs general/of line should then be preferred/introduced.⟩] that is, males and females indiscriminately. He was willing however that all males descending from his grandfather should be preferred to females, but would not extend that privilege to males deriving their descent from a higher source. I on the other hand had [an old Gothick zeal⟩] a zealous partiality for heirs male [for ever/without restriction⟩] however remote, which I maintained by arguments which appeared to me to have [much⟩] considerable weight. As first the opinion of [/some/ eminent/distinguished⟩] some distinguished naturalists, that our species is transmitted through males only the female being [/all along/⟩] all along no

5

10

15

20

25

30

35

---

[a] Statute 1685 Cap.

[2] Lord Auchinleck was one of seven guardians of Elisabeth Sutherland (1765–1839), who succeeded to the title of Countess of Sutherland (*suo jure*) in 1766. Her right to inherit her father's land and title was challenged by George Sutherland of Forse, heir male of the first Earl of Sutherland, and by Sir Robert Gordon of Gordonstoun, heir male of the tenth Earl. This dispute, which was not resolved until the House of Lords ruled in favour of Lady Sutherland in 1771, centred on the issue of inheritance by heirs general versus inheritance by heirs male.

more than a ⟨*nidus* or⟩ nurse, which notion [I thought was∕imagined confirmed I stated my difficulties∕the case with all it difficulties to Johnson. I wrote to Johnson stating the case at∕on∕with all its difficulties at great length⟩] seems to be confirmed by that text of Scripture 'He was yet *in the loins of his Father* when

5   Melchisedec met him', and consequently that a man's grandchild by a daughter instead of being his *surest* descendant as is vulgarly ⟨and in reality⟩ said has [indeed∕in truth *del*] no connection whatever with his blood. — And secondly — independent of this theory (which if [just, must⟩] true, should completely explode heirs general) that if the preference of a male to a female without regard to

10   primogeniture, as a son though much younger nay even a grandson ⟨by a son⟩ to a daughter, be once admitted as it universally is, it must be equally reasonable and proper in the most remote degree of descent from the original proprietor of an estate as in the nearest, because however distant from the representative at the time, that remote heir male, upon the failure of those nearer to the original

15   proprietor than he is, becomes in fact the nearest male to *him*, and is therefore preferable as *his* representative to a female descendant. [An⟩] A little extension of mind will enable us ⟨[at once⟩] easily⟩ to perceive that a son's son, in continuation to whatever length of time is preferable to a son's daughter [and this is the short view of the question between male and female succession∕exclusive] of in an

20   ancient family. Patrimony in which reference∕respect must be had to the original proprietor, and not to one of his descendants.⟩] in the succession to an ancient inheritance in which reference must be had to the representation of the original proprietor, and not to that of one of his descendants.[a]3 [What a man has acquired himself, he may dispose of as he pleases. *del*]

25   [But⟩] And [in∕besides⟩] in the particular case of our family I apprehended that we were under an implied obligation in honour and honesty to transmit the estate by the same tenure which we held it which was as heir male excluding nearer females. I therefore (as I thought conscientiously) [objected to∕opposed leaving out of our entail, two distant male branches one in Scotland, and another which

30   [a] I am aware of Blackstone's admirable demonstration of the reasonableness of the legal succession upon the principle of there being the greatest probability that the nearest heir of the person who last dies proprietor of an estate is of the blood of the first purchaser. But supposing a pedigree to be [authentically ascertained⟩] carefully authenticated through all its branches, instead of mere *probability* there

35   will be a moral[a1] *certainty* [in favour *del*] that the [heir male⟩] nearest heir male at whatever period [is⟩] has the same right of blood with the first heir male [that is⟩] namely the original purchasers eldest son.[a2]

---

3 The second half of this paragraph (from 'As first the opinion' to 'one of his descendants') was eventually moved from the main text to the footnotes, where it joined with note a above ('I am aware' etc.) to form a single lengthy note. JB signalled this change with a marginal note to the compositor, 'All scored round is a Note'.

[a1] The compositor omitted 'moral', and this error went uncorrected.

[a2] By the stage of the revises, italics had been added to 'the nearest heir male, at whatever period' and to 'the original purchasers eldest son' to underscore JB's point.

had about the middle of the last century established itself in Germany.⟩]⁴ objected
to my Father's scheme.

My [opposition/objecting⟩] opposition was very displeasing to my Father [who
was one of the Judges of Scotland a man of respectable character both for abilities
and integrity, and certainly entitled to great deference. There was an apprehen-   5
sion of immediate disagreeable effects but I now believe a groundless one by which
not only myself but my wife and children might suffer, and therefore after much
uneasiness and perplexity⟩] who was entitled to great respect and deference and I
had reason to apprehend disagreable consequences from my non=compliance
with his wishes. After much perplexity and uneasiness I wrote to ∧Dr.∧ Johnson   10
stating the case with all its difficulties at [great/full⟩] full length, [intreating
earnestly/earnestly intreating/requesting him to⟩] and earnestly requesting that
he would consider it at leisure and favour me with his friendly opinion and advice.

TO JAMES BOSWELL ESQ.⁵

                                                                                    15

· ·

To the Same⁶

· ·

[Paper Apart E resumed] I had followed his recommendation and consulted
Lord Hailes [who besides having been/being as well as my Father one of the young   20
Countess of Sutherland's Guardians, had /formed/ a very firm/a firm/a clear
opinion upon this subject in general, contrary to that which I had indulged⟩]
[whose clear opinion upon this question of succession from⟩] who upon this
subject had a firm opinion contrary to mine. His Lordship obligingly took the
trouble to write me a letter, in which he [discussed my difficulties in every view⟩]   25
discussed with legal and historical learning the points in which I saw much
difficulty, maintaining that 'the succession of heirs general was the succession
[of/by⟩] by the law of Scotland from the throne to the cottage, as far as we can
learn it by record' observing that the estate of our family had not been limited to
heirs male and that though an heir male had in one instance been chosen in   30
preference to nearer females that had been an arbitrary act which had seemed best
in the embarrassed state of affairs at the time, and the fact was that upon a fair
computation of the values of land and money at the time, applied to the estate and
the burthens upon it there was nothing given to the heir male but the skeleton of
an estate [and that therefore there was no pretence *del*]. 'The plea of conscience'   35
said his Lordship 'which you put is a most respectable one, especially when
Conscience and *self* are on different sides. But I think that conscience is not well
informed, and that *self* and *she* ought on this occasion to be of a side.'

This letter, [particularly the last consideration that the preference given to the
heir male was unsubstantial had much influence upon my mind, and I sent it⟩]   40

---

⁴ A deleted mark in the margin indicates that at one point JB intended a note here.

⁵ Direction to the compositor, '⟨Take in Dr. Johnson's of 15 Janry. 1776 / 'I am much
impressed'). This sub Paper Apart no longer forms part of the *Life* MS.

⁶ Direction to the compositor, '⟨Take in Dr. Johnson's of Feb. 3 / 'I am going to write').
This sub Paper Apart no longer forms part of the *Life* MS.

which had considerable influence upon my mind, I sent to Dr. Johnson, begging to
hear from him again, upon the interesting question.

    To James Boswell Esq.[4]

. . . .

    To the Same[5]

. . . .

5   [To the Same *del*]
    Mr. Boswell to Dr. Johnson

                                 Edinburgh 20 feb. 1776
                    * * * * *

    You have illuminated my mind and relieved me from imaginary shackles of
10 conscientious obligation. Were it necessary I could immediately join in an entail
upon the series of heirs [chosen›] approved by my Father. But it is better not to act
too suddenly[; it is better to let my mind resolve its new system for some time, that
I may be certain that I shall not again have the *veteres avias*.[6] *del*]
                * * * *

15   Dr. Johnson to Mr. Boswell
Dear Sir
    I am glad that what I could think or say has at all contributed to quiet your
thoughts. Your resolution not to act, till your opinion is confirmed by more
deliberation is very just. If you have been scrupulous do not now be rash. I hope
20 that as you think more, and take opportunities of talking with men intelligent in
questions of property, you will be able to free yourself from every difficulty.
    When I wrote last I sent I think ten packets. Did you receive them all?
    You must tell Mrs. Boswell that I suspected her to have written[7] without your
knowledge, and therefore did not return any answer, lest a clandestine correspond-
25 ence should have been perniciously discovered. I will write to her soon.
                * * * *

          I am Dear Sir, most affectionately yours
Feb 24, 1776   Sam Johnson

---

    [4] Direction to the compositor, 'Take in Dr. Johnson's of Feb. 9 / ("Having not any
acquaintance").' This sub Paper Apart no longer forms part of the *Life* MS.
    [5] Direction to the compositor, 'Take in Dr. Johnson's of Feb. 15 / ("To the letters").'
This sub Paper Apart no longer forms part of the *Life* MS.
    [6] In this deleted allusion, JB quotes from Persius' fifth satire: 'Disce, sed ira cadat naso
rugosaque sanna, / dum veteres avias tibi de pulmone revello': 'Just listen then, and drop
that wrath and those curling sneers from off your nose, while I pluck your old wife's notions
out of your head' (Loeb ed., trans. G. G. Ramsay, *ll.* 91–92). JB may have had in mind
Dryden's translation of *veteres avias* as 'those fond notions of false liberty' (*The Works of John
Dryden*, ed. H. T. Swedenberg, Jr., Berkeley, 1974, iv. 333). In his journal, he uses the tag
to differentiate the shackles of Scottish Calvinism from a buoyant cosmopolitanism
(*Boswell in Holland,* ed. Frederick A. Pottle, 1952, p. 236; *Boswell on the Grand Tour:
Germany and Switzerland*, ed. Frederick A. Pottle, 1953, p. 59).
    [7] In the revises, the following footnote, presumably added in the first proof, is keyed to
'written': 'A letter to him on the interesting subject of the family settlement, which I had
read.' Although the note was printed at the foot of the page in the revises, the superscript
numeral above 'written' was omitted, eliciting a marginal direction from JB: 'Let the note
be upon *written*'.

[MR. BOSWELL to DR. JOHNSON

Edinburgh, 29 Febry 1776

Complaining of melancholy; that *del*]

ₓHaving communicated to Lord Hailes what Dr. Johnson wrote concerning
the question which perplexed me so much his Lordship wrote to me 'Your scruples   5
have produced more fruit than I ever expected from them an excellent dissertation
on general principles of morals and law.'ₓ

I wrote to [him⟩] Dr. Johnson on the 29[8] of february complaining of [gloom and
dejection of mind⟩] melancholy and expressing a strong desire to be with him. I
informed him that the ten packets came all safe that Lord Hailes [is much obliged   10
to you and says you have⟩] was much obliged to him and said he had almost wholly
removed his scruples against entails.

To JAMES BOSWELL ESQ.[9]

. . . .

To the Same[1/2]

. . . .

[Paper Apart W][3] Few things are more unpleasant than the transaction of business   15
with men who are above knowing or caring what they have to do, such as the
Trustees for Lord Cornbury's institution will perhaps appear when you have read
Dr. Douglas's[a] letters.

The last part of the Doctor's letter is of great importance.[b]   The complaint[4]
which he makes I have heard long ago, and did not know but it was redressed. It   20

[a] Now Bishop of Carlisle.[a1]
[b] It related to the management of the Clarendon Press.[b1]

---

[8] The compositor misread the '9' as a zero, and the resulting mistake has never been
corrected.

[9] Direction to the compositor, 'Take in his of March 5'. This sub Paper Apart no longer
forms part of the *Life* MS.

[1] Direction to the compositor, '(Take in his of March 12)'.

[2] Deleted direction to the compositor, 'Go ₓbackₓ to p. 496'. JB replaced this direction
with one reading 'Paper W'.

[3] This Paper Apart is marked 'for P. 496', and has a heading, 'Part of a Letter from Dr.
Johnson to Dr. Wetherel Master of University College Oxford containing the science of
Bookselling' and 'For p. 496'. There is also a marginal note, 'Copied by me J.B. Oxford
1776'. JB made his copy with the permission of SJ and Wetherell (Journ. 21 March 1776).
At a later stage he obtained the text of the first paragraph ('Few things ... Dr. Douglas's
letter'), which he copied onto the blank verso of a fragment of an almanac leaf, with the
heading, 'ₓDr. Johnsonₓ to Mr. Wetherell about establishing Mr. Carter a riding Master at
Oxford'. See *Letters of Johnson* ed. Redford, ii. 183 n. 2, 305–08.

[4] At this point the revises print a note: 'I suppose the complaint was, that the trustees of
the Oxford press did not allow the London Booksellers a sufficient profit upon vending their
publications'.

[a1] In the revises, this note was deleted and Douglas's name was replaced in the main text
by seven asterisks. There is no evidence that Douglas put pressure on JB to delete his name.
[b1] This note does not appear in the revises or in the printed editions.

is unhappy that a practice so erroneous has not yet been altered; for altered it must be or our press will be useless with all it's privileges. The Booksellers who like all other men have strong prejudices in their own favour are enough inclined to think the practice of printing and selling books by any but themselves an encroachment on the rights of their fraternity and have need of stronger inducements to circulate academical publications than those of one another; for of that mutual cooperation by which the general trade is carried on, the University can bear no part. Of those whom he neither loves nor fears and from whom he expects no reciprocation of good offices, why should any man promote the interest but for profit. I suppose with all our scholastick ignorance of mankind we are still too knowing to expect that the Booksellers will erect themselves into Patrons, and buy and sell under the influence of a distinterested zeal for the promotion of learning.

To the Booksellers if we look for either honour or profit from our press, not only their common profit but something more must be allowed, and if Books printed at Oxford are expected to be rated at a high price, that price must be levied on the publick, and paid by the ultimate purchaser not by the intermediate Agents. What price shall be set upon the Book is to the Booksellers wholly indifferent provided that they gain a proportionate profit by negotiating the Sale.

Why Books printed at Oxford should be particularly dear I am however unable to find. We pay no rent; we inherit many of our instruments and materials; lodging and victuals are cheaper than at London and therefore workmanship ought at least not to be dearer. Our expences are naturally less than those of Booksellers, and in most cases communities are content with less profit than individuals.

It is perhaps not considered through how many hands a Book often passes, before it comes into those of the reader, or what part of the profit each hand must retain as a motive for transmitting it to the next.

We will call our primary Agent in London Mr. Cadel who receives our books from us, gives them room in his warehouse and issues them on demand. By him they are sold to Mr. Dilly a wholesale Bookseller who sends them into the Country and the last seller is the Country Bookseller. Here are three profits to be paid between the Printer and the Reader, or in the stile of commerce between the manufacturer and the consumer; and if any of these profits is too penuriously distributed the process of commerce is intercepted.

We are now come to the practical question what is to be done? You will tell me with reason that I have said nothing till I declare how much according to my opinion of the ultimate price ought to be distributed through the whole succession of Sale.

The deduction I am afraid will appear very great. But let it be considered before it is refused. We must allow for profit between thirty and thirty five per cent, between six and seven shillings in the pound, that is for every book which costs the last buyer twenty shillings we must charge Mr. Cadel with something less than fourteen. We must set the copies at fourteen shillings each and superadd what is called the quarterly book or for every hundred books so charged we must deliver an hundred and four.

The profits will then stand thus.

Mr. Cadel who runs no hazard and gives no credit will be paid for warehouse room and attendance by a shilling profit on each Book, and his chance of the quarterly Book.

Mr. Dilly who buys the Book for fifteen shillings and who will expect the
quarterly book, if he takes five and twenty will sell it to his country customer at
sixteen and sixpence by which at the hazard of loss and the certainty of long
credit, he gains the regular profit of ten per cent which is expected in the
wholesale trade.   5

The Country Bookseller buying at Sixteen and Sixpence and commonly
trusting a considerable time gains but three and sixpence, and if he trusts a year,
not much more than two and sixpence, otherwise than as he may perhaps take
as long credit as he gives.

With less profit than this, and more you see he cannot have, the Country   10
Bookseller cannot live; for his receipts are small, and his debts sometimes bad.

Thus Dear Sir I have been incited by Dr. Douglas's[5] letter to give you a detail
of the circulation of Books which perhaps every man has not had opportunity of
knowing and which those who know it, do not perhaps always distinctly consider.

I am etc.   15
SAM: JOHNSON[a]

March 12 1776.

[MS 495 resumed]   [To James Boswell Esq. *del*][6]

. . . .
[MS 497] [7] moment he was in full glow of conversation, and I felt myself
elevated as if brought into another state of being. Mrs. Thrale and I looked to   20
each other while he talked and our looks [fully *del*] expressed our congenial
admiration and affection for [him/the Sage⟩] him. I shall ever recollect this
scene with great pleasure. I called to her '[This is⟩] I am *Hermippus redivivus*. I
am quite restored by him, by transfusion of *mind*.'[8]

. . . .
[MS 497 resumed] I mentioned with much regret the extravagance of the   25
Representative of a great Family in Scotland by which there was danger of its
being ruined, and as Johnson had a great value for it he joined with me in
thinking it would be happy if this person should [die/be cut off⟩] die. Mrs.
Thrale seemed shocked at this, as [feudal barbarity/old fashioned⟩] feudal

[a] I am happy [in having an opportunity by⟩] in giving this full and clear   30
statement to the Publick to vindicate by the authority of the greatest Authour
of his age that respectable body of men the Booksellers of London from the
ₓvulgarₓ reflections of ignorance and malevolence as if their profits were
exorbitant, when in truth Dr. Johnson has here allowed them more than they
usually demand.   35

---

[5]Again, in the revises, asterisks replace Douglas's name.

[6] Deleted direction to the compositor, '"I have not had your letter" (Take it in)'. This
sub Paper Apart no longer forms part of the *Life* MS.

[7] MS 496 has not been recovered; MSS 497–502 are in the collection of the Houghton
Library, Harvard University, shelfmark fMS Eng 1386.

[8] It is likely that the verso of (missing) MS leaf 496 supplied the paragraph that appears
at this point in the printed text.

barbarity and said 'I do not understand this preference of the estate to its owner, of the land to the man who walks upon that land.'[9] *Johnson.* '/Nay/[1] Madam it is not a preference of the land to its owner; it is the preference of a Family to an individual. Here is an establishment, in a country, which is of importance for ages not only to the Chief but to his people, an establishment which extends upwards and downwards; that this should be destroyed by one idle fellow is a sad thing.'

He said 'Entails are good, because it is *[MS 498]* good to preserve in a country serieses of men to whom the people are accustomed to look up as to their [Heads/Leaders>] Leaders. But I am for leaving a quantity of land in commerce to excite industry and keep money in the country; For if no land were to be bought in a country there would be no encouragement to [get/acquire>] acquire wealth because a Family could not be founded there; or if it were [got/acquired>] acquired it must be carried away to another country where land may be bought. And although the land in every country will remain the same and produce as much when there is no money, yet all [the happiness of civil life, which we know is>] that portion of the happiness of civil life, which is produced by money being in a country, would be lost.' BOSWELL. 'Then Sir would it be for the advantage of a country that all its lands were sold at once?' JOHNSON. 'So far Sir as money produces good it would be an advantage; for, then that country would have as much money circulating in it as it is worth. But to be sure this would be counterbalanced by disadvantages attending a total change of proprietors.'

I [was for limiting/wished to limit the power of entailing>] expressed my opinion that the power of entailing should be limited thus — That there should be one third or perhaps *[MS 499]* one half of the land [of/in>] of a country kept free for commerce; — that the proportion allowed to be entailed should be parcelled out so as that no Family could entail above a certain quantity. Let a Family according to the abilities of its representatives be richer or poorer in different generations, or allways rich if its representatives be allways wise. But let its absolute permanency be moderate. In this way we should [have a certainty of so many established roots[2] >] be certain of there being still a number of established roots, and as in the course of nature there is in every age an extinction of [so many/some>] some families, there would be continual openings for men ambitious of perpetuity to plant a stock in the entail ground. — I would not have the very same land to be the entailable proportion, as probably it would not be so well

---

[9] This passage derives from a sentence in JB's journal: 'When I spoke with regret of the Laird of MacLeod's not acting as he should do to preserve the ancient family and that it would be well if he were killed in America, Mrs. Thrale said she did not understand this preference of the estate to its owner, of the land to the man who walks upon that land' (16 March 1776). JB and SJ had visited Norman Macleod (1754–1801), twenty-third Chief of the Macleods of Dunvegan, during their Hebridean tour. At that time they praised his personal qualities and attributed his precarious financial condition to inherited debt (Journ. 3 September, 11 September 1773; *Letters of Johnson* ed. Redford, ii. 87). But MacLeod's neglect of 'feudal principles' had alienated them (Journ. 29 September 1774).

[1] The optional phrase, which JB left unresolved, was printed in the revises.

[2] Interlined above 'so many' is a false start, 'have a certain'. Presumably JB intended 'have a certain number of established roots' as an alternative to 'have so many established roots'.

improved. I mean that a man would/should[3] have an opening in the allotted *quantity*. Indeed I would rather that an old family estate when its entailed proprietors fail, should go into the circle of commerce for a while, than be immediately transferred to a new family and be again fixed. I would have the two races kept distinct.[4] [MS 500] *Johnson*. 'Why Sir, Mankind will be better able to regulate the system of Entails, when the evil of too much land being fixed by them is felt than we can do at present when it is not felt.'

I mentioned Dr. Adam Smith's Book on [*The Wealth of Nations*>] 'The Wealth of Nations' which was just come out and that an eminent Physician had [given it/said to me>] said to me as his opinion that Dr. Smith who had never [been in trade/traded>] been in trade could not be expected to write well on that subject any more than I upon Physick. *Johnson*. 'He is mistaken Sir. A man who has never [traded>] been engaged in trade himself may undoubtedly write well upon trade, and there is nothing which [requires/wants/needs>] requires more to be illustrated by philosophy [/than trade does/>] than trade does. As to mere [riches/wealth>] wealth, that is to say money, it is plain that one nation or one individual cannot get more of it [but/unless>] unless by making another poorer. But trade procures real riches, the reciprocation of the advantages of different countries. A merchant seldom thinks but of his own particular trade. To [have/write>] write a good book upon it [we/a man>] a man must have extensive views. It is not necessary [to practice/to have practiced>] to have practiced to write well upon a subject.' I mentioned Law. *Johnson*. 'Why Sir in England where so much money is to be got by the practice of the Law, most [MS 501] of our writers upon it have been in practice, though Blackstone had not been much in practice when he published his Commentaries. But upon the continent the great writers on law have not all been in practice. Grotius[5] indeed was; but Puffendorf was not, Burlamaqui was not.'

When we had talked of the great consequence which a man acquired by being employed in his profession, I suggested a doubt [as to the general opinion against the propriety or fairness of a Lawyers soliciting employment>] of the justice of the general opinion that it is improper in a Lawyer to solicit employment; for why ∧I urged∧ should it not be equally allowable to solicit that as the means of consequence as it is to solicit votes to be elected a Member of Parliament. Mr. Strahan had told me that a countryman of his and mine who had risen to eminence in the

---

[3] For JB's unresolved alternative, see below, n. 4.

[4] By the stage of revises, JB had deleted four sentences ('I would not have the very same land … two races kept distinct') and replaced them with a footnote keyed to 'entail ground': 'The privilege of perpetuating in a family an estate and arms *indefeasibly* from generation to generation, is enjoyed by none of his Majesty's subjects except in Scotland, where the legal fiction of a *fine and recovery* is unknown. It is a privilege so proud that I should think it would be proper to have the exercise of it dependent on the royal prerogative. It seems absurd to permit the power of perpetuating their representation to men, who having had no eminent merit, have truly no name. The King, as the impartial father of his people, would never refuse to grant the privilege to those who deserved it'.

[5] 'Grotius' appears in the journal entry (16 March 1776), but JB felt uncertain enough to query the name in the revises.

law had when first making his way solicited him to get him employed in City Causes. JOHNSON. 'Sir it is wrong to stir up lawsuits; but when once [lawsuits are/it is certain that lawsuits are⟩] it is certain that a lawsuit is to go on there is nothing wrong in a lawyer's endeavouring that he shall have the benefit rather than

5 another.' *Boswell*. 'You would not solicit employment, Sir, if you were a lawyer.' *Johnson*. 'No Sir. But not because I should think it wrong, but because I should disdain it.' This was a good distinction which will be felt by men of a just pride. He proceeded 'However, I would not have [a Lawyer/You⟩] a Lawyer to be wanting [MS 502] to himself in using fair means. [I would inject a little hint.⟩] I would have

10 him to give a little hint now and then to prevent his being overlooked.'

˄Lord Mountstuart's Bill for a Scotch Militia in supporting which his Lordship had made an able speech in the House of Commons⁶ was now a pretty general topick of conversation. *Johnson*. 'As Scotland contributes so little landtax towards the general support of the Nation, it ought not to have a Militia paid out of the

15 general fund, unless it should be thought for the general interest, that Scotland should be [protected from/secured against⟩] protected from an invasion, which no man can think [necessary⟩] will happen, for what ennemy would invade Scotland where there is nothing to be [had/got⟩] got. No Sir, [because⟩] now that the scotch have not the pay of english soldiers spent among them [because they are⟩]

20 as so many troops are sent abroad, they are trying to get money another way by having a militia payed. If they are affraid, and seriously desire to have an armed force to defend them, they should pay for it. Your scheme is to retain [so much⟩] a part of your little landtax by making us pay and clothe your Militia.' *Boswell*. ['You/Sir You⟩] You should not talk of *we* and *you* Sir; there is now an *Union*.'

25 *Johnson*. 'There must be a distinction of interest while the proportions of landtax are so unequal. If Yorkshire should say "Instead of paying our land tax we will keep so many more militia," it would be unreasonable.' In this argument [the great man⟩] my friend was [certainly⟩] I think [certainly *del*] in the wrong. The landtax is as unequally proportioned between different parts of England as between

30 England and Scotland, nay, it is considerably unequal in Scotland itself. But the landtax is but a small part of the numerous branches of publick revenue all of which Scotland pays precisely as England does. A french invasion made in Scotland would soon penetrate into England.˄

He thus discoursed upon supposed obligations in settling Estates. 'Where a man

35 gets the unlimited property of an Estate, there is no obligation upon him in *justice*

---

⁶ JB inserted, and then deleted, a footnote keyed to 'Commons': 'I am [very *del*] sorry [both *del*] that it has not been published both for the honour of his Lordship and the advantage of Scotland. His Lordship spoke only from a few notes, but he recollected it ⟨as far⟩ as to dictate it to me while I wrote it down. I afterwards made a fair copy of it at his desire, and was [*corner of MS missing*].'

John Stuart (1744–1814), Lord Mountstuart, M.P. for Bossiney (1766–76), moved in the House of Commons, 2 November 1775, for a bill to establish a Scottish militia. The bill was defeated on 20 March 1776 (Namier and Brooke iii. 502–03). JB, who warmly supported the bill, had considered writing 'a pamphlet in favour of Lord Mountstuart's militia for Scotland' (Journ. 4 Jan. 1776). In early May, Mountstuart reconstructed the speech as JB took it down (Notes 1 May, 6 May 1776).

to leave it to one ₍person₎ rather than to another. There is a motive of preference
·from *kindness*, and this kindness is generally entertained for the nearest relation. If
I *owe* a particular man a sum of money, I am obliged to let that man have the next
money I get, and cannot in justice let another have it. But if I owe money to no
man I may dispose of what I get as I please. There is not a *debitum justitiæ* to [my/a   5
man's⟩] a man's next heir; there is only a *debitum charitatis*. It is plain then that I
have morally a choice according to my liking. If I have a brother in want, he has
a claim from affection to my assistance. But if I have also a brother in want, whom
I like better, he has a preferable claim. The right of an heir at law is only this, that
he is to have the succession [/to an estate/⟩] to an estate in case no other person is   10
appointed to it by the [owner /of an Estate/. He has only a preference to the
King.⟩] owner. His right is merely preferable to that of the King.'

We got into a boat to cross over to Blackfriars and as we moved along the
Thames, I talked to [MS 503] him of a little volume which altogether unknown to
him was advertised to be published in a few days under the title of *Johnsoniana*   15
[or/being⟩] or *Bon Mots* of Dr. Johnson. [He said⟩] *Johnson*. 'Sir It is a mighty
impudent thing.' [I asked him if he could have no redress if he⟩] *Boswell*. 'Pray Sir
could you have no redress if you were to prosecute a publisher for bringing out
under [his⟩] your name what [he⟩] you never said, and [that⟩] perhaps ascribing to
you dull stupid nonsense, or [perhaps *del*] making [him⟩] you swear   20
[profanely/bloodily⟩] profanely as many ignorant relaters of his *Bon Mots* [did⟩]
do?' *Johnson*. 'No Sir. There will allways be [so much⟩] some truth mixed with the
falshood and how can it be ascertained how much is true and how much is false?
Besides Sir what damages would a Jury give me for my having been represented as
swearing?'   [I said he⟩] *Boswell*. 'I think Sir, you should at least   25
[contradict/disavow⟩] disavow [the authenticity of *del*] such a publication because
the World and posterity might with much plausible foundation say "Here is a
volume which was publickly advertised and came out in Dr. Johnson's own time,
and by his silence was admitted by him to be genuine."' [He said he should/would
give himself⟩] *Johnson*. 'I shall give myself no trouble about the matter.'   30

He was [/perhaps/ *above*⟩] perhaps above suffering from such fictitious publications; but I could not help thinking that many [a man⟩] men would be much hurt
[/in their reputation/⟩] in their reputation by having absurd and vicious sayings
[MS 504] [ascribed⟩] imputed to them and that it was [very/exceedingly⟩] very
hard if no redress could be obtained.[7]   35

He said 'The value of every story depends on its being true. A story is a picture
either of an individual or of human nature in general. If it be false, it is a picture
of nothing. For instance suppose a man should tell that Johnson before setting
[out for/on his journey to⟩] out for Italy, as he had to cross the Alps sat down to

---

[7] JB supplied but later deleted a note here: 'This Volume however of which I obtained
a copy from Mr. Ridley ₍in St. James's Street₎ the publisher before it was ushered into the
world, though with a few genuine sayings of Johnson ₍intermixed₎ it abounded in
₍dullness and₎ folly [and *del*] had not [₍however₎ *del*] many offensive articles in it. Such
was the power of Johnson's name that even [such a pa⟩] this paultry compilation got to a
second edition to which was gravely prefixed a Notice [that *del*] to enable the reader to
distinguish the species of wit.'

make himself wings. [This many people would believe/Many people would believe this›] This many people would believe; but it would be a picture of nothing. [A worthy friend of ours (naming him)›] [*undeciphered word* (naming a worthy friend of ours)›] _____ (naming a worthy friend of ours)[8] used to think

5   a story a story, till I shewed him that truth was essential to it.' I observed that Foote entertained us with stories which [are/were›] were not true; but that indeed it was properly not as stories that Foote's narratives pleased us but as [ludicrous collections of images/collections of ludicrous images›] collections of ludicrous images. JOHNSON. 'Foote is quite impartial, for he ‚tells‚ lies of every body.'

10   ‚The importance of strict and scrupulous veracity cannot be too often inculcated. Johnson was known to be so rigidly attentive to it that even in his common conversation the slightest circumstance was mentioned with exact precision. The knowledge of his having such a principle and habit made his friends have a perfect reliance on the truth of every thing which he related, however [it might have been

15   doubted›] it might have been doubted if told by many others. As [a whimsical instance›] an instance of this I may mention [a droll anecdote›] an odd incident which he related to have happened to him one night in Fleetstreet. A gentleman begged he would give her his arm to assist her in crossing the street which he accordingly did, upon which she offered him a shilling supposing him to be the

20   watchman. He perceived that the Lady was somewhat in liquor. This if told by most people would have been thought an invention. When told by Johnson it was believed by his friends as much as if they had seen what passed.‚[9]

We landed at the Temple stairs where we parted. [He went home, and I went to the west end of the town. *del*]

25   I found him in the evening in Mrs. Williams's room [/and he entertained me with oysters and porter, while he after eating some of the oysters drank his sweet tea/ *del*].[1] We talked of religious orders. He said, 'It is as unreasonable for a [MS 505] man to go into a Carthusian Convent for fear of being immoral, as for a man to cut off his hands for fear he should steal. There [may be/is›] may be no doubt

30   resolution in the [very/immediate›] immediate act of dismembering himself; but when that is once done, he has no longer any merit for though it is out of his power to steal, yet he may all his life be a thief in his heart. So when a man has once become Carthusian, he is obliged to continue so, whether he chuses it or not. Their silence too is absurd. We read in the Gospel of ‚the Apostles‚ being sent to

35   preach, but not to hold [ones tongue›] their tongues. All severity that does not tend to increase good or prevent evil is idle. ‚I [said to/told›] said to the Lady Abbess of a Convent "Madam, you are here, not for the love of virtue but for the fear of vice." She said she should remember [it/this›] this as long as she lived.' I

---

[8] This 'worthy friend' was Bennet Langton (Journ. 16 March 1776). In the revises, the blank was filled with seven asterisks.

[9] This paragraph amplified a marginal note that JB had written to himself: 'Here mention the importance of strict veracity the confidence in his own truth, and his being taken for a watchman'.

[1] JB at one point considered reinstating this phrase, for after deleting it he wrote 'stet' twice in the left margin. He ultimately decided against its inclusion, and crossed out the 'stet' markings.

thought it hard to give her this view of her situation when she could not help it, and indeed‚ I wondered at [this 'laxity of talk'›]² the whole of what he now said because both in his Rambler and Idler he treats religious austerities with much [solemnity.›] [respect.›] solemnity of respect.

Finding him still persevering in [abstaining›] abstinence from wine I ventured   5
to speak to him of it. *Johnson.* '‚Sir‚ I have no objection to a man's drinking wine, if he can do it in moderation. I found myself apt to go to excess in it, and therefore after having been for some time without it on account of illness I thought it better not to return to it. Every man is to judge for himself according to the effects which he experiences. One of the Fathers tells us he found fasting made him so peevish   10
that he did not practise it.'

‚Though he often enlarged upon the evil of intoxication he was by no means harsh and unforgiving when he knew of occasional excesses in wine. One of his friends I well remember, came to sup at a tavern with him and some other gentlemen, and too plainly discovered that he had drunk too much at dinner.   15
When one who loved mischief thinking to produce a severe censure asked Johnson some days afterwards 'Well Sir, what did your friend say to you, as an apology for being in such a situation?' Johnson answered 'Sir he said all that a man should say. He said he was sorry for it.'³

I heard him once give a very judicious practical advice upon this subject. 'A   20
man' said he 'who has been drinking wine at all freely should never go into a new company. With those who have partaken of wine with him he may be pretty well in unison; but he will probably be offensive or appear ridiculous to other people.'‚ ⁴

[MS 506] He allowed very great influence to education. 'I do not deny Sir but there is some original difference in minds; but it is nothing in comparison of what   25
is formed by education. We may instance the science of [*numbers/figures*›] *numbers* [as what/which›] which all minds are equally capable of attaining yet we find a prodigious difference in the powers of different men in that respect, after they are grown up, because their minds have been more or less exercised in it and I think the same cause will explain the difference of excellence in other things,   30
admitting allways some difference in the first principles.'

This is a difficult subject; but it is best to hope that diligence may do a great deal. We are *sure* of what it can do in [giving us/increasing our›] increasing our [mechanical/corporeal›] mechanical force and dexterity.

I again visited him on Monday forenoon. He took occasion to enlarge as he   35
often did, upon the wretchedness of a sea life. 'A ship is worse than a gaol. There is in a gaol better air better company better conveniency of every kind and a ship has the additional disadvantage of being in danger. When men come to like a

---

² JB had used this expression before (*Life* MS i. 335). The quotation marks connect it to a similar turn of phrase in his *Tour to the Hebrides* (Hill-Powell i. 476 and n. 2).

³ This anecdote originally appeared on MS 451 (see *ante* p. 144) in the context of a passage describing JB's exuberant spirits at a dinner with The Club on 31 March 1775. JB identified himself there as the individual who 'too plainly discovered that he had drunk too much at dinner'.

⁴ This account of SJ's 'judicious practical advice' also appeared originally on MS 451. See *ante* p. 144.

Sea=life they are not fit to live [at>] on land.' — 'Then' said I 'it would be cruel in a Father to breed his [MS 507] son to the sea.' Johnson. 'It would be cruel in a Father who thinks as I do. [Men/People>] Men go to sea before they know the unhappiness of that way of life, and when they have come to know it, they cannot
5   escape [/from it/>] from it because it is then too late to chuse another profession as [is indeed the case with men in general>] indeed is generally the case with men when they have once engaged in [a>] any particular way of life.'

On tuesday [19 March>] March 19 I met him between eight and nine in the morning at the Somerset Coffeehouse in the Strand where we were taken up by the
10   Oxford Coach. He was accompanied by Mr. Gwyn the Architect, and a gentleman of Merton College whom we did not know had the fourth seat. We soon got into [free/easy del] conversation; for it was very remarkable in Johnson that the presence of a stranger was no restraint upon his talk. I observed that [Garrick's quitting the stage would be a relief to him/Garrick would be easier quitting the stage>] Garrick
15   would have an easier life now he had quitted the stage. Johnson. 'I doubt that Sir.' [I said 'Why he>] Boswell. 'Why Sir he will be Atlas with the burthen off his back.' Johnson. 'But I know not ˄Sir˄ if he will be so steady without his load. However he should never play any more but be [quite/entirely>] entirely the gentleman and not partly the player; he should no longer subject himself to be hissed ˄by a mob˄ or to
20   be insolently treated by [the del] performers whom he used to rule with a high hand, and [MS 508] who would gladly retaliate.' Boswell. 'I think he should play once a year for the benefit of decayed Actors as it has been given out he is to do.' Johnson. 'Alas Sir! he will ˄soon˄ be a decayed actor himself.'

He [found fault with/condemned>] expressed his disapprobation of ornamental
25   Architecture such as magnificent columns supporting a Portico, or expensive pilasters supporting merely their own capitals 'because it consumes labour disproportionate to its utility.' For the same reason he satyrised Statuary. 'Painting' said he 'consumes labour not disproportionate to its effect; but a fellow will hack half a year at a block of marble to make something [in/of>] in stone that ˄hardly˄
30   resembles a man. The value of statuary is owing to its difficulty. You would not value the finest head cut upon a carrot.' Here he seemed to me to be [strangely/utterly>] strangely deficient in taste; for surely Statuary is a noble art of imitation, and preserves a wonderful expression of the varieties of the human frame; and although [difficulty/the circumstance of difficulty may enter into the
35   estimation of the value of a marble head I imagine/believe its durability is a principal reason of preference.>] it must be allowed that the circumstance of difficulty enhances the value of a marble head we should consider that if it requires a long time in the performance it has a proportionable value in durability. Gwyn was a fine lively rattling fellow [and even swore a little del]. Dr. Johnson kept him
40   in [pure del] subjection but with a kindly authority [calling him Gwynnie del]. [MS 509] The spirit of the Artist however rose against what he thought a gothick attack and he made a brisk defence. 'What Sir! will you allow no value to beauty in Architecture or in Statuary? Why should we allow it then in writing? Why do you take the trouble to give us so many fine allusions and bright images and elegant
45   phrases you might give us all your instruction without these ornaments.' — Johnson smiled with complacency, but said 'Why Sir all these ornaments are

useful, because they obtain an easier reception for truth; but a Building is not at all more convenient for being decorated with superfluous carved work.'

Gwyn at last was lucky enough to make one [reply/answer>] reply to Dr. Johnson which he allowed to be excellent. Johnson was angry [at>] with him for taking down a church which might have stood many years [only to have a direct/straight road>] and building a new one at a different place, for no other reason but that there might be a direct Road to a new bridge and his expression was 'You are taking a church out of the way, that the people may go in a straight line to the bridge.' 'No Sir' said Gwyn 'I am putting the church in the way that the people may not go out of the way.' *Johnson* (with a ₍hearty loud₎ laugh of approbation). 'Speak no more. Rest your colloquial fame upon this.'

[/Upon our arrival at Oxford/>] Upon our arrival at Oxford [we went/repaired>] Dr. Johnson and I went directly to University College but were disappointed on finding that one of the fellows his friend Mr. Scott who accompanied him from Newcastle to Edinburgh was gone [to/in>] to the country. [MS 510] We [went to/put up at>] put up at the Angel Inn and had the very parlour where he and I and [Sir Robert Chambers and poor Frank /Mr. Francis Stewart>][5] some friends supt in 1768. [He talked of constitutional melancholy and said>] Talking of constitutional melancholy he observed 'A man so afflicted ₍Sir₎ must divert distressing thoughts and not combat with them.' ₍BOSWELL. 'May not he [*think*>] think them down Sir?' JOHNSON. 'No Sir.₎ To attempt to *think them down* is madness. He should have a lamp constantly burning in his bed=chamber during the night, and if wakefully [disturbed/troubled>] disturbed take a book and read and compose himself to rest. To have the management of [the/one's>] the mind is a great art [and/but>] and it may be attained in a considerable degree by experience and habitual exercise.' ₍*Boswell*. 'Should not he provide amusements for himself? Would it not for instance be right for him to take a course of chymistry?' *Johnson*. 'Let him take a course of chymistry, or a course of rope=dancing, or a course of any thing to which he is inclined at the time. Let him contrive to have as many retreats for his mind, as he can, as many things to which it can fly from itself.₎ Burton's Anatomy of Melancholy is a valuable Work. It is perhaps overloaded with quotation. But there is great spirit and great power in what Burton says when he writes from his own mind.'[6] [How much do I regret that I had not diligence enough to record/preserve/register all his conversation this evening/night the recollection of which consoles my mind. *del*]

[Next morning/On Wednesday 20 March after breakfast>] Next morning, we waited on Dr. Wetherell Master of University College with whom Dr. Johnson conferred on the most advantageous mode of disposing of the Books printed at the Clarendon Press as to which I have inserted his Letter to Dr. Wetherell.[7] I often

[5] This meeting took place on 27 March 1768 (Journ.). Francis Stewart (?1747–68), nephew of JB's friend the 10th Earl of Eglinton, was at that time an undergraduate at Christ Church. He died only a few months later.

[6] In this paragraph JB conflates two conversations on the management of melancholy: the advice about 'a course of chymistry' is recorded in the journal for 21 March.

[7] JB here noted in the margin, 'Qu if it should rather come in here?' The letter stayed in its original position: see *ante* p. 182 n. 3 (MS 496).

had occasion to remark that Johnson loved business, loved to have his wisdom actually operate on real life. [MS 511] Dr. Wetherell and I talked of him without reserve in his own presence. *Wetherell.* 'I would have given him a hundred guineas if he would have written a Preface to his "Political Tracts" by way of a Discourse on the British Constitution.' *Boswell.* 'Dr. Johnson though in his writings and upon all occasions a great friend to the Constitution both in Church and State has never written [*per expressum*/expressly/purposely⟩] expressly in support of either. There is really a claim upon him for both. I am sure he could give ⟨a vo⟩lume of no great bulk upon each which[8] ⟨would comprise⟩ all the substance [of the argument *del*], and ⟨with his spirit⟩ would effectually maintain them. He ⟨should erect⟩ a fort on the confines of each.' ⟨I could per⟩ceive that he was [not pleased with/displeased by⟩] displeased by this ⟨dial⟩ogue. He burst out 'Why should *I* be allways writing?' I hoped he was conscious that the debt was just, and meant to discharge it, though he disliked being dunned.

We then went to Pembroke College and waited on ₍his old friend₎ Dr. Adams [now⟩] the Master of it, whom I found to be a most polite pleasing communicative man. Before his [promotion/advancement⟩] advancement [to the Mastership/to be the Head⟩] to the Headship of his College I had intended to [wait/go and⟩] go and visit him at Shrewsbury where he was Rector of St. Chad's, in order to get from him what particulars he could recollect of Johnson's [MS 512] [University/College⟩] academical Life. He now obligingly gave me part of that authentick information, which with what I afterwards owed to his [goodness/kindness has been allready incorporated/interwoven⟩] kindness will be found incorporated in its proper place into this Work.

Dr. Adams had distinguished himself by an able Answer to [/David/⟩] David Hume's Essay on Miracles. He told me he had [met Hume in London at a house where they dined /at dinner⟩] once dined in company with Hume in London; that Hume shook hands with him and said 'You have treated me much better than I deserve' and that [they exchanged visits/he had called on Hume and Hume had called on him⟩] they exchanged visits. I took the liberty ⟨to objec⟩t to treating an infidel Writer wi⟨th smooth civility.⟩ Where there is a contraversy concern⟨ing a passage⟩ in a Classick Authour or concerning a que⟨stion in antiqui⟩ties or any other subject in which human happiness is not deeply interested a man may treat his antagonist with politeness and even respect. But where the contraversy is concerning the truth of Religion it is of such vast importance to him who [maintains/believes⟩] maintains it to [have/get⟩] get the better, that the person of an opponent is not to be spared. If a man firmly believes that Religion is a great/invaluable[9] treasure he will consider a Writer who endeavours to deprive mankind of it as a *robber*; he will look upon him as *odious,* [/even/ *del*] though the Infidel [MS 513][1] may think himself in the right. A robber who reasons as the Gang do in the Beggars Opera who call themselves *practical* [*philosophers*⟩] philosophers and may have as much *bona fides* as pernicious *speculative* philosophers is not

---

[8] The MS is mutilated along the right-hand margin; missing text is supplied in angle brackets from revised proof.

[9] The alternative is resolved by the printing of 'an invaluable' in the revises.

[1] MS 513: current location undetermined (transcribed from a photostat at Yale).

the less an object of just indignation. An abandoned profligate may [have a notion>] think that it is not wrong to debauch my wife; but shall I therefore not detest him? and if I catch him making an attempt shall I treat him with politeness [nay with compliments upon his genteel mistress *del*]. No. I will kick him down stairs [and break his bones>]² or run him through the body. That is, if I really love my wife or have a true ⟨rational⟩ notion of honour. An infidel then should not be treated handsomely by a Christian merely because he endeavours to rob with ingenuity.³ — I do declare that in all this I am exceedingly [reluctant/unwilling>] unwilling to be [provoked/urged>] provoked to [violence>] anger, and could I be persuaded that truth would not suffer [by/from>] from a cool [indifference>] moderation in its defenders I should wish to preserve good humour at least in every contraversy; nor ⟨indeed⟩ do I see why a man should lose his temper while he does all he can to get the better of an opponent. I think [I/we may fairly express it, if an infidel be an>] ridicule may be fairly used against an infidel, for instance if he be an ugly fellow and yet [?supremely>] absurdly vain of his own effigies. We may contrast his appearance with [the>] Cicero's beautiful image of Virtue could she be seen.⁴

[MS 514]⁵ Johnson joined me and said 'When a man voluntarily engages in an important contraversy he is to do all he can to lessen his antagonist, because authority from personal respect has much weight with most people and often more than [reasoning/the arguments>] reasoning. If my antagonist writes bad language, though that may not be essential to the question, I will attack him [for/on>] for his bad language.' *Adams*. 'You would not jostle a chimney [sweep/sweeper>] sweeper.' *Johnson*. 'Yes Sir, if it were necessary to jostle him *down*'.

[Dr. Adams told us/We were told>] Dr. Adams told us that in some of the Colleges at Oxford the Fellows had excluded the [young men/students>] students from social intercourse with them in the Common Room. *Johnson*. 'They are in the right ⟨Sir⟩ for there can be no real conversation, no fair exertion of mind amongst them if the [young men/students>] young men are by; for, a man who has a character does not chuse to stake it in their presence.' *Boswell*. 'But Sir, may there not be very good conversation without a contest for superiority?' *Johnson*. 'No animated conversation ⟨Sir⟩ for, it cannot be but one or other will come off superiour. I do not mean that [he shall have>] the victor must have the better [in/of>] of the argument; for he may take the weak side; but his superiority of parts and knowledge will necessarily appear, and he to whom he thus [MS 515] [appears/shews himself>] shews himself superiour is lessened in the eyes of the young men. You know   said "Mallem cum Scaligero errare quam cum Clavis recte sapere." In the same manner take Bentleys and [Johnsons/Jansens/Jason's>] Jason's Comments upon Horace, you will admire Bentley more when wrong than [Johnson/Jansen/Jason>] Jason when right.'

We walked with Dr. Adams into the Masters Garden and into the Common Room.⁶ *Johnson* (after a reverie of meditation). 'Ay, Here I used to play at drafts

5

10

15

20

25

30

35

40

---

² A tear in the MS makes 'and break his bones' a conjectural reading.
³ JB considered adding a note keyed to 'ingenuity'.
⁴ L. F. Powell suggests that the ugly yet vain infidel may be Gibbon (Hill-Powell ii. 443).
⁵ MSS 514–28: Houghton Library, Harvard University, shelfmark fMS Eng 1386.
⁶ The following paragraph derives from JB's notebook (p. 8).

with Phil. Jones and Fludyer. Jones loved beer and did not get much forward in the
Church. Fludyer turned out a scoundrel a Whig and said he was ashamed of having
been bred at Oxford. He had a living at Putney, and got under the eye of some
retainers to the Court at that time and so [was/became>] became a violent Whig.
5   But he had been a scoundrel all along to be sure.' *Boswell.* 'Was he a scoundrel Sir
in any other [way/respect>] way than being a political scoundrel? Did he cheat at
drafts?' *Johnson.* '[We>] Sir he never played for *money.*'

He then carried me to visit Dr. Bentham Canon of Christ Church and Divinity
Professor with whose learned and lively conversation we were much pleased. He
10   gave us an invitation to dinner which Dr. Johnson told me was a high honour. 'Sir
it is a [MS 516] great thing to dine with the Canons of Christ Church.' We could
not accept, [and we had also been obliged to refuse an invitation from Dr. Adams>]
of his invitation, as we were engaged to dine at University College. We had an
excellent dinner there with the Master and fellows it [being/was>] being St.
15   Cuthberts day which is kept [there>] by them as a festival as he was a Saint of
Durham with which this College is much connected.

We drank tea with Dr. Horne President of Magdalen [Hall>] College ˌnow Bishop
of Norwichˌ of whose abilities in different [respects/ways>] respects the Publick has
had undoubted proofs and [of/by which *del*] the esteem annexed to [his>] whose
20   character [was/will be>] was increased by knowing him personally. He had talked of
publishing an edition of Walton's Lives but had laid Aside the design upon Dr.
Johnson's telling him from mistake that Lord Hailes [was>] intended to do it. I had
wished to negociate between Lord Hailes and him that one or other of them [should
perform so good a work/do so acceptable a service to a numerous class of readers>]
25   should perform so good a work. *Johnson.* 'In order to do it well it will be necessary to
collect all the editions of Walton's Lives. By way of adapting the book to the taste of
the present age they have in a later edition left out a vision which he relates Dr.
Donne had, but it should be restored, and there should be a critical catalogue given
of the works of the different persons [MS 517] whose lives were written by Walton,
30   and therefore their/these[7] works must be carefully read by the Editor.'

We then went to Trinity College where he introduced me to Mr. Thomas
Warton with whom we [sat during>] passed a part of the evening. We talked of
Biography. *Johnson.* 'It is rarely well [done/executed>] executed. [Those>] They
only who live with a man can write his life with any genuine exactness and
35   discrimination, and few people who have lived with a man know what to remark
about him. The chaplain of Dr. Pearce the late Bishop of Rochester [came to me
to assist him>] whom I was to assist in writing some memoirs [of his Lordship/of
him>] of his Lordship,[8] could tell me almost nothing.'[9]

---

[7] The alternative is resolved by the printing of 'their' in the revises.

[8] Zachariah Pearce (1690–1774), D.D., Bishop of Bangor (1747–56) and of Rochester
(1756–74), had contributed twenty etymologies to SJ's *Dictionary* (*Fasti Angl.* i. 108; *Life*
MS i. 212 and n. 2). His chaplain John Derby (c.1720–78) edited Pearce's posthumously
published *Commentary … on the Four Evangelists and the Acts of the Apostles* (1777), for
which SJ supplied the dedication and an accompanying biography (Hazen, *Prefaces &*
Dedications, pp. 154–57).

[9] In the second edition, 'could tell me almost nothing' was replaced by 'could tell me
scarcely any thing' and an explanatory note added: 'It has been mentioned to me, by an

I said Mr. Robert Dodsley's Life should be written, as he had been so much connected with the wits of his time, and by his literary merit had raised himself from the station of a Footman. Mr. Warton said he had published a little volume [under/with⟩] under the title of *The Muse in Livery*. *Johnson*. 'I doubt if Dodsley's brother would thank a man who should write his life. Yet Dodsley himself was not unwilling that his original low condition should be recollected. When Lord Littletons Dialogues of the Dead came out one of which is between *Apicius* an Ancient Epicure and *Darteneuf* a modern epicure Dodsley said to me "I knew Darteneuf well, for I was once his Footman."'

Biography led us to speak of *[MS 518]* Dr. John Campbell who had so great a share in the [great *Biographia Britannica*⟩] Biographia Britannica. Johnson though he valued him highly was of opinion that there was not so much in his great work the 'Political/'A Political Survey of Great Britain'[1] as the World had been taught to expect[2] and had said to me that he believed Campbell's disappointment on account of the bad success of that work had killed him. He this evening observed of it 'That work was his death.' Mr. Warton not [perceiving his meaning/adverting to what he meant⟩] adverting to his meaning answered 'I believe so. From the great [attention/labour⟩] attention which he [employed⟩] bestowed upon it.' *Johnson*. 'Nay Sir he died of want of attention, if he died at all by that Book.'

We talked of [ₓMr. Gibbon's History of the Decline and Fall of the Roman Empireₓ *del*][3] A Work much in vogue at the time written in a very melifluous style and which under pretext of another subject [contained/was a Bolus of⟩] contained much artful infidelity and of which I said it was not fair to attack us thus unexpectedly; He should have warned us of our danger before we entered his [eloquent flower garden/garden of flowery eloquence⟩] garden of flowery eloquence, by advertising 'Spring-guns and mantraps set here.' The Authour had been an Oxonian and was remembered there for having 'turned Papist'. I observed that as he had changed several times from the Church of England to [the Church of Rome/Popery⟩] the Church of Rome — from [the Church of Rome/Popery⟩] the Church of Rome to Infidelity, — I did not despair [/yet/⟩] yet of seeing him a Methodist preacher. *Johnson* (laughing). 'It is said *[MS 519]* that his range has been more [varied⟩] extensive, and that he has /once/[4] been Mahometan. However, now that he has published his infidelity, he will probably persist in it.' *Boswell*. 'I am not quite sure of that Sir.'[5]

---

accurate English friend, that Dr. Johnson could never have used the phrase *almost nothing*, as not being English; and therefore I have put another in its place. At the same time, I am quite convinced it is not good English. For the best writers use the phrase *"little or nothing;"* i.e. almost so little as to be nothing'.

[1] The alternative is resolved by the printing of 'A Political Survey of Great Britain' in the revises.

[2] In the second edition, a footnote is keyed to 'expect': 'Yet surely it is a very useful work, and of wonderful research and labour for one man to have executed'.

[3] The deleted MS reference to Gibbon confirms Hill-Powell's identification.

[4] The optional word, which JB left unresolved, is printed in the revises.

[5] This paragraph conflates two separate discussions of Gibbon's *Decline and Fall*. In the first, JB is provoked by John Smith, Professor of Anatomy at Oxford, 'who indecently talks as an Unbeliever' (Journ. 20 Mar.; *Ominous Years*, p. 282). SJ was not present at this

[You know Sir>] I mentioned Sir Richard Steele having published his Christian Hero, with the avowed purpose of [pledging>] obliging himself to lead a religious life, [yet his practice/tho his conduct>] yet his conduct was by no means strictly suitable.' *Johnson*. 'Steele I believe practised the lighter vices.'

5   Mr. Warton being engaged could not sup with us at our Inn so we had another evening by ourselves. I [put it to him>] asked him whether a man's being forward in making himself known to eminent people, and seeing as much of life and getting as much information as he could in every way was not yet lessening himself by [that/his>] his forwardness. *Johnson*. 'No Sir a man [is growing in reality

10   greater/is making himself in reality greater>] makes himself greater as he increases his knowledge.'

       ₍I censured some ludicrous fantastick dialogues between [a cock and hens>] two coach horses and other such [stuff/nonsense>] stuff which [an acquaintance of his/Baretti>] Baretti had [/lately/>] lately published. He joined with me and said

15   'Nothing odd will do long. Tristram Shandy did not last.' I expressed a desire to be acquainted with Mrs. Rudd[6] at that time universally celebrated for extraordinary address and insinuation. *Johnson*. 'Never believe extraordinary characters which you hear of people. Depend upon it Sir, they are exaggerated. You do not see one man shoot a great deal higher than another.' I mentioned Mr. Burke. [He

20   seemed attempting/beginning to contravert a little; but took himself and said *del*] JOHNSON. 'Yes — Burke *is* an extraordinary man. His stream of mind is perpetual.'[7] It[8] is very agreable to record that Johnson's high estimation of the talents of this gentleman was uniform from their early acquaintance [*undeciphered word del*]. Sir Joshua Reynolds informs me that when Mr. Burke was first [brought into>] elected

25   a member of Parliament and Sir John Hawkins expressed a wonder at such elevation, Johnson said 'Now we who know Burke know that he will be one of the first men in this country.' And once when Johnson was ill and unable to exert himself as much as usual without fatigue, Mr. Burke having been mentioned he

---

conversation. JB joins the two with the sentence beginning, 'The Authour had been an Oxonian...'.

   [6] JB reworked the reference to Caroline Rudd several times. The first MS draft reads simply, 'I mentioned a Lady'. JB then decided to be much more direct: 'I expressed a desire to be acquainted with Mrs. Rudd'. By the stage of the revises, Mrs. Rudd's name had disappeared again: 'I expressed a desire to be acquainted with Mrs.   , as a lady at that time universally celebrated'. Still not satisfied, JB altered the revises to read, 'I expressed a desire to be acquainted with a lady who had been much talked of, and universally celebrated'. It is plausible to link this tinkering to JB's ambivalent, quasi-obsessive fascination with the notorious adventuress whom he interviewed in April 1776 and who later became his lover (*Later Years*, pp. 133–35, 294–95; Gordon Turnbull, 'Criminal Biographer: Boswell and Margaret Caroline Rudd', *Studies in English Literature* 26 [1986], pp. 511–35).

   [7] The phrase 'His stream of mind is perpetual' was printed in the revises 'His rigour of mind is incessant'. It was then changed back to the original wording, accompanied by a marginal explanation from JB: 'I restore. I find the exact words as to Burke'. At the stage of first proof, JB must have altered the wording, but by the time of the revises, he had located the journal entry (for 26 March) that confirmed 'his stream of mind is perpetual'.

   [8] The passage beginning here and extending to the end of the paragraph represents yet a later draft by JB.

said 'that fellow calls forth all my powers. Were I to see Burke now, it would kill me.' So much was he accustomed to consider conversation as a contest, and such was his notion of Burke as an opponent.)

Next morning Thursday March 21 we set out on a post=chaise to pursue our proposed [jaunt/journey>] ramble. It was a delightful day and we drove through 5
Blenheim Park. When I looked at the magnificent Bridge built by John Duke of Marlborough over a small rivulet and recollected the epigram made upon it

> The arch the height of his ambition shows
> The stream an emblem of thy bounty flows

and saw that now by the genius of Brown a magnificent body of water was collected 10
I said 'They have drowned [MS 520] the Epigram' and Johnson did not disapprove of the conceit. [I said to him while in the midst of the noble scene arround us/while in the midst of the noble scene arround us I said to him>] I said to him while in the midst of the noble scene arround us 'You and I Sir have I think now seen together, the extremes of what can be seen in Britain, the wild rough Mull 15
and now Blenheim Park.'

We dined at an excellent Inn at Chapelhouse where he expatiated on the felicity of England in its taverns and Inns and triumphed over France for not having in any perfection the tavern life. 'There is no private house' [/said he/>] said he 'in which people can enjoy themselves so well as at a capital Tavern. Let 20
there be ever so great plenty of good things ever so much grandeur ever so much elegance, ever so much desire that every body should be [easy/at home>] easy. In the nature of things it cannot be. There must [allways/ever>] allways be some degree of [care/anxiety>] care and anxiety. The master of the house is anxious to entertain his guests. The guests are anxious to be agreable to him; and no man but 25
a very impudent dog indeed can as freely command what is in another man's house as if it were his own. Whereas at a tavern there is a general freedom [of>] from anxiety. [You/All>] You are sure [you/they>] you are welcome and the more noise [you/they>] you make the more trouble you give the more good things [you/they>] you call for, the welcomer you are. No servants will attend you with the alacrity 30
which waiters do who are incited by the prospect of an immediate reward in proportion as they please. No Sir [MS 521] There is nothing which has yet been contrived by man by which so much happiness is produced as by a good tavern or Inn.'[9] [Shenstone has finely said/He then repeated with great emotion Shenstone's little Poem>] He then repeated with great emotion Shenstone's lines 35

> He who has travell'd Life's dull round
> Where'er his   may have been
> May sigh to think how oft he found[1]
> The warmest welcome at an Inn.[2]

---

[9] JB's note on Sir John Hawkins's *Memorabilia* first appeared in the second edition.

[1] In the revises, JB, assisted by Tomlins, supplements and corrects the quotation from Shenstone: 'He who' is changed to 'Whoe'er' and 'how oft he' to 'he still has'; the blank in the second line is filled by 'stages'.

[2] In correcting the revises, JB inserted a note keyed to 'Inn': 'It may be mentioned that we happened to lye this night at Henley where Shenstone wrote these lines'; also in the revises, he altered this note to read 'We happened to lye this night at the Inn at Henley the

In the afternoon as we were driven rapidly along in the post=chaise, he said to me 'Life has not many things better than this.'

We stopped at Stratford upon Avon and drank [coffee and tea⟩] tea and coffee, and it pleased me to be with him upon the classick ground of [/his/⟩] Shakespeare's
5   native Place.

He [spoke/talked⟩] spoke slightingly of Dyer's Fleece [saying *del*] 'The subject ⟨Sir⟩ [could not/cannot⟩] cannot be made poetical. How [could one/can a man⟩] can a man write poetically of serges and druggets. Yet you will hear many people talk to you very gravely of 'that *excellent* Poem the Fleece'. He also spoke
10   slightingly of Granger's 'Sugar Cane' [and said *del*] 'Granger did not consider how few could be interested by that subject.'[3] I mentioned to him [a circumstance told me by Mr. Langton how that Poem⟩] Langton having told me that this Poem when read in manuscript at Sir Joshua Reynolds's had made ⟨all⟩ the assembled wits burst into a laugh when after much blank verse pomp, the [MS 522] Poet began a
15   new paragraph thus
              'Now muse lets sing of Rats —
and what increased the ridicule was that [somebody⟩] one of the company who slyly [looked on ⟨with the Authour's friend⟩] overlooked the reader, perceived that the word had been originally mice, and had been altered to Rats as more
20   dignified.[4] Johnson. [Percy/A certain friend of ours⟩] 'Percy was angry [with/at⟩]

---

place where Shenstone wrote these lines'. The first edition conflated these two versions: 'We happened to lye this night at the inn at Henley, where Shenstone wrote these lines'.

In the second edition, JB greatly expanded his commentary on Shenstone, providing both a note on his note as well as an entirely new paragraph discussing 'that elegant gentleman's opinion of Johnson'.

[3] Under intense pressure from Thomas Percy, JB cancelled at the stage of the revises SJ's 'severe Censure' of James Grainger (Percy to JB, 24 March 1791: *Corr. 2*, p. 397; Volume II, Signature E3, pp. 29–30). For the text of the cancellandum, see Hill-Powell iv. 556. Grainger, a close friend of Percy, had introduced him to SJ; after Grainger's death, Percy defended his reputation from attacks in the press (Bertram H. Davis, *Thomas Percy: A Scholar-Cleric in the Age of Johnson*, 1989, pp. 38, 206). In this instance he claimed to be motivated as well by 'a particular solicitude' for Grainger's 'only Daughter a young Lady of great Beauty and Merit' (*Corr. 2*, p. 394).

For the second edition, JB made several changes, all of which restored details that had been eliminated or softened by the cancel. He inserted a new paragraph into the note beginning 'The above was written by the Bishop', as well as a new paragraph in the main text ('This passage does not appear'). JB also reinstated SJ's assertion that Percy was angry with him, placing it this time in a footnote. Most tellingly, he reworked the cancelled passage on Percy's time in the West Indies, and made it the paragraph following that on Percy's history of the wolf. It is difficult not to interpret JB's move as retaliation for Percy's censorship. As Charles Fifer notes, JB 'put back into the second edition of the *Life* matter that he had cancelled in the first edition for fear of offending Percy; and he would hardly have done that unless he had come to feel that his friendship was beyond hope of recovery' (*Corr. 3*, p. lxxxvi). Indeed the restoration of these passages caused mortal offense: even after JB's death, Percy continued to disparage his literary achievements.

[4] In the first edition, a note is keyed to 'dignified': 'Such is this little laughable incident, which has been often related. Dr. Percy, the Bishop of Dromore, who was an intimate friend of Dr. Grainger, and has a particular regard for his memory, has communicated to me the following explanation:

with me for laughing at [the Sugar Cane⟩] 'The Sugar Cane'; for he had a mind to make a great thing of Granger's Rats. There was a Review of it in The London Chronicle said to be written by me; but I only helped Percy with it and was in jest. Granger however might have been made a very good Poet. He was an agreable man, and would have done one any good ⟨in his power⟩; but was I think quite   5
[void/destitute⟩] destitute of principle [/quite without any notion of obligation to rectitude — any principle of duty/⟩] I mean quite without any notion of obligation to rectitude — any principle of duty.⁵ He was [/a/⟩] a very unlucky [/man/⟩] man. He was for some years surgeon to a Regiment. He then got a scotch degree as Physician, and set up in London. Not succeeding well there he got an offer from   10
a rich West Indian to go and live with him as his companion for a [certain short term of years/few years⟩] few years for which he was to have [£200/two hundred a year⟩] an annuity of two hundred pounds during his life. Granger accepted. But in the passage he fell in love with a [girl/young woman⟩] young woman who was a passenger [MS 523] in the ship, — and perhaps grew tired of [the gentleman/his   15
companion⟩] the gentleman gave up his agreement, married the [girl/young woman⟩] young woman, and went to St Christopher's and set up as a Physician. He wrote to Johnston an apothecary in London to send him out a man to compound his medecines. Johnston sent him one such as he could find with an apology for his dullness. This fellow set up as a rival to Granger in the practice of   20
Physick and got so much the better of him in the opinion of the people of St. Christopher's that he carried away all the business; upon which Granger returned to England and soon after died. Granger's Translation of Tibullus is I think very well ⟨done. But what could he make of a sugar=cane?⟩⁶ One may ⟨as well⟩ write

---

"The passage in question was originally not liable to such a perversion; for the authour having occasion in that part of his work to mention the havock made by rats and mice, had introduced the subject in a kind of mock heroick, and a parody of Homer's battle of the frogs and mice, invoking the Muse of the old Grecian bard in an elegant and well-turned manner. In that state I had seen it; but afterwards, unknown to me and other friends, he had been persuaded, contrary to his own better judgement, to alter it, so as to produce the unlucky effect above mentioned."

The Bishop gives this character of Dr. Grainger: — "He was not only a man of genius and learning, but had many excellent virtues; being one of the most generous, friendly, and benevolent men I ever knew."'

⁵ Percy's objection to this sentence was particularly vehement: 'As to the cruel Censure that he was destitute *of any principle*, or *Obligation of Duty*: I know not how we are to judge of Men's principles, but by their operation on their Conduct: and I do declare, that as to the *relative Duties* Dr. Grainger was quite exemplary: His parents died when he was young, but he was one of the most grateful and affectionate Brothers, of the most indulgent husbands, of the most tender Fathers, and, most disinterested Friends I ever knew: as I could support, if needful, by remarkable Instances. Nor did I ever once hear him throw out any sentiment, even *in sport*, that could justify such a severe Imputation, as that "he was quite destitute of principle I mean any Notion of Obligation to rectitude any principle of Duty," etc. etc' (Percy to JB, 24 Mar. 1791, *Corr. 2*, p. 397).

⁶ Having decided upon a cancel, JB changed 'Granger's Translation of Tibullus is I think very well done. But what could he make of a sugar=cane?' to 'His Translation of Tibullus, he thought, was very well done; but "The Sugar=Cane, a Poem," did not please him; for, he exclaimed, 'What could he make of a sugar-cane?'"

The Parsley Bed a Poem, or The Cabbage Garden a Poem.' Boswell. 'You must then pickle your cabbage with the [sal atticum/attick salt>] sal atticum'. Johnson. 'You know there is allready 'The Hop Garden a poem'. — ⟨And I think⟩ One could say a great deal about cabbage. The Poem might begin with the advantages

5 of a civilised society over a rude state exemplified by the Scotch, who had no cabbages till Oliver Cromwell's soldiers introduced them and one might thus shew how arts are [introduced>] propagated by conquest as they were by the Roman Arms.' He seemed to be much diverted with the fertility of his own fancy.

I mentioned that I heard Dr. Percy was writing the History of the Wolf in Great

10 Britain. *Johnson.* 'The Wolf Sir, why the Wolf? Why does he not write [MS 524] of the Bear which we had formerly; nay it is said we had the Beaver. Or why does he not write of the Grey Rat, the Hanover Rat as it is called, because it is said to have come into this country about the time that the family of Hanover came. I should like to see *"The History of the Grey Rat by Thomas Percy D.D. Chaplain in*

15 *ordinary to His Majesty"* ⟨(laughing immoderately)⟩'. *Boswell.* 'I am affraid a Court Chaplain could not decently write of the Grey Rat.' *Johnson.* 'Sir he need not give it the name of the Hanover Rat.' We lay at a good Inn at Henley in Warwick-shire.[7]

On Friday March 22 we got early to Birmingham and after breakfast went to call

20 on his old schoolfellow Mr. Hector [Surgeon here *del*]. A very stupid maid who [answered/opened>] opened the door, told us that her master was [gone out/not at home>] gone out — he was gone to the country — she [did not know/could not tell>] could not tell when he [was to/would>] would return. In short she [was a miserable receiver of his guests>] gave us a miserable reception and [⟨as⟩ *del*]

25 Johnson observed 'She would have behaved no better to people who wanted him in the way of his [profession/business>] profession.' He said to her 'My name is Johnson. Tell him I called. Will you remember the name' [⟨(bawling in her ear)⟩ *del*]. She answered ⟨with rustick simplicity in the Warwickshire dialect⟩ 'I dont understand you Sir.' '[Blochead>] Blochead' (said he) 'I'll write' — I never heard

30 the [word/epithet>] word *Blockhead* applied to a woman before,[8] though I do not/dont see[9] [MS 525] why it should not [/when there is evident occasion for it/>] when there is evident occasion for it.[1] He however [made another attempt/renewed his endeavours>] made another attempt ⟨to make her under-stand him⟩ and roared loud ⟨in her ear⟩ JOHNSON — and then she catched [it/the sound>] the sound.

35 sound>] the sound.

----

[7] The last sentence of this paragraph was omitted in the printing of the revises, apparently having been deleted in first proof. The second edition prints an entirely new sentence, which emphasizes SJ's affection for Percy: 'Thus could he indulge a luxuriant sportive imagination, when talking of a friend whom he loved and esteemed'. This addition may well be considered disingenuous, given the material that JB restored from the cancelled passage (see *ante* p. 199 n. 3).

[8] JB had cause for surprise: SJ defines 'blockhead' in his *Dictionary* as 'a fellow remarkable for stupidity'.

[9] The alternative is resolved by the printing of 'do not see' in the revises.

[1] JB's note on Langton's 'droll illustration of this question' first appeared in the second edition.

We then called on Mr. Lloyd one of the people called Quakers. He too was not at home; but Mrs. Lloyd was, and received us courteously and asked us to dinner. [He>] Johnson said to me 'After the uncertainty of all human things at Hector's, this invitation came very well.' We walked about the town and [were>] he was pleased to see it increasing.   5

I talked of legitimation by subsequent marriage, which obtained in the Roman law and still obtains in the law of Scotland. *Johnson.* 'I think it a bad thing [because/for>] because the chastity of women being of the utmost importance, as all property depends upon it, they who forfeit it should not have any possibility of being restored to good character, nor should the children by an illicit connection   10 attain the full rights of [lawful children/citizens>] lawful children by the posteriour consent of the offending parties.' His opinion upon this subject deserves consid- eration. Upon his principle there may at times be a hardship and seemingly a strange one upon individuals; but the [MS 526] general good of society is better secured and after all, it is [an unreasonable complaint of hardship for/in>]   15 unreasonable in an individual to repine that he has not the advantage of a state which is ₍made₎ different from his ₍own₎ by the social institution under which he [is born/lives>] is born. A woman does not complain that her brother who is younger than her gets their common father's estate. Why then should a natural son complain that a younger brother [/by the same parents/>] by the same parents   20 lawfully begotten gets it. The operation of law is similar in both cases. Besides, [a natural child who has a younger brother by the same father and mother who gets his fathers estate in preference to him, has no better claim to it, than if his brother and he had>] an illegitimate son who has a younger legitimate brother by the same father and mother, has no stronger claim to that father's estate than if that   25 legitimate brother had only the same father from whom alone the estate descends.

Mr. Lloyd joined us in the street and in a little while we met *Friend Hector* as Mr. Lloyd called him. [I loved to observe The joy which Johnson and he expressed on seeing each other again.>] It gave me pleasure to observe the joy which Johnson and he expressed on seeing each other again. Mr. Lloyd and I left them [together   30 at his Fathers/with his Father while I was obligingly shewn>] together while he obligingly shewed me some of the nicer manufactures of this very curious assem- blage of artificers. We all [MS 527] met at dinner at Mr. Lloyd's where we were [excellently entertained/entertained with excellent hospitality>] entertained with great hospitality. Mr. and Mrs. Lloyd had been married the same year with   35 their Majesties and like them had been blessed with a numerous family of fine children their numbers being exactly the same. [*Johnson*/Johnson said>] Johnson said 'Marriage is the best state for a man in general and [a/every>] every man is a worse man in proportion as he is unfit for the married state.'

I have allways liked [the simplicity of manners/the simple manners>] the   40 simplicity of manners and [spiritual/spirituality>] spiritual [exercises>] mindedness of the Quakers and talking with Mr. Lloyd, I said that the essential part of Religion was piety, a devout intercourse with the Divinity — and that many a man was a Quaker without knowing it. [But as Dr. Johnson had expressed a dislike to that sect/their principles, I kept clear of introducing any question   45 concerning their faith.>]

As[2] Dr. Johnson had said to me this forenoon while we walked together, that he liked individuals among the quakers but not the sect ∧when we were at Mr. Lloyd's∧ I kept clear of introducing any question concerning the peculiarities of their faith. But I having asked to look at Baskervilles edition of Barclay's apology

5   Johnson laid hold of it, and the Chapter on Baptism having turned up [he remarked>] [he carelessly remarked>] Johnson remarked 'He says there is neither precept nor practice for baptism, in the scriptures that is false.' Here he was the aggressor by no means in a gentle manner; and the good quakers had the advantage of him; for he had read negligently, and had not observed that Barclay speaks of

10   *infant* baptism, which they calmly made him perceive. Mr. Lloyd however was in as great a mistake; for when insisting that the rite of baptism with water was to cease when the *spiritual* administration of Christ began he maintained that John the Baptist said 'My *baptism* shall decrease but *his* shall increase.' Whereas the words are 'He must increase but I must decrease.'[a]

15   One of them [however *del*] having objected [today *del*] to the 'observance of days and months and years' Johnson answered 'The Church does not superstitiously observe days merely as days, but as memorials of important facts. Christmas might be kept as well upon one day of the year as [another/that on which we keep it>] another. Only there should be a stated day for commemorating the birth of

20   our saviour [because/as>] because there is danger that what may be done upon any day, will be neglected.'[3]

     [MS 528] Mr Hector was so good as to accompany me to see the [great iron works of Mr. Bolton/Mr. Bolton's great iron works>] great Works of Mr. Bolton ∧at a place which he has called Soho∧ about two miles from Birmingham which the very

25   ingenious Proprietor shewed me himself to the best advantage. I wish that Johnson had been with us; for it was a [sight>] scene which I should have been glad to contemplate by his light. The vastness and the contrivance of some of the machinery would have [met his vigorous mind>] 'matched his mighty mind'. I shall never forget Mr. Bolton's expression to me 'I sell here, Sir, what all the world desires

30   to have — Power.' — He had about seven hundred people at work. [He was a sort of an iron Chieftain and seemed>] I contemplated him as an iron Chieftain and he seemed to be a Father to his tribe. One of them came to him complaining grievously of his Landlord for having distrained his goods 'Your landlord is in the right, Smith,' said Bolton. 'But, I'll tell you what. Find you a friend who will lay down one half of

35   your rent and I'll lay down the other half; and you shall have your goods again.'

     [From Mr. Hector I got/Mr. Hector favoured me with several anecdotes/particulars>] From Mr. Hector I now learnt many particulars of Dr. Johnson's early life which with others that [I got from him>] he gave me at different times since, have contributed to the [completion/formation>] formation

40   of this Work [in which I flatter myself he will be faithfully/long preserved *del*].

    [a] John 3.30.

---

[2] The paragraph that follows represents a revision and expansion of the previous sentence ('But ... faith').

[3] Here the second edition inserts a paragraph: 'He said to me at another time ....'

[MS 529]⁴ Dr. Johnson said to me in the forenoon 'You will see ₍Sir₎ at Mr. Hector's his sister Mrs. Careless a Clergymans widow. She was/is⁵ the first woman [with/for>] with whom I [was in love/felt the passion of love>] was in love. It dropt out of my head imperceptibly; but she and I will allways have a kindness for [each other/one another>] each other.' He laughed at the romantick fancy that a man never can be really in love but once. [When I returned with Mr. Hector, we went to>]

On our return from Mr. Boltons Mr. Hector took me to his house where we found Johnson sitting placidly [/at tea/>] at tea with his first love who [/though now/>] though now [well *del*] advanced in [life/years>] years was a genteel woman [and very well bred and agreable>] very agreable and well=bred.

Johnson lamented to Mr. Hector the state of one of their Schoolfellows [/Mr. Charles Congreve/>] Mr. Charles Congreve a Clergyman, which he thus described 'He obtained I believe considerable preferment in Ireland, but now lives in London, quite as a valetudinarian affraid to go into any house but his own. He takes a short airing in a/his⁶ post=chaise every day. he has an old/elderly⁷ woman whom he calls cousin who lives with him, and jogs his elbow when his glass has stood too long empty, and encourages him in drinking, in which he is very willing to be encouraged; not that he gets drunk.

. . . .

[MS 531]⁸ marriages [would in general/in general would>] would in general be as happy and often more so if the parties had no choice in the matter, but they were all [made/united>] made by the Lord Chancellor upon a due [consideration/investigation>] consideration of [their *del*] characters and circumstances'.⁹

I wished to have staid at Birmingham tonight [to have talked more with/learnt more from Mr. Hector>] to have talked more with Mr. Hector but my friend was impatient to [go forward the stage to>] reach his native City. So we drove on ₍that stage₎ in the dark, [/and were long dull and silent/>] /and were long and silent/. When we got within the focus of the Lichfield Lamps 'Now' said he 'we are getting out of a state of death.' We put up at the Three Crowns not one of the [fashionable>] great Inns but a good old fashioned one which had been kept for forty years by Mr. Wilkins, ₍and was₎ the very next house to that in which Johnson was born and brought up and which was still his own property.¹ We had

---

⁴ MS 529: current location undetermined (transcribed from a photostat at Yale).

⁵ The alternative is resolved by the printing of 'was' in the revises.

⁶ The alternative is resolved by the printing of 'his' in the revises.

⁷ The alternative is resolved by the printing of 'elderly' in the revises.

⁸ MS 530: current location undetermined (photostat not available at Yale). MSS 531–532: Houghton Library, Harvard University, shelfmark fMS Eng 1386.

⁹ By the stage of the revises the sequence of clauses in this sentence had been inverted: 'I believe marriages would in general be as happy, and often more so, if they were all made by the Lord Chancellor, upon a due consideration of characters and circumstances, without the parties having any choice in the matter'.

¹ By the stage of the revises, a footnote had been keyed to 'property': 'I went through the birth place of my illustrious friend with a reverence which it doubtless will long be visited. An engraved view of it, with the adjacent buildings, may be found in '"The Gentleman's

a comfortable supper and got into high spirits. I felt all my Toryism glow in this old Capital of the Staffordshire. I could have offered incense *Genio Loci* and I indulged in libations of that ale which Bonniface[2] recommends with [so hearty an eloquence/such an eloquent jollity>] such an eloquent jollity.

5   Next morning [Saturday 22 March *del*] he introduced me to Mrs. Lucy Porter his [daughter in law that is to say Mrs. Johnson's/his wife's daughter>] step daughter. She was now [MS 532] an [elderly maiden Lady>] old maid with much simplicity of manner. She had never been in London. [A>] Her Brother a Captain in the Navy had left her a fortune of ten thousand pounds, about a third of which
10   she had laid out in building a stately house and making a handsom garden [in/on>] in an elevated situation in Lichfield. Johnson when here by himself used to [lodge/live>] live at her house. She reverenced him and he had a parental tenderness for her.

    We then visited Mr. Peter Garrick who [had that morning received/that
15   morning had received>] had that morning received a letter from his brother David announcing our coming to Lichfield. He [was engaged to dinner/*undeciphered word*>] was engaged to dinner, but asked us to tea and to [take beds>] sleep at his house. Johnson however would not quit his old acquaintance Wilkins [of/at>] of the three Crowns. The family likeness of the Garricks was very striking, and
20   Johnson thought that David's vivacity was not so peculiar to himself as was supposed. 'Sir' said he 'I dont know but if Peter had cultivated all the arts of gayety as much as David has done, he might have been as brisk and lively. Depend upon it Sir [vivacity/gayety>] vivacity is much an art and depends greatly on habit.' I believe [MS 533][3] there is a good deal of truth in this notwithstanding the
25   ludicrous story ₍told me by a Lady abroad₎ of a heavy German Baron who had lived much with the young english at Geneva and was ambitious to be as lively as they with which view he with assiduous exertion was jumping over the ₍tables &₎ chairs in his lodgings and when the people of the house ran in [to see>] and asked with surprise what was the matter answered *S'h apprens tétre fif*.

30   We dined at our Inn and had with us a Mr. Jackson one of Johnson's schoolfellows, whom he treated with much kindness, though he seemed to be a low man, dull and untaught. He had a coarse grey=brown coat black waistcoat greasy leather breeches and a yellow uncurled wig, and his countenance had the ruddiness which [bespeaks/betokens>] betokens one who is in no haste to 'leave his
35   can'. He drank only ale. He had tried to be a cutler at Birmingham, but had not succeeded, and now he lived poorly at home, and [was upon/was trying>] had some scheme of dressing leather in a better manner than [common/usual>] common, to his indistinct account of which Dr. Johnson listened with patient attention, that he might assist him with his advice. Here was an instance of genuine humanity

---

Magazine" for February, 1785.' In correcting the revises, JB altered the note to read as follows: 'I went through the house where my illustrious friend was born with a reverence with which it doubtless will long be visited. An engraved view of it, with the adjacent buildings, is in "The Gentleman's Magazine" for February, 1785.'

   [2] JB keys in an addition from the (missing) verso that can be conjecturally supplied from the printed text: 'in "The Beaux Stratagem"'.

   [3] MS 533: Hyde Collection.

[MS 534] [4] and real kindness in this great man who has been [so/most>] most unjustly represented as altogether harsh and destitute of [tenderness/gentleness>] tenderness. [A thousand such/Thousands of such>] A thousand such instances might have been recorded in the course of his long [life. That his temper was hasty>] life though that his temper was warm and hasty and his manner often   5 rough cannot be denied. [But nothing could be juster or better said than what Goldsmith once observed to me 'Johnson has nothing of the Bear but his skin' *del*][5]

I saw here for the first time *oat ale,* and oat=cakes not hard as in Scotland but soft like a brown wheaten cake[6] were served at breakfast. It was pleasant to me to find that 'Oats' the *food of horses* ∧were∧ so much used ∧as the *food of the people*∧   10 in Dr. Johnson's own town. He [ran out>] expatiated[7] in praise of Lichfield and its inhabitants who he said were 'the most sober decent people in England, the genteelest in proportion to their wealth, and spoke the purest english.' I doubted as to the last article [/of this eulogium/>] of this eulogy; for they had several provincial sounds as *there* pronounced like *fear* instead of like *fair once* pronounced   15 *woonse* instead of *wunnse.* Johnson himself never got entirely free of *[MS 535]* his provincial accent. Garrick used to take him off squeesing a lemon into [the Bowl>] a Punch Bowl with strange gesticulations,[8] and calling out 'Who's for *Poonsh*'.[9]

I perceived [little doing in Lichfield>] very little business going forward in Lichfield. I found two strange manufactures for so inland a place sail=cloth and   20 streamers for ships, [but these very limited/to no extent *del*]. I observed them making some saddle cloths and dressing a good many sheep=skins. But upon the whole the busy hand of industry seemed to be quite slackened. 'Surely Sir' said I 'you are an idle set of people.' [Who could have replied as he readily did/with such ingenuity *del*] JOHNSON. 'Sir we are a City of Philosophers. We work with our heads   25 [not with our hands. We make>] and make the Boobies of Birmingham work for us with their hands.'

There was at this time a company of Players performing at Lichfield. The Manager Mr. Stanton sent [/in/*del*] his compliments and that he would be glad to wait on [us/Dr. Johnson>] Dr. Johnson. Johnson received him very courteously   30 ∧and he drank a glass of wine with us∧. He was a plain decent well=behaved man, and expressed his gratitude to Dr. Johnson for having once got him permission from Dr. Taylor at Ashbourne to play there upon moderate terms. [Garrick was soon introduced.>] Garrick's name was soon introduced. *Johnson.* 'Garrick's

---

[4] MSS 534–37: Houghton Library, Harvard University, shelfmark fMS Eng 1386.

[5] In the left margin is a note in JB's hand that explains the logic behind the deletion: 'See if not in'. JB had already included this material in his passage for 7 April 1775. See *ante* p. 152 (MS 462).

[6] In correcting the revises, EM suggests two alternatives to 'brown wheaten cake': 'muffin' and 'Yorkshire cake'. JB selects 'Yorkshire cake'.

[7] JB would seem to have turned to SJ's *Dictionary* in making this revision: there, 'to expatiate' is listed as the primary definition of 'to run out'.

[8] In the revises, JB experimented with a further descriptive detail after 'strange gesticulations'. He first added 'and hands not overclean', but in response to a marginal note from EM ('Would not this be better omitted?'), he substituted 'looking round the company'.

[9] In the revises JB adds and then deletes an additional sentence: '[He'd be a stout>] He must have been a stout man said Garrick who would have been for it'.

conversation [MS 536] is gay and grotesque. It is a dish of all sorts, but all good things. There is no solid meat in it; There is a want of sentiment in it; not but that he has sentiment sometimes, and sentiment too very powerful and very pleasing; but it has not its full proportion in his conversation.'

5   ‹When we were by ourselves he told me [that forty years ago he had›] 'Forty years ago Sir I was in love with an actress here, Mrs. Emmet who acted Flora in "Hob in the Well". What merit this Lady had as an actress, or what was her figure or her manner I [have not/never heard›] have not been informed. But if we may believe Mr. Garrick his old Masters taste in theatrical merit was by no means refined he was
10   [by no means›] not an *elegans formarum Spectator*. Garrick used to tell [how Johnson used to praise›] that Johnson said of an actor who played Sir Harry Wildair at Lichfield 'There is a courtly vivacity about the fellow' when said Garrick this was the most vulgar ruffian that ever went upon boards. [Johnson's description of one of his literary friends 'Sir ____ is courtly and airy' was by no means *del*][1]
15   We had promised to Mr. Stanton to be at his theatre on Monday. Dr. Johnson jocularily proposed to me to write a Prologue for the occasion 'A Prologue by James Boswell Esq from the Hebrides'. I was really inclined to take the hint, and write 'Prologue spoken before Dr. Johnson at Lichfield 1776' like 'Prologue Spoken before the Duke of York at Edinburgh' in Charles the Second's Time. Much might
20   have been said of what Lichfield had done for Shakespeare by Johnson and Garrick. But I [*undeciphered word*/found›] found he was averse to it.›

We went and viewed the Museum of Mr. ‹Richard› Green apothecary here who told me he was proud of being a relation of Dr. Johnson's. It was indeed a wonderful Collection both of Antiquities and Natural curiosities and ingenious
25   works of art. He had all the articles accurately arranged, with their names upon labels printed at his own little press, and on the [first flat of his *del*] staircase leading to it was a Board with the names of Contributors marked in gold [letters. A printed Catalogue of the Collection/letters and there was a printed Catalogue of the Collection›] letters. A printed Catalogue of the Collection [/was to be had at the
30   Bookseller's/›] was to be had at the[2] Bookseller's. Johnson expressed his admiration of the activity and diligence and good fortune of Mr. Green in getting together so great a variety of things in his situation and Mr. Green told me that Johnson once said to him 'Sir I should as soon have thought of building a man of War as of [getting/making›] collecting such a museum.' Mr. Green's obliging alacrity in
35   shewing it was very pleasing. He [/has/›] has favoured me with his engraved Portrait which has a motto very characteristical of his disposition *Nemo sibi vivat*.

‹A Physician[3] who had quitted practice, because his whimsically changing his Religion had made people distrustful of [him I thought/maintained this unreason-able, as›] him being mentioned I maintained that this was unreasonable, as
40   Religion is unconnected with medical skill. *Johnson*. 'Sir it is not unreasonable; for

---

[1] The adjective 'airy' points toward the Hon. Mrs. Cholmondeley as the 'literary friend' in question (Hill-Powell v. 248; *Letters of Johnson* ed. Redford, iii. 22).

[2] In response to a query from EM in the margin of the revises ('Is there only one Bookseller in Litchfield?'), JB changed 'the' to 'a'.

[3] JB's journal entry for 23 March 1776 reveals that the physician was his uncle, Dr. John Boswell.

when people see a man absurd in what they understand, they may conclude the same of him in what they do not understand. If a Physician were to take to eating of horse=flesh nobody would employ him, though one may eat horse=flesh and be a very skillful Physician. If a man were educated in an absurd religion his continuing to profess it would not hurt him [as a change/his changing would do.⟩] though his changing to it would.   5

I went and viewed the House in which my illustrious Friend was born and which remained his own property as long as he lived. Mr. Hinxman the tenant of it obligingly allowed me to go through it. It was a good large house; and an engraved view of it with the adjacent buildings is to be seen in the Gentleman's   10 Magazine for   ₓ⁴

[MS 537] We drank [tea and coffee/coffee and tea⟩] tea and coffee at Mr. Peter Garrick's where was Mrs. Aston one of the Maiden sisters of Mrs. Walmsley, Wife of Johnson's first [Patron⟩] Friend and sister also of the Lady of whom Johnson used to speak with the warmest admiration by the name of Molly [Aston. She⟩] Aston   15 who was afterwards married to Captain Brodie of [the Navy/His Majesty's Navy/the Royal Navy⟩] the Navy.

One Sunday [24 March⟩] March 24 we breakfasted with Mrs. Cobb a Widow Lady who lived in a sweet old sequestered place close by the town called the *Friary* it having been formerly a religious house. She and her niece Miss Adey were great admirers of   20 Dr. Johnson, and he behaved to them with that kindness and easy pleasantry such as we see between old and intimate acquaintance. He accompanied Mrs. Cobb to Church⁵ and I went to the Cathedral, where I was very much pleased with the musick finding it to be peculiarly solemn and accordant with the words of the service.

We dined at Mr. Peter Garrick's who was in a very lively humour, and [MS   25 538]⁶ justified Johnson's saying that if he had cultivated gayety as much as his brother David he might have [been equally excellent/equally excelled⟩] equally excelled in it. He was today quite a London Narrator telling us a variety of anecdotes with that earnestness and mimickry which we often [find/*undeciphered word* with⟩] find in the wits of the Metropolis. Dr. Johnson went with me to the   30 Cathedral⁷ in the afternoon. It was grand and pleasing to contemplate this illustrious writer now full of fame, worshipping in the Cathedral of his native city, [where he had appeared conspicuously when an infant. *del*]

I returned to coffee & tea/tea & coffee⁸ at Mr. Peter Garrick's, and then found Dr. Johnson at the Reverend Mr. Sewards Canon Residentiary who inhabited the   35 Bishop's Palace in which Mr. Walmsley lived and which had been the scene of many happy hours in Johnson's early life. Mr. Seward had ₓwith eclesiastical

---

⁴ This sentence trails off and JB notes in the margin, 'Qu Shall I get the Plate and have it here?' By the time of the revises (which omit this paragraph) he had decided to handle the reference to SJ's birthplace and the 'engraved view' through a footnote keyed to part of the narrative for 22 March. See *ante* p. 204 and n. 1 (MS 531); see also *Ominous Years*, p. 293 n. 6.

⁵ By the stage of the revises, the name of the church, St. Mary's, had been supplied.

⁶ MS 538: current location undetermined (transcribed from a photostat at Yale).

⁷ In the revises, JB changed 'Cathedral' to '"solemn temple"', thereby introducing an allusion to *The Tempest* (IV. i. 153).

⁸ The alternative is resolved by the printing of 'tea and coffee' in the revises.

hospitality and politeness,ᴧ asked me in the forenoon merely as a stranger, to dine
with him; and in the afternoon when I was introduced to him he asked Dr.
Johnson & me to spend the evening and sup with him. He was a genteel [polite⟩]
well=bred dignified [eclesiastick⟩] Clergyman, had travelled *[MS 539]*[9] with Lord
5   Charles Fitzroy uncle of the present Duke of Grafton who died when abroad and
had lived much in the great World. He was an ingenious and literary man, had
published [/an edition of/⟩] an edition of Beaumont and Fletcher, and [/written/⟩]
written verses in Dodsley's Collection. His Lady was the daughter of Mr. Hunter
Johnson's first schoolmaster. And now for the first time I had the pleasure of
10   seeing his celebrated daughter Miss Anna Seward [to whose obliging communications concerning Johnson I have since been so much indebted.⟩] to whom I have
since been indebted for many civilities as well as some obliging communications
concerning Johnson.

     Mr. Seward mentioned to us the observations which he had made upon the
15   Strata of earth in Volcanoes from which it appeared that they were so very
different in depth in different periods that no calculation whatever could be made
as to the time required for their formation. This fully refuted an antimosaical
remark introduced into Captain Brydone's Tour, I hope heedlessly, from a kind of
vanity which is too common in those who have thought only superficially upon
20   the most important of all subjects. Dr. Johnson *[MS 540]* indeed had said before,
independent of this observation 'Shall all the accumulated evidence of the History
of the World, — shall the authority of what is unquestionably the most ancient
writing[1] be overturned by an uncertain remark such as this?'

     On Monday [25 March⟩] March 25 we breakfasted at Mrs. Lucy Porters. He
25   had sent an express to Dr. Taylor's acquainting him of our being at Lichfield and
[he⟩] Taylor had returned an answer that his post chaise should come for us [this
day/on Monday⟩] this day. While we sat at breakfast Dr. Johnson received a letter
by the post, which seemed to agitate him very much. When he had read it he
[said⟩] exclaimed 'One of the most dreadful things that has happened in my time.'
30   The phrase *my time* like the word *age* is usually [understood to refer/applied⟩]
understood to refer to [something of a publick or general nature⟩] an event of a
publick or general nature. I figured something like an Assassination of the King —
like a gunpowder plot carried into execution — or like another fire of London. —
When asked 'What is it Sir?' He answered 'Mr Thrale has lost his only son.' This
35   was [to be sure/no doubt⟩] no doubt a very [great/heavy⟩] great affliction to Mr.
and Mrs. Thrale [and which their friends must/would consider as an event of
sorrowful *[MS 541]* magnitude.⟩] which their friends would consider accordingly.
[MS 541] But from the manner in which the intelligence of it was communicated
ᴧby Johnsonᴧ it appeared for the moment to be comparatively small. I was
40   however soon affected with sincere concern and was curious to [see/observe⟩]
observe how Dr. Johnson would feel. He said 'This is a total [end to their family⟩]
extinction of their family as much as if they were sold into captivity.' — Upon my

---

[9] MSS 539–50: Houghton Library, Harvard University, shelfmark fMS Eng 1386.
[1] JB appears to have considered adding something after 'writing': marks denoting an
insertion are added and then deleted on both MSS 540r and 539v.

[observing/mentioning⟩] mentioning that Mr. Thrale had daughters [to⟩] who
might inherit his wealth 'Daughters' said Johnson ⟨warmly⟩ 'He'll no more value
his daughters than' — I was going to speak — 'Sir,' said he, 'Don't you know how
you yourself think. Sir, he wishes to propagate his name.' In short I saw male
succession strong in his mind, even where there was no name, no family, of any   5
standing. I said it was lucky he was not present when this misfortune happened.
Johnson. 'It is lucky for me. People in distress never think that you feel enough.' —
Boswell. 'And Sir they will have the hope of seeing you, which will be a relief in the
mean time and when you get to them, the pain will be so far abated that they will
be capable of being consoled by you, which in the first violence of it I believe   10
would not be the case.' *[MS 542] Johnson.* 'No Sir; Violent pain of mind as violent
pain of body *must* be severely felt.' *Boswell.* 'I own Sir, I have not so much feeling
for the distress of others as some people have, or pretend to have. But I have this,
that I would do all [I could/in my power⟩] in my power to relieve them.' *Johnson.*
'Sir it is affectation to [appear/pretend⟩] pretend to feel the distress of others as   15
much as they do themselves. It is equally so, as if one should pretend to feel as
much pain while a friend's leg is cutting off, as he does. No Sir. You have
expressed the [true effect of concern⟩] rational and just nature of sympathy. I
would have gone to the extremity of the earth to have preserved this boy.'

He was soon quite calm. The letter was from Mr. Thrale's Clerk, and concluded   20
'I need not say how much they wish to see you in London.' He said 'We shall
hasten back from Taylor's.'

Mrs. Lucy Porter and ⟨some⟩ other Ladies of the Place talked a great deal of
him when he [had left/was out of⟩] was out of the room not only with veneration
but affection. [It was delightful to me/I was highly gratified to find⟩] I was   25
delighted to find that he was *beloved* in his native City.

Mrs. Aston whom I had seen [last night/the night before⟩] the preceeding
night *[MS 543]* and her sister Mrs. Gastrel a widow Lady had each a house and
garden ⟨and pleasure ground⟩ prettily situated upon Stowhill a gentle eminence
adjoining to Lichfield. He walked away to dinner there, leaving me by myself   30
without any apology. I wondered at his want of that [facility of manners/easy
freedom⟩] 'facility of manners' from which [one/a man⟩] a man has no difficulty in
carrying a friend to a house where he is intimate; [or of that PETITE MORALE as the
french happily express an attention to those small particulars of which human
happiness is composed, for to be thus cast off into solitude for the best part of a day   35
made me uneasy and somewhat fretful/angry⟩] [and that attention to those small
particulars of which human happiness is composed, for it was very unpleasant to be
thus left in a country town where I was a stranger. I know not how it happened, or
was managed, but I was relieved by getting a note⟩] I felt it very unpleasant to be
thus left in solitude in a country town where I was an entire stranger and began to   40
think myself unkindly deserted; but I was soon relieved, and convinced that my
friend instead of being deficient in delicacy had conducted the matter with perfect
propriety for I received the following note in his handwriting. 'Mrs. Gastrel at the
lower house on Stowhill desires Mr. Boswell's company to dinner at two.' I [went
and was well entertained, and again had a/another proof⟩] accepted of the   45
invitation, and had here another proof how amiable his character was in the

opinion of those who knew him best. I [did not know>] was not informed till afterwards that Mrs. Gastrel's husband was the Clergyman of Stratford upon Avon who [barbarously>] with gothick barbarity cut down Shakspeare's mulberry tree,[2] and as Dr. Johnson told me, did [MS 544] it to vex his parishioners. [But his Lady

5   was not answerable for this poetical sacrilege.>] His Lady I have reason to believe participated in the guilt of what the enthusiasts for our immortal Bard deem almost a species of sacrilege.

     [Here>] After dinner Dr. Johnson wrote a letter to Mrs. Thrale on the death of her son. I said it would be hard upon Thrale, but she would soon forget it as she had

10   so many things to think of. *Johnson.* 'No Sir Thrale will forget it first. *She* has many things that she *may* think of. *He* has many things that he *must* think of.' — This was [an admirable/a most just>] a very just remark upon the [difference between>] different effect of those light pursuits which occupy a vacant and easy mind, and those serious [engagements/occupations>] engagements which arrest

15   attention and keep [us/a man>] us from brooding over grief.

     He observed of Lord Bute 'It was said of Augustus, that it would have been better for Rome that he had never been born, or had never died. So it would have been better for this Nation if Lord Bute had never been Minister, or had never resigned.'

20   [We went to the Theatre in their Town Hall and>] In the evening we went to the Town=hall which was converted into a temporary Theatre and saw [*Theodosius*>] 'Theodosius' with 'The [*Jubilee*>] Stratford Jubilee.' It was pleasing to see [him>] Dr. Johnson sitting in [the front>] a conspicuous part of the Pit, and receiving [kindly>] affectionate homage from all his acquaintance. We were quite

25   gay and merry. I afterwards mentioned [MS 545] to him that I reflected upon myself for being so, when poor Mr. and Mrs. Thrale were in such distress. *Johnson.* 'You are [wrong/*undeciphered word*>] wrong Sir. Twenty years hence Mr. and Mrs. Thrale will not suffer much from the death of their son. ‸Now Sir you are to consider that‸ Distance of place as well as distance of time [lessens distress>]

30   operates upon the human feelings. I would not have you be gay in the presence of the distressed, because it would shock them; but you may be gay at a distance. Pain for the loss of a friend or of a relation whom we love, is occasioned by the want which we feel. In time the vacuity is filled with something else; or, sometimes the vacuity closes up of itself.'

35   Mr. Seward and Mr. Pearson [another/a>] another clergyman here supt with us at our Inn, and after they left us, we sat up late as we used to do in London.

     Here I shall [give/record>] record some [gleanings/fragments>] fragments of my friend's conversation during this [jaunt/excursion>] jaunt.

     'Marriage ‸Sir‸ is much more necessary to a man than ‸to‸ a woman, for he is

40   much less able to supply himself with domestick comforts. ‸You will recollect my saying to some Ladies the other day that‸ I had often wondered [at women marrying/why young women should marry>] why young women should marry [when an unmarried woman has>] as they have so much more freedom, and so

---

[2] The second edition prints a note that refers the reader to EM's edition of Shakespeare for 'an accurate and animated statement of Mr. Gastrel's barbarity'.

much more attention paid ⸢to them⸣ *[MS 546]* [than one who is married/an unmarried one›] while unmarried than when married. I [have not mentioned›] indeed did not mention the *strong* reason ⸢for their marrying⸣, the *mechanical* reason.' *Boswell.* 'Why that *is* a strong one. But [imagination makes it much›] does not imagination make it seem much more important than it is in reality. It is a delusion in us as well as in women.' *Johnson.* '[Yes/True›] Yes, Sir; and a delusion that is allways beginning again.' *Boswell.* 'I [don't know but/imagine›] don't know but there is³ [more evil than good›] more misery upon the whole than happiness produced by that [appetite›] passion.' *Johnson.* 'I don't think so Sir.'

'Never speak of a man in his own presence. It is allways indelicate and may be offensive.'

'Questioning is not the mode of conversation [of/among›] among Gentlemen. It is assuming a superiority and it is particularly wrong to question a man concerning himself. [He may not wish to have parts of his former life brought under his own view, or made known to other people.›] There may be parts of his former life [which he may not wish to have brought under his view.›] which he may not wish to be made known to other persons, or even brought to his own recollection.'

'A man should be careful never to tell tales of himself to his own disadvantage. People may be amused, and laugh at the time, but they will be remembered, and brought out against him, upon some after occasion. *[MS 547]* Much may be done if a great man puts his whole mind to a particular [business/study›] object. By doing so Norton [is›] has made himself the great Lawyer that he is allowed to be.'

⸢I mentioned an acquaintance of mine a sectary who was a very religious man who not only attended regularly on publick worship with those of his Communion, but made a particular study of the Scriptures, and even wrote a Commentary on some parts of them, yet was known to be very licentious in indulging himself with [common women of the town maintaining/alledging›] women maintaining that men [were›] are to be saved by faith alone, and that the Christian Religion had not prescribed any fixed rule [of›] for the intercourse between the sexes.⁴ *Johnson.* 'Sir, there is no trusting to that crazy piety.'

I observed that it was strange how well scotchmen were known to one another in their own country though born in very distant counties; for we do not find that even the gentlemen of [two or three *del*] neighboring counties in England [even known to one another/actually known to each other›] are mutually known to each other. [He›] Johnson at once with his usual acuteness saw and explained this. 'Why Sir, you have Edinburgh where the [people›] gentlemen from all your counties meet, and which is not so large but that they are all known. There is no such common place of collection in England, except London where from its great

---

³ Two or three undeciphered words are interlined above 'there is'.

⁴ This religious yet licentious man was John Boswell (1710–80), M.D., JB's uncle, who 'forsook the Kirk for the more "primitive" society of the Glassites, preached the extreme doctrine of salvation by faith, demonstrated his antinominianism practically by frequenting bawdy houses, and was excommunicated by his sect' (*Earlier Years*, p. 21). The journal records a response to SJ's forthright comment that expresses JB's motivation in bringing up his uncle's case: 'I was humbled by this strong saying' (23 Mar. 1776).

size and diffusion, [but a few can be known to each other>] many of those who
reside in contiguous counties of England may remain unknown to each other [in
the metropolis del].λ

5　　On tuesday [26 March>] March 26 λthere came for us an equipage
[well/properly>] properly suited to a wealthy well=beneficed Clergymanλ Dr.
Taylor's large [undeciphered word del] roomy post=chaise drawn by four stout plump
horses and driven by two steady jolly postilions conveyed us to Ashbourne where
I found my friend's school=fellow [upon an establishment all of a piece with>]
living upon an establishment perfectly corresponding with his substantial credit-
10　able equipage. His house garden, λpleasureλ grounds table in short every thing
good and [no scantiness/?nothing of scantiness>] no scantiness λappearingλ. [It
is agreable to see a man have such>] [Let a man have such>] Every man should form
such a plan of living as he can execute compleatly. [One should not/Let him not>]
Let him not draw [an outline wider/a wider outline>] an outline wider than he can
15　fill up. I have seen many skeletons of shew and [high=living>] magnificence
λwhich excited at once ridicule and pityλ. Dr. Taylor had a good estate of his own
and good preferment in the church λbeing a Prebendary of Westminster and
Rector of Bosworth.λ He was a diligent Justice of the Peace, and presided
[over/in>] over the town of Ashbourne, to the the inhabitants of which I was told
20　he was very liberal, [an instance of which — he had the winter before given
away/distributed two hundred pounds [MS 548] among such of them as
required/wanted/stood in need of his assistance>] and as a proof of this it was
mentioned to me he had the winter before distributed two hundred pounds [MS
548] among such of them as stood in need of his assistance. He had [of course>]
25　consequently a considerable political interest λin the county of Derbyλ which he
[carried>] employed to support the Devonshire family; for though the
school=fellow and friend of Johnson he was a Whig. I could not perceive in his
character much congeniality of any sort with that of Johnson, who however said
λto meλ 'Sir, he has a very strong understanding.' His size and figure and
30　countenance and manner were that of a hearty english squire with the Parson
superinduced, and I took particular notice of his upper=servant Mr. Peters a
decent grave man in purple clothes and a large white wig [like/most like>] like the
[Butler/Major Domo>] Butler or Major Domo of a Bishop.

　　Dr. Johnson and Dr. Taylor met with great cordiality, and Johnson λsoonλ gave
35　him the same sad account of their school=fellow Congreve that he had given to
Mr. Hector, adding a remark of such moment to the rational [comfort/conduct of
age>] conduct of a man in the decline of life that it deserves to be imprinted upon
every mind 'There is nothing [of which an old man should be so much
aware/against which an old man should guard more>] against which an old man
40　should be so much upon his guard as putting himself to nurse' — Innumerable
have been the [wretched>] melancholy instances of men [/who were/>] who were
once distinguished for firmness resolution and spirit [yet in the evening of life>]
and in their latter days were governed like [MS 549] children by interested female
artifice.
45　　Dr. Taylor [commended/spoke in praise>] commended a Physician who was
known to him and Dr. Johnson and said 'I fight many battles for him, as a number

of people in the country dislike him.' *Johnson*. 'But you should consider Sir that by every one of your victories he is a loser, for every man of whom you get the better will be very angry, and will resolve not to employ him. Whereas if people get the better of you in argument about him, they'll think "We'll send for Dr. ___⁵ nevertheless."' This was [an observation/a remark›] an observation deep and sure   5
in human nature.

ₓWe talked of [some letters to Lord Mansfield which had been published arraigning an eminent›] a Book in which an eminent Judge was arraigned before the bar of the Publick as having given an unjust decision in a great Cause.⁶ Dr. Johnson maintained that this Publication would not give uneasiness to [the   10
Judge/his Lordship›] the Judge. 'For' (said he) 'either he acted honestly, or he meant to do injustice. If he acted honestly his own consciousness will protect him. If he meant to do injustice he will be glad to see [the man/Stuart›] the man who attacks him so much vexed. [And after all/For Sir those letters are but the wailings of a dog who has been licked.' — 'But Sir,' said I, 'a dog may bite'.   15

Upon the subject of education he observed 'There is no man whatever who is so grossly unfaithful as the Master of a Great School. He professes to teach all the boys who come to him equally; yet he does nothing but for a very few who are forward to learn, and he does not inform the relation of the rest that they are unfit to be made scholars'. *del*]ₓ   ·   20

[On Wednesday 27 March as Dr.›] Next day as Dr. Johnson had acquainted Dr. Taylor of the [strong *del*] reason for his returning speedily to London, it was resolved that we should set out after [dinner at which a few of Dr. Taylor's neighbours appeared.›] dinner. A few of Dr. Taylor's neighbours were his guests that day.   25

Dr. Johnson talked with approbation of [some=one›] one who had attained to the state of the philosophical wise=man that is to have no want of any=thing. 'Then Sir' said I 'the Savage is a wise man'. 'Sir' said he 'I do not mean simply being without but not having a want'. I maintained against his proposition that it was better to have fine clothes, for instance, than not to want them/feel the want.⁷   30
Johnson. 'No, Sir; fine clothes [MS 550] are [only good/good only›] good only as they supply the want of other means of [having›] procuring respect. Was Charles the Twelfth think you less [respected/respectable›] respected [in›] for his coarse blue coat and black [neckcloth/stock›] stock? And you find the King of Prussia dresses plain because the dignity of his character is sufficient'. [A gentleman   35
present brought himself›] I here brought myself into a scrape, for [he›] I heedlessly said 'Would not *you* Sir be the better for velvet and embroidery?' *Johnson*. 'Sir you put an end to [an/all›] all argument when you introduce [a man/your opponent›]

---

⁵ By the stage of the revises, this blank had been replaced with six asterisks. JB's journal entry for 26 March 1776 identifies the physician as William Butter (1726–1805), M.D., of Derby. For a detailed biographical account, see Hill-Powell iii. 467–68.

⁶ In the revises this paragraph begins 'Next day we talked of', the compositor having misread JB's 'Next day'—intended as a substitution for 'On Wednesday 27 March' (see line 21)—as belonging to this passage on Lord Mansfield.

⁷ The alternative is resolved by the printing of 'feel the want of them' in the revises.

your opponent himself. Have you no better manners? [That you want.⟩] There is *your* want.'   [The gentleman apologised by saying he mentioned/had mentioned/*undeciphered words*⟩] I apologised by saying I had mentioned him as an instance of one who wanted as little as any man in the world, and yet perhaps
5   might receive some additional lustre from [dress/fine clothes⟩] dress.

Appendix

A Provisional List of *Errata* in Volume 1

Frontispiece. The corrector's note alluded to in the editorial note beneath the illustration was cut off in the reproduction. It reads: 'The above was the first Master pulled in H. Baldwin's Own Printing Office. Unionstreet. Bridge Street Blackfriars. Monday 9 Nov. 1789'.

p. xvii, Appendices, H. *Delete misprinted initial quotation mark*
Illustrations. for Title-page for the first edition *read* Proof-sheet of an early version of the title-page for the first edition

p. xix, last line of text. *Delete misprinted initial quotation mark*

p. xx, n. 3. Making of the *should be italic*

p. xxxi, *l.* 7. *Delete misprinted initial quotation mark*

p. xxxviii, *l.* 2 from foot. *For* simultaneously *read* soon after

Facsimile pages of the manuscript (following p. xxxix). Page 8 should have been printed on the right and the opposite unnumbered page on the left. See Introduction, p. xxii.

p. 127, n. 7. *For* p. *read* pp.

p. 130, n. 6. *For* decipherable *read* deciphered

p. 197, n. 10. *For* 1732 *read* 1723

p. 208, n. 5, *l.* 2. *Delete misprinted comma*

p. 232, n. 8, last line. *For* has been *read* was

p. 254, *l.* 7. *Supply missing terminal hooked caret*

p. 303, n. 8. *For* 4–11 *read* 3–10

p. 349, n. 2. *For* is now owned by *read* was acquired by the late

p. 365, Appendix E, heading. *For misprinted* Bowell's *read* Boswell's

p. 383, last line. *Delete* 21

p. 395, n. to page 53 *l.* 14. *For l.* 1 *read* p. 52 *l.* 26

p. 398, n. to p. 62 *ll.* 16–2. *For* post *read* ante

APPENDIX

p. 400, n. to p. 70 *l.* 15. *Delete misprinted initial quotation mark before* dined

p. 404, second n. to p. 85 *l.* 13. *Within the quotation SJ's inscription should be set off by double quotation marks*

p. 408, second n. to p. 95 *l.* 18. *For* 93 *read* 79

p. 416, n. to p. 122 *l.* 34. *For* 24–28 *read* 5–9
n. to p. 123 *ll.* 5–9. *For* 12 *read* 34

p. 421, n. to p. 132 *l.* 13. *Delete misprinted* vc *before* himself

p. 427, first n. to p. 147 *l.* 23. *In place of the misprinted apostrophe before* Sir *supply double initial quotation marks*

p. 429, n. to p. 152 *l.* 1. *For* ω *read* ὡ

p. 433, n. to p. 161 *l.* 23. *For* p. 172 *l.* 10 *read* p. 153 *l.* 16

p. 445, n. to p. 192 *l.* 15. *For* l. 7 *read* ll. 13–14

p. 460, first n. to p. 235 *l.* 20. *Replace misprinted terminal italic bracket with roman bracket*
n. to p. 236 *l.* 30. *Delete misprinted apostrophe before and misprinted* l *after* Shakespeare

p. 466, n. to p. 253 *l.* 15. *For* 288 *read* 253

p. 468, n. to p. 260 *l.* 14. *Delete repeated* first draft
first n. to p. 262 *l.* 11. *for* 8 *read* 7

p. 469, n. to p. 464 *l.* 11. *Delete* l.
first n. to p. 264 *l.* 17. *For* 15 *read* 14

p. 470, second n. to p. 266 *l.* 7. *For* 13 *read* 4

p. 471, n. to p. 268 *l.* 5. *Within the quotation* heaven's mercy *should be set off by double quotation marks*
n. to p. 268 *l.* 8. *For* 302 *read* 265

p. 472, n. to p. 270 *l.* 23. *The line reference should read* 25 *and a* 25 *should read* l. 24

p. 474, n. to p. 274 *l.* 20. *Change single quotation mark to double in the second line*

p. 480, n. to p. 287 *l.* 29. Vicar of Wakefield *should be set off by double quotation marks*

p. 482, n. to p. 295 *l.* 6. *For* 340 *read* 294

p. 489, second n. to p. 318 *l.* 7. London *should be set off by double quotation marks*

APPENDIX

p. 490, first n. to p. 319 *l.* 17. Douglas *should be set off by double quotation marks throughout note*

p. 494, n. to p. 331 *l.* 5. *Quotation marks before* Sir *should be double*

p. 501, n. to Frontispiece, *l.* 7 from foot. *Replace semicolon with colon*

p. 503, headnote, *l.* 2. *Delete misprinted hyphen*

p. 503, Augusta of Saxe-Gotha etc. *Delete entry here and enter as* Princess Dowager of Wales (Augusta of Saxe-Gotha) etc. *on p.* 515

p. 504, Brett. *For* 24 *read* 1724

p. 505, Cave, Edward, *l.* 2. *Delete misprinted hyphen*

p. 505, Davis. *For* Lockyear *read* Lockyer

p. 506, Des Maizeaux. *Transpose* 1666–1745 *and* Pierre

p. 507, Hawkins, Sir John, *l.* 6. *Insert* 'Ad *after* translation of
l. 7. *Insert* (second) *before* n. 3,

p. 508, Johnson, Rev. John. *Insert comma after* John

p. 511, Levett, Robert. *For* Levett *read* Levett or Levet

p. 511, LIFE OF SAMUEL JOHNSON, 1st col., *ll.* 7–6 from foot. *For* a composite … mss *read* its composite structure

p. 517, Thornton, *l.* 2. *Delete hyphen*
Warton, Rev.Thomas, *l.* 3 from end of article. *Delete misprinted hyphen*

p. 518, Whitehead. *Delete misprinted comma after* Poet

p. 518, Williams, Anna. *Change* appearance in *Life to* JB plans to introduce in *Life*

page 1

1   Both in] Third edition, 'In'.

11   he] Third edition, 'Dr. Johnson'.

14–15 wrote to him frequently ... single letter in return] Changed in the revises to 'He did not favour me with a letter for more than two years.'

20   Poetry'] There is an undeciphered deletion interlined above this word.

page 2

1   prevented him] Accidentally omitted in the first draft; supplied in revision.

1–2   a great] Changed by JB in the revises to 'a very great'.

2   Dedications] MS orig. 'dedications'.

2–3   After all the diligence ... my inquiries.] Changed in the first edition to 'Some of these, the persons who were favoured with them are unwilling should be mentioned, from a too anxious apprehension, as I think, that they might be suspected of having received larger assistance; and some, after all the diligence I have bestowed, have escaped my inquiries'.

3   my inquiries] MS orig. 'me'.

3   He told me] Changed in the first edition to 'He told me, a great many years ago,'.

6   providing only that] Printed in the revises 'provided'.

9   from] Added in the same draft.

9   ceased from writing] Printed in the revises 'omitted to write'.

13   my letters] Printed in the revises 'the greater part of mine'.

18   visit] In the revises JB changed 'visit' to 'Tour', then had second thoughts, and reverted to the original word by writing 'stet'.

page 3

17–18 it. Come] Originally run on; marked for new paragraph in revision.

23   novelty] Inserted by JB in a space left blank in the copy.

24   feasted] Inserted by JB in a space left blank in the copy.

page 4

5   very] Omitted in the revises.

11–12 Voltaire in a conversation with me had distinguished ...] False start, 'Voltaire had distinguished to me in'.

12   Pope and Dryden] MS orig. 'Pope's couplet and Dryden's sentence'.

22   Much no doubt ... expression] MS orig. 'It was no doubt submitted to his friendly revision'. JB seems to have abandoned this beginning altogether and started the sentence afresh with 'Much no doubt ...'.

23   conversing] Printed in the revises 'conversation'.

28   distinguish] MS orig. 'mark'.

page 5

7–8   bear ... verses] MS orig. 'are a small portion of the whole which consists of 438 lines'.

13   quite] Omitted in the revises.

15   at a loss with] Printed in the revises 'perplexed by'.

15   here as with] Printed in the revises 'as by'.

17   rebellion] Printed in the revises 'in the year 1514'.

20   *corona ferrea candescente*] A later addition.

19–21 the punishment ... his head] Printed in the revises '*George*, not *Luke*, was punished by his head being encircled with a red hot iron crown: *corona condescente ferrea coronatur'.*

21 was exercised on] MS orig. 'occurs in'.
22 King] A later addition.
23 me by] False start, 'me with'.
23 at the same time favoured] False start, 'at the same time marked'.
25 four last] Third edition, 'last four'.
29–30 sky. Talking of education] Originally run on; marked for new paragraph in revision.
36–37 lectures.' At night] Originally run on; marked for new paragraph in revision.
37 met] Printed in the revises 'supped with'.
38 Original Place] Printed in the revises 'Original Place of meeting'.

page 6

3–4 lemonade. I told him] Originally run on; marked for new paragraph in revision.
27–28 small. Dr. Johnson] Originally run on; marked for new paragraph in revision.

page 7

6 a Lawyer] First draft, 'an Advocate'.
8 beneath you] First draft, 'beneath/below'.
11 I] The deleted 'I' is preceded by an undeciphered word which was first partially erased and then deleted.
17 if you do] Added in the same draft.
17–18 court. He said] Run on in the first draft; marked for new paragraph in revision.
21 A youthful passion] MS orig. 'Youthful passions'. Although he added 'A' to the beginning of the sentence, JB initially failed to change 'passions' to 'passion', a change here corrected.
22–23 encouraged. I] Originally run on; marked for new paragraph in revision.
23 talked] Printed in the revises 'introduced the subject'.
25 they] MS orig. 'these'.
26–27 fortuitous. I] Originally run on; marked for new paragraph in revision.
28 by] Added in the same draft.
32 having been mentioned] First draft 'had been mentioned'.
32–33 some remarks ... Italy] First draft 'and I quoted Mr. Wilkes for something'.
36 15 Febry] Printed in the revises 'the 15th of February'.
36–37 old and intimate] Changed by JB in the revises to 'old and most intimate'.
37–38 *undeciphered word*] Perhaps the letter 'H', as if JB had originally intended to begin the next sentence with 'Having' instead of 'I having'.
31, 38 can.' I having] Originally run on; marked for new paragraph in revision.
40 passed] Printed in the revises 'spent'.
40 said] Changed by JB in the revises to 'said (sarcastically)'.
45 if you are to talk] Printed erroneously in the revises 'if you are talk' and then changed by JB to 'if you are talking'.

page 8

3 Sir] Added in the same draft, 'Sir' is preceded by 'that', which has been deleted.
3 his] Printed in the revises 'but that his'.
12 'Why] Printed in the revises 'Why, Sir'.

13–14 them.' This violence⌉ Originally run on; marked for new paragraph in revision.

19 singularities⌉ MS 'in which however' deleted.

19 proofs rather⌉ MS orig. 'rather proofs'.

22 *Confession du Foi du Curé Savoyarde*⌉ Changed by Plymsell in the revises to 'Profession de Foi du Vicaire Savoyard'.

23 mind⌉ Printed in the revises 'man'.

25–26 though ... doubts⌉ A later addition.

26 state of mind⌉ MS orig. 'principle'.

26 sometimes⌉ A later addition.

26–27 which after ... candid man⌉ Printed in the revises 'to be viewed with pity rather than with anger'.

27 Johnson⌉ MS orig. 'he said'.

29–35 the other.' I⌉ Originally run on; marked for new paragraph in revision.

31 the advice⌉ MS orig. 'a consolatory'.

36–37 than ourselves.⌉ In the revises, JB changed 'than ourselves' to 'than we are', then had second thoughts and reverted to the original wording.

38 worse than they are⌉ MS orig. 'beneath them'.

page 9

10 teised⌉ MS 'with' deleted.

13 Why⌉ In the revises, a word was added and then deleted after 'Why'. It has not been deciphered.

16 Sir. The⌉ MS orig. 'Sir, the'.

28 while now⌉ Printed in the revises 'while our friend, now'.

page 10

3–4 wonder.' He⌉ Originally run on; marked for new paragraph in revision.

7 up and down⌉ Added in the same draft.

8 wrote⌉ Printed in the revises and the first edition, 'have wrote', but changed for the second edition to 'have written'.

18 wrote⌉ Printed in the revises 'mentioned'.

18 to him⌉ Printed in the revises 'to him in a letter'.

22 to him⌉ Omitted in the third edition.

25 Thesis⌉ MS orig. 'Theses'.

30 Theses⌉ The copyist, Margaret Boswell, originally wrote 'Thesis'. JB himself appears to have changed it to 'Theses'. In the revises, it is printed 'Thesis'.

33 not to urge⌉ In JB's hand.

page 11

4–5 dead. I have⌉ Originally run on by the copyist; marked for new paragraph in revision by JB.

6 enchain⌉ Written in JB's hand over another word, which has not been deciphered.

11 (*second*) have⌉ Omitted in the revises.

20 deliberations⌉ Printed in the revises 'deliberation'.

23 faculties⌉ Corrected by JB from 'faculty'.

27 perplexities⌉ Corrected by JB from 'perplexity'.

28 Vacancy⌉ Written in JB's hand over another word, which has not been deciphered.

29–30 *Haec sunt ... age.*⌉ Inserted in JB's hand.

page 12

14   Modo namq] Printed in the revises 'modo namque' and changed to 'in modo namque'.

20   his] Third edition, 'Johnson's'.

20   at this year Mr. Thrale's] Printed in the revises 'this year at Mr. Thrale's'.

22   now] Printed in the revises 'then'.

page 13

4   pieces] Omitted in the revises.

4   'Epitaph ... an Ode'] Printed in the revises '"Epitaph on Philips" "Translation of a Latin Epitaph on Sir Thomas Hanmer" and "Friendship an Ode"'.

4–5   there ... and] A later addition.

5   have in] False start, 'have see'. JB apparently intended 'seen'.

5   I have in his own handwriting 'The Ant'] Printed in the revises '"The Ant," a paraphrase from the Proverbs, of which I have a copy in his own hand-writing'.

8   them] Third edition, 'the pieces in this volume'.

12   on reading it] A later addition.

13   if it was not] Printed in the revises 'whether it was not his.'

15   repeating] A later addition.

18   'The Fountains'] False start, 'With such'.

18   fairy] A later addition.

22   But] Omitted in the revises.

28   justly] Added in the same draft.

29   in Scotland] Added in the same draft.

35   To Mr. William Drummond] Added and deleted by JB in the revises 'at Edinburgh'.

page 14

3   is] Printed in the revises 'be'.

25   the Revolution] Printed in the revises 'of the revolutions'.

28   desired] Changed in the revises to 'desire'.

page 15

13–14 The opposers ... to go on.] Printed in the revises 'The opponents of this pious scheme being made ashamed of their conduct, the benevolent undertaking was allowed to go on.'

16   now] Omitted in the revises.

21–22 for his genius ... misconduct] Printed in the revises 'by his genius, misfortunes, and misconduct'.

page 16

1   differed] Printed in the first edition 'disagreed'.

4   proved] Printed in the first edition 'ascertained'.

4   to Johnson] Added in the same draft.

4–5   Mr. Hervey ... to it] Printed in the revises 'in answer to it, Mr. Hervey printed'.

5   Dr.] A later addition.

16   expostulating] Printed in the revises 'remonstrating'.

22   by] Printed in the revises 'of'.

25   memorable] Printed in the revises 'remarkable'.

29   that splendid room] Printed in the revises 'those splendid rooms'.

30   numerous] MS 'and choice' deleted.

page 17

1–2   one of the librarians whom Dr. Johnson knew and esteemed⌉ Printed in the revises 'the librarian'.

3   convenience⌉ MS orig. 'comfort'.

5–6   leisure hours. His Majesty.⌉ Originally run on; marked for new paragraph in revision.

6   [these⟩]⌉ In EM's hand.

6   [his frequent⟩]⌉ In EM's hand.

7   he should be told⌉ Deleted and then marked 'stet' by EM.

8   next came⌉ Printed in the revises 'came next'.

8   [next visited⟩] next came to the library⌉ In EM's hand.

9   as soon as⌉ MS orig. 'when'.

9   fairly⌉ MS orig. 'fairly/once'.

9   on⌉ Added in the same draft.

12   then⌉ In EM's hand.

13   then⌉ Written and deleted by EM.

17   hastily⌉ In EM's hand.

18   a *del*⌉ JB's deleted 'a' is printed in the revises.

18–19   here is⌉ MS orig. 'heres'.

page 18

1   to Dr. Johnson⌉ Omitted in the printing of the revises.

7   sometimes⌉ Added in the same draft.

12   (*second*) at⌉ Omitted in the revises.

16   do⌉ MS orig. 'did'.

18   is⌉ MS orig. 'was'.

18   have⌉ MS orig. 'had'.

20   (*first*) then⌉ Omitted in the revises.

20   inquired⌉ In EM's hand.

20   The King then inquired⌉ Printed in the revises 'His Majesty enquired'.

page 19

4   written⌉ MS orig. 'done'.

12   whole⌉ Added in the same draft.

18   had not indeed neglected reading⌉ Omitted in the revises.

19   earlier⌉ Printed in the revises 'early'.

page 20

6   was⌉ Printed in the revises 'is'.

18–19   very ... Kings⌉ First draft, '[very partial when they characterise/speak of⟩] in their characters of'.

24   to be praised⌉ First draft, 'to praise'.

30   Henry the Second⌉ MS orig. 'Richard the Third'.

30   says⌉ MS orig. 'said'. Printed 'said' in the revises.

31   answered Johnson⌉ Printed in the revises '(answered Johnson)'.

page 21

1   easier⌉ Third edition, 'more easily'.

6   His Majesty⌉ Printed in the revises 'The King'.

8   mentioned⌉ In EM's hand.

8   (*second*) an⌉ MS orig. 'that'.

8   Dr. Hill⌉ MS orig. 'Dr. Hill's'.

8   Dr. Hill⌉ Printed in the revises 'that writer'.

8   objects⌉ MS orig. 'things'.
10   than by using one⌉ Added by EM.
10   (added Johnson)⌉ In EM's hand.
10–11 acquainted with microscopes⌉ MS orig. 'who has seen a microscope'.
11   of them⌉ Added in the same draft.
12   the object will appear⌉ In EM's hand.
19   down⌉ Omitted in the printing of the revises.
21   He⌉ In EM's hand.
21   therefore⌉ In EM's hand.
24   man⌉ MS orig. 'figure'.
26   talked⌉ MS orig. 'began to speak'.
30   on⌉ Added in the same draft.
37   that⌉ Added in the same draft.
43   arranging⌉ In EM's hand.
44   than formerly⌉ Added by EM.

page 22
2   undertake it⌉ In EM's hand.
6   During ... Interview⌉ Added in the same draft.
7   firm⌉ Added in the same draft.
8   which⌉ MS orig. 'such'.
8   used⌉ MS orig. 'practised'.
8   at⌉ JB first wrote 'at,' then deleted it and replaced it with 'in,' and finally
             deleted 'in' and reinstated 'at'.
9   then⌉ In EM's hand.
9–10   the King withdrew⌉ In EM's hand.
12   seen⌉ MS orig. 'met with'.
15   At Sir Joshua Reynolds's⌉ JB originally wrote 'At Sir Joshua Reynolds's,'
             then added 'Mr Langton informs me that at Sir Joshua Reynolds's,' then
             returned to his original wording.
17   interview⌉ Changed by JB in the revises to 'conversation'.
18   and⌉ In EM's hand.
19   him⌉ MS orig. 'Johnson'.
19   give⌉ Printed in the revises 'mention'.
20   with ... humour⌉ MS orig. 'very kindly'.
22   man⌉ MS orig. 'man's'.
25   particulars⌉ Printed in the revises 'circumstances'.
28   restrained from intemperance⌉ In EM's hand.
33   sate⌉ Perhaps JB intended 'sat'.
35   assigned⌉ In EM's hand.
40   chagrin and⌉ In EM's hand.
40   wch⌉ Omitted in the revises.
40   Dr. J.⌉ Printed in the revises 'Dr. Johnson'.
40–41 at the singular ... enjoyed⌉ In EM's hand.
42   sprung⌉ Changed in the revises to 'sprang'.

page 23
3   received ... him⌉ MS orig. 'did not receive a single letter'.
3   In 1767 I received no letter from him,⌉ Printed in the revises 'I received
             no letter from Johnson this year'.
4   he⌉ A later addition that replaced 'his'.
7   insight into⌉ Printed in the revises 'light as to'.
9   near/about⌉ Omitted in the revises.

11–12   as a harsh and savage character⌐ Printed in the revises 'as a man of a harsh and stern character'.
14   often found⌐ False start 'am[ong]'.
20   labours and attainments ... ⌐ MS ', as he compare' deleted.

page 24
4   science⌐ Printed in the revises 'sciences'.
7   scotch⌐ In correcting the revises, JB deleted 'scotch'; he later reinstated it by writing 'stet'.
9   might⌐ MS orig. 'may'.
11   could do no harm to⌐ MS orig. 'could not affect'.
17   of⌐ Added in the same draft.
17   in which ... as it was⌐ False start, 'he ⌄*undeciphered word*⌄ runs the paralel b.'
20   who are⌐ A later addition.
21   others⌐ MS orig. 'all'.
26   humour⌐ MS orig. 'merriment'.
32   at⌐ MS orig. 'gone to'.

page 25
3   my latinity⌐ Printed in the revises 'the Latinity of my Thesis'.
5   followed him⌐ MS orig. 'went'.
6   was⌐ False start 'shall'.
8   to me to Scotland⌐ MS 'the da' deleted.
10   with the circumstances of time and place⌐ Added in the same draft.
14   in continuation. I⌐ Originally run-on; marked for new paragraph in revision.
21   be⌐ Inadvertently omitted by JB.
23   (*second*) must be⌐ Added in the same draft.
23   thinking⌐ Printed in the revises 'supposing'.
24   arguments weak and inconclusive⌐ Printed in the revises 'arguments to be weak and inconclusive'.
25   to⌐ MS orig. 'before'.
36   therefore⌐ Added in the same draft.

page 26
12   prolix⌐ Omitted in the revises.
15   knew⌐ MS orig. 'could'. JB apparently intended originally to refer first to the 'man who could tell the hour' and then to the 'man who knew how a Watch was made'.
16   the hour⌐ MS orig. 'what o'clock'.
19   Fielding⌐ MS '[*undeciphered word*]' deleted.
20   his⌐ MS orig. 'the'.
25   used ... a saying⌐ First draft, 'gave it as his opinion'.
27   tendency⌐ Added in the same draft.
32   a higher ... perfection⌐ MS orig. 'higher attainments in Ethicks'.
34   exceedingly well⌐ Printed in the revises 'very happily'.
35   credulous account⌐ MS orig. 'foolish story'.
41   however talked of it and⌐ Added in the same draft.
43   of⌐ MS orig. 'from'.
43   (*second*) the⌐ Added in the same draft.
43   decide⌐ MS orig. 'give the cause'.
44   but⌐ Added in the same draft.

44   allowing⌝ Printed in the revises 'granting'.
45   to be⌝ MS orig. 'as'.

page 27

1   because⌝ MS orig. 'for this reason'.
1   very⌝ Added in the same draft.
3   sort of⌝ Printed in the revises 'kind of'.
7   troubled⌝ MS orig. 'plagued'.
9   literally/absolutely>]⌝ Added in the same draft.
20   He⌝ Printed in the revises 'Johnson'.
21   such⌝ Added in the same draft.
28   Of Guthrie⌝ False start, 'Talk'.
32   very very weary⌝ Printed in the revises 'very weary'.

page 28

2   your⌝ Italicized for emphasis in the revises.
2–3   native place.' His⌝ Originally run on; marked for new paragraph in revision.
13   and solicitous⌝ Printed in the revises 'and being solicitous'.
14   of Scotland⌝ Added in the same draft.
19–21   A Book ... was mentioned⌝ Printed in the revises 'An essay, written by Mr. Deane, a divine of the Church of England, maintaining the future life of brutes, by an explication of certain parts of the scriptures, was mentioned'.
26   a blow of reprehension⌝ MS orig. 'due chastisement'.
27   metaphysical⌝ Added in the same draft.
28   dont know⌝ MS orig. 'know not'.
29   rowling⌝ MS orig. 'growling'.
29   rowling⌝ Printed in the revises 'rolling,' a correction of the obsolete 'rowling'.
29   at ... eye⌝ Added in the same draft.
30   No⌝ Printed in the revises 'True'.
31   him⌝ Printed in the revises '*him*'.
32   up rose⌝ Printed in the revises 'rose up'.
39   center⌝ Here, as elsewhere, printed in the revises 'centre'. Although Johnson's *Dictionary* lists 'centre' as the correct spelling, the OED notes that 'center' was 'the prevalent spelling from the 16th to 18th c.'.

page 29

8   one⌝ Printed in the revises 'a scorpion'.
13   A number⌝ MS orig. 'Many'.
15   glowworm.⌝ Printed in the revises 'I am sorry I did not ask where it was to be found.' Presumably this sentence was inserted in the first set of proofs.
17   if⌝ Printed in the revises 'whether'.
17   Du Halde's China⌝ Printed in the revises 'Du Halde's account of China'.
20   He ... constitutes⌝ MS orig. 'He said confusion of progeny constituted'.
21   so⌝ Omitted in the revises.
25   would⌝ MS orig. 'should'.

page 30

6–7   dreaded ... talents⌝ Printed in the revises 'was afraid of her superiority of talents'.
8   you'll⌝ MS orig. 'thou'll'.
9   may be justified⌝ MS orig. 'was justified'.

10–15 He doubtless ... a blaze] A later addition.
31   go to back to] MS orig. 'be in'.
31   to go back to] Printed in the revises 'to go in' and then corrected by JB to 'to go to'.

page 31
3   was] Added in the same draft.
5   embracing him] Added in the same draft.
7   being published] MS orig. 'having published'.
8   if] Printed in the revises 'whether'.
11   especially if] Added in the same draft.
14   will] MS orig. 'please'.
16   universal] Printed in the revises '*universal*'.
17   indeed] Added in the same draft.
17   private] Printed in the revises '*private*'.
18   a] Omitted in the revises.
22   the Nation] MS orig. 'the people of England'.
25   inconveniences] Printed in the revises 'inconveniencies'.
34   [Paper Apart K]] In JB's hand.
35   in] MS orig. 'by'.
37   this] Changed in the revises to 'this pamphlet'.
38–39   gratify ... away] MS orig. 'keep/bring into more notice'.
39   away, if left to itself] Printed in the revises 'away of itself'.

page 32
2   farther] Changed by JB in the revises to 'further'.
2–3   had him now placed] Changed by JB in the revises to 'now placed him'.
8   Soon after this] Changed in the revises to 'Soon afterwards'.
9   There] Changed in the revises to 'They'.
10   Dr. ... Dromore] Added in the same draft.
13   but] MS 'he at' deleted.
22   but] False start, 'w'. Perhaps JB began to write 'when', then realized he had omitted 'but' and so wrote 'but' over the 'w' of 'when'.
31–32   his life. He] Originally run on; marked for new paragraph in revision.
32   old] Added in the same draft.
40   this man] In a single draft, JB started with 'him' which became 'this fellow' and ended as 'this man'.

page 33
2   tell us] MS orig. 'say'.
3   nor] Printed in the second edition 'or'.
5   is it] MS orig. 'it is'.
11–12   as ... Authour] Added in the same draft.
12   Some of us] MS orig. 'One or two of our number'.
12–13   by various arguments] MS orig. 'in different'. JB's first thought was apparently, 'in different ways'.
14   ability] MS orig. 'merit'.
16–17   is that to] MS orig. 'has that to do with'.
27   in presence of] MS orig. 'bef'. JB probably began to write 'before' and then changed his mind.
29   his punishment] MS orig. 'the matter'.
30   (*first*) over] Printed in the revises 'o'er'.
35   Alexander] Added in the same draft.

page 34

1   often] Changed in the revises to 'sometimes'.

3   men ... distinction] MS orig. 'literati'.

6–7   answered the Earl with a pleasing smile] Printed in the revises '(answered the Earl, with a smile)'.

8   To] MS orig. 'As'. Apparently a false start.

14   (*first*) his] Printed in the revises 'Johnson's'.

17   and devotional] Added in the same draft.

19   his] MS '[*undeciphered word*]' deleted.

20   character] MS orig. 'mind'.

21–22 Royal Academy] Printed in the second edition 'Royal Academy of Arts in London'.

22   had] Printed in the second edition 'had now'.

25   this] Changed in the revises to 'the'.

25–28 In the course ... Letter] Printed in the revises 'In the course of the year he wrote some letters to Mrs. Thrale, passed some part of the summer at Oxford and at Litchfield, and when at Oxford wrote the following letter:'.

page 35

7   Autumn] MS 'very desireous' added and deleted in the same draft.

8   going] Added in the same draft.

11   my] MS orig. 'me'.

14   Stratford upon Avon] Added in the same draft.

24   dies] Printed in the revises 'dyes'.

24   their] False start, 'co'.

page 36

1   which] 'They' appears above 'which', a sign that JB briefly considered beginning a new sentence at this point. Though JB forgot to delete the word, it was (correctly) passed over by the compositor.

3   a less ardent desire for literary fame] Printed in the revises 'less ardent feelings'.

13   histories] A correction, perhaps by JB, written over 'history'.

14   deligh[t]ful] MS orig. 'entertaining'. The copyist corrected this by writing 'delighful' above 'entertaining'.

23   be very unwilling] A correction, perhaps by JB, written over several undeciphered words.

24   (*second*) you] The insertion is in JB's hand.

28   is a long time] Omitted by the copyist, this phrase was reinserted by JB.

29   ever] A correction of 'even', perhaps by JB.

33   with his company] Added in the same draft.

page 37

4   his brave countrymen] MS orig. 'the brave islanders'.

8   attend] MS orig. 'wait'.

13   blended] MS orig. 'melted'.

16   behaviour. I] Originally run on; marked for new paragraph in revision.

18–19 them.' He] Originally run on; marked for new paragraph in revision.

22   cases of necessity] MS orig. 'exigencies'.

23   administrate] Changed by JB in the revises to 'administer'.

25   offer ... exemption] MS orig. 'grant exemption'.

36–38 for ... me] MS orig. 'for life appears to me'.

41   that of other countries] MS orig. 'others'.

42   30 September] Printed in the revises '30th of September'.

page 38

1   such] Added in the same draft.

1   on't] Printed in the revises 'of't'.

1–2   It ... instruct] MS orig. 'It cannot entertain. It cannot instruct'.

11   any] MS orig. 'every'.

16   my] Added in the same draft.

18   abstractly] Changed in the revises by JB to 'abstractedly'.

22   I ... say] Added in the same draft.

24   rest of the] Added in the same draft.

30   promised] MS orig. 'proposed to'.

30   instructive] MS orig. 'good'.

page 39

7   sensible and] Added in the same draft.

8–9   Sir Thomas Overbury] MS orig. '*Sir Thomas Overbury*'.

10   intelligence] MS orig. 'wit'.

17   censured] MS orig. 'found fault with'.

17   marrying a second time] MS orig. 'making/entering into a second marriage'.

18   wife] Printed in the revises 'he said'.

19   not] MS orig. 'never'.

20   to] MS orig. 'at'.

23   So] 'With' del. above 'So'.

26–27 a promise of Mrs. Johnson] MS orig. 'Mrs. Johnson's promise'.

page 40

8–9   He ... Maid] MS orig. 'He has married a Widow. He might have had a
Maid'.

10   had the pleasure of seeing] MS orig. 'seen'.

21   6] Printed in the revises '6th'.

23   pleasing] MS orig. 'valuable'.

24   tempered by] MS orig. 'mixed'.

25   the care of] MS orig. 'venerated by'.

26–27 happy. He] Originally run on; marked for new paragraph in revision.

29   I, having] False start, 'Talkin'.

35–36 perfection. I] Originally run on; marked for new paragraph in revision.

38–1   them. Mrs. Thrale] Originally run on; marked for new paragraph in
revision.

page 41

2   said] In the revises, two words (possibly 'of him') added and deleted after
'said'.

6   body] Printed in the revises 'one'.

11–12 deserved praise. Mrs. Thrale] Originally run on; marked for new paragraph in revision.

12   for] MS orig. 'at'.

20   as a poet] Added in the same draft.

21   sooth] MS orig. 'console'.

22   his friends] Printed in the revises 'us'.

26–27 of Johnson] Added in the same draft.

28   Johnson] False start, 'he'.

31   which] Omitted in the revises.
32   or] Printed in the revises 'and'.
40   yet] Added in the same draft.

page 42

1   the] Printed in the revises 'their'.
2   They might] False start, 'In twenty years Sir'.
4   He] MS orig. 'His powerful imagination'.
5   On ... 10 October] False start, 'On the 10 October'.
8   one] Added in the same draft.
8   one of each other] Printed in the revises 'of each other'.
11   Upon Johnson's] False start, 'It was a most'.
15   language] Printed in the revises 'languages'.
15   notions] MS orig. 'ideas'.
16   people] MS orig. 'country'.
17   direct] Added in the same draft.
22   Sir] Added in the same draft.
23   Spirit] MS orig. 'prevailing Spirit'.
30   as ... life] MS orig. 'in real life'.
31   That] MS orig. 'This'.
34   lies] MS orig. 'lyes'.

page 43

5   passé] MS orig. 'passè'.
6   prevalu] Printed in the revises 'prevalue'.
6   ‹ montagnes] MS orig. 'montaignes'.
7   compagne] MS orig. 'compaigne'.
9   immediately] A later addition.
13   allways] MS orig. 'in general'.
17–18   *l'homme d'epee*. He] Originally run on; marked for new paragraph in revision.
18   He] Printed in the revises 'Dr. Johnson'.
20   on't] Printed in the revises 'of't'.
21   16] Printed in the revises '16th'.
22–23   Mr. Garrick] Added in the same draft.
29   hour that was fixed] Changed by EM in the revises to 'appointed hour'.
33   answered] False start, 'sai'.
33   answered Johnson] Printed in the revises 'answered Johnson with a delicate humanity'.
34   There was a delicate humanity in this observation.] Omitted in the revises.
37   that passion] Printed in the revises 'such impressions'.

page 44

5   could] MS orig. 'might'.
5–6   a colour. When] Originally run on; marked for new paragraph in revision.
8   those of] Added in the same draft.
15   thou] Printed in the revises '*thou*'.
16–17   as a peculiar circumstance] Added in the same draft.
20   his] Added in the same draft.
22   his] Changed by EM in the revises to 'some fine'.
30   must not] MS orig. 'is not to'.

page 45

1   only] MS orig. 'but'.

6   the night] MS orig. 'the field'.

10   Someone] MS orig. 'Somebody'.

11   diminished] MS orig. 'minute'.

28   to be] Added in the same draft.

28   he would] MS orig. 'he'd'.

30   though] MS orig. 'but'.

31–32 no character. I] Originally run on; marked for new paragraph in revision.

35   attacked] MS orig. 'affected to attack'.

38   provoked the lash of wit] JB crossed out this phrase but then reinserted by writing 'stet' in the left margin.

38   cannot complain that] Originally JB wrote 'cannot complain of'. He apparently changed his mind immediately about this wording, deleted 'of', and replaced it with 'that'.

43   by ... farther] Added in the same draft.

43   farther] Printed in the revises 'further'.

page 46

1   one] MS orig. 'a'.

4   And] MS orig. 'But'.

7   in] Printed in the revises 'on'.

10   slighting] JB apparently briefly considered changing course here, for he crossed out 'slighting'. He obviously thought better of it, however, for he then wrote it again and carried on as originally planned.

10   considered] Printed in the revises 'remembered'.

10   let it be considered that] MS orig. 'this'.

21   cried] MS orig. 'said'.

29   which] Printed in the revises 'whom'.

33   vindicating] Printed in the revises 'to vindicate', and then altered to 'vindicated'.

35   the merit of] Omitted in the printing of the revises.

37   saying] Printed in the revises 'saying (with reference to Voltaire)'.

page 47

8–9   *Essay on the*] Added in the same draft.

10   depends] MS orig. 'depend', the consequence of incomplete alternative phrasing.

19   important] Added in the same draft.

22   The ... turn] Added in the same draft.

23   eminence] False start, 'cons' (for 'consequence') deleted before 'eminence'.

24   how] Printed in the revises 'how it happened that'.

29   much] Added in the same draft.

29   much] Omitted in the revises.

40   not] MS orig. 'never'.

40   Shakespeare] MS orig. 'Shakspeare'.

page 48

2   for instance] MS orig. 'is'.

3   No] Printed in the revises 'Indeed'.

7   entertaining] 'a' deleted before 'very'.

14   would] MS orig. 'did'.

14   him ... end⌉ MS orig. 'his Ode out'.

16   that⌉ MS orig. 'how'.

20   Man⌉ MS orig. 'us all' deleted before 'Man'.

23   conduct himself⌉ MS orig. 'behave'.

24   know not⌉ MS orig. 'am uncertain'.

26–27 myself. Talking of⌉ Originally run on; marked for new paragraph in revision.

33   were⌉ MS orig. 'had committed'.

33   apprehended⌉ MS orig. 'taken'.

38   he⌉ MS orig. 'you'.

40   yet⌉ MS orig. 'but'.

40   them⌉ MS orig. 'those friends'.

42–1 the mind. I⌉ Originally run on; marked for new paragraph in revision.

page 49

4   would⌉ Changed by EM in the revises to 'might'.

4   him⌉ MS orig. 'Baretti'.

6   true⌉ Omitted in the revises.

7   (first) or⌉ Printed in the revises 'and'.

9   himself⌉ Added in the same draft.

11   those⌉ MS orig. 'these'.

14   And Sir⌉ Omitted in the revises.

16   pay⌉ Printed in the revises 'pay'.

16, 19 feeling.' Boswell⌉ Originally run on; marked for new paragraph in revision.

22   that of⌉ Added in the same draft.

25   broke⌉ Changed by EM in the revises to 'broken'.

31   Sir⌉ Added in the same draft.

33   readily⌉ MS orig. 'soon'.

36   pretty coarse jocularity⌉ Printed in the revises 'coarse jocularity'.

39   sterling wit⌉ Printed in the revises 'some sterling wit'.

45   a man who was for years⌉ Printed in the revises 'a man who for years'.

34–1 before him. 'Buchanan⌉ Originally run on; marked for new paragraph in revision.

page 50

1   Buchanan⌉ Changed in the revises to 'Buchanan (he observed)'.

6   does not refute⌉ MS orig. 'is not against'.

7   (third) and⌉ Printed in the revises 'who'.

8   three⌉ MS orig. 'two'.

8   tells me⌉ MS orig. 'says'.

9   I should laugh at him⌉ Added in the same draft.

10   do⌉ An inadvertent omission in the first draft, 'do' was added by JB at a later stage.

18   October 20⌉ MS orig. '20 October'.

19   Mr.⌉ MS orig. 'Signor'.

20   having⌉ MS orig. 'had'.

20   street⌉ MS 'and' deleted.

20   at the Old Bailey⌉ Added in the same draft.

22   aweful⌉ Added in the same draft.

22   Sessions⌉ MS orig. 'Session'.

22   Sessions House⌉ Printed in the second edition 'Sessions-House, emphatically called JUSTICE HALL'.

23   due⌉ MS orig. 'much'.

29   tavern] Added in the same draft.
33   be entertained] MS orig. 'live'.
34   entertain] MS orig. 'have'.
34   very] Added in the same draft.
35–36 whom he exposes] Added in the same draft.
36–37 action.' Talking] Originally run on; marked for new paragraph in revision.
39   for] Printed in the revises 'from'.
39   trade] MS orig. 'it'.
42   foreign] Added in the same draft.

page 51
6   grow] Added in the same draft.
7   are] Printed in the revises 'being'.
8–9   no growing weary] MS orig. 'no wearying'.
16   better.] Changed by JB in the revises to 'less'.
17   he fancies so] MS orig. 'that is'.
18   sufficient] MS orig. 'much'.
20   down] MS orig. 'in'.
22   Dr.] Added in the same draft.
23   willingly drank] MS orig. 'was willing to drink'.
25–26 peevish temper. There] Originally run on; marked for new paragraph in revision.

page 52
16   Sir] Added in the same draft.
19   He seemed ... subject] JB made two tentative false starts here. He first wrote and crossed out 'Johnson'. He then wrote and crossed out 'He seemed and no wonder as may well be supposed'.
33   makes] JB inadvertently wrote 'make' here.
34   this] MS orig. 'the'.
35   Would] False start, 'Why'.
39–40 about that.' *Boswell*] Originally run on; marked for new paragraph in revision.
40   what is called] Added in the same draft.

page 53
4   Empire] MS orig. 'nation'.
18   now] Omitted in the revises.
19   the raising of] MS orig. 'raise'.
19   plentiful and] Added in the same draft.
22   disturb] MS orig. 'spoil'.
24   Why] MS orig. 'Sir'.
24   Why] Changed in the revises to 'But'.
25   But] Changed in the revises to 'For'.
27   (*second*) land] MS orig. 'it'.

page 54
4   reason] MS orig. 'argue'.
5   only] Omitted in the revises.
5   cannot] Printed in the revises 'can't'.
5–6   were ... agree] MS orig. 'that they could not agree'.
10   quit] MS orig. 'leave'.
20   not] An inadvertent omission corrected by JB at a later stage of revision.

23   if] Printed in the revises 'whether'.
23   Roman Catholick] 'was' deleted before 'should'.
29   upon honour I] Printed in the revises 'I really'.
32   an apostolical institution] MS orig. 'apostolical'.
34   of prayer] Added in the same draft.
34   are to] MS orig. 'can'.
35   are] Added in the same draft.
40   with ... be] MS orig. 'as little positively as could be'.
40   Sir] Added in the same draft.

page 55
2   the Deity] MS orig. 'GOD'.
7   do] Inadvertently omitted by JB in the first draft, 'do' was added later.
7   how] MS orig. 'why'.
10   farther] Printed in the revises 'further'.
11   from] MS 'denying its' and 'in' deleted.
15   and] Added in the same draft.
16–17 asunder. I proceeded] Originally run on; marked for new paragraph in
       revision.
20–21 merit being] MS orig. 'deserve to be'.
27   The] False start, 'But'.
41   thus] Added in the same draft.
41   mention] MS orig. 'throw out'.
42   I might hear] Added in the same draft. Probably an inadvertent omission
       in the first place.
43   here] Added in the same draft.

page 56
1   (*second*) record] Printed in the revises 'mention'.
2   Roman] Added in the same draft.
3   was exerting himself] MS orig. 'wished'.
4   convert] MS orig. 'man'.
5   (*second*) He] MS orig. 'It'.
36   drove] Printed in the revises 'drives'.
39   in passion] Printed in the revises 'in a passion'.

page 57
3   must be] Printed in the revises 'must be so'.
3–4   whine.' I attempted] Originally run on; marked for new paragraph in
       revision.
6   agitation] MS orig. 'tumult'.
9–10   tomorrow.' I went] Originally run on; marked for new paragraph in
       revision.
12   (*second*) the] MS orig. 'a'.
14   stating] MS 'acknowledging' added and deleted in the same draft.
17   that day] MS orig. 'to=day'.
17   call] Printed in the revises 'call on him'.
18   said I] Added in the same draft.
22–23 or his own reflection] Added in the same draft.
23   him] MS orig. 'his ferocity'.
24–25 the conversation. He] Originally run on; marked for new paragraph in
       revision.
25   by] MS orig. 'in'.

26   That his Creation⌉ Changed by EM in the revises to 'That in his "Creation" he'.

page 58

1   a⌉ MS 'Writer of' deleted.

4   incidental⌉ MS orig. 'incident which'.

4–5   I may be perhaps thought⌉ Printed in the revises 'perhaps, I may be thought'.

8   *humour*⌉ Printed in the revises 'humour'.

8   good=*natured*⌉ Printed in the revises 'good-natured'.

11   it up⌉ MS orig. 'amends'.

11   making it up⌉ Printed in the revises 'reconciliation'.

14   and that the other was now⌉ Printed in the revises 'and the other as now'.

15   10⌉ Printed in the revises '10th'.

16   at⌉ MS orig. 'to'.

20   10th⌉ Printed in the revises 'tenth of'.

31   Song of mine on Matrimony⌉ MS orig. 'Song entitled a Matrimonial Thought'. After deleting his original version of this phrase, JB made a false start by writing 'Song of mine wh' before settling on the final version as transcribed.

32   set to Musick⌉ Second edition, 'set to music by the very ingenious Mr. Dibden'.

page 59

10   their⌉ MS orig. 'a'.

11   virtually⌉ Added in the same draft.

15   justly⌉ Added in the same draft.

17   Pamphlet⌉ MS 'and I believe he really thought so' added and deleted in the same draft.

17   But⌉ False start, 'That'.

17   But⌉ MS 'he' deleted.

18   constitutional⌉ Added in the same draft.

19   offensive⌉ A later addition.

24   in general⌉ Added in the same draft.

25   and contract⌉ Added in the same draft.

28   at that time⌉ Added in the same draft.

28   at that time with great avidity⌉ Printed in the revises 'with great avidity at the time'.

28–29 and ... composition⌉ Added in the same draft.

29   this Pamphlet⌉ Printed in the revises 'it'.

31   people⌉ MS 'is but too evident' deleted.

page 60

2   pays a grateful⌉ False start, 'expre'.

3   railers⌉ Printed in the revises 'rulers', this misreading of the MS was not corrected in the first three editions.

3–4   have endeavoured⌉ MS orig. 'attacked not'.

7   the faction⌉ MS orig. 'it'.

11   which ... Johnson's⌉ Added in the same draft.

12   care⌉ MS 'special' added and deleted in the same draft.

16   his present Majesty] MS orig. 'George III'.

19   Protector⌉ MS orig. 'friend'.

20   The following⌉ False start, 'Take in from Prayers'.

20   minute⌉ MS 'of his' deleted.

page 61

16 During this year] False start, 'As during'.

17 without any coldness] In the original version of MS 356, JB settled on this phrase after altering 'without any difference or any offence' to 'without any cause of difference or any offence.'

page 62

1 merely] The first draft of the original MS 356 qualified 'merely' with 'I suppose'. This was a same-draft addition which was deleted in that very draft and hence was not carried over to the new version of MS 356.

1 I ... London] Added in the same draft.

3 To supply... present] False start, 'I shall ther'. JB probably intended 'therefore'.

11 upon] Added in the same draft.

13 accept of] False start (?'su') interlined above (a rejected alternative to 'accept of').

13 limited] Added in the same draft.

24 still] Omitted in the revises.

24–25 in this Pamphlet of its miseries] Printed in the revises 'of its miseries in this pamphlet'.

32 argumentative] 'liter[ary]' deleted before 'argumentative'.

page 63

5 Mr] Added in the same draft.

9 a flat unmeaning addition] False start, 'beat out into'.

15 when] First draft, 'as'.

17 to be employed] First draft, 'to be employed/to have an active share in political negociation'.

18 be ... getting] First draft, 'obtain for him/be the means of his getting'.

page 64

41 at a later period of his life] MS orig. 'as late in his life or later'.

page 65

2 the greatest figure there] Changed from 'a great figure of'.

5 gone] Printed in the revises 'come'.

7 now] MS orig. 'yet'.

17 that] Added in the same draft.

22 speaking] Added in the same draft.

24 in his opinion] Added in the same draft.

25 one who is himself so eminent] False start, 'an', apparently with the intention of writing 'an eminent orator ...'.

26–27 It was confirmed ... Johnson] MS orig. 'Dr. Scott of the Commons said he'.

28 From] False start, 'I have'.

29 William] Added in the same draft.

32 acknowledged that he rose] False start, 'he acknowledged that when he rose'.

34 however] Added in the same draft.

34 'tried his hand'] Printed in the revises '"tried his hand" in parliament'.

35 Ministry] MS orig. 'Ministers'.

36 tried his hand] Printed in the revises 'tried his hand in parliament'.

37–38 I ... discontinued] JB made two false starts here. He first wrote 'I at length broke through'. This phrase was then crossed out and replaced by 'I renew', which in turn was replaced by the final version transcribed in the main text.

page 66

1 I gave him] False start, 'Proceed to give'.
1 I gave him] Printed in the revises 'In the subsequent part of this letter, I gave him'.
2–3 promised ... Hebrides] MS orig. 'I will promise to attend him to the highlands or even to the Hebrides'.
9 last letter and his] Added in the same draft.
10 at] False start, 'in the'.
11 In] In EM's hand.
11 I again wrote to him] In EM's hand.
12 informing him] In EM's hand.
14 In his religious record] False start, 'To Dr. Joh'. Presumably this refers to the same potential insertion as above (see *ante* p. 66 n. 4).
14 than usual] Added in the same draft.
19 (*first*) as] Omitted in the revises.
24 Easter Eve] MS 'his judgement imperceptibly corrects the too great anxiety of his apprehensions' added and deleted in the same draft.

page 67

6 Rambler] Printed in the revises 'the Rambler'.
7 as to this] Printed in the revises 'on this subject'.
16 Feb. 27. 1772.] A later addition. JB had originally placed the date after Johnson's name at the very end of the letter.
16 etc.] A later addition.
16 Sir ... servant] JB originally deleted this phrase, but later reinstated it by writing 'stet' in the margin.
24 some] MS orig. 'a'.
25 that of] Omitted in the revises.

page 68

1 21] Printed in the revises '21st of'.
1 to be] Printed in the revises 'to find myself'.
1–2 Dr. Johnson's] Printed in the revises 'my friend's'.
2 Francis] Added in the same draft.
3 to him] Omitted in the revises.
4 He] Printed in the revises 'Dr. Johnson'.
6 (meaning to support the Schoolmaster)] Printed in the revises '(alluding to the cause of the schoolmaster)'.
13 own] Added in the same draft.
15 No] Omitted in the revises.
19 on] Printed in the revises 'concerning'.

page 69

17 debate arrose] MS orig. 'conversation ensued'.
19 When Dr. Johnson] False start, 'Mr. Stock'.
27 where she was born] MS orig. 'her country'.
30 mysterious] Added in the same draft.
42–43 buffoonery.' He] Originally run on; marked for new paragraph in revision.
44 said he] Added in the same draft.
43–44 He recommended ... exhibition] Omitted in the revises.
45 March 23] MS orig. '23 March'.
45 fourth] MS orig. 'new'.

page 70

2   for] MS orig. 'to'.

4–5   if it could be allowed to be] Printed in the revises 'it to be'.

5   legitimate] Added in the same draft.

16   on that account] MS orig. 'for severity/on that account'.

21   upon] Printed in the revises 'on'.

22   as I had taken a good deal of pains] Printed in the revises 'having myself taken some pains'.

27   from] Printed in the revises 'from the'.

33   the] Added in the same draft.

30–35   The prim prating ... alike] Printed in the revises 'A studied and factitious pronunciation, which requires perpetual attention, and imposes perpetual constraint, is exceedingly disgusting. A small intermixture of provincial peculiarities may, perhaps, have an agreeable effect, as the notes of different birds concur in the harmony of the grove, and please more than if they were all exactly alike.'

36   a] MS orig. 'the'. After deleting 'the', JB wrote and deleted 'a'. He apparently did not deliberate long about another possible wording, for he promptly wrote 'a' again and carried on with the sentence.

39   was] Printed in the revises 'has been'.

page 71

1   it roused] Printed in the revises 'as it rouses'.

1   it was] Printed in the revises 'and is'.

2   english speaker] False start, 'english speaker's declama'. This was in turn replaced by 'english speaker's orations' before JB settled on the present and final version.

3   the pronunciation] MS orig. 'that mode of pronunciation'.

5   the master of a shop in London] False start, 'in a shop in London'.

7   Sir] Added in the same draft.

14   great] Added in the same draft.

15   March 31] MS orig. '31 March'.

16   A] MS orig. 'The'.

16   the state of] Added in the same draft.

16   was] MS 'an' added and deleted in the same draft.

17   to man] Added in the same draft.

17   Sir] Added in the same draft.

33   by lending] MS orig. 'is to lend'.

page 72

8   April 5] MS orig. '5 April'.

10   defective] MS orig. 'faulty'.

11   is mighty awkward] MS orig. 'faulty'.

13   whom] Deleted false start (interlined above) which appears to read 'wh'.

15–16   very well. I mentioned] Originally run on; marked for new paragraph in revision.

18   ordained] MS orig. 'in orders'.

21   insurmountable/sufficient] Added in the same draft.

24   sentiment] MS orig. 'thought'.

27   transgressions as] False start, 'indulgences in to'. Perhaps JB intended 'indulgences in to which ...'.

28   excluded ... betrayed] MS orig. '[excluded from heaven though they may have been /unguardedly/ betrayed/excluded from heaven for having been

/unguardedly/ betrayed]'.

28   have been betrayed] Changed by JB in the revises to 'have been betrayed into'.

30   reflection] Added in the same draft.

32   immoral acts] MS orig. 'immoralities'.

page 73

14   does to keep you in mind of him] Printed in the revises 'talks merely'.

14   lest ... company] MS orig. 'for fear you should forget he is there'.

15   should] MS orig. 'would'.

19   April 14] MS orig. '14 April'.

20   upon] Printed in the revises 'after'.

23   On] False start, 'Th'.

27–28 by the obliging aid of Mr. Longlands the Solicitor who compared notes with me] Changed by JB in the revises to 'by the aid of Mr. Longlands the solicitor on the other side, who obligingly allowed me to compare his note with my own'.

31   talked] False start, 'mention'.

31   recent] Added in the same draft.

31   who] MS orig. 'because they'.

33–34 What ... teach] MS orig. 'What had people to do in an University who were not willing to be taught but who would insist to teach'.

35   Sir] Added in the same draft.

36   am told] MS orig. 'believe'.

38   an illustration uncommonly happy] MS orig. 'one of the best things that Johnson ever said'.

39   Johnson] MS orig. 'him'.

40–41 ventured ... humour] MS orig. 'undertook the defence of drinking, although he looked very aweful and cloudy upon me'.

41–42 After ... maxim] MS orig. 'At last I said 'Sir you know the maxim'.

page 74

8   inclined to work] MS orig. 'industrious'.

14   (first) for] Printed in the revises 'from'.

14   remote] Written over an undeciphered erasure.

14   consequential] Omitted in the revises.

14   consequential evil] MS orig. 'consequences of evil'.

15   if he had not candles] MS orig. 'had he not candles'.

18   and] MS orig. 'or'.

19   withholds it] MS orig. 'not'.

21   seasons] False start, 'pl'.

21   of the northern] Added in the same draft.

24   penetration] MS 'and' added and deleted in the same draft.

25   therefore too difficult] MS orig. 'not full enough'.

25   easily] Omitted in the revises.

26   opinion] MS 'saying' deleted after opinion.

36   she had it from me] Printed in the revises 'it was communicated to her by me'.

page 75

1   had been] MS orig. 'was'.

3   Week,] MS 'and' deleted.

5   Religions] MS orig. 'piety'.

5   Religions] Printed in the revises 'religion'.

7   most] Added in the same draft.
8   paid] MS orig. 'visited'.
21   sunday] MS 'the' deleted.
21   On sunday 19] Printed in the revises 'On Sunday, April 19'.
22–23   the notion ... distinguish] MS orig. 'the received notion that the blind are able to distinguish'.
23   the great Sanderson] Printed in the revises 'Professor Sanderson'.
27–28   those cards ... commonly are] Printed in the revises '"the cards used by such persons must be less polished than ours commonly are"'.
28–29   are. We talked] Originally run on; marked for new paragraph in revision.
29–30   harmonious composition] MS orig. 'harmony'.
29–30   The General said no simple sound was pretty but only a harmonious composition of sounds.] Printed in the revises 'The General said there was no beauty in a simple sound but only in an harmonious composition of sounds.'
32   beautiful] MS orig. 'fine'.
34   ill] Printed in the revises 'little'.
41   is] Omitted in the revises.

page 76
1   Those of the two tastes] Changed by JB in the revises first to 'Those of the two opposite tastes' and then to 'The two classes of persons'.
9   what was said] Added in the same draft.
19   indignant] Added in the same draft.
23   having] Added in the same draft.
24   and] Added in the same draft.
24   us] MS orig. 'one'.
25   a man] MS orig. 'one'.
26   liking] MS orig. 'fondness'.
29   to] Added in the same draft.
30   have] MS orig. 'am'.
31   in a style] Added in the same draft.
31   quaint] MS orig. 'quaintly'.
31   however] Added in the same draft.
31   His book] False start, 'The style gives the substance'.
32–33   We figure ... us] MS orig. 'He figures an ancient gentleman talking away;'.
35   When ... maintain] MS orig. 'When I one day maintained/threw out'.
36   life] MS orig. 'time'.
37   permitted] MS orig. 'left'.

page 77
6   Great] MS 'would have' added and deleted in the same draft.
6–7   Greece.' A] Originally run on; marked for new paragraph in revision.
10   in] False start, 'to'.
17   Johnson] False start, '*Johnson*'. JB apparently intended to allot dialogue to SJ here.
19   It is a pity] MS orig. 'It is too bad'.
19   a flea/you have] JB rejected 'you have' as a false start.
23   *caught*] MS orig. 'taken'.
25–26   young.' He said] Originally run on; marked for new paragraph in revision.
33–34   Historian.' He said] Originally run on; marked for new paragraph in revision.

page 78
4–6   away. I mentioned] Originally run on; marked for new paragraph in revision.

5   home] Omitted in the revises.
13   go and] Added in the same draft.
14   and] Omitted in the revises.
15   I spent ... Mr. Thrale's] First draft, 'I had some very good days with him at Mr. Thrale's'.
16   what he called with high relish] Added in the same draft.
18   Mr.] Added in the same draft.
18   agreed] MS orig. 'appointed'.
22   spent] MS orig. 'passed'.
23–24   passed. He said] Originally run on; marked for new paragraph in revision.
25–26   Adjunct. 'The misfortune] Originally run on; marked for new paragraph in revision.
26   this;] Added in the same draft.
28   but he were] Printed in the revises 'he is not'.
29   but he were] Printed in the revises 'he is not'.

page 79
2   guard] False start, 'secure/in'. Perhaps the latter option was meant to be 'insure'.
5–6   where ... inconsiderable] False start, 'so as not to enforce/apply it as a general sanction, upon presumptive fraud, but to require'.
6–8   I had laboured the winter before in a case *Wilson* against *Smith and Armour* to persuade the Judges to return to the ancient law.] Printed in the revises 'In a case which came before that Court the preceding winter, I had laboured to persuade the Judges to return to the ancient law.' In the revises, the name of the case is supplied in a footnote.
8   adhere to it] MS orig. 'preserve it/maint[ain it]'.
8   had] Added in the same draft.
14   it is urged] Added in the same draft.
32   sentence] False start, 'opini[on]'.
33   nor] Printed in the revises 'not'.

page 80
7   end] MS orig. 'use'.
9–10   possession is] MS orig. 'possessions are'.
14   As the law] Originally run on; marked for new paragraph in revision.
16   fraud] Printed in the revises 'frauds'.
20–21   by ... further] False start, 'to cover it over no not cover it over'.
21   folly] MS orig. 'mistake'.
32   'Some ages ago] Printed in the revises 'Some ages ago (says he)'.

page 81
1   moveable] MS orig. 'moveables'.
3   in order to subdue] MS orig. 'to subdue'.
9–10   or may pass] Added in the same draft.
20   Open] MS 'to' deleted.
23   It ... but] False start, 'It is not for times of ferocity but for times'.
28–29   relaxed.' Whatever] A deleted 'Wh' after 'relaxed' makes it clear that JB did not originally intend a paragraph break.
31–32   fraudulent. Since] Originally run on; marked for new paragraph in revision.
32   as] MS 'a' deleted.
36   are] Omitted in the revises.

page 82

10 intromiss⌉ Printed in the revises 'intromit'.

16–17 If ... law⌉ False start, 'If the law wc duty enjoined'.

24 recepit⌉ Corrected to '*recipit*' for the second edition.

37 intellectual⌉ Added in the same draft.

38 other⌉ Added in the same draft.

38–39 which had been used⌉ Added in the same draft.

35–39 It is astonishing ... of the question.⌉ Printed in the revises 'With such comprehension of mind and such clearness of penetration did he thus treat a subject altogether new to him, without any other preparation than my having stated to him the arguments which had been used on each side of the question.'

40–41 one of no mean fame⌉ Printed in the revises 'a writer of so much fame'.

41 Opinion⌉ False start, 'Argument'.

42 Johnson⌉ MS orig. 'he'.

42 though⌉ Added in the same draft.

43 may be found⌉ MS orig. 'is/is to be found'.

41–43 for the Opinion which Johnson so ably refutes though in the most courteous terms towards its authour may be found in his Lordship's 'Historical Law Tracts'⌉ Omitted in the revises.

page 83

1 Sir David Dalrymple Lord Hailes one of their number⌉ Printed in the revises 'My respected friend Lord Hailes, however, one of that honourable body'.

3 honoured⌉ Printed in the revises 'favoured'.

3 His Lordship⌉ Printed in the revises 'His Lordship, with wonderful *acumen*,'.

4 his⌉ False start, 'th'.

4 composition⌉ MS orig. 'argument'.

4 But that I may do⌉ False start, 'But to give'.

6 *a very well drawn*⌉ False start, 'a very good'.

8 thus⌉ False start, 'thereby'.

8 made⌉ Printed in the revises 'made to me'.

8 made by one⌉ False start, 'which one'.

11 SAMUEL⌉ Added in the same draft.

15 would⌉ MS '[*undeciphered word*]' added and deleted in the same draft.

15–16 (Renewed ... to Scotland.)⌉ Printed in the revises 'I renewed my solicitations that he would this year accomplish his long-intended visit to Scotland.'

23 In 1773 he published nothing except in giving⌉ Printed in the revises 'In 1773 his only publication was'.

24 he⌉ False start, 'supply'.

28 as⌉ False start, 'to'.

28 in a very high degree⌉ Added in the same draft.

page 84

1 high⌉ MS orig. 'great'.

4 but⌉ Printed in the revises 'and'.

6 (*first*) and⌉ Printed in the revises 'but'.

9 (*second*) his⌉ MS orig. 'the'.

9–10 great and valuable additions⌉ False start, 'great additions and va'.

9–10 taste and who ... considerable reputation⌉ Printed in the revises 'taste. It is almost unnecessary to say, that by his great and valuable additions to

Dr. Johnson's work he justly obtained considerable reputation'.
16   newspaper] Added in the same draft.
20   his] False start, 'When Dr. Johnson c'.
21   came] MS 'he' deleted before 'home'.
26   a thing] False start, 'as'.

page 85

2   very] Added in the same draft.
4   new] Added in the same draft.
5   must be] Added in the same draft.
7   Why Sir I believe] MS orig. 'I suppose'.
8–9   him.' I mentioned] Originally run on; marked for new paragraph in revision.
14–15 have been willing to] Added in the same draft.
21–22 stuff.' I could not] Originally run on; marked for new paragraph in revision.
22–23 this] MS orig. 'the'.
27   the evening of] Added in the same draft.
28   repeated] MS orig. 'renewed'.
29   said he] MS 'may enforce' deleted.
35–36 people.' I thought it] Originally run on; marked for new paragraph in revision.
38   stages] MS orig. 'states'.
42   celebrated] Added in the same draft.
42   pun] Printed in the revises 'puns'.
43–44 when both very old and failed] Added in the same draft.
44   failed] Printed in the revises 'infirm'.

page 86

1   He talked] Originally run on; marked for new paragraph in revision. Before JB made the deletions and additions recorded in the main text above, 'He talked' was to follow immediately after 'perceptions/perceptive faculty'.
1   *The Spectator*] False start, 'Shakspe'.
2   prepared] MS orig. 'done'.
4   observed] MS orig. 'said'.
6   he had told all he knew that] JB made two false starts in this draft, first writing 'he told', then replacing it with 'he said', before settling on the final version of the first draft, 'he had told all he knew...'.
8   throwing out] MS orig. 'broaching'.
9   sentiments] MS orig. 'topicks'.
17   modern imitations of] Added in the same draft.
19   this] MS orig. 'the'.
31   ludicrous] Printed in the revises 'improper'.
31   applying] MS orig. 'introducing'. JB also made an initial false start by writing 'an irrever' before deleting it and proceeding.
32   (*first*) to] MS orig. 'into'.
34   April 8] MS orig. '8 April'.
35   indeed] Added in the same draft.
35   (*second*) is] MS 'that of' added and deleted in the same draft.
37   much] Added in the same draft.
37   took no pains] MS orig. 'did not try'.
39–1 not.' Though he was] Originally run on; marked for new paragraph in revision.

page 87

1   not disposed⌉ MS orig. 'indisposed'.

2   (*second*) at⌉ Added in the same draft.

8   breakfasted⌉ False start, 'was with him at breakfast'.

8   breakfasted on tea⌉ Printed in the revises 'breakfasted with him on tea'.

8   *Doctor*⌉ MS orig. '*Dr*.'.

11   tremulous⌉ Added in the same draft.

13–14 *us*.' We went to church⌉ Originally run on; marked for new paragraph in revision.

16   turned over⌉ MS orig. 'in'.

16–17 In Arch=Bishop Laud's ... Johnson⌉ False start, 'In Laud's Life [MS 375] by ∫Life of Laud I found a saying of King Charles II that'.

25   *Johnson* ... is⌉ MS orig. 'Mr. Johnson said it was'.

26   lawyer⌉ MS orig. 'man'.

28   that⌉ MS orig. 'how'.

28   had⌉ Added in the same draft.

28   before⌉ MS orig. 'ago'.

30   Johnson, 'Sir⌉ MS orig. '"Sir" said Johnson'.

31   nothing⌉ MS 'completely' added and deleted in the same draft.

35   meat⌉ Added in the same draft.

page 88

1   a publick oven⌉ MS orig. 'an oven'.

1–2   because ... it⌉ Added in the same draft.

2   so there is the advantage⌉ Printed in the revises 'and thus the advantage is obtained'.

3   from⌉ MS orig. 'at'.

4   April 11⌉ MS orig. 'On the 11 April'.

4   Sunday⌉ MS orig. 'day'.

7   in the gloomy recess of Bolt Court⌉ Added in the same draft.

8   dusky⌉ Added in the same draft.

8   hardly⌉ Printed in the revises 'scarcely'.

9   uncouth⌉ MS orig. 'vulgar'.

12   company⌉ MS orig. '[*undeciphered word*]'.

15   One of his dishes⌉ MS orig. 'The Lamb'.

16   A⌉ Added in the same draft.

19   curious⌉ Changed by JB in the revises to 'desirous'.

21   But the fact was⌉ Two false starts, 'But the fact was' and 'But this luxurious wit might have'.

23   (*first*) the⌉Added in the same draft.

26   a church⌉ First draft, 'one/a church'.

28–29 practice.' He owned that⌉ Originally run on; marked for new paragraph in revision.

33   estimation⌉ MS orig. 'eye'.

33   *Johnson*⌉ MS 'is much owing to you' added and deleted in the same draft.

page 89

4   handsome and⌉ Added in the same draft.

4–5   which he expresses⌉ Printed in the revises 'which he at this time expressed'.

5   entitled⌉ In EM's hand.

7   He⌉ Printed in the revises 'Johnson'.

8   complete⌉ Added in the same draft.

11   a] MS orig. 'his'.

15–16 take pleasure in helping] MS orig. 'be glad to help'.

17   should] MS orig. 'might'.

19   upon a fact in common life] Added in the same draft.

22   a great proportion] False start, 'the chief'.

26   He advised me to do it.] Added in the same draft.

26–27 said he 'to be recorded] Printed in the revises '"to be recorded," (said he)'.

28   remember] MS orig. 'can'.

30   afterwards] MS orig. 'after'.

31   again] Added in the same draft.

31   to communicate ... early years.] False start, 'for Anecd'.

39   3 Edit.] Printed in the revises '3d edit'.

page 90

6   April 13] MS orig. 'tuesday 13 April'.

6   April 13] Printed in the revises 'Tuesday April 13'.

6   Oglethorpe's.] MS 'no other company there but two Ladies/Miss Lockwood and Miss Scott. The General' deleted.

8–9   We found ... London] MS orig. 'Signor Martinelli of Florence who Authour of a/an/the History of England in Italian [/printed in/at London-/>] printed in London was also there'.

9   in London.] Printed in the revises 'at London'.

9–10   London. I spoke] Originally run on; marked for new paragraph in revision.

11   with] False start, 'being'.

14   Dr.] MS orig. 'Mr.'.

15–16   it.' This brought] Originally run on; marked for new paragraph in revision.

21   (second) to] An inadvertent omission.

24   poetry] MS 'as Horace's odes' deleted.

24–25   poetry. The General] Originally run on; marked for new paragraph in revision.

28   Do you think so, Sir?] Presumably in first proof, this sentence was altered to, 'I know not why you think so, Sir.' In the revises, JB inserted 'should' between 'you' and 'think'.

31   An animated debate took place] MS orig. 'A question was started'.

32   day.] MS orig. 'times.'

33   have to] Added in the same draft.

34   do not] MS orig. 'would not'.

page 91

7   in a man] Added in the same draft.

7   *live*] Printed in the revises 'live'.

7   his] MS orig. 'ones'.

8   live] Printed in the revises '*live*'.

8–9   I would advise him to be] MS orig. 'Let him be'.

10   who] MS orig. 'is'.

10   attaches ... country] MS orig. 'takes a party /in/ politicks'.

11   imagined] Added in the same draft.

12   Boswell. 'Or principle.] Added in the same draft.

15   lies,] MS 'a day' added and deleted in the same draft.

20   should chuse] MS orig. 'wish'.

25   had engagements for] MS orig. 'been engaged for'.

27   for several years] Added in the same draft.
28   ventured to tell] MS orig. 'told'.
29   thus] MS orig. 'this'.
30–31 his carriage] MS orig. 'the post=chaise'.
31   who] Added in the same draft.
33   carry] MS orig. 'take'.
40   at least] Added in the same draft.

page 92
16   do] Printed in the revises '*do*'.
17   in] MS orig. 'of'.
26   happy] Printed in the revises '*happy*'.
33   It] MS orig. 'This'.

page 93
1   to write him] Printed in the revises 'write for him'.
3   a man] MS orig. 'one'.
5   I would] MS orig. 'I'd'.
6   now] Added in the same draft.
8   *Johnson*] False start, '*Goldsmith*'.
9   the last Royal Family] Printed in the revises 'the last generation of the Royal Family'.
12   coming to] Printed in the revises 'applying to'.
13   Why Sir] Added in the same draft.
19   Sir] Added in the same draft.
22   musical performers] MS orig. 'performers in musick'.
23   I am told] Added in the same draft.
23   £700] Printed in the revises 'seven hundred'.
24   endeavour] MS orig. 'strive'.
26   on] Added in the same draft.
26   Any] MS orig. 'A'.
33–34 sufficient to enable him to keep] Printed in the revises 'sufficient to keep'.
35–36 Mr. Strahan ... several] MS orig. 'Mr. Strahan to set up his coach but had kept his several'.
38–39 better.' Mr. Elphinston] Originally run on; marked for new paragraph in revision.

page 94
7   strained] MS orig. 'forced'.
8–9   in my opinion] MS orig. 'if'.
14   who] MS orig. 'whose vanity'.
15   (*second*) it can be conceived] Printed in the revises 'can be conceived'.
19   *Johnson*] False start, 'I remember one from Lord Chatham to him, in which he'.
26   be lashed] Printed in the revises 'be, Sir, lashed'.
30–31 *Ennosigæum*. This does] Originally run on; marked for new paragraph in revision.
32   mentioning them] Printed in the revises 'they are mentioned'.
34   passage] Printed in the revises 'passage in Juvenal'; 'in Juvenal' deleted in the revises.

page 95
1   him] Inadvertently omitted in MS.

6 their⌉ Added in the same draft.
6 intellect⌉ Printed in the revises 'intellects'.
7 destroy themselves⌉ Printed in the revises 'commit suicide'.
12 And⌉ Added in the same draft.
12–13 disposition to fear⌉ Printed in the revises 'timid disposition'.
20–21 he might if he pleased⌉ MS 'have' deleted.
30 Letters to Lord Mansfield⌉ Printed in the revises 'Letters to Lord Mansfield; a copy of which had been sent by the authour to Dr. Johnson'.
34 work⌉ MS orig. 'publication'.

page 96
1 do no⌉ MS orig. 'not do'.
3 her⌉ MS orig. 'the'.
9 for my argument⌉ A later addition.
9 or the other⌉ A later addition.
10 which leg⌉ Printed in the revises 'which leg I move first'.
11 dubious⌉ MS orig. 'doubtful'.
12 figured⌉ Printed in the revises 'imagined'.

page 97
3 composed partly⌉ MS orig. 'partly composed'.
15 nothing⌉ MS 'when' added and deleted in the same draft.
16 forcible⌉ Added in the same draft.
23 requires⌉ In EM's hand.
24 most⌉ MS 'of our' deleted after most.
23–24 observed ... character⌉ In EM's hand.
25 He ... instance⌉ In EM's hand.
26 saw⌉ In EM's hand.
27–28 the skill continued⌉ In EM's hand.
28 them⌉ In EM's hand.
30 shaking⌉ In EM's hand.

page 98
3 this ... for⌉ In EM's hand.
4 those⌉ Added in the same draft.
4 those little fishes⌉ Printed in the revises 'little fishes'.
4 they would⌉ In EM's hand.
7 except ... beautiful⌉ In EM's hand.
9 however⌉ In EM's hand.
9 among⌉ MS orig. 'in'.
14 him⌉ False start, 'in'.
15 Lower⌉ Added in the same draft.
22 Miss Lockwood⌉ Added in the same draft.
22 in company with Dr. Goldsmith⌉ Added in the same draft.
23 Oglethorpe's⌉ False start, 'in'.
24 (second) Dr.⌉ MS orig. 'Mr'.
28–29 and I ... Tour⌉ Added in the same draft.
32 to visit Scotland this year⌉ Printed in the revises 'to fulfil his engagement'.
32–33 year. The custom⌉ Originally run on; marked for new paragraph in revision.

page 99
1 of his quarter⌉ Added in the same draft.
4–5 no matter what animals he has killed.'⌉ Printed in the revises 'let the

animals he has killed be what they may'.

8 Nay 'tis] Printed in the revises 'Nay, Sir, it is'.
14 wo] A false start for 'would'.
17–18 and spoken of slightingly by Goldsmith,] A later addition.
19–20 is doing a good deal] Printed in the revises 'is a good deal'.
20 a good deal] First draft, 'very well'.
20 literary] A later addition.
21–22 I consider ... name] False start, 'I consider literary reputation to be alive only while any thing'.
22–23 will ensure him a] Printed in the revises 'will ensure a'.
23 him a ... from] First draft, 'a sale with'.
30 Goldsmith having said] False start, '*Goldsmith*'.
35 formular. It] False start, 'formular, it'.
36 church service] MS orig. 'prayers'.
38 graciously pleased] Printed in the revises 'graciously pleased to grant'.
39 Emperour] MS orig. 'Emperor'.

page 100

1 it was right] Printed in the revises 'it is right'.
10 guineas,] False start, 'Garrick'.
11 shilling.] False start, 'How'.
12 fee] MS 'Nay [in>] from one point of view a lawyer is worse, for he' deleted.
13 nonsence or] Added in the same draft.
13 absurdity] False start, 'tho'.
14 a play or a part which] MS orig. 'what'.
15 now] Added in the same draft.
26 as candidate ... that] MS orig. 'as a proposed candidate to be of that'.
28 me.] Deleted false start, 'As one bl'. Probably JB intended 'blackball' (see MS 398, *ante* p. 103).
29 Goldsmith being mentioned] Originally run on; marked for new paragraph in revision. The original run-on (that which existed prior to the replacement of 'company' with 'members of the Literary Club ...') was from 'company' to 'Goldsmith being mentioned'.
33 a Writer] MS, 'to be' added and deleted in the same draft.
36–37 study ... it] MS orig. 'closet'.
44 Historian!] Printed in the revises 'An Historian!'

page 101

2 (growing ... scotch)] Added in the same draft.
12 look upon] False start, 'cons[ider]'.
25–26 which you think particularly fine] Printed in the revises 'which you think is particularly fine'.
26 that of] Added in the same draft.
28–29 you will find him better] Printed in the revises 'you will find that he excels Vertot'.
33 I cannot ... that] Two false starts, 'That Dr. Johnson' and 'I have no doubt that'.
34 often owned that he] Changed by JB in the revises to 'owned that he often'.
34 who often owned that he 'talked for victory'] Three false starts, 'must upon this occasion in the ardour', 'was upon this occasion in the ardour', 'expressed himself upon this occasion in the ardour'.
34 rather urged] MS orig. 'urged rather'.
36 opinion] MS 'whatever that may have been' deleted.

36   for] MS orig. 'and'.
37   so widely differ] MS orig. 'seriously differ so much'.
38   I remember] Originally run on; marked for new paragraph in revision.
      The original run-on (that which existed before the insertion of the
      paragraph beginning 'I cannot dismiss' and of '*Johnson*' at the head of this
      paragraph) was from 'Persian Tale' to 'I remember'.
40   illis] Printed in the revises 'istis'.

page 102
3   *illis*] Printed in the revises '*istis*'.
4   Johnson] MS orig. 'He'.
13   monuments] False start, 'should be e[rected]'.
18   come first] Printed in the revises 'to be first'.
20   our poets] MS orig. 'them'.
21   Some] False start, 'While some'.
23   figured] Printed in the revises 'assigned'.
26   Theology.] MS orig. 'divinity'.
27   practice] MS orig. 'conduct'.

page 103
6   half] Added in the same draft.
14–15 Dr. Goldsmith] Added in the same draft.
17   Goldsmith] MS 'and the' deleted.
20   leant] Printed in the revises 'leaned'.
20   with humourous formality] False start, 'humourously'.
22   from] MS orig. 'of'.
23   Goldsmith] Originally run on; marked for new paragraph in revision.
      Before the additions and the deletions to the previous paragraph, the run-
      on was from 'I had dined' to 'Goldsmith'.
23–24 rehearsed] MS orig. 'read'.
25–26 There was a Poem] False start, 'In a Poem'.

page 104
5–6   pry. Talking] Originally run on; marked for new paragraph in revision.
13   work] False start, 'narr[ative]'.
16   did,] MS 'that' deleted.
23   that I have known] Added in the same draft.
25   with exquisite wit] Added in the same draft.

page 105
1   were he to visit Ireland] Added in the same draft.
2–3   a fair people] First draft, 'a fair people; they never/are not in a combina-
      tion to'.
5–6   so much agitated] Printed in the revises 'much agitated'.
6   whether] False start, 'how'.
9   is] MS orig. 'being'.
9   judicatures] False start, 'before which this matter may be cont'.
17   to me] Added in the same draft.
23   apologise for] MS orig. 'excuse'.
28   mere] MS 'appearance of' added and deleted in the same draft.
32   while thus unhappily] False start, 'in these un'.
33   Seduced] False start, 'As I proceeded w'.
40   of his county] Added in the same draft.

page 106

1   He] MS 'and Mrs. Thrale' deleted.
1   would] Changed by JB in the revises to 'did'.
1   when] False start, 'for'.
2   by signs] Added in the same draft.
4   He ... understand] Added in the same draft.
11–12 a steady calvinist teacher] Added in the same draft.
17   Hawkesworth's] Originally run on; marked for new paragraph in revision. Before changes were made to the preceding paragraph, the run on extended from 'Johnson' to 'Hawkesworth'.
24   twenty thousand] MS orig. '20 000'.
25–26 way.' Talking of birds] Originally run on; marked for new paragraph in revision.
31   (first) a] Added in the same draft.
38   may remain] Printed in the revises 'may be found'.

page 107

2–3   migrate.' Boswell] Originally run on; marked for new paragraph in revision.
4   readily] Omitted in the revises.
4   serves them readily for bread] Printed in the revises 'serves them for bread'.
4   heartily] Added in the same draft.
6   as] Added in the same draft.
11   he] False start, 'the'.
17   brute] False start, 'animals'.
22–23 In ... mention] MS orig. 'Afterwards'.
24   it ... slight] MS orig. 'slightly'.
27–28 the propagation of] Added in the same draft.
36   (second) with] Added in the same draft.
38   inform himself] Printed in the revises 'inform himself and think justly'.
41   may and] Added in the same draft.

page 108

10   without] MS 'a' deleted.
11   moral] Added in the same draft.
18   who has] Added in the same draft.
27   another] MS orig. 'one'.
29   to Christianity] Added in the same draft.
42   Sir] Added in the same draft.
43   had] Added in the same draft.

page 109

5   the subject] MS orig. 'it'.
7   erroneous doctrines] MS orig. 'errours'.
8   in] Added in the same draft.
9   this] Printed in the revises 'that'.
10   (second) the] Printed in the revises 'a'.
16   So,] Printed in the revises 'So, Sir,'.
18   Dr.] Omitted in the printing of the revises, no doubt because the compositor overlooked JB's later draft insertion of the word.
24–25 soon proceed to] Added in the same draft.
27   put to] Printed in the revises 'put forth'.
35   back to] Added in the same draft.

page 110

1   were] Added in the same draft.

5   tolerate ... tolerable] First edition, "'tolerate all things that are tolerable'".

10   great] Printed in the revises 'restless'.

14   to] False start, 'for'.

17   obtain] MS orig. 'seise'.

18   crying] Printed in the revises 'exclaiming'.

18   it] Printed in the revises '*it*'.

19   which Goldsmith supposed to be] Printed in the revises 'which led Goldsmith to think that he was'.

20   word] Printed in the revises 'words'.

21   envy and] Added in the same draft.

25   very] Added in the same draft.

30   in] False start, 'to'.

32   Johnson] False start, '*Johnson*'.

page 111

5   It may] False start, 'The Que[stion]'.

9   he did not think it fit that] False start, 'though, in a mixed company he did not obtrude'. This false start was altered to 'though, when in a mixed company he did not obtrude' before it, too, was struck out and replaced with the final wording.

9   aweful] False start, 'm'.

10   at this time] Added in the same draft.

15   *Boswell*] Written over '*Johnson*'.

17   forth] MS orig. 'out'.

18   a most] MS orig. 'an'.

18   we see there] Added in the same draft.

24   by ... penalties] Added in the same draft.

24   is] Printed in the revises 'was'.

30   Johnson.] False start, [*one or two undeciphered words del*].

30   only] Added in the same draft.

35   think] Added in the same draft.

38   silently] Added in the same draft.

40   and] Added in the same draft.

42   from you] Printed in the revises 'from you, Sir'.

page 112

2   as usual] Printed in the revises 'as ever'.

2   rattled away] Printed in the revises 'rattled away as usual'.

3   tonight] False start, 'Mr. Langton'.

6   excelling] Printed in the revises 'excellency'.

7   and that] Added in the same draft.

10   cabinet at home] Printed in the revises 'cabinet'.

10   not content] Added in the same draft.

16   (*first*) his] False start, 'suc[h]'.

19   of the wits] First edition, 'of wits'.

21–22   republick'. But he was] Originally run on; marked for new paragraph in revision.

22   But he was exceedingly mortified] Printed in the revises 'He was still more mortified'.

22   he was] Added in the same draft.

24   present,] False start, 'he was suddenly stopped by'.

31–32 Beauclerk ... Bozzy'] Printed in the revises 'Beauclerk, Beau; Boswell, Bozzy; Langton, Lanky; Murphy, Mur; Sheridan, Sherry'.
36 minute] Supplied in an unidentified hand to remedy an inadvertent omission.

page 113
12 him] Printed in the revises 'Johnson'.
13 company] MS 'most judicious' deleted after company.

page 114
3 an exclusive right to] MS orig. 'a Patent for'.
5 curious] Printed in the revises 'strange'.
6 Sir, it is all] False start, 'All that, Sir'.
7 useless if] Printed in the revises 'useless even were it'.
8 it] Added in the same draft.
10 May 9] MS orig. 'May 9th'.
10 for] Printed in the revises 'to'.
14 broke out violently] Deleted but then reinstated through 'stet' markings.
19 he was so open] Printed in the revises 'he was so candid in owning it'.
23–24 freely. He now seemed] Originally run on; marked for new paragraph in revision.
28 called out] Printed in the revises, 'exclaimed'.
31–32 cradle.' I dined] Originally run on; marked for new paragraph in revision.
38 as is] MS 'foolishly' added and deleted in the same draft.
42–43 respectable families. His zeal on] False start, 'his zeal for'.

page 115
2–3 subordination and] Added in the same draft.
8 He] Printed in the revises 'Johnson'.
15 *Towser*] First edition, '*Towzer*'.
19 _____] This line is omitted in the revises.
19–20 a thing, a mighty thing] Printed in the revises 'a mighty thing'.
20 home] Printed in the revises 'home to his seat in the country'.
22 upon] MS 'human' added and deleted in the same draft.
26 (to Chambers)] Printed in the revises 'Chambers'.
26 hope] Printed in the revises 'trust'.
29 In] In the revises a new paragraph begins here.
35 is] False start, 'pre[served]'.
35 my *del*] JB's deleted 'my' was printed in the revises, presumably having been reinstated in the first proof.
36–37 a man. Mr. Chambers] Originally run on; marked for new paragraph in revision.
38 of which] MS orig. 'Quorum'.
40 laughing] Printed in the revises 'it'.

page 116
3 foot] Added in the same draft.
4 night] One word interlined and deleted; this may be 'wat', for 'watches of the night'.
6–7 posts which were at that time at the side of the foot pavement] Printed in the revises 'posts at the side of the foot pavement'.
16 admits] MS orig. 'retracts'.
21 the desire of] Added in the same draft.

22   on different days] Added in the same draft.
22   of this year] Added in the same draft.

page 117

6   I wrote] False start, 'I again'.
8   August] MS 'and' deleted.
15   18] Printed in the revises '18th'.
15   on which] Printed in the revises 'on which day'.
15   22] Printed in the revises '22d'.
16   on which] Printed in the revises 'when'.
16   I suppose] Printed in the revises 'I believe'.
17   passed] MS orig. 'spent'.
17   in] MS orig. 'with'.
18   by Berwick] Printed in the revises 'by the way of Berwick'.
18   He ... Edinburgh] This was preceded by two false starts, 'He was some days at Edinburgh' and 'He came to Edinburgh by Berwick upon Tweed'.
20   Hebrides ... in view] MS orig. 'Hebrides, which was the principal object/were his principal objects'.
20   visited] MS orig. 'saw'.
22   Dumbarton] Printed in the revises 'Dunbarton'.
22   by Loudon] Added in the same draft.
22–1   by Loudon, then to Auchinleck] Printed in the revises 'then by Loudon to Auchinleck'.

page 118

1   in Ayrshire] Added in the same draft.
2   then] Added in the same draft.
3   thus] Added in the same draft.
8   wherever] False start, 'in the'.
11   How he was considered] False start, 'As brilliant proofs both'.
14   as] Added in the same draft.
14   topicks] False start, 'I trust from'.
18   separate and] Added in the same draft.
20   as] MS 'any of' deleted.
20   his] MS 'smaller' added and deleted in the same draft.
23   a great many of] Added in the same draft.
26–27   of my Journal] MS orig. 'it'.
26–27   of my Journal] Printed in the revises 'of that work'.

page 119

1   he] JB made two false starts, 'he was not unmindful of any source of intelligence' and 'His'.
1–2   he ... London] JB made two false starts here, the first one reading, 'he continued' and the second one reading, 'he did not remit his inquiries on that'.
5   His humane] False start, 'In 1774'.
5   forgiving] Added in the same draft.
8   he] MS orig. 'were'.
10   and] False start, 'in'.
17   In the course] False start, 'When in the course'.
18   self=examination this year] Printed in the revises 'self-examination with retrospect to this year'.
19   1774] Added in the same draft.

22   heartily⌉ Printed in the revises 'seriously'.

22   our Travels⌉ MS orig. 'his Journey'.

23   he became⌉ False start, 'I was favoured'.

page 120

3   Steevens⌉ Printed in the revises 'Mr Steevens'.

6   state of health⌉ Printed in the revises 'situation'.

6   the⌉ Printed in the revises 'that'.

8   mentioning⌉ Printed in the revises 'mentioned'.

10   that⌉ Added in the same draft.

12   influence⌉ Printed in the revises 'influence on my mind'.

page 121

3   His⌉ Printed in the revises 'This'.

5   a⌉ Added in the same draft.

9   the castles⌉ Added in the same draft.

13–14 a contested election⌉ MS orig. 'an election'.

14–15 The Patriot,'⌉ In the revises a footnote is keyed to this title: 'In the newspapers'.

15   addressed ... Britain⌉ Added in the same draft.

15   title⌉ False start, 'taking'.

18   to⌉ Added in the same draft.

18   an⌉ MS orig. 'a violent'.

19   appear⌉ False start, 'cons'.

20   however⌉ MS orig. 'not only'.

20   energetick⌉ MS orig. 'energy and'.

21   still⌉ Added in the same draft.

22   endeavours to vindicate] MS orig. 'attempted to defend'.

24   attempt⌉ MS orig. 'attempts'.

25   contained⌉ MS orig. 'contains'.

27   sincere⌉ Added in the same draft.

28   of his country⌉ Printed in the revises 'of his King and country'.

page 122

2   gentleman⌉ MS orig. 'man'.

2–3   This letter ... I insert it⌉ Printed in the revises 'This letter, which shews his tender concern for an amiable young gentleman to whom we had been very much obliged in the Hebrides, I have inserted'.

3–4   I insert it according⌉ First edition, 'I have inserted according to its date'.

5   October 1st⌉ MS orig. 'the 1 October'.

2–8   This letter ... unfortunately drowned⌉ Printed in the revises 'This letter, which shews his tender concern for an amiable young gentleman to whom we had been very much obliged in the Hebrides, I have inserted according to its date, though before receiving it I had informed him of the melancholy event that the young Laird of Coll was unfortunately drowned'.

17   in⌉ Added in the same draft.

17   sixty fourth⌉ Printed in the second edition 'sixty-fifth'.

20   always⌉ Printed in the revises 'very'.

page 124

7–8   a robust ... life⌉ Added in the same draft.

10   very⌉ Added in the same draft.

11   argumentative⌉ Added in the same draft.

15–16 appeared in the newspapers of the day] False start, 'appeared at the time'.
16 republished] Printed in the revises 're-published; but not with perfect accuracy'.
23 can be] MS orig. 'is'.
23 known can be] Printed in the revises 'known, and going into a new and unknown state of being, can be'.
25 consideration] MS orig. 'reflection'.
27 one day] Added in the same draft.
33 danger] MS 'of' deleted.

page 125
1 it] False start, 'Another friend o'.
9 possession of] Added in the same draft.
14 declaring] First draft, 'and declared'.
17 material/corporeal] Added in the same draft.
23 Round=house] A correction of 'Watch=house'.
25 scenes. Having] JB's correction. Veronica had punctuated it 'scenes; having'.
23–25 Mr. Garrick ... a moment] Printed in the revises 'In the play-house at Lichfield, as Mr. Garrick informed me, Johnson having for a moment quitted a chair which was placed for him between the side-scenes'.
26 quit it] Printed in the revises 'relinquish it' and changed by JB to 'give it up'.
27 the chair he sat on into] Changed by JB in the revises to 'the chair into'.
29 mimick] Changed by JB in the revises to 'imitate'.
31 and being at dinner] False start, 'next to dine with'. Both the false start and the correction are in Veronica's hand.
31 bookseller's] Printed in the revises 'bookseller'.
32 he] Added in JB's hand.
37 the wit] Printed in the revises 'the mimick'.

page 126
1–2 as much ... intellectual] In JB's hand.
6 painted] Added in the same draft.
7–8 and abounds in ingenious sentiments] Printed in the revises 'and in ingenious sentiments'.
14 which] At this point JB considered an alternative participatorial construction, 'owing both [to his original genius and long residence in Asia].'
17 though] 'indeed' deleted after 'though'.
17 these] Printed in the revises 'those'.
18 a] Printed in the revises 'the'.
24 must be allowed] MS orig. 'is certainly true'.
28–1 The Account ... some/individuals] Added in the same draft.
30 observations] MS orig. 'remarks'.

page 127
4 he said] Added in the same draft.
4 that] Printed in the revises 'which'.
5–6 published as the compositions of Ossian] Printed in the revises 'ascribed to Ossian'.
9 authenticity] MS 'by a strange infatuation' added and deleted in the same draft.
10 there were certainly many] Printed in the revises 'there were many'.

14   upon a subject ... uninteresting] Added in the same draft.

14   that] MS 'I believe more than some and less than others' deleted.

15   first] Added in the same draft.

23–24 there came forth an Epick Poem in Six Books] False start, 'an Epick Poem in Six Books'. Presumably, JB originally intended something along the lines of 'an Epick Poem in Six Books came forth ...'.

25   former Compositions] False start, 'other perf[ormances]'.

26   such a recurrence] Printed in the revises 'a perpetual recurrence'.

26   that were] Printed in the revises 'which appear'.

26–27 there was found such a ... and when] MS orig. 'there was a mere recurrence of the same images that were to be found in the fragments that it seemed like a large quantity of printed/stamped linen or paper of the same patern consisting of five or six varieties, and when'.

27   no] MS orig. 'the'.

31   James] Added in the same draft.

33   Johnson] In EM's hand.

35   his conduct] MS orig. 'a letter written by him'.

38   inserted in the newspapers] First draft, 'had'.

page 128

1   do any thing so well myself upon] False start, 'close this sub[ject]'.

1–4   But I ... Journey] In the revises this paragraph is printed as follows: 'The observations of my friend Mr. Dempster in a letter written to me, soon after he had read Dr. Johnson's book, are so just and liberal, that they cannot be too often repeated.'

5   And] Omitted in the revises.

5   native of Scotland] MS orig. 'scotchman'.

6   his] Printed in the revises 'an'.

6   says] Printed in the revises 'is equally liberal'.

8   his] MS orig. 'the'.

8   at the time] MS orig. 'of the moment'.

10   rugged] MS orig. '[undeciphered word]'; printed in the revises 'harsh'.

10   sour] MS orig. 'malignant'.

12   parsimony] MS 'and meaness' deleted.

13   the] MS 'contempt of the' deleted.

16   virulence] Changed by JB in the revises to 'rancour'.

18   in his 'Journey'] Added in the same draft.

page 129

3   nay I have] Added in the same draft.

5   the merit of] Added in the same draft.

5–6   which in old times was renowned for its valour and maintained] Garbled in the revises 'which has even renowned for its valour, which in former times maintained' and changed by JB to 'which has been ever renowned for its valour, which in former times maintained'.

41   more] Added in the same draft.

41   even] Omitted in the printing of the revises.

page 130

2   No Sir] Added in the same draft.

4   He] Printed in the revises 'Johnson'.

6   to the office of] Printed in the revises 'to be'.

7   who] MS orig. 'that'.

9   attempt] Printed in the revises 'conduct'.

11   in newspapers ... publications] Added in the same draft.

17–18 as is said raised by purse pride/swollen with purse pride] Added in the same draft.

18   a man better known in both countries] Changed in the revises by Plymsell to 'another Scotchman, who has found means to make himself well known both in Scotland and England'.

19–20 to Mr. Seward] Added in the same draft.

25   21 March] Printed in the revises 'March 21'.

26   in repairing to Dr. Johnson] Printed in the revises 'on repairing to Bolt court' and then changed by EM to 'on repairing to Dr. Johnson's'.

27   him] Printed in the revises 'Dr. Johnson' and changed by EM in the revises to 'him'.

27   in his study] Deleted in the revises by EM, then reinstated with 'stet'.

page 131

1   strongly resembling him] MS orig. 'resembling him much'.

5   in the evening] Added in the same draft.

6–7   he was violent upon the Ossian controversy] Printed in the revises 'he was vehement on the subject of the Ossian controversy'.

12   what they think] Printed in the revises 'any thing'.

19   The doubts] False start, 'He had now'.

19   state] MS orig. 'mention to him'.

21   American colonies] MS orig. 'people [MS 436] of America'.

23   and] MS 'he' added and deleted in the same draft.

26–27 fellow subjects in America] MS orig. 'Colonists'.

28   had] Added in the same draft.

29   anything] False start, 'anything sh[ort]'.

37   so inconsistent with] Printed in the revises 'so unsuitable to'.

42   Positive] MS orig. 'Strong'.

43   rage] Changed by JB in the revises to 'severity'.

44   this Ministerial Rhapsody] Printed erroneously in the revises 'this severity rhapsody' and then corrected by JB to 'this rhapsody'.

46   and gore] Added in the same draft.

page 132

3   and curtailed] Added in the same draft.

6   while] Added in the same draft.

17   here] Added in the same draft.

18   struck out either] Changed by JB in the revises to 'struck out, it does not appear why,'.

23   European intelligence from] Added in the same draft.

page 133

2   If a new monarchy is erected] False start, 'He who first takes into his hand the sceptre of America'.

17   will not long contain] Printed in the revises 'will not contain'.

18   let not the] Printed in the revises 'let the' and then changed to 'let not ours'.

18   with delight] Added in the same draft. In the printing of the revises, these words were omitted; JB reinserted them when he corrected the revises.

26   various attacks] First draft, 'variety of censure in different writings'.

26   weapons of literary warfare] First draft, 'style of attack'.
28–29   which I ... much] First draft, 'which he really felt'.
31   general] Added in the same draft.
32   expostulated ... thus] First draft, 'expostulated with him thus in a strain of able and affecting argument'.

page 134

1   I ... *moral*] Added in the same draft.
1–2   support ... which] First draft, 'reconcile his principles of morality and Religion with writing for a wicked Ministry in such a manner. A task which'.
2–3   ask... defend?] First draft, 'suppose/ask of even their infidel pensioner Hume'.
8   the measures of] Added in the same draft.
12   These pamphlets] MS orig. 'This unlucky pamphlet'.
18–19   One was a Pamphlet entitled 'A Letter] Printed in the revises 'One was, "A Letter"'.
22   man] MS orig. 'character'.
23   boldly and] Added in the same draft.
23   pointedly] False start, 'and b'. JB must originally have intended 'pointedly and boldly' before settling on the present version.

page 135

12   that subject] Printed in the revises 'politicks'.
25   very ready] Printed in the revises 'willing'.
25   will] MS orig. 'must'.
36   he] False start, 'it'.
36   Confident ... he] Printed in the revises 'However confident of the rectitude of his own mind, Johnson'.
38   and the influence] Printed in the revises 'and that the influence'.
38–39   be on that account] Printed in the revises 'should on that account be'.

page 136

4   this] Printed in the revises 'such a measure'.
5   signified] Printed in the revises 'once signified'.
9   (*second*) Mr.] Printed in the revises 'and Mr.'.
11   willing to believe the second sight'] The revises print a footnote identifying the source of this quotation: 'Johnson's "Journey to the Western Islands of Scotland," edit. 1785, p. 256'.
14   me] False start, 'that'.
18   formal] Added in the same draft.
19   (*first*) formal] Added in the same draft.
21–22   I answered 'I was ... my Lord.'] The revises end this sentence with 'Dr. Johnson'.
24   heard him speak] Printed in the revises 'saw and heard him'.
26   Johnson] MS orig. 'He'.
26   great] Printed in the revises 'high'.
29   much] Added in the same draft.
32   say of 'Gulliver's Travels'] MS orig. 'treat "Gulliver's Travels" slightingly, saying/of which he said'.
38   observed that] MS orig. 'said'.

page 137

3   This] False start, 'Now'.
10   But] In the revises, the sentence begins with 'Sheridan'.
12   Strahan's] MS 'the Printers' added and deleted in the same draft.

13 that] MS orig. 'how'.

19 so that] First draft, 'and'.

22 having been] MS orig. 'being'.

25 He said, 'I do not think] Printed in the revises '"I do not think (said he)'.

27 Methodists] MS 'as Bickerstaff has' added and deleted in the same draft.

29 I believed] Printed in the revises 'perhaps'.

35 His opinion ... for] Printed in the revises 'This was not merely a cursory remark; for'.

37 about the [*undeciphered word del*] year] Printed in the revises 'about the beginning of this century'.

37–38 ill-formed] Printed in the revises 'ill informed'.

40–41 which he ... integrity.] Printed in the revises 'This conduct, Johnson calls "perverseness of integrity"', and changed by JB to 'perverseness of rectitude'.

page 138

6 nonjuring clergymen] MS orig. 'nonjurant clergy'.

10 taken the oaths] Printed in the revises 'complied with the requisition of government'.

12 have been more violent against a swearing Jacobite] Printed in the revises 'have thought more unfavourably of a Jacobite who took the oaths'.

15 observing] MS orig. 'observed'.

18 He] Printed in the revises 'Mr. Strahan'.

19 Mr. Strahan] Printed in the revises 'him'.

23–24 Johnson desired ... and] Printed in the revises 'Johnson having inquired after him, said,'.

28 I] False start, 'h'. Perhaps JB originally intended 'he had professed' instead of 'I had heard him profess'.

35 also] Omitted in the printing of the revises.

40 a hearty gentleman] Printed in the revises 'a very zealous gentleman', and changed by JB to 'a very sanguine gentleman'.

page 139

3–4 I can.' 'Well, my boy,] Originally run on; marked for new paragraph in revision.

15 but] Added in the same draft.

20 however slight my title] Omitted in the revises.

25 spoke] Printed in the revises 'said'.

33 and took] First draft, 'taking'.

page 140

1 omit] First draft, 'not to omit/to preserve'.

2 misunderstood] First draft, 'misunderstood/misconceived'.

3 indicated] False start, 'int[imated]'.

5 At Mr. Beauclerk's] Printed in the revises 'At Mr. Beauclerk's, where I supped,'.

5 whom] MS orig. 'who'.

5 I] JB briefly considered an addition here, writing on the verso of MS 446 'whom I met frequentl', and then deleting the clause.

8 Come] False start, 'Why'. The 'Why' appears now two sentences on.

9 men as] Changed by JB in the revises to 'as any'.

9–10 as in the world] Printed in the revises 'as any in the world'.

10 But I don't know how] Changed by JB in the revises to 'but, I don't know

how it is'.

13 He took ... repeating⌉ Printed in the revises 'He imitated the manner of his old master with ludicrous exaggeration; repeating, with pauses and half whistlings interjected,'.

16 downwards⌉ MS orig. 'down'.

18 best⌉ Added in the same draft.

18–19 being able to imitate most exactly⌉ False start, 'as being the most exact imita'.

19 affords⌉ First draft, 'is'.

21–22 while perusing his conversation⌉ A later addition.

page 141

4 Next day⌉ In the original, a run on from 'contorted gesticulation'.

5–6 I understood⌉ Printed in the revises 'I understand' and then changed by JB to 'I understand, Sir,'.

10 which escaped⌉ Changed by JB in the revises to 'which have escaped'; EM responded, 'certainly better.'

20 "Church=yard"⌉ Printed in the revises "'Elegy in a Country Church-yard'".

page 142

1 prey⌉ Printed in the revises 'prey," &'.

5 young⌉ Added in the same draft.

7–13 and I cannot but be struck ... mildness and forgiveness⌉ In the revises, the comparable passage differs considerably: 'and, while I recapitulate the debate, and recollect what has since happened, I cannot but be struck in a manner that delicacy forbids me to express. While I contended that she ought to be treated with an inflexible steadiness of displeasure, Mrs. Thrale was all for mildness and forgiveness'.

9 It⌉ Originally, this was a lowercase 'it', as the text ran directly from 'and' to 'it is not'.

11 displeasure⌉ False start, 'Mr[s. Thrale]' deleted after 'displeasure'.

15 Madam⌉ Added in the same draft.

17 rank⌉ Printed in the revises 'station'.

18 the rank which⌉ Printed in the revises 'that which'.

23 so as⌉ Added in the same draft.

25–26 the opinion which I then expressed⌉ Printed in the revises 'what I then meant to express'.

29 in such cases⌉ Added in the same draft.

29 It is weak ... such cases⌉ Printed in the revises 'It is weak, and contempt-ible, and unworthy, in a parent to relax in such a case.'

30–34 and those too ... to which she has descended⌉ Printed in the revises 'And let it be considered, that the claim of a daughter who has acted thus, to be restored to her former situation, is either fanatical or unjust. If there be no value in the distinction of rank, what does she suffer by being kept in the situation to which she has descended? If there be a value in that distinction, it ought to be steadily maintained.'

35 shorter or longer⌉ Printed in the revises 'longer or shorter'.

page 143

8 which⌉ Added in the same draft.

16 as I could⌉ Added in the same draft.

19 one long accustomed⌉Added in the same draft.

20   March 31⌉ MS orig. '31 March'.
20   wicked⌉ Added in the same draft.
24   (*first*) Dr.⌉ Added in the same draft.
25   did⌉ MS orig. 'do'.
28   attempted⌉ False start, 'being in'.
30   On Friday March 31⌉ Added in the same draft.

page 144
2   No.⌉ Printed in the revises "'No, Sir.'"
3   No.⌉ Printed in the revises "'No, Sir.'"
3   Why then⌉ Printed in the revises "'Why then, Sir'".
3   Because⌉ Printed in the revises 'Because, Sir'.
5   you⌉ Presumably JB here intended 'her'.
18   the peel of the seville oranges which he squeesed⌉ Printed in the revises 'the Seville oranges, after he had squeezed the juice of them'.
19   Beauclerk⌉ False start, 'G[arrick]'.
19   told me of it⌉ Printed in the revises 'talked of it to me'.
22   with all the pulp taken out and⌉ Omitted in the first edition.
23   see so far⌉ Printed in the revises 'partly see'.
24   orange peels⌉ Printed in the revises 'squeezed oranges'.
27   farther⌉ Printed in the revises 'further'.
28   The World then⌉ Printed in the revises 'Then the world'.
30   with⌉ Changed in the revises to 'upon'.
31   with⌉ Changed in the revises to 'upon'.

page 145
34   some⌉ Printed in the revises 'a few'.
34   corrections⌉ False start, 'This'.

page 146
4   was⌉ Printed in the revises 'is'.
5   in writing⌉ Added in the same draft.
8   where⌉ Printed in the revises '*where*'.
9   with great propriety have added⌉ False start, 'with great truth have'.
10   we⌉ Added in the same draft.
11   Mr. William Gerrard Hamilton's⌉ MS orig. 'the Right Honourable Mr. Hamilton's'.
14   very⌉ Added in the same draft.
22   will you not allow him⌉ MS orig. 'has he not'.
22–23 a nobleness of resolution⌉ Printed in the revises 'a nobleness of resolution, in penetrating into distant regions'.
25   Hoole's⌉ MS orig. 'Holle's'.

page 147
9   that⌉ MS orig. 'fame'.
13–14 He mentioned ... 'They are'⌉ MS orig. 'The odes to Obscurity and Oblivion in ridicule of Mason and Gray being mentioned, He said, "They are..."'
12, 14 them'. The Odes⌉ Originally run on; marked for new paragraph in revision.
20   had⌉ MS 'several times' added and deleted in the same draft.
21–23 suspicion of treason ... the King'⌉ MS orig. 'suspicion of treason while concerting the plot of a Tragedy/their different shares in the conduct of a Tragedy, and one of them was overheard saying to the other, "I'll kill the

King.'"
25   Mr.] Added in the same draft.
27–28   manner.' I often wondered at] Originally run on; marked for new paragraph in
        revision.
31   Mr.] Added in the same draft.
35   Who among us can read] First draft, 'Who can read'.

page 148
2   the works of] Added in the same draft.
7   ever was] Changed in the revises by JB to 'can be'.
8–9   Organ? His 'Taxation no Tyranny'] Originally run on; marked for new para-
        graph in revision.
10   the] Added in the same draft.
12   of small arms] Added in the same draft.
13   might I think] MS orig. 'may'.
19   Mrs.] Added in the same draft.
19   like] Added in the same draft.
22   heard he] Added in the same draft.
28   *Bouts rimés*] Printed in the revises '"*Bouts rimés*" (said he)'.
30   for the vase] Added in the same draft.
31   *Boswell*] MS orig. 'Bos'.
32   *Johnson*] Added in the same draft.

page 149
5   (*second*) the] MS 'tedious and weary' deleted.
7   want of] Added in the same draft.
9   figured] Printed in the revises 'imagined'.
9   in London] Added in the same draft.
11   in the vicinity] Printed in the revises 'near town'.
12   desired] False start, 'told'.
13   which he accordingly did] Added in the same draft.
16   Mr. Dilly's] Printed in the revises 'Messieurs Dillys'.
16   with] MS orig. 'where were'.
19   Mr. Dilly's table] Printed in the revises 'Messieurs Dillys' table'.
23   which though a tall] First draft, 'though a tall'.
24   a favourite/pleasing child] First draft, 'a child'.

page 150
3   however] MS orig. 'but'.
5–6   Johnson. We talked] Originally run on; marked for new paragraph in revision.
5–6   Speaking in publick] Printed in the revises 'publick speaking'.
10–11   For my own part I] MS orig. 'I /myself/'.
12   it] Added in the same draft.
12   beat] Printed in the revises 'beaten'.
15   said I] Printed in the revises '(I asked)'.
15   it] MS 'universally' added and deleted in the same draft.
21   virtue] Added in the same draft.
21   (*third*) others] Printed in the revises 'other'.
30   Davies's] False start, 'or as he taught us to call him'.
31   a] Printed in the revises 'the'.

page 151
7   good] False start, 'reg[ulation]'.

12 those of] Added in the same draft.
13 take out] Printed in the revises 'except'.
14 said] First draft, 'said/observed'.
15 Brydone] Printed in the revises 'Brydone's'.
15 better] MS 'now' added and deleted in the same draft.
17 (first) on] Printed in the revises 'in'.
17 (second) on] Printed in the revises 'in'.
18 It would seem] Printed in the revises 'It would seem (he added)'.
20–21 qui.' I mentioned] Originally run on; marked for new paragraph in revision.
23 another Italian Authour] MS orig. 'Cappaccio'.

page 152
2 Mr.] Omitted in the revises.
11 The mention] False start, 'This mentioned'.
14 (I forget what)] Printed in the revises '[what he added, I have forgotten]'.
14–16 while he being ... his remarks] Printed in the revises 'which he being dull of hearing, did not perceive, or, if he did, was not willing to break off his talk; so he continued to vociferate his remarks'.
18 (second) him] MS 'sufficiently' deleted.
21 that] Added in the same draft.
23 Mr. Gibbon muttered (in a low voice)] Printed in the revises 'Mr. Gibbon muttered, in a low tone of voice'.
24 I suppose] Added in the same draft.
25 judicious truth] Printed in the revises 'prudent resolution'.
34 Some of us] Printed in the revises 'I'.
34–37 that all Patriots were not scoundrels] Printed in the revises 'that certainly all Patriots were not scoundrels'.
36 an] Altered from 'An' (JB at one point having planned an independent sentence, 'An eminent ... was mentioned').
38–39 not honest] Changed for emphasis in the revises to '*not* honest'.

page 153
1 (second) for] Printed in the revises 'of'.
5 Mrs. Pritchard being mentioned] MS orig. 'Of Mrs. Pritchard'.
7 all] Added in the same draft.
10 April 8] Printed 'May 8' in the revises; the first three editions perpetuate the error.
10 was] Printed in the revises 'we met'.
11 He] Printed in the revises 'Johnson'.
13–14 circle. Mrs. Thrale] Originally run on; marked for new paragraph in revision.
14 trite] Changed by JB in the revises to 'coarse'.
19 nothing better than] Added in the same draft.
21 our] False start, 'yo[ur]'.
22 the man at the door] Printed in the revises 'the man who is stationed at the door'.
23 peoples] Added in the same draft.
23 That is to be done] Changed in the revises to 'that is done'.
28–29 and that upon this Mr. Fitzherbert had observed] Printed in the revises 'and that upon this being mentioned to Mr. Fitzherbert, he observed'.
32 bring.] Printed in the revises 'bring with me'.
32–33 I thus had it in my power to gratify him] Printed in the revises 'This

learned gentleman was thus gratified'.

33   high⟧ Added in the same draft.

33–34 being with Dr. Johnson⟧ Printed in the revises 'being in company with Dr. Johnson'.

35–1   abroad. I must⟧ Originally run on; marked for new paragraph in revision.

page 154

2   the half⟧ Printed in the revises 'the whole'.

4   I have preserved⟧ Printed in the revises 'I have preserved, however'.

6   challenge ... Writer⟧ MS orig. 'challenge any Biographical Writer'.

6   as⟧ MS orig. 'show'.

10   Johnson⟧ Printed in the revises 'He'.

12   Johnson⟧ Printed in the revises 'He'.

25–26 that it ... conferred⟧ Printed in the revises 'because my first acquaintance with him was unexpected and unsolicited'.

39–40 other occasions⟧ Printed in the revises 'a subsequent occasion'.

41   parts⟧ Printed in the revises 'particulars'.

41–42 in collecting ... as he did⟧ Printed in the revises 'in obtaining more from him, not apprehending that his friends were so soon to lose him'.

45   disorder⟧ Printed in the revises 'fever'.

page 155

7   for here⟧ Printed in the revises 'for here (I observed)'.

7   a number of people⟧ Printed in the revises 'many readers'.

15   No⟧ False start, 'Th'.

15   that⟧ Added in the same draft.

22–23 drest.' On friday⟧ Originally run on; marked for new paragraph in revision.

26   even⟧ Added in the same draft.

26   to⟧ Printed in the revises 'with'.

32   (second) his⟧ Added in the same draft.

page 156

4–5   I suppose⟧ Added in the same draft.

13   grow⟧ MS orig. 'become'.

16   Bute⟧ False start, 'gave up £___'.

23–24 and let it be remembered⟧ MS orig. 'Johnson should also have recollected'.

page 157

3   to go errands⟧ Changed by JB in the revises to 'to go on errands'.

4   to go errands⟧ Changed by JB in the revises to 'to go on errands'.

26   to support itself⟧ Printed in the revises 'to maintain its authority'.

page 158

1   as nobody⟧ Printed in the revises 'nobody'.

3–4   and as it is kept in country towns⟧ Added in the same draft.

13   Never fear Sir⟧ Added in the same draft.

23   chosen⟧ Added in the same draft.

23   singularly⟧ Printed in the revises 'extremely'.

26   up to his study⟧ MS orig. 'up stairs'.

27   in a calm undisturbed frame⟧ Printed in the revises 'in a serene undisturbed frame of mind'.

34   it⟧ Added in the same draft.

page 159

3 places of fame] Printed in the revises 'places in the Temple of Fame'.

3–5 so that ... can have it] Printed in the revises 'so that as but a few at any period can possess poetical reputation, a man of genius can now hardly acquire it.'

15 *Johnson.* 'Sir] False start, '"Sir," said he'.

17 he said] Printed in the revises 'he said in his acid manner'.

19–20 hanged.' Dr. Johnson] Originally run on; marked for new paragraph in revision.

20 but] False start, 'that'.

23 I am affraid a deist] False start, 'unset'.

34 however] Added in the same draft.

36 to an acquaintance] Printed in the revises 'talking to an acquaintance on this subject'.

page 160

1 April 15] Printed in the revises 'April 16'.

2 and] MS 'nobody there but' added and deleted in the same draft.

8 We] MS 'however' added and deleted in the same draft.

19 superficial] Added in the same draft.

29 Twittenham] Printed in the revises 'Twickenham'.

page 161

2–4 along. Our conversation] Originally run on; marked for new paragraph in revision.

10 he may join them] MS orig. 'may he go also'.

11 invited to abuse him] Printed in the revises 'invited on purpose to abuse him," (smiling).'

13 perhaps] Printed in the revises 'rather'.

14 did not at all proceed from] MS orig. 'had no participation with'.

14 I] False start, 'he'.

14–15 I give ... conversation] MS orig. 'the following dialogue/conversation / actually/ passed between us'.

15 conversation] Printed in the revises 'dialogue'.

17 *acid*] MS orig. '*acrimonious*'.

18 to the others] False start, 'none'.

23 light] Added in the same draft.

30 with me] Added in the same draft.

32–33 and knowing ... to him] Printed in the revises 'and I read a great part of them to him, knowing they would afford him entertainment'.

36 scotch] Added in the same draft.

36 with] First draft, 'by/with'.

39 Scotland. He confirmed] Printed in the revises 'Scotland; and confirmed'.

page 162

8 of them] Added in the same draft.

9 (*second*) that] MS orig. 'how'.

17 very generally] MS orig. 'most people'.

18 what he says.] Printed in the revises 'what he says to be true'.

20 be flattered] MS orig. 'say so'.

23 Said Sir Joshua] Printed in the revises 'Sir Joshua observed'.

23 (aside)] A later addition.

23   *(second)* the⌉ A later addition.

23   Books⌉ Printed in the revises 'books' and then changed by JB to 'the books'.

31   *(first)* can⌉ Interlined above 'can' is a false start, 'eit[her]'.

31   a⌉ False start, 'that a th[ing]'.

42   amongst⌉ Printed in the revises 'among'.

page 163

2–3   Islands. The common remark⌉ Originally run on; marked for new paragraph in revision.

3   having been made⌉ Printed in the revises 'being made'.

18–19 reason nay though our senses approved of⌉ Changed by JB in the revises to 'reason approved, nay, though our senses relished'.

21   many⌉ False start, 'ever[y]'.

23   almost⌉ Added in the same draft.

26   contrary⌉ MS orig. 'contrary/a'.

28   'The Beggar's Opera'⌉ False start, '"The Beggar's Opera" being/having been introduced with'.

36–37 whose discernment of the human character is acute and pentrating as in⌉ Changed by JB in the revises to 'whose discernment is as acute and penetrating in judging of the human character as it is in'.

page 164

2   all⌉ Added in the same draft.

3–4   Morality.' While he⌉ Originally run on; marked for new paragraph in revision.

6   In his Life of Gay⌉ Added in the same draft.

10   private⌉ Printed in the revises 'adventurous'.

10–12 and the allusions ... so artfully put⌉ Printed in the revises 'the allusions so lively, and the contrasts with the ordinary and more painful modes of acquiring property are so artfully displayed'.

14   London⌉ Added in the same draft.

15   that⌉ Printed in the revises 'which'.

15   early⌉ Added in the same draft.

16–17 no Performance which the Theatre exhibits delights me more⌉ MS orig. 'no theatrical Performance delights me more'.

18   'worthy'⌉ Printed in the revises '*worthy*'.

20   I am satisfied that⌉ Added in the same draft.

21–22 The agreable alternative we know was in the event conspicuously evident.⌉ Printed in the revises 'It proved the former, beyond the warmest expectations of the authour or his friends'.

22   however⌉ Added in the same draft.

22   confirmed to us⌉ Printed in the revises 'shewed us'.

24   during ... appearance⌉ Added in the same draft.

page 165

1   be not severe⌉ Added in the same draft.

2   Captain⌉ Added in the same draft.

3   *(second)* such⌉ Printed in the revises 'great'.

5   We talked of a young Gentleman's⌉ False start, 'A Gentleman's'.

18   modern⌉ Added in the same draft.

20   do⌉ Added in the same draft.

23   after the Restoration⌉ Added in the same draft.

24   much⌉ In the revises JB started to replace 'much' with an alternative, partially

deleting 'much' and writing in the margin 'great' (presumably with 'great a' in mind). This substitution, however, was abandoned.

25   had] Printed in the revises 'had then'.

30   Nation] Printed in the revises 'nation'.

page 166

1   (second) ever] Omitted in the revises.

2   Monarch] Printed in the revises 'monarch'.

2   a few] Added in the same draft.

9–10   had made it his sole object] Added in the same draft.

11   And he would have done] Abandoned alternative, 'there would h[ave]'.

15   sad] Added in the same draft.

23   Johnson] MS orig. 'He'.

28–29   I never could see] False start, 'I cannot account'.

33   words] False start, 'without' added and deleted in the same draft.

page 167

1   are] MS orig. 'is'.

2   at once] Added in the same draft.

8   thus] Added in the same draft.

13   for a considerable time] False start, 'again till'.

17   and] MS 'record' added and deleted in the same draft.

17   few] False start, 're' added and deleted in the same draft.

17   his] Added in the same draft.

19   arguments upon two Law Cases] MS orig. 'two Essays'.

21   saturday] Added in the same draft.

21–22   he dictated to me] Added in the same draft.

22   formerly] Printed in the revises 'already'.

27   Paterson etc. against Alexander etc.] Printed in the revises 'Paterson and others against Alexander and others'.

29   determining] False start, 'disfranchising'.

page 168

2   May 8] MS orig. '8 May'.

7   and while] Printed in the revises 'and who, while'.

11–12   with him. Talking of an acquaintance] False start, 'An acquaintance'. Originally run on; marked for new paragraph in revision.

17   who] False start, 'having had'.

21   sit] False start, 'late'.

24   him] Printed in the revises 'Johnson'.

24   attend] Printed in the revises 'go to'.

25   upon] False start, 'a' ('Consultation at a').

27   a man of any other profession] Printed in the revises 'an artisan'.

28   for] MS orig. 'to'.

34   what is of moral and what is of ritual obligation] MS orig. 'what is moral and what is ritual'.

35   On saturday] Originally run on; marked for new paragraph in revision.

36   Advocate] Printed in the revises 'a Scotch Advocate'.

page 169

2–3   how he had heard so much said] Printed in the revises 'at his having heard so much'.

3   Johnson's] MS 'uncouth' added and deleted in the same draft.

4   no more] Printed in the revises 'nothing'.
13–14 known. It being asked] Originally run on; marked for new paragraph in revision.
15   (second) preferred] Printed in the revises 'had preferred'.
18   preferred] Printed in the revises 'has preferred'.
18   But] Added in the same draft.
24   of a passage] Added in the same draft.
26   any] Added in the same draft.
29   in my life] A false start 'who' is interlined above this phrase.
32   on] Added in the same draft.
32–33 took leave of him] Added in the same draft.
35   during this period] Added in the same draft.

page 170
1   would] Third edition, 'should'.
6   circumstance] MS orig. 'thing'.
6   kind of] Added in the same draft.
7   described] False start, 'used'.
14   excerpt] Printed in the revises 'extract'.
18   in Edinburgh] Added in the same draft.
20   evening.] False start, 'Monboddo argued for the second sight and McQueen like a true highlan[der]'.

page 171
14   after] Printed in the revises 'afterwards'.
20–22 There ... preserved] Printed in the revises 'There can be no doubt that many years previous to 1775, he corresponded with this lady, who was his step-daughter, but none of his earlier letters to her have been preserved'.

page 172
2   an account of] Added in the same draft.
3   is reported to have] Added in the same draft.
4   such a number of] Printed in the revises 'so many'.
5   that can be found] Printed in the revises 'subject for remark'.
7–8   thinking and illustrating] Printed in the revises 'thought and illustration'.
8–9   which lasted but about two months] Added in the same draft.
12   but one titled] MS orig. 'the one titled'.
9–17   saw in two Small ... a specimen.] Printed in the revises 'saw. He promised to shew me them, but I neglected to put him in mind of it; and the greatest part of them have been lost, or, perhaps, destroyed in that precipitate burning of his papers a few days before his death, which must ever be lamented: One small paper-book, however, entitled "FRANCE, II." has been preserved, and is in my possession. It is a diurnal register of his life and observations, from the 10th of October to the 4th of November, inclusive, being twenty-six days; and shews an extraordinary attention to various minute particulars. Being the only memorial of this tour that remains, my readers, I am confident, will peruse it with pleasure, though his notes are very short, and evidently written only to assist his own recollection.'
16   shews] Replaced by 'shows' in the second edition.

page 173
1   of his french Tour] Added in the same draft.
3   an] Added in the same draft.

5   Sir⎤ Added in the same draft.
9   in France⎤ Added in the same draft.
14   magnificently⎤ False start, 'misera'.
24   tea⎤ Added in the same draft.
28   while there⎤ Added in the same draft.
33   Johnson⎤ Added in the same draft.
36   *Johnson*. 'Yes Sir⎤ Added in the same draft.
40   imperfectly⎤ False start, 'imperfectly; and'.
42   When⎤ Added in the same draft.

page 174
8   I imagine⎤ Added in the same draft.
11   May⎤ Printed in the revises 'July'.
15   me⎤ Printed in the revises 'ne'. Presumably the correction was made in the first proof.
23   rely⎤ Two false starts, 'a' and 'on every'.
23   both⎤ Added in the same draft.
23   observation and memory⎤ Printed in the revises 'memory'.
31   had hurried⎤ Changed by JB in the revises to 'was hurrying'.
31   timber⎤ Omitted in the revises.
34   coach, while he was drest in his⎤ Printed in the revises 'coach. His dress was a'.
36   knees⎤ Printed in the revises 'the knees'.
37   gathered⎤ False start, 'to'.
39   He⎤ In the revises JB changed 'He' to 'Johnson' and then back to 'He'.
39   eloquence⎤ First edition, 'elegance'.

page 175
1   Reynolds⎤ Printed in the revises 'Reynolds's'.
1   Douglas⎤ Printed in the revises 'Douglas's'.
8   many⎤ MS orig. 'frequent and'.
17   get⎤ MS orig. 'give'.

page 176
5   had⎤ Added in the same draft.
14–15   at an after time⎤ Printed in the revises 'on a subsequent day'.
20   Why Sir⎤ Printed in the revises 'Why, Sir, you are not to wonder at that'.
30–32   executed so far as I can discover no work of any sort for the Publick.] Printed in the revises 'wrote, so far as I can discover, nothing for the publick'.
32   collected⎤ First draft, 'published'.
32   last four⎤ First draft, 'four last'.
32   under⎤ First draft, 'with/under'.
33   this⎤ First draft, 'the following/this'.

page 177
2   to⎤ Added in the same draft.
5   will by and by be proved by his private notes of this year.⎤ Printed in the revises 'is proved by his private notes of this year, which I shall insert in their proper place'.
7–8   At this time ... family⎤ MS orig. 'At this time a matter of great consequence to me and my family was in agitation'.
12   may be understood⎤ False start, 'may be subject'.

15–16   which ... (*Affleck*)] Added in the same draft.
15–16   Auchinleck in Ayrshire ... (pronounced *Affleck*)] Printed in the revises 'Auchinleck (pronounced *Affleck*) in Ayrshire, which belonged to a family of the same name with the lands'.
26   are] False start, 'At this'.

page 178

7   the estate ... daughters] MS orig. 'large portions having been given to the daughters'. This draft was preceded by a false start, 'having large portions'.
16   advantage/use] False start, 'the privile'.
16   our law of Scotland] In correcting the revises, JB changed 'our law' to 'the law of Scotland' and then back to 'our law'.
23   declared] Added in the same draft.
28   however] Added in the same draft.
28   succession] MS orig. 'descendants'.
31–32   all males descending] False start, 'males should'.
39   Statute 1685 Cap.] Changed by JB in the revises 'Acts of the Parliament of Scotland 1685, Cap. 22'.

page 179

1   nurse, which] Printed in the revises 'nurse, as Mother Earth is to plants of every sort; which'.
5   him,'] Printed in the revises 'him", Heb. vi. 10)'.
5   grandchild] Printed in the revises 'grandson'.
6   as is vulgarly and in reality said has] Printed in the revises 'as is vulgarly said, has, in reality'.
22   reference must] Printed in the revises 'regard should'.
26   honesty] Printed in the revises 'good faith'.
29   distant] Added in the same draft.

page 180

6   but ... one] Added in the same draft.
20   young] Added in the same draft.
23   this] MS orig. 'the'.
25   discussed my difficulties] MS orig. 'treated the points'.
26   and historical] Added in the same draft.
26–27   in which ... maintaining] MS orig. 'which perplexed me, shewing'.
30   and that] Added in the same draft.
31   which] False start 'appe[ared]'.
31   seemed best] Printed in the revises 'seemed to be best'.
32   (*second*) the] Printed in the revises 'that'.
31–32   that had been ... and] Added in the same draft.
39   consideration] MS orig. 'circumstance'.
39   preference] MS 'of' deleted.

page 181

2   the] Changed by Selfe in the revises to 'this'.
7   20 feb.] Printed in the revises 'Feb. 20'.
11   upon] MS orig. 'on'.

page 182

4   what Dr. Johnson] False start, 'Dr. Johnson's'.
8   gloom and] Added in the same draft.

9   be with⌉ JB deleted these words and then reinstated them with 'stet'.

9–10 him. I informed⌉ Printed in the revises 'him, informing'.

9–10 him. I informed ... ten⌉ JB made two false starts, 'him and the' and 'him. That the'.

10   (*second*) that⌉ Added in the same draft.

page 183

12   the promotion of learning⌉ MS orig. 'literature'.

33   intercepted⌉ First edition, 'interrupted'.

page 184

19   in full⌉ Printed in the revises 'in a full'.

23   I am *Hermippus redivivus.*⌉ Printed in the revises 'I am now, intellectually, *Hermippus redivivus*'.

25   I⌉ False start, 'We'.

27   had a great value for it⌉ Printed in the revises 'respected it for its antiquity'.

30–35 I am happy ... usually demand⌉ Printed in the revises, 'I am happy in giving this full and clear statement to the Publick to vindicate by the authority of the greatest Authour of his age that respectable body of men the Booksellers of London from vulgar reflections, as if their profits were exorbitant, when, in truth Dr. Johnson has here allowed them more than they usually demand.'

page 185

16   being⌉ Printed in the revises 'circulating'.

24   kept⌉ Added in the same draft.

30   still⌉ Printed in the revises 'always'.

page 186

2   entailed⌉ Added in the same draft.

4   be⌉ Added in the same draft.

6   the system of⌉ Added in the same draft.

6   fixed⌉ Printed in the revises 'locked up'.

7   can⌉ MS orig. 'could/can'.

9   come out⌉ Printed in the revises 'published'.

9   an eminent Physician⌉ Printed in the revises 'Sir John Pringle'.

9–10 had said to me as his opinion⌉ Printed in the revises 'had observed to me'.

12   I⌉ Printed in the revises 'a lawyer'.

18–19 But trade ... countries.⌉ Printed in the revises 'but trade procures what is more valuable, the reciprocation of the peculiar advantages of different countries'.

21   necessary⌉ False start, 'for'.

22   I mentioned Law.⌉ Expanded by the stage of the revises to read, 'I mentioned law as a subject on which no man could write well without practice'.

26   all⌉ Added in the same draft.

32   that⌉ False start, 'mean'.

34   who had risen to eminence⌉ MS orig. 'in great eminence'.

page 187

7   (*second*) a⌉ Added in the same draft.

10   give⌉ Printed in the revises 'inject'.

11–12 in supporting ... Commons] A later draft addition.
14   support] False start, 'fund'.
24   (*second*) Sir] A later draft addition.
27   more] False start, '/men as/'.
27   so many more militia] Printed in the revises 'a greater number of militia'.
28   certainly *del*] By the stage of the revises 'certainly' had been reinstated.
32   made] False start, 'soon'.
34   Where] MS orig. 'When'.

page 188

6   *charitatis*] Printed in the revises '*caritatis*'.
13   over to Blackfriars] MS orig. 'the Thames'.
14–15 altogether unknown to him] Added in the same draft.
19   perhaps] Omitted in the revises.
21   his] Printed in the revises 'your'.
22–23 with the falshood] Added in the same draft. MS 'trash and' deleted before 'falshood'.
24   Besides Sir] MS orig. 'And'.
30–31 matter. He was] Originally run on; marked for new paragraph in revision.
32   fictitious] Printed in the revises 'spurious'.
32   hurt] Printed in the revises 'injured'.
34–35 it was very hard if no redress could be obtained] Printed in the revises 'redress ought in such cases to be given'.

page 189

7   properly] Added in the same draft.
7   stories] Printed in the revises 'narratives'.
7   narratives] Printed in the revises 'stories'.
7   ludicrous] Added in the same draft.
8   (*second*) ludicrous] Added in the same draft.
11   that] Added in the same draft.
14   which he related] Printed in the revises 'that he told'.
14–15 it might have been doubted] Interlined above this phrase is an undeciphered alternative, possibly 'its tr[uth] might from its str[angeness]'.
15   told] MS orig. 'related'.
17   to have happened] Printed in the revises 'as having happened'.
17   gentleman] It is clear that JB meant 'gentlewoman'.
17–20 A gentle[wo]man ... He perceived] Printed in the revises '"A gentlewoman (said he) begged I would give her my arm to assist her in crossing the street, which I accordingly did; upon which she offered me a shilling, supposing me to be the watchman. I perceived"'.
29–30 may be no doubt resolution] Printed in the revises 'is, indeed, great resolution'.
31   though] Added in the same draft.
33   Carthusian] Changed in the revises by JB to 'a Carthusian'.
34   too] Added in the same draft.

page 190

3   religious] Added in the same draft.
5–6   ventured to speak] MS orig. 'spoke'.
12   intoxication] First draft, '[drinking>] [indulging to excess in wine]'.
12   was] False start, 'very ready to make allowance for' deleted.
13   when he knew of occasional excesses] Printed in the revises 'to those who engaged in occasional excess'.

15   and] MS 'was' deleted.

16   thinking to produce a severe censure] Added in the same draft.

16   censure] MS orig. 'rem[onstrance]'.

18   being] MS orig. 'coming'.

18   should] Printed in the revises '*should*'.

21   at all freely] Added in the same draft.

23   probably] False start, 'of[fe nd]'.

23–24   people.' He allowed] Originally run on; marked for new paragraph in revision.

24   very] Added in the same draft.

28   find] MS orig. 'found'.

31–32   principles.' This is] Originally run on; marked for new paragraph in revision.

35   Monday forenoon] Printed in the revises 'Monday'.

page 191

4   have come to] Added in the same draft.

6   (*second*) indeed] Added in the same draft.

8–9   On tuesday March 19 I met him between eight and nine in the morning] Printed in the revises 'On Tuesday March 19 which was fixed for our proposed jaunt, we met in the morning'.

11   whom we did not know] Added in the same draft.

12   in] Printed in the revises 'of'.

14–15   (*second*) Garrick ... stage] Printed in the revises 'Garrick, who was about to quit the stage, would soon have an easier life'.

21   BOSWELL. 'I think] MS orig. 'I said I thought'.

21   play] False start, 'pe[rform]'.

22   it has been given out] Printed in the revises 'it has been said'.

24   He] Printed in the revises 'Johnson'.

26   'because] MS 'said he' added and deleted in the same draft.

31   head cut] MS orig. 'cut head'.

35   the value of] Added in the same draft.

35   I imagine/believe its] MS orig. 'I take it'.

38   proportionable] Printed in the revises 'proportionate'.

38   Gwyn] Printed in the revises as the beginning of a new paragraph.

41   attack] False start, 'on'.

45   give us] Printed in the revises 'convey'.

page 192

1   at all] Added in the same draft.

2   being decorated with] MS orig. 'having'.

2–3   work.' Gwyn at last] Originally run on; marked for new paragraph in revision.

4   was angry with] Printed in the revises 'censured'.

5   years] MS 'and rebuilding it in another place for no other reason than' added and deleted in the same draft.

9   in] Italicized in the revises.

10   go out of the way] Italicized in the revises.

13   on] MS orig. 'in'.

14   one of the fellows] Added in the same draft.

17   Sir Robert] Added in the same draft.

17   poor Frank] Added in the same draft.

17   Francis] Added in the same draft.

17   supt] MS 'with [*undeciphered word*]' added and deleted in the same draft.
27   for instance] Added in the same draft.
31–32   It ... quotation] MS orig. 'There is perhaps too much quotation in it.'
32   Burton] Interlined above is a false start, 'When'.
37   waited on] Printed in the revises 'visited'.
39   as to which I have inserted his Letter to Dr. Wetherell] Printed in the revises 'on which subject his letter has been inserted in a former page'.

page 193

1   that] Omitted in the revises.
1–2   to have ... life] MS orig. 'that his wisdom should operate in real action'.
3   guineas] Interlined above is a false start, 'for'.
4   (*first*) a] Interlined above is a false start, 'as'.
12   burst out] MS orig. 'said'.
15   on] MS 'his old friend and who should have been his Tutor' added and deleted in the same draft.
22   authentick] Added in the same draft.
32   Authour] Added in the same draft.
40   may] Third edition, 'might'.
42   *bona fides*] Printed in the revises 'sincerity'.

page 194

8   I do declare] Printed in the revises 'I do declare, however'.
13   get the better of] Printed in the revises 'refute'.
14   for instance if he be] A later addition.
15   effigies] Changed by JB in the revises first to 'figure' and then to 'person'.
17   joined me] Printed in the revises 'coincided with me'.
17   Johnson joined me and said] MS orig. '*Johnson*'.
26–27   in the] Added in the same draft.
28   amongst them] Added in the same draft.
30   very good] Added in the same draft.
36   You know   said] Printed in the revises 'You know it was said'.
38   Jason's] Printed erroneously in the revises 'Jason de Neres' and corrected for the third edition to 'Jason de Nores'.

page 195

1   much] Printed in the revises 'very'.
3   and] Added in the same draft.
6   being] Added in the same draft.
7   he] Printed in the revises 'we'.
15   there] MS orig. 'here'.
16–17   connected. We drank tea] Originally run on; marked for new paragraph in revision.
17   President] MS orig. 'Master'.
19   undoubted] Printed in the revises 'eminent'.
36   Dr. Pearce ... Rochester] Changed by JB in the revises to 'a late Bishop'. At the same time that JB decided to delete Pearce's name, he considered rewriting the entire sentence; 'although he' is added and then deleted before 'could tell'.
38–1   nothing.' I said] Originally run on; marked for new paragraph in revision.

page 196

4   if] Printed in the revises 'whether'.
9–10   Footman.'" Biography led us] Originally run on; marked for new paragraph in

revision.

10–11 who had ... the] Printed in the revises 'who had written a considerable part of the'.

15 account of] Added in the same draft.

18 upon] Printed in the revises 'on'.

19–20 Book.' We talked of] Originally run on; marked for new paragraph in revision.

20 We talked of] Added in the same draft, and then omitted from the printing of the revises.

22 and] Added in the same draft, and then changed by the stage of the revises to 'but'.

23 of] Added in the same draft.

23 and of which] Deleted by the stage of the revises.

26 Spring-guns] MS orig. 'Gun-springs'.

28 several times] Added in the same draft.

34–1 Sir.' You know] Originally run on; marked for new paragraph in revision.

page 197

1 having] Added in the same draft.

6 (*second*) him] Printed in the revises 'Johnson'.

7 of life] Added in the same draft.

9 No] Added in the same draft.

9–10 a man makes] Printed in the revises 'a man always makes'.

16 universally] Added in the same draft.

19 Mr.] Added in the same draft.

22 record] False start, 'menti[on]'.

22 to record] Printed in the revises 'to the record'.

23 gentleman] First draft, 'extraordinary man'.

23 uniform] Added in the same draft.

23–24 Sir Joshua Reynolds] False start, 'When Mr.'

25–26 at such elevation] Printed in the revises 'at his attaining a seat'.

28 Mr. Burke having been mentioned] False start, 'the conversation having'.

page 198

4 morning] MS orig. 'day'.

4 March 21] MS orig. '21 March'.

5 proposed] Omitted from the revises, apparently having been deleted in first proof.

6 built] False start, 'upon'.

8 his] MS orig. 'the'.

8 The arch the height of his ambition shows] Changed by JB in the revises to 'The lofty arch, his high ambition shows'.

11–12 and Johnson ... conceit] Deleted in the revises.

12 conceit] MS orig. 'turn'.

12 said] Printed in the revises 'observed'.

15 wild rough Mull] Changed by JB in the revises to 'wild rough Island of Mull'.

16 now] Omitted in the revises, apparently having been deleted in first proof.

16–17 Park.' We dined] Originally run on; marked for new paragraph in revision.

18 France] Printed in the revises 'the French'.

18–19 not having in any perfection the tavern life] MS orig. 'the inferiority of its tavern life'.

20   said he⌉ Printed in the revises '(said he)'; presumably JB's deleted op-
        tional markings were mistaken for a set of parentheses.
20   enjoy themselves so well⌉ MS orig. 'be so happy'.
20   at⌉ MS orig. 'in'.
26   another man's house⌉ MS orig. 'his neighbour's house'.
29   the more trouble you give⌉ Added in the same draft.

page 199
5–6   Place. He⌉ Originally run on; marked for new paragraph in revision.
12   Langton having⌉ Printed in the revises 'Langton's having'.

page 200
3   with it⌉ Added in the same draft.
5   good⌉ Printed in the revises 'service'.
10   he got an offer from⌉ Printed in the revises 'and an offer being made to
        him'.
11   go and⌉ Added in the same draft.
12   have⌉ Printed in the revises 'receive'.
13   accepted⌉ Changed by JB in the revises to 'accepted it'.
15   grew⌉ Added in the same draft and altered from 'growing'.
17   Physician⌉ Printed in the revises 'Physician there'.
19   such as he could find⌉ Added in the same draft.
23   Granger's⌉ Printed in the revises 'His'.
24   may⌉ Printed in the revises 'might'.

page 201
6   thus⌉ Added in the same draft.
19   March 22⌉ MS orig. '22 March'.
19   On Friday ... Birmingham⌉ Printed in the revises 'On Friday, March 22,
        having left Henley, where we had lain the preceding night, at an early
        hour, we arrived at Birmingham about nine o'clock'.
28   dialect⌉ Printed in the revises 'pronunciation'.

page 202
1   then⌉ Printed in the revises 'next'.
5–6   increasing. I talked⌉ Originally run on; marked for new paragraph in
        revision.
19   common⌉ Added in the same draft.
20   younger⌉ Added in the same draft.
24   and he⌉ Added in the same draft.
27   Mr. Lloyd⌉ MS orig. 'he'.
28–29   I loved to observe ... other again⌉ MS orig. 'The joy which Johnson and
        he expressed on seeing each/one other again was truly cordial'.
40   liked⌉ Printed in the revises 'loved'.
42   with⌉ MS orig. 'of'.
42   Lloyd⌉ MS 'while we walked' deleted.
42   said⌉ Printed in the revises 'observed'.
44   Dr.⌉ Added in the same draft.
45   introducing⌉ Added in the same draft.

page 203
4   I⌉ Added in the same draft.
4   apology] MS 'for the Quakers Dr' deleted.

5   laid⸃ MS orig. 'took'.
5   having turned up⸃ Printed in the revises 'happening to open'.
6   (*first*) remarked⸃ False start, 'said'.
10   perceive⸃ False start, 'They insisted that the rite of baptism'.
15   One of them⸃ This sentence was designated the beginning of a new
        paragraph, as a consequence of JB's decision to expand the original brief
        mention of Quaker principles.
17   merely⸃ Added in the same draft.
19   Only⸃ Printed in the revises 'but'.

page 204

1   forenoon⸃ Printed in the revises 'morning'.
4   It dropt⸃ False start interlined above, 'The passion'.
4   will⸃ Second edition, 'shall'.
6   really⸃ Added in the same draft.
5–6   He laughed ... once⸃ Printed in the revises, 'He laughed at the notion
        that a man never can be really in love but once, and considered it as a
        mere romantick fancy'.
6–8   once. On our⸃ Originally run on; marked for new paragraph in revision.
9   first love⸃ Printed in the revises '*first love*'.
11–12   well=bred. Johnson⸃ Originally run on; marked for new paragraph in
        revision.
12   (*first*) Mr.⸃ Added in the same draft.
12   the state ... Schoolfellows⸃ MS orig. 'the state of their Schoolfellow'.
17   whom⸃ False start, 'a'.
22   a⸃ Added in the same draft.
25–26   to have ... Mr. Hector⸃ Added in the same draft.
26   my friend⸃ False start, 'he'.
28   and were long and silent⸃ In the revises, the optional phrase became 'and
        were long pensive and silent'.
29   got⸃ Changed by JB in the revises to 'came'.
29–30   getting out of⸃ MS orig. 'in'.
30   Crowns⸃ False start, 'he'.
30   not one⸃ False start, 'none'.
31   which had been⸃ Added in the same draft.
31–32   which had been kept for forty years⸃ Printed in the revises 'which was kept'.
31–32   for forty years⸃ Added in the same draft.

page 205

9   ten thousand pounds⸃ MS orig. '10,000'.
24   the⸃ Changed by JB in the revises to 'a'.
27   (*first*) with⸃ JB made two false starts here, 'in order to' and 'which'.
32   brown⸃ Omitted in the printing of the revises.

page 206

16   *wunnse*⸃ Printed in the revises '*wunse, or wonse*'.
16–17   his provincial accent⸃ Second edition, 'those provincial accents'.
17   Garrick used⸃ Printed in the revises 'Garrick sometimes used'.
18   strange⸃ Printed in the revises 'uncouth'.
18–19   *Poonsh.*' I perceived⸃ Originally run on; marked for new paragraph in
        revision.
19–20   I perceived ... Lichfield.⸃ Printed in the revises 'Very little business
        appeared to be going forward in Lichfield'.

25   JOHNSON. 'Sir⌉ Printed in the revises 'Sir (said Johnson)'.

29–30 and that he would be glad to wait on⌉ Printed in the revises 'requested leave to wait on'. The second edition prints 'begged leave to wait on'.

34   Garrick's name was soon introduced.⌉ First draft, 'Mr. Garrick's name was soon introduced into our conversation'.

page 207

9   Mr.⌉ MS 'David' added and deleted in the same draft.

12   when said Garrick⌉ Printed in the revises 'When in fact, according to Garrick's account'.

13   Johnson's description⌉ False start, 'Johnson used to describe'.

17–18 I was really ... like⌉ Printed in the revises 'I was really inclined to take the hint. Methought, "Prologue, spoken before Dr. Samuel Johnson at Lichfield, 1776;" would have sounded as well as'.

19   Edinburgh⌉ Printed in the revises 'Oxford'.

20–21 Johnson and Garrick⌉ Printed in the revises 'by producing Johnson and Garrick'.

23   proud of being⌉ Added in the same draft.

23   indeed⌉ Changed by JB in the revises to 'truly'.

24–25 and ingenious works of art⌉ Added in the same draft.

31   activity and⌉ Added in the same draft.

34   Mr. Green's obliging⌉ False start, 'Mr. Green obligingly'.

35–36 He has favoured ... very characteristical⌉ Printed in the revises 'His engraved portrait, with which he has favoured me, has a motto truly characteristical'.

37–39 A Physician ... being mentioned⌉ Printed in revises 'A physician being mentioned who had lost his practice, because his whimsically changing his religion had made people distrustful of him'.

39   being mentioned⌉ In EM's hand.

page 208

12   tea and coffee/coffee and tea⌉ MS orig. 'tea'.

19   a sweet old⌉ Printed in the revises 'an agreeably'.

21   that⌉ MS orig. 'a'. By the stage of the revises, the wording had reverted to 'a'.

23   pleased⌉ Changed by JB in the revises to 'delightful'.

24   to be⌉ Added in the same draft.

24–25 service. We dined⌉ Originally run on; marked for new paragraph in revision.

26   justified⌉ Changed by JB in the revises to 'verified'.

29   often⌉ Printed in the revises 'usually'.

33–34 infant. I returned⌉ Originally run on; marked for new paragraph in revision.

35   Sewards⌉ MS orig. 'Seywards'.

37   Seward⌉ MS orig. 'Seyward'.

page 209

1   forenoon⌉ Printed in the revises 'morning'.

5   when⌉ Added in the same draft.

5   and⌉ MS 'in his travels' added and deleted in the same draft.

6   World. He was⌉ MS orig. 'World and was'.

9   now⌉ MS orig. 'here'.

11   concerning Johnson⌉ Added in the same draft.

14   Seward⌉ MS orig. 'Seyward'.

16   (second) in⌉ MS orig. 'at'.

16   different⌉ Added in the same draft.

18   Captain Brydone's Tour⌉ Changed by JB in the revises to 'Captain Brydone's

entertaining Tour'.

19   thought only superficially upon⌉ Changed in the revises to 'not sufficiently studied'.

21   all⌉ Added in the same draft.

22   what is⌉ Added in the same draft.

26   post⌉ Added in the same draft.

31   (*first*) of a⌉ Added in the same draft.

31   nature⌉ Added in the same draft.

32   figured⌉ Printed in the revises 'imagined'.

38   of it⌉ Added in the same draft.

39–40 I was however soon affected with sincere concern⌉ Printed in the revises
'I however, soon felt a sincere concern'.

41   would feel⌉ Printed in the revises 'would be affected'.

42   as much⌉ Added in the same draft.

page 210

1   daughters⌉ False start, 'to'.

5–6 any standing⌉ Printed in the revises 'any long standing'.

11–12 violent pain⌉ Added in the same draft.

13   (*third*) have⌉ Printed in the revises 'know'.

25–26 I was delighted⌉ Printed in the revises 'It pleased me'.

26   *beloved*⌉ Printed in the revises 'so much *beloved*'.

30   He⌉ Printed in the revises 'Johnson'.

40   stranger⌉ False start, 'but soon'.

page 211

3   Shakspeare's⌉ MS orig. 'Shakespeare's'.

3–4 who with gothick ... vex his parishioners⌉ Printed in the revises 'where he
was a proprietor of Shakspeare's Garden, with Gothick barbarity cut
down his mulberry-tree, and, as Dr. Johnson told me, did it to vex his
neighbours'.

6   participated⌉ Before settling on 'participated' as the appropriate verb to
describe Mrs. Gastrel's involvement in the destruction of the mulberry
tree, JB made a false start, 'was an accesso[ry]' and then wrote and deleted
'shared with him'.

7–8 sacrilege. After⌉ Originally run on; marked for new paragraph in revision.

9   hard upon Thrale⌉ Printed in the revises 'very distressing to Thrale'.

9   it would ... but⌉ Added in the same draft.

22   It was pleasing⌉ Changed by JB in the revises to 'I was happy'.

25   reflected upon⌉ Printed in the revises 'condemned'.

28   suffer much⌉ Printed in the revises 'suffer much pain'.

28   suffer much from the death of their son⌉ MS orig. 'be severely pained by
the death of their son'.

30   be⌉ Added in the same draft.

35   Seward⌉ MS orig. 'Seyward'.

36–37 London. Here I⌉ Originally run on; marked for new paragraph in revision.

39–40 'Marriage ... to⌉ MS orig. 'A man stands much more in need of marriage
than a woman, for he can do much less to'.

40–41 my saying⌉ First draft, 'that I mentioned'.

page 212

5–6 It is ... in women⌉ Printed in the revises '"Is it not, to a certain degree, a
delusion in us as well as in women?"'

6   and⌉ Printed in the revises 'but it is'.

12   mode of⌉ Added in the same draft.

15   own⌉ Added in the same draft.

17   be⌉ First draft, 'have'.

19   A man⌉ False start, 'Never'.

19   to his own disadvantage⌉ Added in the same draft.

21   after⌉ Printed in the revises 'subsequent'.

24   a sectary⌉ Added in the same draft.

27   be⌉ MS 'what is thought' added and deleted in the same draft.

27   in⌉ Added in the same draft.

33   in their own country⌉ A later addition.

34   (*first*) even⌉ Interlined in the same draft, originally part of 'this is the case with'. Omitted in the printing of the revises, presumably because the compositor overlooked the interlineation.

34   the gentlemen⌉ Deleted interlineation, 'this is the case with'.

36   with his usual acuteness⌉ A later addition.

36   Johnson at once ... explained this⌉ Printed in the revises 'Johnson, with his usual acuteness, at once saw and explained the reason of this'.

page 213

1   many of those who⌉ False start, 'of those who'.

7   conveyed⌉ Printed in the revises 'which conveyed'.

10   garden⌉ Added in the same draft.

11   appearing⌉ Altered from 'appearance' in the same draft.

16   which excited⌉ Printed in the revises 'excite'.

23   before⌉ Changed by JB in the revises to 'preceeding'.

25   of Derby⌉ A later addition.

32   large⌉ Added in the same draft.

41   (*second*) who were⌉ Omitted in the revises, apparently having been deleted in first proof.

42   in⌉ Interlined above 'in' is a false start, 'upo[n]'.

page 214

1   But⌉ MS 'Sir' added and deleted in the same draft.

7   of⌉ False start, 'Mr. Andrew Stuart'.

7   to Lord Mansfield⌉ Added in the same draft.

10   uneasiness⌉ Printed in the revises 'any uneasiness'.

14   but⌉ Added in the same draft.

16   observed⌉ First draft, 'said/observed'.

19   rest⌉ First draft, 'rest/dunces'.

23   a few⌉ deleted interlineation, 'we saw'.

25–26 day. Dr. Johnson⌉ Originally run on; marked for new paragraph in revision.

29   against his proposition⌉ Added in the same draft.

Index

The indexes of this edition of the *Life* are designed to complement the index of the Hill-Powell edition. They contain matter that will be found in the text, notes, introduction, and appendices of this edition only. Just as the two editions will ordinarily be used together for scholarly purposes, so will their indexes. The following abbreviations are employed here: JB (James Boswell), SJ (Samuel Johnson), EM (Edmond Malone), *Life* (Boswell's *Life of Johnson*), GM (*The Gentleman's Magazine*). Peers are listed under their titles. Places are indexed selectively. The index was compiled by Carrie Roider and Nancy Johnson.